Baby Names YOUR CHILD CAN LIVE WITH

Thousands of Names to Help You Make the Perfect Choice

By Lisa Shaw
Edited by Andrea Norville

ADAMS MEDIA
Avon, Massachusetts

Published by Adams Media, an F+W Publications Company
57 Littlefield Street
Avon, MA 02322
www.adamsmedia.com
Printed in Canada
ISBN: 1-59337-284-1

J I H G F E D C B A

Contains portions of material adapted and abridged from *The Everything® Baby Names Book* by Lisa Shaw, © 1997, F+W Publication Inc.

Library of Congress Cataloging-in-Publication Data
Shaw, Lisa.
Baby names your child can live with / Lisa Shaw.
p. cm.
ISBN 1-59337-284-1
1. Names, Personal--Dictionaries. I. Title.

CS2377.S427 2005
929.4'4'097303--dc22

2004026893

This publication is designed to provide accurate and authoritative information with regard to the subject matter covered. It is sold with the understanding that the publisher is not engaged in rendering legal, accounting, or other professional advice. If legal advice or other expert assistance is required, the services of a competent professional person should be sought.

—From a *Declaration of Principles* jointly adopted by a Committee of the American Bar Association and a Committee of Publishers and Associations

The point of view reflected in this book does not reflect all international standards. It is written with a "typically American" sensibility in mind, based on names that are more familiar within this culture at present.

Contents

F

G

H

I

J

K

L

M

N

O

P

Q

R

S

G

H

I

J

K

L

M

Introduction

CHOOSING the right name for your baby is a tall order. There are thousands of options to consider in this book, and yet you have to boil them all down to just one first name and one middle name. But what is it, exactly, that makes a name "right" for a child? There are lots of ways to slice this complex question. Maybe you're looking for a name that reflects your ethnic heritage, or perhaps you want to choose a name with a meaning that is particularly significant to you and your partner. Regardless of the criteria you use, the fact remains you're choosing something that will be your child's primary touchstone of identification. It's bound to feel a bit odd selecting something that will affect your baby in such an integral way, before he or she's even born!

The name you pick for your child is something that she will carry with her always and everywhere, for the rest of her life. Wow, there's a lot riding on that decision . . . So are you stressed out yet? Don't be. This book will help you to weigh up the many possibilities. In the following pages, you'll find boys' names and girls' names organized alphabetically, with names for each letter of the alphabet organized into three categories. As you read on, you'll learn if you're partial to tried and true classics; if you're prepared to make a slightly daring choice; or if you're ready to choose a name that will have your child living on the edge.

But that stuff is designed to help you make sense of all the choices, in order to find the name that *you* can live with. That still doesn't bring you any closer to finding the name that *your child* can live with. How do you figure that out? Ultimately, choosing a name your child can live with happily means choosing wisely. It entails weighing up possibilities carefully, not just jumping on the latest fad or following some silly celebrity's lead.

Of course, you want to be careful to consider how the first and middle names you choose sound together, and how those two names in combination sound with your last name. And then there's that major matter of nicknames. Do you or don't you want your child to be called by a particular nickname? Don't automatically assume that just because *you* call your child by his or her full name, everyone else will follow suit. If a name *can* be shortened, you can bet many people *will* shorten it. Of course, you're no mind reader, and you can't possibly anticipate every nickname that could someday come your child's way. All we're saying here is think logically, and then take your best shot. And remember that some kids are merciless teasers, and it's a pretty safe bet that a kid named Charles Brown is in for trouble.

That said, there's no denying that the names different cultures bestow upon their children vary tremendously. Baby names, like so many other cultural constructs, are quite subjective. You'll find myriad names from all sorts of ethnic backgrounds in these pages. Certainly, although some of them might be classified as "Living on the Edge" in this book, they might strike you as downright common if you are from that particular ethnic background. However, we have tried to present the names in this book according to the common standards that are most familiar to "typical" American culture, as we know it in this present day.

Ultimately, selecting a name for your baby is a very personal decision. You'll know it when a name feels right. Make this choice count. Also make sure the name you do pick means something to you so that someday, as he grows, your child can hold on to that meaning as well. Congratulations on the soon-to-be birth of your baby, and best of luck choosing the perfect name that you *and* your child can live with!

Part 1

BOYS' NAMES

A

Tried and True Classics

AARON *(Hebrew)* Exalted; enlightened. The older brother of Moses, appointed by God to be his brother's keeper. Aaron has actually been one of the more popular names since the early days of the United States in the 1600s. Famous people from the past and present with the name include a vice-president, Aaron Burr, the American composer Aaron Copland, and the singer Aaron Neville. Variations: *Aarao, Aharon, Arek, Aron, Aronek, Aronne, Aronos, Arran, Arren, Arrin, Arron.*

ABRAHAM *(Hebrew)* Father of many. If the name Abraham conjures up an image of a wise old man to you, you may scoff at the idea of making an infant put up with the name until it fits, say, oh, in sixty years or so. But as more and more parents decide to give their children names that conjure up American history, Abraham will continue to have a growing place in baby names. Variations: *Abe, Abrahamo, Abrahan, Abram, Abramo, Abran, Abrao, Avraham, Avram, Avrum.*

ADAM *(Hebrew)* Man of the red earth. Adam was the first man who made it into the world, and his name has always been popular in many countries and in many religions. In this country, the popularity of Adam increased during the '60s. Adam West, who played Batman in that television series, undoubtedly served as the inspiration for many men named Adam today. Many parents pick the name for their first son. Variations: *Adamec, Adamek, Adamh, Adamik, Adamka, Adamko, Adams, Adamson, Adamsson, Adan, Adao, Addam, Addams, Addamson, Addie, Addis, Addy, Adhamh, Adnet, Adnot.*

ADRIAN *(Latin)* Black; dark. Variations: *Adrean, Adren.*

AIDAN *(Irish, Gaelic)* Fiery. Aidan has become popular in recent years due to the success of the ice-blue-eyed actor Aidan Quinn. *Sex and the City* also brought the name back into the mainstream with Carrie's fiancé, Aidan.

The Most Popular Boys' Names from the 1940s

In the 1940s, the number one thing on most Americans' minds was World War II, and when it was going to be over. Parents-to-be in the 1940s chose simple no-nonsense names for their children—a clear indication of the serious tenor of the times. Following are the most popular boys' names during the 1940s:

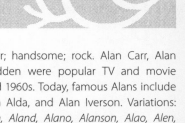

1. James
2. John
3. Robert
4. William
5. Charles
6. David
7. Jerry
8. Thomas
9. Richard
10. José

ALAN *(Irish, Gaelic)* Fair; handsome; rock. Alan Carr, Alan Ladd, and Allen Ludden were popular TV and movie stars in the 1950s and 1960s. Today, famous Alans include Alan Jay Lerner, Alan Alda, and Alan Iverson. Variations: *Ailean, Ailin, Al, Alain, Aland, Alano, Alanson, Alao, Alen, Alin, Allan, Allayne, Allen, Alleyn, Alleyne, Allin, Allon, Allyn, Alon, Alun.*

ALBERT *(Old English)* Bright; brilliant. Variations: *Alberto, Albie, Albin, Albrecht.*

ALDEN *(English)* Wise; old.

ALDRICH *(English)* An old and wise leader.

ALEXANDER *(Greek)* Protector; helper and defender of mankind. Alexander is one of those great, strong names that stands well on its own as well as in one of its many versions. So if you like the name as is, fine. If your boy later decides that he'd rather be called Alex, Alek, or chooses the wonderfully sensual Spanish name Alessandro, it's all possible. Famous Alexanders include Alexander the Great, Alexander Hamilton, actor Alec Baldwin, Alexander Haig, and Aleksandr Solzhenitsyn. Variations: *Alasdair, Alastair, Alaster, Alec, Alejandro, Alejo, Alek, Alekos, Aleksander, Aleksandr, Alesandro, Alessandre, Alessandri, Alessandro, Alex, Alexandre, Alexandro, Alexandros, Alexei, Alexi, Alexio, Alik, Alisander, Alissander, Alissandre, Alistair, Alister, Alistir, Allistair, Allister, Allistir, Alsandair, Alsandare, Sacha, Sande, Sander, Sanders, Sanderson, Sandey, Sandie, Sandor, Sandy, Sascha, Sasha, Sashenka, Sashka (Russian), Saunders, Saunderson.*

ALFRED *(English)* Elf; wise listener; counselor. Variation: *Alfredo.*

ALPHONSE *(German)* One who is ready to fight; noble. Variations: *Alfonse, Alfonso, Alfonze, Alfonzo, Alonzo, Alphonso.*

ALTON *(English)* One who lives in an old town.

ALVIN *(German)* Friend. A couple of generations ago, Alvin was a common choice among new parents for their infant sons. One famous Alvin is choreographer Alvin Ailey. Variations: *Ailwyn, Alion, Aluin, Aluino, Alva, Alvan, Alven, Alvie, Alvino, Alvy, Alvyn, Alwin, Alwyn, Alwynn, Aylwin.*

AMOS *(Hebrew)* Strong one. Famous Amoses in the past have been named after the Book of Amos in the Old Testament; Amos was a prophet. Variations: *Amotz, Amoz.*

ANDRÉ *(French)* Manly. French version of Andrew. Variations: *Ahndray, Andrae, Andray, Aundray.*

ANDREW *(English)* Manly; brave. Andrew has always been a popular name for boys in this century, not only in English but in many languages. The name Andrew conjures up both dignity and informality, traits that served United States presidents Andrew Johnson and Andrew Jackson. Other famous Andrews include Andy Warhol, Andrew Wyeth, Andy Griffith, Prince Andrew, Andy Rooney, and Andrew Carnegie. Variations: *Aindrea, Aindreas, Anders, Andi, Andonis, Andor, Andre, Andreas, Andrei, Andres, Andrey, Andy.*

ANGELO *(primarily Italian; also Greek, Portuguese, Spanish)* Messenger; angel. Though the name Angel used to be the most popular form of this name, Angelo has come into favor because Angel has been used more often as a girls' name. Variation: *Angel.*

ANGUS *(Scottish, Gaelic)* Only or unique choice. Variation: *Aengus.*

ANTHONY *(Latin)* Praiseworthy; valuable. Saint Anthony was a hermit who lived in the third century in what is today Italy; he is the patron saint for poor people. Today, even though the name Anthony may often conjure up images of Little Italy and doo-wop singers in the 1950s, it is one of the more popular names of the last twenty-five years. A list of famous people who have Anthony as their first names is a veritable Who's Who of class: Anthony Quinn, Anthony Hopkins, Anton Chekhov, and Anthony Perkins. Variations: *Andonios, Andonis, Anntoin, Antin, Antoine, Anton, Antone, Antonello, Antoney, Antoni, Antonin, Antonino, Antonio, Antonius, Antons, Antony, Antos.*

ARMAND *(German)* Man of the army. Variations: *Arman, Armande, Armando, Armin, Armon, Armond, Armonde, Armondo.*

ARNOLD *(German)* Strong as an eagle. This definition could certainly describe one of this century's most famous golfers, Arnold Palmer. Undoubtedly, Arnold Schwarzenegger has also helped to rejuvenate the reputation of this name and its popularity in American culture and among its boys. Variations: *Arnaud, Arne, Arnie, Arno, Arnolde, Arnoldo.*

ARTHUR *(Celtic)* Bear; rock. Although Arthur is not a common name today, it was used in the early part of the century with some frequency. With its Celtic origin, most people will associate this name with King Arthur. Who wouldn't want to be named after royalty? Other famous Arthurs include Arthur Ashe, Art Linkletter, and playwright Arthur Miller. Variations: *Art, Artair, Arte, Artek, Artie, Artis, Arto, Artur, Arturo, Arty, Atur.*

AUGUST *(Latin)* Worthy of respect. Variations: *Agostino, Agosto, Aguistin, Agustin, Agustino, Augie, Augustin, Augustine, Augustino, Augusto, Augustus, Augy.*

AUSTIN *(English)* Majestic. Austin, along with its variants, is currently one of the more popular names. Especially with the recent newfound popularity of writer Jane Austen, this name seems to be at the forefront of an explosion in "veddy British" names on these shores. Austin has recently held the honor of being the most popular name for newborn boys in a few of the western U.S. states. Famous Austins are still few and far between, until those in the current crop hit their stride. Variations: *Austen, Austyn.*

AVERY *(English)* Counselor. This name fits tidily into the trend of naming a baby after a town or place, and also as an androgynous name that suits both boys and girls equally well.

Slightly Daring Choices

ABDUL *(Arabic)* Servant of God.

ABEL *(Hebrew)* Breathing spirit or breath. In the Bible, Abel was the second son of Adam.

ABNER *(Hebrew)* Father of light. Biblical. Variations: *Aviner, Avner.*

ACE *(English)* Unity. Nickname given to one who excels. It's also the name of a member of the rock group Kiss.

ACTON *(English)* Town in Great Britain.

ADAIAH *(Hebrew)* Witness of God. Variations: *Adaia, Adaya.*

ADDISON *(English)* Son of Adam.

ADE *(African: Nigerian)* Royal.

ADLAI *(Hebrew)* God's justice.

ADLER *(English)* An eagle.

ADMON *(Hebrew)* Red peony.

ADONIAH *(Hebrew)* The Lord is my God. Variations: *Adonia, Adonijah, Adoniya, Adoniyah.*

ADONIS *(Greek)* Handsome.

ADRIEL *(Hebrew)* God's flock.

AHMAD *(Arabic)* More deserving. Variation: *Ahmed.*

AJANI *(African: Nigerian)* He fights for possession.

AKELA *(Hawaiian)* Noble. Variation: *Asera.*

ALASTAIR *(Greek)* One who rules. Variation: *Alister.*

ALBANY *(English)* The city.

ALI *(Arabic)* Elevated; kind.

ALLARD *(English, French)* Brave; noble one.

AMADEUS *(Latin)* Beloved of God. Of course this name was popularized in the mid-'80s movie *Amadeus* about the composer Wolfgang Amadeus Mozart. Will your child turn out to be a prodigy if you give him this name? Variations: *Amadeo, Amado.*

AMBROSE *(English)* Immortal being.

AMMAR *(Arabic)* Long life.

ANASTASIO *(Italian)* Resurrection. Variation: *Anastasius.*

ANSEL *(French)* One who follows a nobleman. Variations: *Ancel, Anselm.*

ANSON *(English)* Son of Anne. Anson can also mean son of God. A famous Anson is actor Anson Williams, who played Potsy on *Happy Days*. Variations: *Annson, Ansson.*

Creating a Name from Scratch

Okay, maybe you've been reading through the names in this book, but nothing's hit you yet. Perhaps you're not looking for a name that's just "unusual"—you want a name that goes beyond the realm of typical conventionalities.

Well, you could make up your own unique name by creating a word that doesn't mean anything, or you could use a word that is a name for *something* else—just not usually a person. That's how the fad for naming babies after geographic places came about. One day out of the blue, a couple named their son or daughter Montana, and someone else heard it and thought it was a good idea. Now, while Montana isn't exactly commonplace, these days people don't look at you funny when you tell them it's the name you've chosen for your little girl.

If you want to give your baby a newly created name, you might start by looking around you at the things that really mean the most. Choosing a name that represents something close to your heart is a great way to transfer that love to your new baby.

Just be careful that you don't go too far out on a limb here. Just because *you* think "Nirvana" embodies everything you're aiming for with a name—maybe for you, having a baby is just like Heaven, or maybe you're just a huge fan of the band—that doesn't mean the kids in school will share your sentiments someday!

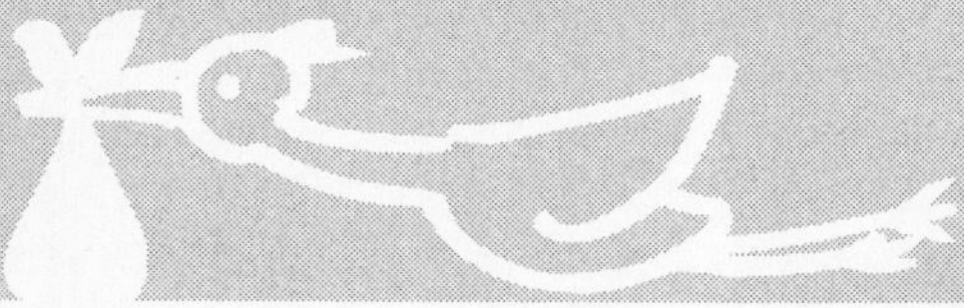

APOLLO *(Greek)* Manly; destroyer. Apollo, the god of medicine and healing, is known as one of the more powerful Greek gods. He is best known for flying through the sky in a chariot and giving a famous oratory at Delphi. Variations: *Apollon, Apollos, Apolo.*

ARCHER *(English)* Bowman; archer. Variations: *Archibald, Archie, Archy.*

ARDEN *(Celtic)* Eager.

ARES *(Greek)* The god of war.

ARI *(Hebrew)* Lion. Variation: *Arie.*

ARISTOTLE *(Greek)* Superior. The Greek philosopher who was known only by his first name was the most famous example of Aristotle until Jacqueline Kennedy married the Greek shipping tycoon Aristotle Onassis. Variations: *Ari, Arie, Arri, Ary.*

ARLEN *(Irish, Gaelic)* Pledge; oath. Variations: *Arlan, Arlin, Arlyn.*

ARLO *(Spanish)* Bayberry tree. Even though the only Arlo you may have heard of is Arlo Guthrie, the name is actually a common Italian version of Charles.

ARMON *(Hebrew)* High place.

ARMSTRONG *(English)* One who has a strong arm.

ARRIO *(Spanish)* Fierce; warlike. Variations: *Ario, Arryo, Aryo.*

ARSENIO *(Greek)* Virile; masculine. The first time you probably ever heard this name was when you got your first glimpse of talk show host Arsenio Hall.

ARTEMUS *(Greek)* One who follows Artemis, the Greek goddess of the hunt. Variations: *Artemas, Artemis, Artimas, Artimis, Artimus.*

ASAD *(Arabic)* More fortunate. Variation: *Assad.*

ASHBY *(English)* Ash tree farm. Variations: *Ash, Ashbey, Ashbie, Ashburn.*

ASHER *(Hebrew)* Happy. Asher was one of Jacob's sons in the Bible. Variations: *Anschel, Anshel, Anshil, Ashu.*

ASHLIN *(English)* Ash trees that encircle a pond. Variation: *Ashlen.*

ASHTON *(English)* Town with ash trees. Actor Ashton Kutcher is quickly making this unique name popular. It will probably be even more popular when his die-hard fans have children of their own in ten or fifteen years.

ASRIEL *(Hebrew)* Prince of God.

ATLEY *(English)* Meadow. Variations: *Atlea, Atlee, Atleigh, Attlee, Attleigh, Attley.*

AVERILL *(English)* Fighting boar. Variations: *Ave, Averel, Averell, Averil, Averyl, Averyll, Avrel, Avrell, Avrill, Avryll.*

AVIRAM *(Hebrew)* My father is strong. Variation: *Abiram.*

AZRAEL *(Hebrew, Greek)* Help from God. Variation: *Azriel.*

Living on the Edge

AADI *(Hindu)* Beginning.

ABBA *(Hebrew)* Father.

ABDAL KARIM *(Arabic)* One who serves the generous one. Variations: *Abdel Kerim, Abdel Krim.*

ABDAL RAHIM *(Arabic)* One who serves the compassionate. Variations: *Abder Rahim, Abdul Rahim.*

ABDAL SALAM *(Arabic)* One who serves peace. Variations: *Abdel Salam, Abdul Salam, Abdus Salam.*

ABDUL JABBAR *(Arabic)* Servant of the mighty.

ABDUL KARIM *(Arabic)* Servant of a generous man. Variation: *Abdul Kareem.*

ACESTES *(Greek)* Mythological Trojan king.

ACHAIUS *(Irish)* Horseman.

ACHILLES *(Greek)* The mythological hero who appears in

Homer's *Iliad*, where he successfully fights the Trojans. His mother helped to make him unbeatable when she held him by the ankle and submerged him in the River Styx. His ankle was the only part of him that could be injured, which is why today we refer to that part of the anatomy as an Achilles' heel.

ACHIYA *(Hebrew)* God is my brother. Variations: *Achiyahu, Ahia, Ahiah.*

ACTAEON *(Greek)* Ancient mythological figure.

ADAMNAN *(Irish)* Little Adam. Variation: *Adhamhnan.*

ADAMYA *(Hindu)* Difficult.

ADAR *(Syrian)* Ruler or prince; (Hebrew) noble; fiery.

ADEBEN *(African: Ghanian)* Twelfth-born son.

ADIKA *(African: Ghanian)* First child from second husband.

ADIL *(Arabic)* Fair.

ADITYA *(Hindu)* The sun. Variation: *Aaditva.*

ADIV *(Hebrew)* Gentle.

ADOLPH *(German)* Noble wolf. Variations: *Adolf, Adolfo, Adolphe.*

AEACUS *(Greek)* Son of Zeus.

AILESH *(Hindu)* King of all.

AILILL *(Irish)* Sprite.

AINMIRE *(Irish)* Great lord.

AISEA *(Polynesian)* God saves.

AKE *(Scandinavian)* Ancestor. Variation: *Age.*

AKIHITO *(Japanese)* Bright.

AKONIIA *(Hawaiian)* The Lord is my God. Variation: *Adoniia.*

ALGOT *(Scandinavian)* Last name.

ALITZ *(Hebrew)* Happy. Variation: *Aliz.*

ALLON *(Hebrew)* Oak tree. Variation: *Alon.*

ALOIKI *(Hawaiian)* Famous war. Variation: *Aloisi.*

ALPHEUS *(Greek)* God of the river.

ALTAIR *(Greek)* Bird.

AMARIAH *(Hebrew)* God has spoken. Variations: *Amaria, Amariahu, Amarya, Amaryahu.*

AMASA *(Hebrew)* Hardship. Variations: *Amasai, Amasia, Amasiah, Amasya.*

AMIRAM *(Hebrew)* Powerful country.

ANAD *(Hindu)* God. Variation: *Anaadi.*

ANAEL *(Greek)* Guardian for Librans.

ANANYA *(Hindu)* Unique.

APIA *(Hawaiian)* God is my father. Variation: *Abia.*

ARCAS *(Greek)* The son of Jupiter and Callisto.

ARNOST *(Czech)* Determined.

ARUN *(Cambodian)* Sun.

ARVIN *(German)* Friend of the people. People might recognized this name from actor Arvin Sloane in the popular television series *Alias.* Variations: *Arv, Arvid, Arvie, Arvy, Arwin, Arwyn.*

ATID *(Thai)* Sun.

AULAY *(Scottish)* Forefather.

AXEL *(Scandinavian)* Father of peace; reward from God. Axel is a common name in both Norway and Sweden, but the first that Americans got wind of the name was from the lead singer of the rock group Guns 'N Roses, Axl Rose. Variations: *Aksel, Ax, Axe, Axell, Axil, Axill, Axl.*

AZAD *(Turkish)* Free.

AZIEL *(Hebrew)* God is my power.

AZIM *(Arabic)* Defender. Variations: *Aseem, Asim, Azeem.*

Learn a Lesson from Celebrities' Baby Names

Most of us know that those Hollywood types have a penchant for the unusual. No surprise, then, that many stars choose unusual names for their kids. But there's a fine line between unusual and just plain outlandish. Case in point: By now, anyone who hasn't been living under a rock probably knows that actress Gwyneth Paltrow and her husband, Coldplay rocker Chris Martin, named their daughter Apple Blythe Alison. What would make these parents mess with a perfectly lovely name like "Blythe Alison" by affixing the name of a fruit in front of it. Maybe she's the Apple of their eyes, but who else will see things that way?

Here are some other bizarre celebrity baby names, guaranteed to get you to think twice about making the same kinds of mistakes:

ZOWIE BOWIE
MOON UNIT and DWEEZIL ZAPPA
SAGE MOONBLOOD STALLONE
PILOT INSPEKTOR LEE
CRUMPET COHEN
DIEZEL KY LEWIS
JAZ ELLE AGASSI
BANJO PATRICK TAYLOR
RYDER RUSSELL ROBINSON *(Okay, this one's not so bad, but maybe Kate Hudson and Chris Robinson could have let up a little on the alliteration.)*

These are just some of the many silly celebrity names, which just goes to show that in spite of all that Hollywood money and beauty, there's no accounting for taste—or brains, apparently.

Tried and True Classics

BAILEY *(English)* This name has also become popular for girls in the last decade; it originally meant a steward or bailiff. Variations: *Bailee, Bailie, Baillie, Baily, Baylee, Bayley, Bayly.*

BALDWIN *(German)* Brave friend. Variations: *Bald, Baldovino, Balduin, Baldwinn, Baldwyn, Baldwynn, Balldwin, Baudoin.*

BARCLAY *(English)* Valley of the birches. Variations: *Barcley, Barklay, Barkley, Barklie, Barrclay.*

BARRY *(Gaelic)* Pointed object; spear. Barry is also increasingly being used as a girls' name with the spelling of Barrie. The name, however, is not as popular as it was a couple of decades ago. Variation: *Barrymore.*

BARTHOLOMEW *(English)* Farmer's son. The basic version of this English surname may be given as a first name, usually after a family member. There are countless derivatives that come from Bartholomew, which was the name of one of the twelve apostles. Today, the most famous celebrity who goes by a shortened version of Bartholomew is none other than Bart Simpson. Variations: *Bart, Bartel, Barth, Barthel, Barthelemy, Barthelmy, Barthlomeo, Bartholome, Bartholomieu, Bartlett, Bartoli, Bartolo, Bartolomeo, Bartram.*

BEAU *(French)* Beautiful. Variation: *Bo.*

BENJAMIN *(Hebrew)* In the Bible Benjamin was the youngest son of Jacob. The name translates to son of my right hand. The name Benjamin has become extremely popular in recent years, but it has been a great American staple since the days of Benjamin Franklin. Other famous Benjamins include Benjamin Disraeli and Dr. Benjamin Spock. Variations: *Benejamen, Beniamino, Benjaman, Benjamen, Benjamino, Benjamon, Benji, Benjie, Benjiman, Benjimen, Benjy,*

Bennie, Benny, Minyamin, Minyomei, Minyomi.

BERNARD *(German)* Brave. Bernard has a long and illustrious history, even though it is not frequently on the top fifty lists. Two saints from medieval days went by the name Bernard, as does the heroic type of dog that is considered to be the patron saint for hikers. Variations: *Barnard, Barnardo, Barney, Barnhard, Barnhardo, Barnie, Barny, Bernardas, Bernardel, Bernardin, Bernardino, Bernardo, Bernardyn, Bernhard, Bernhardo, Bernie, Berny, Burnard.*

BERT *(English)* Bright light. Bert is more common in the United States as a shortened version of Robert, Gilbert, and other names that end in "-bert." Famous Berts include Burt Reynolds, Burt Lancaster, Burt Bachrach, and the best friend of Ernie. Variations: *Berthold, Bertie, Bertold, Bertolde, Berty, Burt, Burtt, Burty.*

BILL *(English)* Bill is rarely a given first name. It is a variation of the more formal name William, which most parents of "Bills" choose to name their boys. Variations: *Billy, Byll.*

BLAINE *(Gaelic)* Thin. Blaine is also used as a girls' name. Variations: *Blain, Blane, Blayne.*

BLAIR *(English)* Flat piece of land. Like Blaine, Blair is also commonly given to girls. Variations: *Blaire, Blayr, Blayre.*

BLAKE *(English)* This name could be given to both boys and girls and, strangely enough, could mean either light or dark. Blake is a name that became synonymous with the most famous TV character of the '80s, *Dynasty*'s Blake Carrington, who was played by John Forsythe. The husband of actress Julie Andrews, Blake Edwards, has long been known for his offbeat movies. Variations: *Blaike, Blayke.*

BOB *(English)* Bright; famous. Like its common counterpart Bill, Bob is rarely given as the name that will appear on the birth certificate; Robert is typically the given name of choice. Famous Bobs include singer Bob Dylan and the late comedian Bob Hope. Variations: *Bobbey, Bobbie, Bobby.*

BORIS *(Slavic)* Warrior. Boris is one of those names that brings up memories of Saturday-morning cartoons or monster movies. Famous Borises include Boris Karloff, Boris Pasternak, Boris Yeltsin, and Boris Becker. Variations: *Boriss, Borris, Borys.*

BOYD *(Gaelic)* Blonde. Variation: *Boid.*

BRADFORD *(English)* A wide stream. Variations: *Brad, Bradburn, Braddford, Bradfurd.*

BRADLEY *(English)* A wide meadow. Bradley is one of those names that seems to always skirt the edge between extreme popularity and obsolescence. The name is undoubtedly popular today due to the fame of movie star Brad Pitt. Variations: *Brad, Bradlea, Bradlee, Bradleigh, Bradlie, Bradly.*

BRADSHAW *(English)* Wide forest.

BRADY *(English)* Wide island.

BRANDON *(English)* Sword; hill afire. Brandon is one of those names that appears to be suddenly cool. Famous Brandons include Brandon Cruz, who played Bill Bixby's son in the TV show *The Courtship of Eddie's Father*, and network heads Brandon Tartikoff and Brandon Stoddard. Variations: *Bran, Brandan, Branden, Brandin, Brandyn.*

BRENDAN *(Irish, Gaelic)* Little raven. Famous Brendans include Brendan Gill, Brendan Fraser, and Brendan Behan. Brendan was also an Irish saint nicknamed "The Voyager," who, rumor has it, was the first Irishman to sail to America. Variations: *Brenden, Brendin, Brendon.*

BRENNAN *(Irish)* Raven. Variation: *Brennen, Breneon.*

BRENT *(English)* Mountaintop. Though Brent is very popular today, it has been used as a first name only for the last fifty years or so. Famous Brents include Brent Musburger, Brent Scowcroft, and the fictional character Brent Tarleton. Variations: *Brentan, Brentin, Brenton, Brentyn.*

BRETT *(English)* British man. Brett is a name that is more popular in Australia than it is on these shores. Brett is also frequently used as a girls' name today, which unlike many popular androgynous names, hasn't diminished its popularity among boys. Famous Bretts include authors Bret Harte and Bret Easton Ellis, and James Garner's cowboy character, Bret Maverick. Variations: *Bret, Brette, Bretton, Brit, Britt.*

BRIAN *(Irish, Gaelic)* Brave; virtuous. If English names are currently popular among American parents-to-be, Irish names are a close second, and Brian leads the pack. Brian seems to be popular because it's a solid name with lots of possibilities for variety, yet it has a bit of a lilt to it, and it doesn't seem overexposed—yet. There are many famous Brians, including Brian Wilson, Brian Boitano, Bryan Ferry, Brian De Palma, and Brian Dennehy. Variations: *Briano, Brien, Brion, Bryan, Bryon.*

BRODERICK *(Scottish)* Brother. Variations: *Brod, Broddy, Broderic, Brodric, Brodrick.*

BRODY *(Scottish)* Second son. Variations: *Brodee, Brodey, Brodi, Brodie.*

BRONSON *(English)* Dark man's son. With the popularity of other boys' names that start with "B-r-" and have two syllables, Bronson certainly seems like a candidate for an increase in usage. Actor Bronson Pinchot may help further the cause. Variations: *Bron, Bronnson, Bronsen, Bronsin, Bronsonn, Bronsson.*

BRUCE *(English)* Thick brush. Variations: *Brucey, Brucie.*

BRYCE *(Celtic)* Swift moving; ambitious; go-getter. Variation: *Brice.*

Slightly Daring Choices

BAIRD *(Irish)* A traveling singer. Variations: *Bard, Barde, Barr, Bayerd, Bayrd.*

BAKER *(English)* One whose job is to bake. Last name. Variations: *Bax, Baxter.*

BALDER *(English)* Brave warrior; (*Scandinavian*) Prince. Variations: *Baldur, Baudier.*

BALDRIC *(German)* Brave ruler. Variations: *Baldrick, Baudric.*

BALIN *(Hindu)* Soldier. Balin is also the name of the monkey king in Hindu mythology, who is said to be able to instantly weaken any of his enemies by just wishing it. Variation: *Bali.*

Political Names

Look at a list of past U.S. presidents as well as other politicians who have made the news in the last couple of decades, and you'll see that as far as their names go, plain works. James, John, and William are the names that have appeared more than once on the list of presidential names. On the other hand, there are some vice-presidents who never made it to the top spot. Could it be because of their names? Just think about Garret, Levi, and Schuyler. So does that mean you should stay away from Spiro if you've got political aspirations for your child?

BALLARD *(German)* Mighty.

BALTHASAR *(Greek)* One of the Three Kings of Christmas. Variation: *Balta.*

BANAN *(Irish)* White.

BARKER *(English)* Shepherd.

BARNES *(English)* The barns.

BARNETT *(English)* Baronet.

BARON *(English)* Warrior. Variation: *Barron.*

BARTON *(English)* Field of barley.

BASIL *(English)* Royal. The great British actor Basil Rathbone is the most famous person to have come along with this name, but the Catholic Church also has its own Saint Basil. Variations: *Basile, Basilio, Basilios, Basilius, Bazil, Bazyl.*

BASSETT *(English)* Short person. Because the most popular usage of Bassett in this country, excepting its service as a last name, is as the name of a hound, the name hasn't become as popular as it could be, given the great interest in giving today's American babies British names. Variation: *Basset.*

BEACAN *(Irish)* Small. Variations: *Beag, Bec, Becan.*

BEACHER *(English)* Near beech trees. Variations: *Beach, Beachy, Beecher, Beechy.*

BEAL *(French)* Handsome. Variations: *Beale, Beall, Beals.*

BECK *(English)* Brook.

BELA *(Czech)* White. The most famous person with this name is legendary actor Bela Lugosi.

BELDON *(English)* Beautiful valley. Variations: *Belden, Beldin, Bellden, Belldon.*

BELLAMY *(English)* Handsome companion. Variations: *Belamy, Bell, Bellamey, Bellamie.*

BENEDICT *(Latin)* Blessed. Though the Benedict that Americans most commonly remember is the Revolutionary War traitor Benedict Arnold, the name was actually given to fifteen different popes. And in his play *Much Ado about Nothing,* Shakespeare used the name for a bachelor who married with great hesitation. Some parents have been choosing Benedict as an alternative to the prospect of their child's facing kindergarten rooms filled with Benjamins—the names are similar but Benedict may be more distinctive. Variations: *Bence, Benci, Bendek, Bendict, Bendix,*

Benedek, Benedetto, Benedick, Benedicto, Benedictus, Benedik, Benedikt, Benito.

BENNETT *(English)* Formal version of Benedict. Variations: *Benet, Benett, Bennet.*

BENSON *(English)* Son of Ben. Last name. Variations: *Bensen, Benssen, Bensson.*

BENTLEY *(English)* Meadow. Though Bentley had its origins as a name for boys, it is starting to catch on among girls as well. Parents who dream of great things for their children—including fancy cars—may opt for the name Bentley. Variations: *Bentlea, Bentlee, Bentlie.*

BENTON *(English)* Town in Britain.

BERGER *(French)* Shepherd.

BERKELEY *(English)* Last name. Town in Britain. Berkeley is also sometimes used as a girls' name. Parents who attended the University of California at Berkeley or the Berklee School of Music in Boston may choose this name for their child as a way to influence later career choices. Variations: *Barcley, Barklay, Barkley, Barklie, Berkley.*

BERTRAM *(German)* Brightly colored raven. Variations: *Bert, Bertrand.*

BEVAN *(Welsh)* A son of a man named Evan. Its usage today is becoming popular among parents who like the name Evan, but are looking for something a little different. Variations: *Beavan, Beaven, Beven, Bevin, Bevon.*

BING *(German)* This literally means a hollow in the earth that's shaped like a pot; also, a type of cherry. Although the most famous person known by this name had the last name of Crosby, his birth name was actually Harry.

BIRCH *(English)* A tree. The most famous American with this name was the senator Birch Bayh. If nature names ever catch on again the way they did in the 1970s, an arbor-loving family might decide to name all their children after trees. Variations: *Birk, Burch.*

BIRNEY *(English)* Brook with an island. Variations: *Birnie, Birny, Burney, Burnie.*

BISHOP *(English)* Bishop.

BJORN *(Scandinavian)* Bear.

BLAISE *(Latin)* Stutterer. Variations: *Blaize, Blase, Blayse, Blayze, Blaze.*

BLAKELY *(English)* Dark or light meadow. Variations: *Blakelee, Blakeley, Blakelie.*

BLISS *(English)* Joy.

BLYTHE *(English)* Happy. Variation: *Blithe.*

BOAZ *(Hebrew)* Quick. Boaz is an obscure name from the Old Testament, and although the last time it appeared with any regularity in this country was during the seventeenth century, it does seem to be making tiny inroads among American parents who are looking for something that's completely different, but can be shortened to a familiar nickname: Bo. Variations: *Boas, Boase.*

BODEN *(French)* One who delivers the news. Variations: *Bodin, Bowden, Bowdoin.*

BOGART *(French)* Strength of a bow. Of course, the most famous Bogart went by the name Humphrey, and even though it appears most often as a last name in this country, Bogart is gaining in popularity as a first name. Variations: *Bogey, Bogie, Bogy.*

BOOKER *(English)* Slang for the Bible. One famous American with this name was Booker T. Washington.

BOONE *(French)* Good.

BORDEN *(English)* Boar's house. Variations: *Bordin, Bordon.*

BOSTON *(English)* Named for the capital city of Massachusetts.

BOWIE *(Gaelic)* Blond. Famous Bowies include David Bowie; Bowie Kuhn, a past commissioner of baseball; and the Bowie knife, named for its inventor, Colonel James Bowie.

BRADEN *(English)* Broad meadow. Variations: *Bradon, Braeden, Brayden, Braydon.*

…ic) Raven. Variations: *Bramm, Bran, Brann.*

…Welsh) Raven.

BREWSTER *(English)* Brewer. Variation: *Brewer.*

BRIGHAM *(English)* Village near a bridge. Variations: *Brigg, Briggs.*

BROCK *(English)* Badger. Variations: *Broc, Brockley.*

BRUNO *(German)* Dark-skinned. Variation: *Bruns.*

BRYDEN *(English)* Town in Britain.

BRYSON *(English)* Nobleman's son.

BUCKLEY *(English)* Meadow where deer graze. Variations: *Bucklie, Buckly.*

BUDDY *(English)* Friend. Buddy, along with its derivatives, has rarely been the name that appears on a baby's birth certificate; its common usage is as a nickname, which such notables as actors Bud Abbott and Buddy Ebsen, and football coach Bud Anderson picked up. Variations: *Bud, Budd, Buddey, Buddie.*

BURGESS *(English)* Citizen. Variations: *Burges, Burgiss.*

BURKE *(French)* Fortress dweller. Variations: *Berk, Berke, Birk, Birke, Bourke, Burk.*

BURTON *(English)* Fort. Variations: *Bert, Burt.*

BYRON *(English)* Cow barn. Variation: *Biron.*

Living on the Edge

BABAR *(Hindu)* Lion. Variation: *Baber.*

BACCHUS *(Latin)* God of wine.

BACHIR *(Hebrew)* Oldest son.

BADAR *(Arabic)* Full moon.

BADEN *(English)* Last name.

BAINBRIDGE *(English)* Bridge. Variations: *Bain, Baynbridge, Bayne, Baynebridge.*

BALFOUR *(Gaelic)* Grazing land. Town in northern Scotland. Variations: *Balfor, Balfore.*

BARDOLF *(English)* Wolf that wields an ax. Variations: *Bardolph, Bardou, Bardoul, Bardulf, Bardulph.*

BARDRICK *(German)* Soldier with an ax. Variation: *Bardric.*

BAREND *(Scandinavian)* Firm bear.

BARNABAS *(Hebrew)* Comfort. If you were an aficionado of afternoon TV in the late '60s, you undoubtedly were familiar with the spooky soap opera *Dark Shadows,* and its resident vampire, Barnabas Collins. Another famous Barnabas was Barnaby Jones, a TV detective in the '70s. Variations: *Barnabie, Barnabus, Barnaby, Barnebas, Barney, Barnie, Burnaby.*

BARNUM *(English)* A baron's home. Variation: *Barnham.*

BEANON *(Irish)* Good. Variations: *Beinean, Beineon, Binean.*

BENAIAH *(Hebrew)* God builds. Variations: *Benaya, Benayahu.*

BERDY *(Russian)* Very smart.

BERTIN *(Spanish)* Good friend. Variation: *Berton.*

BERWIN *(English)* Friend at harvest time. Variations: *Berwyn, Berwynn, Berwynne.*

BEVERLY *(English)* A stream of beavers. Beverly is more commonly a girls' name. Just don't do this to your son! Variations: *Beverlee, Beverleigh, Beverley.*

BEVIS *(French)* A town in France, though a recent popular variation of the spelling—Beavis, from MTV's *Beavis and Butthead* cartoon—will probably make you think twice about giving your baby boy this name. Variations: *Beauvais, Beavis.*

BIALAS *(Polish)* White. Variation: *Bialy.*

BIRKETT *(English)* Area with birch trees. Variations: *Birket, Birkit, Birkitt, Burket, Burkett, Burkitt.*

BONIFACE *(Latin)* Fortunate. Variations: *Bonifacio, Bonifacius.*

BOYNE *(Irish)* White cow. Variations: *Boine, Boyn.*

BRANDEIS *(German)* One who dwells in a land burned by fire.

BRASIL *(Irish)* War. Variations: *Brazil, Breasal, Bresal, Bressal.*

BRYCHAN *(Welsh)* Speckled.

BRYNMOR *(Welsh)* Great hill. Variation: *Bryn.*

BUCK *(English)* Male deer. Buck Owens and Buck Henry are two famous men with this name, which in Greek is defined as "weaver," but because of its stag-like association, some parents will shy away. It's not too bad until you realize the many nicknames your child might be called like Bucky or Buck Tooth. Variations: *Buckey, Buckie, Bucky.*

BURLEIGH *(English)* Town in Britain. Variations: *Burley, Burlie, Byrleigh, Byrley.*

BURNABY *(Norse)* Warrior's land.

BURNE *(English)* Brook. Town in Britain. Variations: *Bourn, Bourne, Bourne, Burn, Byrn, Byrne, Byrnes.*

BURNELL *(French)* Small child with brown hair. Variation: *Burnel.*

BUSBY *(Scottish)* Village in the forest.

Angelic Names

The word "angel" means "messenger" in the Bible, and angels appear in both the Old and New Testaments. The most well-known angels are:

GABRIEL: *Guardian angel of fire, Gabriel is a messenger of God. In the Bible, he appears to the prophet Daniel in the Old Testament and to Elizabeth and Zecchariah in the New Testament, announcing the birth of their son, John the Baptist. Perhaps most importantly, Gabriel is the angel who visits Mary to announce she will bear a son, Jesus.*

MICHAEL: *Guardian angel of the threshold, St. Jude describes Michael as the archangel, or chief angel (Jude 9).* In the Book of Revelation, Michael leads the angels in Heaven in a battle against the devil, and he is credited with throwing Satan out of Heaven (Rev. 12: 7–9). Michael is also described as Israel's guardian angel in the Book of Daniel.

RAPHAEL: *The angel Raphael appears in the Book of Tobit, which is accepted as part of the Catholic, Anglican, and Orthodox Bibles, although not the Protestant Bible.*

Following are some other angels' names that might not sound quite so familiar to you:

ATTARIB: *Guardian angel of winter.*

TORQUARET: *Guardian angel of autumn.*

TUBIEL: *Guardian angel of summer.*

ZADKIEL: *Guardian angel of benevolence, mercy, and memory.*

C

Tried and True Classics

CALEB *(Hebrew)* Brave; dog. Caleb was a popular name among Puritans in the United States, since the Biblical Caleb was one of the people who spent time wandering with Moses on his excursion in the wilderness. Starting in the nineteenth century, common usage of the name began to fall off. However, in the current trend to look for baby names that are traditional yet different, the prevalence of Caleb among American boys has grown. Variations: *Cale, Kalb, Kaleb.*

CALVIN *(English)* Bald. There have been a wide variety of Calvins who have been on the pinnacle of fame since the twentieth century began. The great thing about them is that they're all radically different from one another: *Calvin Coolidge, Calvin Klein, Cal Ripken, and last but not least, Calvin of the late, great comic strip "Calvin and Hobbes."* Variations: Cal, Calvino, Kalvin.

CAMERON *(Gaelic)* Crooked nose or river. Variation: *Camron.*

CAMPBELL *(Gaelic)* Crooked mouth. Variations: *Cam, Camp.*

CARL *(English)* Man. Carl is one of those names that rolls off the tongue and sounds like it has more than one syllable. Famous Carls include Carl Sagan, Carl Sandburg, and Carl Bernstein. Variation: *Karl.*

CARLETON *(English)* Farmer's land. Variations: *Carlton, Charleton.*

CARLOS *(Spanish)* Man. Spanish version of Charles. Variations: *Carlino, Carlo, Carolo.*

CARMINE *(Latin)* Garden. Variations: *Carmel, Carmelo.*

CARROLL *(English)* Man. Version of Charles. Though Carol is more popular as a girls' name, it does seem to be making inroads into the male side of the chart, which is where it originally started out. Famous Carrolls include actors Carroll O'Connor and Carroll Spinney, who plays Big Bird on *Sesame Street*. Variations: *Caroll, Carolus, Carrol, Caryl.*

CARSON *(English)* Son who lives in a swamp. Popular MTV veejay Carson Daly has brought this name to the mainstream. Variation: *Karsen.*

CARTER *(English)* Driver of the cart. President Carter may be responsible for this surname catching on as a first name among both boys and girls.

CASEY *(Irish)* Observant. Popular among both girls and boys, Casey is being chosen by many parents today because it sounds like a name that suits both a kid and an adult. Some names are great for children but falter when you try them out on an adult, and vice versa. Casey works well for all ages, and both sexes, which will only continue to contribute to its popularity. Famous Caseys include Casey Stengel, Casey Kasem, and infamous engineer Casey Jones. Variations: *Cacey, Cayce, Caycey, Kasey.*

CASSIDY *(Irish)* Smart. It literally translates from O'Caiside, which means one who dwells in an area of Ireland called Caiside. Caiside itself means bent love, which somehow turned into smart. Cassidy is another wildly popular name for both boys and girls that may have begun to bloom at the peak of the TV show *The Partridge Family*, back in the 1970s. Variation: *Cassady.*

CECIL *(English)* Blind. Famous Cecils include Cecil B. de Mille, Cecil Taylor, and the companion of Beany in the children's cartoon called *Beany and Cecil.* Variations: *Cecilio, Cecillo, Cecillus, Celio.*

CEDRIC *(Welsh)* Leader of war. Variations: *Cedrick, Cedrych.*

CHAD *(English)* Protector. Strong, one-syllable names became popular for a while in the late '60s and early '70s, mostly owing to TV actors with such names. Among the most popular was Chad Everett of the show *Medical Center.* Variations: *Chadd, Chadwick.*

CHANDLER *(English)* Candle maker. This name has become popular in the last few years, due perhaps to its appearance as first and last names among both male and female TV characters. The most notable character is Chandler Bing from the hit TV series *Friends.*

CHARLES *(English)* Man. Charles has spawned a number of variations in all cultures throughout the centuries. The name has a rich and varied history, as the name of the patron saint of Catholic bishops, cartoon characters, and a slew of actors, from Charles Bronson to Charlie Chan. Other famous Charleses include Chick Corea, Charles Darwin, Charley Weaver, Charles Dickens, and Charlie Chaplin. Variations: *Charley, Charlie, Chas, Chaz, Chick, Chip, Chuck.*

CHESTER *(English)* Campsite. Chester seems to be a fussy name that conjures up Victorian tea in the afternoons and bow ties. What's more popular, however, is one of Chester's nicknames: *Chet.* Chet Huntley and Chet Atkins are two celebrities with the name. Variations: Cheston, Chet.

CHRISTIAN *(Greek)* Anointed one; Christ. Variations: *Chresta, Chris, Christiaan, Christianos, Chrystian, Cris, Kris, Kriss, Kristian.*

CHRISTOPHER *(Greek)* One who holds Christ in his heart. Famous Christophers include St. Christopher, the patron saint of people who travel, the actor Christopher Plummer, Winnie-the-Pooh's friend Christopher Robin, and explorer Christopher Columbus. Christopher just started to become popular among new parents in the '80s; now classrooms are filled with Christophers and its variations. Variations: *Chris, Christof, Christofer, Christoff, Christoffer, Christoforus, Christoph, Christophe, Christophoros, Christos, Christos, Cris, Cristobal, Cristoforo, Kit, Kitt, Kristofer, Kristofor.*

CLARENCE *(English)* Clear. Variations: *Clair, Clarance, Clare, Clarey.*

Athletic Names

Whatever their passion for sports, some parents-to-be are naming their babies after a top athletic figure. There's lots of fertile name territory to be covered in football, basketball, baseball, hockey, and tennis. Just be sure if you're living in Yankees land, you don't inadvertently name your child after a Red Sox player—you'll be risking your child's life and limb!

The Olympics is always sure to draw some unusual names to the public's attention. After all, who ever heard of the name Picabo before the 1994 Winter Olympics? Today, over a decade later, it wouldn't be that surprising to find a young lady in school with that name. Remember, however, naming your child after a top athlete *du jour* runs the risk of sounding dated in ten or twenty years. So what will people think about kids named Misty ten years from now?

CLARK *(English)* Scholar. You can't really go wrong with this name for your son. It has a few good associations like Clark Kent or Clark Gable. Variations: *Clarke, Clerc, Clerk.*

CLAUDE *(Latin)* With a limp. Claude was quite a prolific name in the arts in the sixteenth and seventeenth centuries, including luminaries such as Debussy, Monteverdi, and Monet. Variations: *Claud, Claudio, Claudius, Klaudio.*

CLAY *(English)* Maker of clay. Clay can stand on its own, but it's also short for some of the following names that have Clay as their first syllable. *American Idol* star Clay Aiken has made this name more familiar.

CLAYTON *(English)* House or town near a clay bed. Clayton is a name that has always been popular to some extent; today, however, when it is given to a newborn baby, parents are more likely to use its nickname, Clay, and not the full version. Variations: *Clayten, Claytin.*

CLEMENT *(English)* Gentle. The American we know best with the name Clement was Clement Moore, who penned "'Twas the Night Before Christmas" earlier in this century. The most common nickname for Clement is Clem. Variations: *Clem, Cleme, Clemen, Clemens, Clemente, Clementius, Clemento, Clemmie, Clemmons, Clemmy.*

CLIFFORD *(English)* Place to cross a river near a cliff. Cliff has been a good name for celebrities: think of Cliff Richard, Clifford Irving, Cliff Robertson, and Cliff Claven from *Cheers.* However, it also is associated with a Big Red Dog. Variations: *Cliff, Clyff, Clyfford.*

CLINTON *(English)* Town near a hill. Before President Clinton came into national prominence, the name Clinton had appeared now and then as a first name: *Clint Eastwood and Clint Black are two examples.* Variations: Clint, Clynt.

CODY *(English)* Cushion. Cody used to be known as a town in Wyoming and the name of various Western outlaws from the nineteenth century. Today, it is undoubtedly most famous for being the name of TV personality Kathie Lee Gifford's baby, which is all it took for the name to skyrocket in popularity in the mid-'90s. Cody is also popular for girls. Variations: *Codey, Codie, Coty, Kodey, Kodie, Kody.*

COLIN *(English)* Triumphant people; also, young boy. Colin and its various spellings have become popular for boys, and to a lesser extent, girls, in the last ten years or so. The name sounds British and worthy of respect. Another reason for its popularity is that General Colin Powell has become an American hero since his victory in the Gulf War. Variations: *Colan, Cole, Collin, Colyn.*

CONAN *(Irish)* Elevated. Conan the Barbarian aside, Conan is beginning to appear on these shores with a little more regularity. Talk show host Conan O'Brien is probably the reason. Variation: *Conant.*

CONNOR *(Irish)* Much desire. Another popular name that could serve as last name or first, male or female; it is starting to appear in both sexes more frequently. Variations: *Conner, Conor.*

CONRAD *(German)* Courageous adviser. Variations: *Conn, Connie, Conny, Conrade, Conrado, Konrad, Kurt, Kurtis.*

COOPER *(English)* Barrel maker.

COREY *(Irish)* The hollow. This name is red hot and it's not difficult to see why. It fits several of the criteria for why certain names are popular today: it's unisex—both girls and boys are comfortable with the name. It originates from across the big sea, and in the '90s in America, anything British or Irish is much sought after. In addition, a number of popular young actors and singers have the name: *Corey Feldman, Corey Haim, and Corey Hart.* However, it does show signs of being overtaken by other popular names. Variations: *Corin, Correy, Cory, Korey.*

CRAIG *(Welsh)* Rock. Craig was once very popular, with actors Craig Stevens and Craig Lucas claiming it for themselves. Variation: *Kraig.*

CURTIS *(English)* Polite. Variations: *Curt, Kurt, Kurtis.*

Slightly Daring Choices

CADMAN *(Welsh)* Soldier.

CAELAN *(Irish)* Powerful warrior. Variations: *Caelin, Calin, Caulan.*

CAIN *(Hebrew)* Spear.
CALDER *(English)* Brook.
CALEY *(Irish)* Slender.
CALLAGHAN *(Irish)* An Irish saint.
CALLUM *(Irish)* Dove. Variation: *Calum.*
CAMDEN *(English)* Twisting valley.
CANICE *(Irish)* Handsome. Variation: *Coinneach.*
CAREY *(Welsh)* Near a castle. Variation: *Cary.*
CARLIN *(Gaelic)* Little champion. Variations: *Carling, Carly, Carolan, Carollan.*
CARMICHAEL *(Gaelic)* One who follows Michael.
CARVER *(English)* Woodcarver.
CARY *(English)* Stream.
CASSIUS *(Latin)* Narcissistic. Legendary boxer Muhammad Ali's real name is Cassius Clay.
CHANCE *(English)* Good fortune.
CHARLTON *(English)* House where Charles lives. Variations: *Carleton, Carlton.*
CHASE *(English)* Hunter. Variations: *Chace, Chaise.*
CHAUNCEY *(English)* Chancellor. Variations: *Chance, Chancey, Chaunce, Chauncy.*
CHAYIM *(Hebrew)* Life. Variations: *Chaim, Chaimek, Chayyim, Chayym, Haim, Hayyim, Hayym.*
CHEYENNE *(English)* A city in Wyoming.
CHI *(African: Nigerian)* God.
CHIP *(English)* Nickname for Charles that is sometimes given as the full name.
CIAN *(Irish)* Ancient; old. Variation: *Cianan.*
CIARAN *(Irish)* Black; black hair. Variations: *Ciardha, Ciarrai*
CID *(Spanish)* Rooster; God.
CLANCY *(Irish)* Son of a red-headed soldier. Variation: *Clancey.*
CLIFTON *(English)* Town near a cliff. Variations: *Clift, Clyfton.*
CLIVE *(English)* Cliff. Horror buffs will notice this name from the famous horror director, Clive Barker. Variation: *Clyve.*

CLYDE *(Scottish)* River in Scotland.

COLBY *(English)* Dark farm. Variation: *Collby.*

COLEMAN *(English)* Dove; one who follows Nicholas; (Irish) Little dove. Cole Porter helped to make this name popular earlier in this century. Variations: *Cole, Colman.*

CORT *(German)* Courageous. Variation: *Kort.*

Boys' Names from the New Testament

The Bible is a rich source of ideas when it comes to names. These classic names have endured for thousands of years, and they are full of meaning. No wonder so many parents go this route. For boys, names might come from a specific book of the Bible—Matthew, Mark, Luke, John, Timothy, James, or Peter—or one of the twelve apostles: Thomas, Andrew, or Philip, for example. Here are some other options:

ALEXANDER: *Son of the man who carried Jesus' cross*
DEMAS: *A colleague of Paul*
ELIAS: *Variation of the Old Testament's Elijah*
GALIO: *Older brother of Seneca*
JAIRUS: *Leader of the synagogue at Capernaum*
JASON: *Colleague of Paul*
JOSEPH: *Father of Jesus*
NATHANIEL: *Disciple of Jesus*
PAUL: *Apostle*
STEPHEN: *Martyr*

COSMO *(Greek)* Order. Cosmo is the patron saint of Milan and of doctors. Fans of the television series *Seinfeld* will recognize this name as Kramer's first name. Variations: *Cos, Cosimo, Cosme.*

COSTA *(Greek)* Stable, steady. Variation: *Kostas.*

COTY *(French)* Comforter. Variation: *Koty.*

CRISPIN *(Latin)* Curly hair. Variations: *Crepin, Crispen, Crispian, Crispino, Crispo, Crispus.*

CROSBY *(English)* By the cross. Variations: *Crosbey, Crosbie.*

CYRUS *(Latin)* Sun. The most famous person with this name is baseball great Cy Young. Variation: *Cy.*

Living on the Edge

CAESAR *(Latin)* Hairy. Variations: *Caezar, Cesar, Cesare, Cesareo, Cesario, Cesaro, Cezar, Cezary, Cezek.*

CAFFAR *(Irish)* Helmet.

CALVERT *(English)* Calf herder. Variation: *Calbert.*

CARTWRIGHT *(English)* One who builds carts.

CARVEL *(French)* One who lives in a swamp. Variation: *Carvell.*

CASIMIR *(Polish)* He brings peace. Variations: *Casimire, Casimiro, Castimer, Kazimir.*

CASPAR *(English)* Wealthy man. Unless you want your child to be called "the friendly ghost," you should steer clear of this one. Variations: *Cash, Casper, Cass.*

CASTOR *(Greek)* Beaver.

CHAL *(Gypsy)* Boy.

CHALIL *(Hebrew)* Flute. Variations: *Halil, Hallil.*

CHAND *(Hindu)* Shining moon. Variations: *Chanda, Chandak, Chander, Chandra, Chandrabha, Chandrak, Chandrakant.*

CHANNING *(English)* Wise; church official.

CHE *(Spanish)* God will add. Hispanic nickname for Joseph.

CHEVALIER *(French)* Knight. Variations: *Chev, Chevi, Chevy.*

CHIRAM *(Hebrew)* Exalted brother. Variation: *Hiram.*

CHRISTMAS *(English)* The holiday. Christmas used to be a somewhat popular name through the 1800s. Perhaps parents who loved the holiday—and who were fondly remembering their own holiday celebrations before the children arrived—hoped that with a boy with this name, every day would be Christmas. Of course, after the annual rites of the kids waking up at 4 A.M., anxious to see what Santa brought, any sane parent would have second thoughts about the wisdom of being reminded of this day the other 364 days of the year.

CICERO *(English)* Chickpea. Variation: *Ciceron.*

CLEON *(Greek)* Famous. It is also a popular African-American variation of Cleo or Leon.

COLBERT *(English)* Famous sailor. Variations: *Colvert, Culbert.*

COLLEY *(English)* Black hair. Variation: *Collis.*

COLLIER *(English)* Coal miner. Like Colin, the name Collier evokes a lot of professional respect.

COLSTON *(English)* Unknown property owner. Variations: *Colson, Colt.*

CONARY *(Irish)* Last name.

CONSTANTINE *(Latin)* Stable, steady. Variations: *Constant, Constantin, Constantino, Constantinos, Costa, Konstantin, Konstanz.*

COURTLAND *(English)* Farm land. Variations: *Cortland, Cortlandt, Courtlandt.*

COURTNEY *(English)* One who lives in the court. This is another name that should be left for the girls. Variations: *Cortney, Courtenay, Courtnay.*

CRANDALL *(English)* Valley of cranes. Variations: *Crandal, Crandell.*

CUNNINGHAM *(Gaelic)* Village with a milk pail.
CUTLER *(English)* Maker of knives.
CYNAN *(Welsh)* Chief. Variation: *Kynan.*

Tried and True Classics

DALE *(English)* One who lives in a dale or valley. Variations: *Dal, Daley, Daly, Dayle.*

DAMIAN *(Greek)* Tame. Damian was a popular name in the 1970s, until it was used as the name of a character who was supposed to be the devil's son in *The Omen* movie trilogy. After that, parents might have thought twice, fearing the child might actually live up to the name's potential. Damian is also the name of the patron saint of hairdressers. Variations: *Dameon, Damiano, Damien, Damion, Damyan, Damyen, Damyon.*

DAMON *(Greek)* Gentle one. Variations: *Daemon, Daimen, Daimon, Daman, Damen, Damone, Daymon.*

DANA *(English)* A resident of Denmark. Dana can be either a girls' or boys' name.

DANIEL *(Hebrew)* God is my judge. The name is Biblical in origin—as in the tale of Daniel being thrown to the lions—but it is an approachable name, not stuffy at all. There are a slew of famous Daniels to help cement your choice: Danny DeVito, Danny Kaye, Danny Thomas, Daniel Webster, Daniel Boone, Daniel Barenboim, and Daniel Day-Lewis. Variations: *Dan, Danakas, Danek, Dani, Daniele, Daniels, Danil, Danila, Danilkar, Danilo, Danko, Dannie, Danniel, Danny, Dano, Danya, Danylets, Danylo, Dasco, Donois, Dusan.*

DARREN *(Gaelic)* Great. Variations: *Daran, Daren, Darin, Darran, Darrin, Darron, Darryn, Daryn.*

DARRYL *(English)* An English last name. Darryl was a popular name in the '80s. Famous Darryls include baseball player Darryl Strawberry and musician Darryl Hall. Darryl was so popular, in fact, that there were three of them on the

Newhart TV show. Variations: *Darrel, Darrell, Darrill, Darrol, Darryll, Daryl, Daryll.*

DAVID *(Hebrew)* Cherished. Even though the name David has been in this country since the 1700s, it has never really gone out of style. The fact that David is a Biblical name—David opposed mighty Goliath—and that so many famous people have lived with the name may combine to account for its continued popularity: David Bowie, David Mamet, David Cassidy, David Letterman, Davy Jones, and Dave Winfield. The name has significance in both the Christian and Jewish religions: David is one of the patron saints of Wales, while the Star of David is the cornerstone symbol of Judaism. Variations: *Dave, Daveed, Davi, Davidek, Davie, Davy, Dewey, Dodya.*

DAWSON *(English)* Last name. This name was made popular because of the hit TV series *Dawson's Creek.*

DEAN *(English)* Valley. Dean was wildly popular back in the '50s and '60s, probably because of actor Dean Martin; today actor Dean Cain carries the torch for the name. Variations: *Deane, Dene.*

DENNIS *(Greek)* One who follows Dionysius, the Greek god of wine. Denis is also the patron saint of France. Dennis the Menace is undoubtedly the most famous Dennis around, but a number of other Dennises have made their mark on the world: Dennis Weaver, Denis Diderot, Denis Papin, and Dennis O'Keefe, among others. Variations: *Denies, Denis, Denka, Dennes, Denney, Denny, Dennys, Denys.*

DENZELL *(African-American)* Unknown definition. Variations: *Denzel, Denziel, Denzil, Denzill, Denzyl.*

DEREK *(English)* Leader. Eric Clapton and his group Derek and the Dominoes probably gave Americans their first exposure to this name. It is also distinguished by the many British actors who share it: Derek Bond, Derek Jacobi, Derek Farr, and Derek de Lint are just a few on this prestigious list.

Variations: *Dereck, Derick, Derik, Derreck, Derrek, Derrick, Derrik, Deryck, Deryk.*

DEVEN *(Hindu)* God.

DEVIN *(Irish)* Poet. Variations: *Dev, Devan, Deven, Devon, Devonn, Devyn.*

DIEGO *(Spanish)* Hispanic form of James. Diego is starting to become popular because it is a place name—San Diego. It was also the first name of Frida Kahlo's husband, the famous Mexican artist Diego Rivera.

DILLON *(Irish)* Loyal. Variations: *Dillan, Dilon, Dilyn.*

DIMITRI *(Russian)* Lover of the earth. Variations: *Dimitr, Dimitre, Dimitrios, Dimitry, Dmitri.*

DOMINICK *(English)* Lord. Variations: *Dom, Dome, Domek, Domenic, Domenico, Domicio, Domingo, Domingos, Dominic, Dominik, Dominique, Domo, Domokos, Nic, Nick, Nik.*

DONALD *(Scottish)* Mighty. For decades, Donald has been a very popular name, with Donald Trump, Donald Sutherland, Donald Barthelme, Donald O'Connor, Donnie Osmond, and Donnie Wahlberg all succeeding with the name. Variations: *Don, Donal, Donaldo, Donalt, Donnie, Donny.*

DORIAN *(Greek)* A region in Greece. Variations: *Dorean, Dorien, Dorion, Dorrian, Dorryen.*

DOUGLAS *(English)* Dark water. River in Ireland. Common Scottish last name. It was used as frequently for girls as for boys when it first began to catch on back in the seventeenth century. Famous Douglases include General Douglas MacArthur, Douglas Fairbanks, Douglas Edwards, and Douglas Moore. Variations: *Doug, Douglass.*

DREW *(English)* Wise. Diminutive of Andrew. Drew also became a popular girls' name in the '80s. Variations: *Drewe, Dru.*

DUANE *(Irish)* Dark-skinned. Variations: *Duwayne, Dwain, Dwaine, Dwane, Dwayne.*

DUNCAN *(Scottish)* Brown-skinned soldier. Duncan is a great name—just the sound of it, the heft of it, along with its roots, makes it a great candidate to become more popular. Variations: *Dun, Dune, Dunn.*

DUSTIN *(English)* Dusty place or courageous soldier. When Dustin Hoffman's career first began to take off back in the '60s and '70s, parents didn't respond to the possibility of using this name for their own babies. Today's parents are, as little Dustins are walking around everywhere. You may decide to go the same route, or to choose one of the variations. Variations: *Dust, Dustan, Duston, Dusty, Dustyn.*

DWIGHT *(Flemish)* Blond.

DYLAN *(Welsh)* Son of the ocean. Variations: *Dillan, Dillon.*

Slightly Daring Choices

DACEY *(Gaelic)* A man from the south. Variations: *Dace, Dacia, Dacian, Dacy.*

DACIAN *(Latin)* One from Dacia in Rome.

DAKOTA *(Native American)* Friend. Dakota is also used as a name for girls, as are many of the other currently popular names that describe locations.

DALLAS *(Scottish)* Town in Scotland. Dallas can also be used as a name for girls. Dallas Green and Dallas Townsend are two big reasons for the popularity of the name.

DALLIN *(English)* Proud. Variations: *Dalan, Dallan, Dallen, Dallon, Dalon.*

DALTON *(English)* A town in a valley. Variations: *Dallton, Dalten.*

DALY *(Irish)* To gather together. Variations: *Dailey, Daley.*

DANE *(English)* Brook. Variations: *Dain, Dayne.*

DANTE *(Latin)* Everlasting. This name has an illustrious literary history, belonging to two great poets—Dante Alighieri and Dante Gabriel Rossetti. Variations: *Dontae, Donte.*

DARBY *(English)* Area where deer graze. Darby is also commonly used as a girls' name. Variations: *Dar, Darb, Derby.*

DARCY *(Irish)* Dark one. Like Darby, Darcy is also occasionally used to name girls. Variations: *Darce, Darcey, Darsey, Darsy.*

DARIUS *(Greek)* Wealthy. Variations: *Dario, Darrius.*

DARNELL *(English)* Hidden area. Variations: *Darnal, Darnall, Darnel.*

DAVIN *(Scandinavian)* Shining.

DAVIS *(English)* Son of David. Variations: *Davison, Dawson.*

DAYTON *(English)* Illuminated town.

DEACON *(Greek)* Servant. Variations: *Deke, Dekel, Dekle.*

DECLAN *(Irish)* Irish saint. Declan is slowly but surely becoming more popular among parents with Irish roots who want to give their boys a name that reflects their family background and has a somewhat romantic sound to it. Variation: *Deaclan.*

DELANEY *(Irish)* Child of a competitor. Variations: *Delaine, Delainey, Delainy, Delane, Delany.*

DELBERT *(English)* Sunny day. Though Delbert seems a bit old-fashioned, singer Delbert McClinton and baseball player Del Unser keep this name in the public consciousness.

DELL *(English)* Valley. Dell has been used both as a boys' and girls' name, though in this country it has appeared more as a female name, sometimes spelled with only one "l." Variation: *Del.*

DEMETRIUS *(Greek)* Lover of the earth. Variations: *Demeter, Demetre, Demetri, Demetrio, Demetris, Demetrois, Dimetre, Dimitri, Dimitry, Dmitri, Dmitrios, Dmitry.*

DEMPSEY *(Irish)* Proud.

DENTON *(English)* Valley town. Variations: *Dent, Denten, Dentin.*

DENVER *(English)* Green valley. Capital of Colorado. Denver is also popularly used as a girls' name.

The Most Popular Boys' Names from the 1950s

Americans in the 1950s were ripe with postwar optimism about the future of the country and their own kids. Parents chose safe, almost corporate names that also provided for some degree of variation as a baby grew into an adult.

1. Robert
2. Michael
3. James
4. John
5. David
6. William
7. Thomas
8. Richard
9. Gary
10. Charles
11. Ronald
12. Dennis
13. Steven
14. Kenneth
15. Joseph
16. Mark
17. Daniel
18. Paul
19. Donald
20. Gregory
21. Larry
22. Lawrence
23. Timothy
24. Alan
25. Edward
26. Gerald
27. Douglas
28. George
29. Frank
30. Patrick
31. Anthony
32. Philip
33. Raymond
34. Bruce
35. Jeffrey
36. Brian
37. Peter
38. Frederick
39. Roger
40. Carl
41. Dale
42. Walter
43. Christopher
44. Martin
45. Craig
46. Arthur
47. Andrew
48. Jerome
49. Leonard
50. Henry

DERMOT *(Irish)* Free of jealousy. This name is not too popular but actor Dermot Mulroney might change that. Variations: *Dermod, Dermott.*

DESMOND *(Irish)* From South Munster, an old civilization in Ireland. South African archbishop Desmond Tutu and author Desmond Morris have helped to make this name more visible in the last decade. Variations: *Desmund, Dezmond.*

DESTIN *(French)* Fate. Variation: *Deston.*

DEVLIN *(Irish)* Courageous. Variations: *Devland, Devlen, Devlyn.*

DIALLO *(African)* Bold.

DION *(African-American)* God. Dallas Cowboys star Deion Sanders is the most popular celebrity with this name. Variations: *Deion, DeOn, Deon.*

DOLAN *(Irish)* Black hair.

DONOVAN *(Irish)* Dark. Variations: *Don, Donavan, Donavon, Donoven, Donovon.*

DORAN *(Irish)* Stranger. Variations: *Doron, Dorran, Dorren.*

DRAKE *(English)* Dragon.

DUKE *(English)* Leader. Shortened version of Marmaduke.

DYSON *(English)* Last name. Shortened version of Dennison.

Living on the Edge

DAGAN *(Hebrew)* Earth. Variation: *Dagon.*

DALBERT *(English)* Bright one. Variation: *Delbert.*

DANFORTH *(English)* Town in Britain.

DARIUS *(Greek)*; also a Persian king.

DARRIE *(Irish)* Red hair. Variation: *Darry.*

DARTON *(English)* Place where deer graze.

DARWIN *(English)* Friend. Variations: *Danvin, Derwin, Derwynn.*

DASAN *(Native American)* Chief.

DEKER *(Hebrew)* To pierce.

DENBY *(Scandinavian)* Denmark village. Variations: *Danby, Denbey.*

DENHAM *(English)* Town in a dell.

DENNISON *(English)* Son of Dennis. Variations: *Denison, Dennyson, Dyson.*

DEONTAE *(African-American)* Newly created. Variations: *D'Ante, Deante, Deonte, Diante, Diontay, Dionte, Donte.*

DEORSA *(Scottish)* Farmer.

DERBY *(English)* Village with deer.

DERNAS *(Hebrew)* A colleague of Paul's.

DEVAL *(Hindu)* Divine.

DEVERELL *(English)* Riverbank.

DEVINE *(Irish)* Ox.

DEWEY *(English)* Last name.

DEXTER *(Latin)* Right-handed. Variation: *Dex.*

DIAMOND *(English)* Jewel.

DICKENS *(English)* Last name. Variations: *Dickon, Dickons.*

DIDIER *(French)* Desire.

DIEDERIK *(Scandinavian)* Ruler of the people. Variations: *Diderik, Didrik, Dierk.*

DIETER *(German)* People's army.

DIETRICH *(German)* Leader of the people.

DIMA *(Russian)* Powerful warrior.

DINO *(Italian)* Small sword. Nickname for Dean.

DINSMORE *(Irish)* Fort on the hill.

DIONYSUS *(Latin)* God of wine. Variations: *Dionis, Dionusios, Dionysius.*

DIPAK *(Hindu)* Lamp. Deepak Chopra has made this name recognizable in the American mainstream. Variation: *Deepak.*

DIRK *(German)* Dagger.

DOBRY *(Polish)* Good.

DONAHUE *(Irish)* Dark. Variations: *Donahoe, Donohue.*

DONATO *(Italian)* Present. Variations: *Don, Donat, Donatello, Donati, Donatien, Donatus.*

DONNAN *(Irish)* Brown. Variation: *Donn.*

DONNELLY *(Irish)* Dark-skinned man. Variations: *Don, Donnell.*

DOUGAL *(Scottish)* Dark-skinned stranger. Variations: *Dougald, Dougall, Dugal, Dugald, Dugall.*

DOWAN *(Irish)* Black.

DOYLE *(Irish)* Dark stranger.

DUDLEY *(English)* Field where people gather. Variation: *Dudly.*

DUFF *(Celtic)* Dark-skinned. Variations: *Duffey, Duffy.*

DUNHAM *(Celtic)* Dark-skinned man.

DUNLEY *(Celtic)* Meadow on a hill.

DUNLOP *(Scottish)* Muddy hill.

DUNMORE *(Scottish)* Fort on a hill.

DUNN *(Scottish)* Brown. Variation: *Dunne.*

DUNSTAN *(English)* Rocky hill.

DUNTON *(English)* Town on a hill.

DWYER *(Irish)* Dark wisdom.

DYER *(English)* One who dyes clothing for a living.

Tried and True Classics

EARL *(English)* Leader; nobleman. Famous Earls include Erle Stanley Gardner, Earl Warren, and Earl Scruggs. Rarely used as a first name these days, Earl is often chosen as a good middle name. Variations: *Earle, Earlie, Early, Erl, Erle, Errol, Erryl.*

EDGAR *(English)* Wealthy man who holds a spear. Edgar Winter, Edgar Allan Poe, and Candice Bergen's father, Edgar, are all notable men with this name. Variations: *Edgard, Edgardo.*

EDMUND *(English)* Wealthy guardian. As a given name, Edward is more popular than Edmund, even though the variations and nicknames that derive from each are basically the same. Variations: *Ed, Eddie, Eddy.*

EDWARD *(English)* Guardian of property. Edward has a touch of nobility to it, along with a number of famous, distinguished men who go by the name: Edward Albee, Edward Hopper, and Edouard Manet. Of course, some of the more exotic spellings can only help to enhance the image of Edward. Variations: *Ed, Eddie, Edouard, Eduardo, Edvard.*

EDWIN *(English)* Rich friend. Variation: *Edwyn.*

ELI *(Hebrew)* God is great. Variations: *Elie, Ely.*

ELIJAH *(Hebrew)* The Lord is my God. Elijah Wood played Frodo in the *Lord of the Rings* trilogy. Variations: *Elek, Elias, Eliasz, Elie, Eliya, Eliyahu, Ellis, Elya.* Elliot (English) God on high. Variations: *Eliot, Eliott, Elliott.*

ELTON *(English)* Ella's town; old town. Not a very popular name but it belongs to one of the greatest singer/songwriters of our time, Elton John.

ELVIN *(English)* Old friend.

The Most Popular Boys' Names from the 1960s

Who could predict that the decade following the tranquil 1950s would bring such turmoil in national events? You'd think this shift would also follow suit when it came to choosing children's names, but to the contrary, the names parents were choosing for their babies were actually quite conventional. Most of the radical shifts in political activity and social outlook did not occur until the second half of the decade, and that's when the change in baby-name choices began to take place. These new choices quietly averaged in with the more sedate names of the decade's first half, and so unusual choices didn't surface on top name lists until the 1970s.

1. Michael
2. David
3. James
4. John
5. Robert
6. William
7. Mark
8. Richard
9. Jeffrey
10. Charles

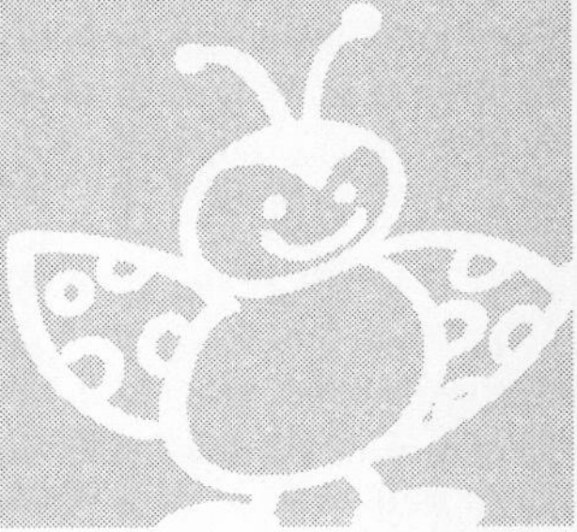

ELVIS *(Scandinavian)* Wise.

EMANUEL *(Hebrew)* God is among us. The name given to the Messiah. Biblical names are hot, and Emanuel, which appears in Isaiah 7:14, signifies prophecy and promise and is given by parents to a son whom they believe is capable of accomplishing great things. Though the shortened versions of Manny and Manuel are directly derived from Emanuel, today's parents are tending toward the full, more formal version. Variations: *Emmanuel, Emmanuil; Immanuel, Manny, Manuel.*

EMILE *(French)* Eager. The French novelist Emile Zola is perhaps the most famous Emile around, although actor Emilio Estevez has helped to make the name more visible in recent years. Variations: *Emil, Emilek, Emilio, Emilo, Emils.*

EMMETT *(German)* Powerful. Clown Emmett Kelly, Jr., popularized this name, but it is beginning to catch on for girls as well. Variations: *Emmet, Emmot, Emmott.*

ENRICO *(Italian)* Leader of the house. Variations: *Enric, Enrikos, Enrique.*

ERIC *(Scandinavian)* Ruler of the people. Eric is a very popular name that appears to have reached its peak in the mid-'70s, helped along, no doubt, by the fame of Eric Clapton, Eric Severeid, and speedskater Eric Heiden. Like its feminine counterpart, Erica, Eric first became popular in the United States in the mid-nineteenth century as the result of a popular children's book called *Eric; or, Little by Little*, by an author named Frederic William Farrar. Variations: *Erek, Erich, Erick, Erico, Erik.*

ERNEST *(English)* Earnest. Variations: *Earnest, Ernestino, Ernesto, Ernie, Ernst.*

ERWIN *(English)* A boar and a friend. A number of men with the name Erwin have been involved behind the scenes in movies, including producer Erwin Allen. Author Irwin Shaw wrote the book *Rich Man, Poor Man.* Variations: *Erwinek, Erwyn, Erwynn, Irwin.*

ETHAN *(Hebrew)* Steady. The novel *Ethan Frome* and the Revolutionary War hero Ethan Allen are the best-known examples of this name. It should be among the top contenders for parents who are looking for a dignified name that fits a child as well as it does an adult. Variations: *Eitan, Etan.*

EUGENE *(Greek)* Well born. Eugene O'Neill and Eugene Ormandy were christened with this name, as well as four popes, but today its nickname—Gene—is more popular as a given name than its source. Variations: *Eugen, Eugeni, Eugenio, Eugenius, Gene.*

EVAN *(Welsh)* God is good. Evan is a version of John that is picking up speed as a common name for American boys today. However much they like the name, we wouldn't suggest that parents with the last name of Evans go so far as the parents of Evan Evans, a Welsh poet from the eighteenth century. Variations: *Ev, Evann, Evans, Evin, Ewan.*

Slightly Daring Choices

EAMON *(Irish)* Rich protector. Variation: *Eamonn.*

EATON *(English)* Town on a river. Variations: *Eatton, Eton, Eyton.*

EDAN *(Celtic)* Fire.

EDEN *(Hebrew)* Delight. Variations: *Eaden, Eadin, Edan, Edin.*

EDISON *(English)* Edward's son. Variations: *Ed, Eddison, Edson.*

EIMHIN *(Irish)* Quick.

ELAN *(Hebrew)* Tree. Variation: *Ilan.*

ELDON *(English)* Consecrated hill; in England.

ELLERY *(English)* Island with elder trees. Last name. Variation: *Ellary.*

ELLISON *(English)* Son of Ellis. Variations: *Elison, Ellyson, Elson.*

ELROY *(African-American)* The king. Variations: *El Roy, Elroi.*

ELWOOD *(English)* Old wood. Variation: *Ellwood.*

ELWYN *(Welsh)* Fair.

EMBER *(English)* Ashes.

EMERSON *(German)* Emery's son.

EMERY *(German)* Leader of the house. Variations: *Emmery, Emory.*

ENNIS *(Gaelic)* Only choice.

ENOS *(Hebrew)* Man. Variations: *Enosa, Enosh.*

ENZO *(Italian)* To win.

EOIN *(Irish)* God is good.

ERCOLE *(Italian)* Gift.

ERROL *(Scottish)* Area in Scotland. Variations: *Erroll, Erryl.*

ESMOND *(English)* Rich protector.

ÉTIENNE *(French)* Crown. Variation of Stephen.

EVANDER *(Scottish)* Good man. Boxer Evander Holyfield is the most well-known person with this name.

EVERETT *(English)* Wild boar. Everett is most commonly known as a last name. Variations: *Everard, Everet, Everhard, Everitt.*

EZRA *(Hebrew)* Helper. It seems that names with an unusual letter like "z" or "x" are becoming very popular; this may be one explanation for why Ezra is starting to appear more often on boys' birth certificates. The poet Ezra Pound is the most famous holder of this name. Variations: *Esra, Ezera, Ezri.*

Living on the Edge

EBENEZER *(Hebrew)* Ebenezer literally means rock that helps, but who could hear this name without thinking of the Dickens' story *A Christmas Carol*? In many old cemeteries in northern New England you undoubtedly would come across a whole slew of Ebenezers among the Johns and Davids. Surprisingly enough, Ebenezer was once one of the top ten names to give boys. Variations: *Ebbaneza, Eben, Ebeneezer, Ebeneser, Ebenezar, Ebenezeer.*

EDEL *(German)* Noble.

EDENSAW *(Native American: Tlingit)* Glacier.

EDSEL *(English)* Home of a rich man.

EGINHARD *(German)* Power of the sword. Variations: *Eginhardt, Egon, Einhard, Einhardt.*

EGOR *(Russian)* Farmer. Variation: *Igor.*

EIFION *(Welsh)* Last name.

EILWYN *(Welsh)* White brow. Variation: *Eilwen.*

ELAZAR *(Hebrew)* God helps.

ELBERT *(English)* Noble; shining.

ELIAZ *(Hebrew)* My God is powerful.

ELIRAN *(Hebrew)* My God is song. Variation: *Eliron.*

ELMAN *(German)* Elm tree.

ELMER *(English)* Noble. Variations: *Aylmar, Aylmer, Aymer, Ellmer, Elmir, Elmo.*

ELMO *(Latin)* Helmet from God. The *Sesame Street* character has brought attention to this name.

EPHRAYIM *(Hebrew)* Fertile. Another Bible name for boys that starts with an "E" and is beginning to appear among American children again. The name of Efrem Zimbalist, Jr., became familiar to people in the '60s through the popular TV show *The FBI.* Variations: *Efraim, Efrain, Efrayim, Efrem, Efren, Ephraim, Ephrain.*

ERASMUS *(Greek)* Loved. A famous high school in Brooklyn, Erasmus High, produced several of today's celebrities, including Barbra Streisand. Variations: *Erasme, Erasmo, Erastus.*

ERVIN *(Scottish)* Beautiful. Also a form of Irvin. Variations: *Erving, Ervyn.*

ESTÉBAN *(Spanish)* Crown. Variation of Stephen.

EVERTON *(English)* Boar town.

EWAN *(Scottish)* Youth. Variations: *Euan, Euen, Ewen.*

EZEKIEL *(Hebrew)* The strength of God. Variation: *Zeke.*

Tried and True Classics

FERDINAND *(German)* Brave traveler. Ferdinand is a very old name. It was used by Shakespeare in *Love's Labour's Lost* as well as *The Tempest*. More recently, Fernando Lamas and Jelly Roll Morton—whose real name was Fernando—are the most stellar examples of the name. The name is currently enjoying a renaissance in some of its variations. Variations: *Ferdinando, Ferdynand, Fernand, Fernando.*

FLETCHER *(English)* One who makes arrows. Actor Chevy Chase has helped to make the nickname of Fletcher more visible through his *Fletch* movies, but the full name is also an attractive choice for a boy today. Variation: *Fletch.*

FLOYD *(Welsh)* Gray hair. Famous Floyds include boxer Floyd Patterson.

FRANCIS *(Latin)* Frenchman. Francis and its derivatives were very popular earlier in this century; top names include Frank Sinatra, Franco Zeffirelli, Franco Harris, Frank Lloyd Wright, Frankie Valli, Frank Capra, and Frank Loesser, among many others. Though Francis was frequently in the top ten list of names from the late nineteenth century through the 1940s, it doesn't even crack the top fifty names today. All that may be about to change, however, as more parents opt for traditional names from their own family trees. Variations: *Fran, Franc, Franchot, Francisco, Franco, Francois, Frank, Frankie, Franky.*

FRANKLIN *(English)* A free property owner. Variations: *Frank, Franki, Frankie, Franklyn, Franklynn, Franky.*

FRANZ *(German)* Frenchman. Franz Kafka and composers Franz Liszt and Schubert are the men who come to mind with this name. Variations: *Frans, Franzen, Franzl.*

FRASIER *(English)* Town in France. Undoubtedly, Fraser will become a popular name in the next decade, due to the success of the TV character played by Kelsey Grammer. Variations: *Fraser, Fraze, Frazer, Frazier.*

FREDERICK *(German)* Merciful leader. Fred Astaire, Fred Mertz, Fred MacMurray, and even Mister Fred Rogers serve as the most popular men with this name. Variations: *Fred, Freddie, Freddy, Fredek, Frederich, Frederico, Frederik, Fredric, Fredrick, Friedrich, Fritz.*

Slightly Daring Choices

FABIAN *(Latin)* One who grows beans. The singer Fabian from the '50s—whose full name was Fabian Forte—may make this name a good choice for parents who fondly remember that decade. Variations: *Faba, Fabek, Faber, Fabert, Fabiano, Fabien, Fabio, Fabius, Fabiyan, Fabyan, Fabyen.*

FABRICE *(French)* He who works with his hands. Variations: *Fabrizio, Fabrizius.*

FALKNER *(English)* Falcon trainer. Falkner is a first name/last name that is ripe for an increase in use among parents who are looking for something distinctive and distinguished. Variations: *Falconer, Falconner, Faulkner, Fowler.*

FARON *(English)* Unknown definition. Last name. Variations: *Faran, Farin, Farran, Farrin, Farron, Farrun, Farun.*

FARRELL *(Irish)* Courageous man. Variations: *Farall, Farrel, Farrill, Farryll, Ferrel, Ferrell, Ferrill, Ferryl.*

FARROW *(Irish)* Unknown definition. Last name.

FELIPE *(Spanish)* Lover of horses. Derivative of Philip.

FELIX *(Latin)* Happy; lucky.

Scandinavian Boys' Names

Scandinavian names are certainly distinctive, but they're not all that different from what we Americans are used to, in many cases. Here are some of the top Scandinavian boys' names:

ANDERS	**HANS**	**OLAF**
BJORN	**INGVAR**	**OSKAR**
DAG	**JENS**	**PER**
ERIK	**KARL**	**ROLF**
GUNNAR	**LARS**	
GUSTAF	**NILS**	

FENTON *(English)* Town by a swamp.

FINAN *(Irish)* Blonde child. Variation: *Fionan.*

FINIAN *(Irish)* Fair. The musical *Finian's Rainbow* is how most people were first exposed to this name. Its wonderful lilt and Irish connotations may cause Finian to become more popular than it's been. Variations: *Finnian, Fionan, Fionn.*

FINLAY *(Irish)* Fair hero. Variations: *Findlay, Findley, Finleigh, Finley.*

FINN *(Irish)* From Finland.

FINNEGAN *(Irish)* Fair. Like Finian, Finnegan seems to be poised for an increase in popularity among boys' names because it meets the popularity criteria of last name, unisex usage, and the association with Ireland. Variation: *Finegan.*

FIORELLO *(Italian)* Little flower. The longtime mayor of New York earlier in this century, Fiorello LaGuardia, is the main reason that this name continues to be visible.

FITCH *(English)* Name of a mammal similar to a ferret.

FITZ *(English)* Son.

FLANNERY *(Irish)* Red hair. Though Flannery is more popularly known as a girls' name, the choice seems appropriate for a red-haired boy. Variations: *Flaine, Flann, Flannan.*

FLORIAN *(Latin)* In bloom. Variations: *Florien, Florino, Floryan.*

FLYNN *(Irish)* Red-haired man's son. Variations: *Flin, Flinn, Flyn.*

FORBES *(Scottish)* Field.

FORD *(English)* River crossing.

FOREST *(French)* Woods. Forrest Gump isn't the only popular figure with this name: Forrest Sawyer, Forrest Whittaker, and Forrest Tucker were around long before Tom Hanks' character was. Variations: *Forester, Forrest, Forrester, Forster, Foster.*

FULLER *(English)* One who shrinks cloth.

FULTON *(English)* Town of the people.

FYNN *(African: Ghanian)* River in Ghana.

Living on the Edge

FADEY *(Russian)* Bold. Variations: *Faddei, Fadeaushka, Fadeuka.*

FADIL *(Arabic)* Generous.

FAGAN *(Irish)* Eager child. Variation: *Fagin.*

FAIRLEIGH *(English)* Meadow with bulls. Variations: *Fairlay, Fairlee, Fairlie, Farleigh, Farley.*

FAISAL *(Arabic)* Stubborn. Variation: *Faysal.*

FALAN *(Hindu)* Fertile. Variations: *Faleen, Falit.*

FAOLAN *(Irish)* Little wolf. Variations: *Felan, Phelan.*

FARNELL *(English)* Hill of ferns.

FARNHAM *(English)* Meadow of the ferns. Variations: *Farnam, Farnum, Fernham.*

FARQUHAR *(Scottish)* Dear one. Variations: *Farquar, Farquarson,*

Farquharson, Fearchar.

FAUST *(Latin)* Good luck. Variations: *Faustino, Fausto, Faustus.*

FEIVEL *(Hebrew)* Bright one. Variation: *Feiwel.*

FENWICK *(English)* Farm by a swamp.

FERGUS *(Scottish)* Best choice. Variation: *Ferris.*

FERGUSON *(Scottish)* Son of Fergus.

FIDEL *(Latin)* Faith. The major connection that people have with this name is with the ruler of Cuba, Fidel Castro, who by chance is the literal embodiment of the definition of the name—faithful. The variations for the name are highly lyrical and lack the connotations. For a baby born during the month of December, Fidel may be a good choice because of the Christmas carol "Adeste Fidelis." Variations: *Fidal, Fidele, Fidelio, Fidelis, Fidello.*

FIELDING *(English)* In the field. Variation: *Field.*

FINEEN *(Irish)* Fair birth. Variations: *Finghin, Finin, Finneen, Finnin.*

FIRTH *(English)* Forest.

FISK *(English)* Fish. Variation: *Fiske.*

FITZGERALD *(English)* Son of the mighty spearholder.

FLAMINIO *(Spanish)* Priest.

FLAVIAN *(Latin)* Yellow hair. Variations: *Flavia, Flavien, Flavio.*

FLEMING *(English)* Man from the valley. Variation: *Flemming.*

FLINT *(English)* Stream. Flint rhymes with Clint, another macho name, but Flint is even tougher-sounding.

FLORENT *(French)* Flower. Variation: *Florenz.*

FORTUNÉ *(French)* Lucky. Variations: *Fortunato, Fortunatus, Fortunio.*

FRAYNE *(English)* Foreign. Variations: *Fraine, Frayn, Freyne.*

FREEDOM *(English)* Liberty.

FREY *(Scandinavian)* Supreme Lord.

FRITZ *(German)* Peaceful ruler. Fritz started out as a nickname for Frederick, but started to appear as an independent name among babies born in the late nineteenth century. Variations: *Fritzchen, Fritzroy.*

Tried and True Classics

GABRIEL *(Hebrew)* Man of God. Gabriel is a wonderfully diverse name with plenty of choices for the parent—and later, the son—who wants a variant of the name, yet wishes to remain true to the root. Famous Gabriels include Gabe Kaplan, Garbriel Garcia Marquez, and Gabriel Byrne. Variations: *Gab, Gabby, Gabe, Gabi, Gabko, Gabo, Gabor, Gabriele, Gabrielli, Gabriello, Gabris, Gabys, Gavi, Gavriel.*

GARRETT *(Irish)* Brave with a spear. Variations: *Garett, Garrat.*

GARTH *(English)* Gardener. Garth is most popular today because of the country singer Garth Brooks, but it was even more popular in the nineteenth century, when a number of writers, from George Eliot to Charlotte Yonge, chose the name for main characters in their novels.

GARY *(English)* Spear. Gary Cooper is singlehandedly credited with creating this name as a possibility for modern use in the '40s and '50s. Before he began using it as his first name—his real name was Frank—its only use was as a last name and as a town in Indiana immortalized in the musical *The Music Man.* Today, while Gary isn't as popular as it was in the middle part of this century, celebrities currently in the spotlight include Garry Trudeau and Garry Shandling. Variations: *Garey, Garrey, Garry.*

GAVIN *(Welsh)* White falcon. Variations: *Gavan, Gaven, Gavyn, Gawain, Gawaine, Gawayn, Gawayne, Gawen.*

GENE *(English)* Well born. Derived from Eugene. Gene is a friendly, approachable name, probably made so by actors Gene Kelly, Gene Wilder, and Gene Hackman. Variations: *Genek, Genio, Genka, Genya.*

GEOFFREY *(German)* Peace. Alternative spelling for Jeffrey.

GEORGE *(Greek)* Farmer. While George as a given name has not been the most popular choice in the last couple of decades, it seems to be making a mini-comeback, particularly among parents who wish to honor an older relative with the name. Famous Georges include George Washington, George Patton, Giorgio Armani, and George Bush. Although a woman novelist in the nineteenth century became famous under the pseudonym George Sand, the name George is overwhelmingly more popular for boys than for girls. Variations: *Georg, Georges, Georgi, Georgios, Georgy, Giorgio, Giorgos.*

GERALD *(German)* Ruler with a spear. The fact that a recent president had this name may have increased its popularity among parents who like the nicknames that are created from Gerald, but prefer something a bit more formal as the given name. Once a particularly popular choice among African-American families, today it is chosen equally frequently by parents of many backgrounds. Variations: *Geralde, Geraldo, Geraud, Gerrald, Gerrold, Gerry, Jerald, Jeralde, Jeraud, Jerold, Jerrald, Jerrold, Jerry.*

GERARD *(German)* Brave with a spear. Variations: *Garrard, Gerhard, Gerrard, Gerrit, Gerry.*

GILBERT *(German)* Bright pledge. In the past, Gilbert hasn't been a name to choose if you're looking for your son to grow into a suave, debonair adult, but Johnny Depp's role in the movie *What's Eating Gilbert Grape?* may do a lot to change all that. Variations: *Gib, Gil, Gilberto.*

GINO *(Italian)* Living forever.

GIOVANNI *(Italian)* God is good. Italian version of John.

GIUSEPPE *(Italian)* God will increase. Italian version of Joseph.

GLEN *(Irish)* Narrow valley. In the past, parents have chosen Glen for their children—boys and, to a lesser extent, girls—because the name is a smooth one, nonthreatening, and already claimed by such equally unflappable celebrities as Glenn Miller and Glen Ford. Today, it may seem a bit plain for some parents, but others are choosing it just for that reason alone. Variation: *Glenn.*

GORDON *(English)* Round hill. A relative of Gordon—Jordan—is currently popular and making the rounds among new parents. Those who want to be a bit different might choose Gordon, the original. Famous Gordons include Gordon Lightfoot and Gordie Howe. Variations: *Gordan, Gorden, Gordie, Gordy.*

GRAHAM *(English)* Gray house. Singer Graham Nash and novelist Graham Greene, make this name a possibility for parents who are looking to give their sons a name that couldn't be mistaken for anything but British. Variations: *Graeham, Graeme, Grahame, Gram.*

GRANT *(French)* Great.

GREGORY *(Greek)* Observant. Gregory and its offshoots have been popular in this country since Gregory Peck appeared in *To Kill a Mockingbird.* Before that watershed event, it was more frequently chosen by popes—sixteen of them, to be precise. Today, the most famous Gregorys include Greg Louganis, the Olympic diver, and TV character Greg Brady. Variations: *Greg, Gregg, Gregoire, Gregor, Gregorio, Gregorios, Gregos, Greig, Gries, Grigor.*

GUS *(English)* Majestic. Gus was originally a shortened form of Augustus, but came into its own as an independent name over the course of the last century.

Slightly Daring Choices

GAGE *(French)* Pledge.

GALE *(Irish)* Foreigner. Variations: *Gael, Gail.*

GALEN *(Greek)* Healer. Variation: *Galeno.*

GALLAGHER *(Irish)* Foreign partner.

GALT *(Scandinavian: Norwegian)* One from a region in Norway called Galt. A famous designer named Jean Paul Gaultier has given this name some panache. Variations: *Galtero, Gaultier, Gautier.*

GALVIN *(Irish)* Sparrow. Variations: *Gallven, Gallvin, Galvan, Galven.*

GARETH *(Welsh)* Gentle. Variations: *Garith, Garreth, Garyth.*

GARLAND *(French)* Wreath. Variations: *Garlan, Garlen, Garlyn.*

GARNER *(English)* To harvest grain. Variation: *Gar.*

GARNET *(English)* Shelter; jewel; red. Variation: *Garnett.*

GARRISON *(English)* Fort.

GEARY *(English)* Changeable. Variation: *Gearey.*

GENOS *(Phoenician)* Sun worshipers.

GERMAIN *(French)* One from Germany. Variations: *Germaine, German, Germane, Germayn, Germayne, Jermain, Jermaine, Jermane, Jermayn, Jermayne.*

GIANCARLO *(Italian)* Combination of John and Charles.

GIANNIS *(Greek)* God is good; variation of John. Variations: *Giannes, Gianni, Giannos.*

GIBSON *(English)* Son of Gilbert. Variations: *Gibb, Gibbons, Gibbs.*

GIDEON *(Hebrew)* One who cuts down trees. Variations: *Gideone, Gidon, Gidoni.*

GIFFORD *(English)* Brave provider; also, puffy-faced. Variations: *Gifferd, Giffyrd.*

GILES *(English)* Young goat. Variations: *Gil, Gilles, Gyles.*

GILLEAN *(Scottish)* Servant of Saint John. Variations: *Gillan, Gillen, Gillian.*

GILMER *(English)* Famous hostage.

GILMORE *(Irish)* Servant of the Virgin Mary. Variations: *Gillmore, Gillmour, Gilmour, Giolle Maire.*

GIONA *(Italian)* Italian version of Jonah.

GIPSY *(English)* Wanderer. Variation: *Gypsy.*

GLENDON *(Scottish)* Town in a glen. Variations: *Glenden, Glendin, Glenton, Glentworth.*

GRAY *(English)* Gray. Last name. Variations: *Graydon, Grey, Grayson.*

GRIFFIN *(Latin)* One with a hooked nose. Variations: *Griff, Griffon, Gryphon.*

GRIFFITH *(Welsh)* Powerful leader. Variations: *Griff, Griffyth, Gryffyth.*

GROVER *(English)* Grove of trees. Grover is a name that both sounds cute for a baby and appropriately grownup for an adult. Grovers who have been famous include the *Sesame Street* muppet and Grover Cleveland.

GUNNAR *(Scandinavian)* Battle. Variations: *Gun, Gunder.*

GUNTHER *(Scandinavian)* Warrior. Variations: *Guenther, Gun, Gunnar, Guntar, Gunter, Guntero, Gunthar.*

GUY *(French)* Guide; forest; man. Variations: *Gui, Guion, Guyon.*

GYAN *(Hindu)* Knowledge. Variation: *Gyani.*

Living on the Edge

GADIEL *(Hebrew)* Fortune from God. Variation: *Gadiel.*

GAIR *(Irish)* Small one. Variations: *Gaer, Geir.*

GAIUS *(Welsh)* Rejoice.

GAMALIEL *(Hebrew)* God is my reward. Variation: *Gamaliel.*

GANESH *(Hindu)* Lord of them all.

GANNON *(Irish)* Light-skinned.

GARBHAN *(Irish)* Small, tough child. Variation: *Garvan.*

GARDNER *(English)* Gardener.

GAREK *(Polish)* Wealth with a spear. Variation of Edgar. Variations: *Garreck, Garrik.*

GARFIELD *(English)* Field of spears. Both a cartoon cat and a president have had this name, but it is a relatively rare choice today.

GARNOCK *(Welsh)* River of alder trees.

GARRICK *(English)* He who rules with a spear. Variations: *Garreck, Garryck, Garyk.*

GARRIDAN *(Gypsy)* He who hides.

GARSON *(English)* Son of Gar.

GARVEY *(Irish)* Peace. Variations: *Garvie, Garvy.*

GARVIN *(English)* Friend with a spear. Variations: *Garvan, Garven, Garvyn.*

GASTON *(French)* Man from Gascon. An area in France. Many children—and parents—today are familiar with Gaston only as the name of a villain in the Disney movie *Beauty and the Beast.* Variation: *Gascon.*

GAUTIER *(French)* Powerful leader. Variations: *Gauther, Gauthier.*

GEMINI *(Latin)* Twins.

GERONIMO *(Native American: Apache)* A famous Apache Indian chief.

GEVARIAH *(Hebrew)* God's might. Variations: *Gevaria, Gevarya, Gevaryah, Gevaryahu.*

GHALIB *(Arabic)* Conqueror; dominant.

GILAD *(Arabic)* Camel's hump. Variations: *Giladi, Gilead.*

GILAM *(Hebrew)* Joy of a people.

GILLANDERS *(Scottish)* Servant of St. Andrew. Variations: *Gille Ainndreis, Gille Anndrai.*

GILLESPIE *(Irish)* Servant of the bishop. Variations: *Gilleasbuig, Gillis, Giolla Easpaig.*

GILLETT *(French)* Young. Variations: *Gelett, Gelette, Gillette.*

GILROY *(Irish)* Servant of the redhead. Variations: *Gilderoy, Gildray, Gildrey, Gildroy, Gillroy.*

GILSON *(English)* Unknown definition. Last name.

GLASGOW *(Scottish)* Capital of Scotland.

GODDARD *(German)* A hard God. Variations: *Godard, Godart, Goddart, Godhardt, Godhart, Gothart, Gotthard, Gotthardt, Gotthart.*

GODFREY *(German)* God is peace. Variation of Geoffrey. Variations: *Goddfrey, Godfried, Gotfrid, Gottfrid, Gottfried.*

GOLDWIN *(English)* Golden friend. Variations: *Goldewin, Goldewyn, Goldwinn, Goldwyn, Goldwynn.*

GOLIATH *(Hebrew)* Exile. Variation: *Golliath.*

GOMER *(English)* Good fight. To me this name has an indelible association with the actor Jim Nabors as Gomer Pyle.

GONZALO *(Spanish)* Wolf. Variation: *Gonzales.*

GORE *(English)* Spear.

GORMAN *(Irish)* Child with blue eyes.

GOWON *(African: Nigerian)* Rain maker.

GRADY *(Irish)* Famous. Variations: *Gradey, Graidey, Graidy.*

GRANTLY *(English)* Gray meadow. Variations: *Grantlea, Grantleigh, Grantley.*

GRANVILLE *(French)* Big town. Variations: *Granvil, Granvile, Granvill, Grenville.*

GRAYSON *(English)* Son of a man with gray hair. Variation: *Greyson.*

GREELEY *(English)* Gray meadow. Variations: *Greelea, Greeleigh, Greely.*

GRISWOLD *(German)* Gray forest.

GUADALUPE *(Spanish)* Valley of the wolf. Variations: *Guadaloup, Guadaloupe.*

GUILDFORD *(English)* Ford with yellow flowers. Variations: *Gilford, Guildford.*

GULSHAN *(Hindu)* Garden.

GULZAR *(Arabic)* Blooming.

GUSTAF *(Scandinavian: Swedish)* Staff of the gods. Variations: *Gus, Gustaff, Gustav, Gustave, Gustavo, Gustavs, Gusti, Gustik, Gustus, Gusty.*

GUTHRE *(Irish)* Windy area. Variations: *Guthrie, Guthry.*

Tried and True Classics

HAMILTON *(English)* Fortified castle. Variation: *Hamelton.*

HANK *(English)* Ruler of the estate. Diminutive of Henry. Hank is a down-home, unpretentious name that, because of the famous men who have lived with it—Hank Aaron and Hank Williams—is a good choice for parents who are also down-home and unpretentious. However, most people use Hank as the nickname and instead give Henry as the full name.

HAROLD *(English)* Army ruler. The name Harold conjures up a feel of the good life as it was experienced about a hundred years ago, in smoking jackets and book-lined parlors. Variations: *Hal, Harailt, Harald, Haraldo, Haralds, Haroldas, Haroldo.*

HARRISON *(English)* Harry's son. Actor Harrison Ford has made this name famous. Variation: *Harrisen.*

HARRY *(English)* Ruler at home. Variation of Henry. Today Harry seems to be one of those old-fashioned names that is on its way back into style. Britain's young Prince Harry may have something to do with the revival. Variations: *Harrey, Harri, Harrie.*

HARVEY *(French)* Eager for battle. Harvey is back with a vengeance, and growing in popularity. Playwright Harvey Fierstein may have helped the reputation of the name, with his activism and outspokenness. Variations: *Herve, Hervey.*

HAYDEN *(English)* Hill of heather; (Welsh) Valley with hedges. Though Hayden and its variants are quite popular across the ocean in Great Britain and Wales, the name is just beginning to catch on in this country. Actor Hayden Christensen, who plays Anakin Skywalker in the new *Star Wars* movies, has made this name more mainstream. Variations: *Aidan, Haddan, Haddon, Haden, Hadon, Hadyn, Haydn, Haydon.*

HEATHCLIFF *(English)* Cliff near an open field. Heathcliff is probably equally famous as a cartoon cat and a character in *Wuthering Heights.* The shortened version Heath is more common than the full name these days, as is the case with actor Heath Ledger. Variation: *Heath.*

HECTOR *(Greek)* Holding fast. Actor Hector Elizondo and composer Hector Berlioz are the most famous Hectors in the last one hundred years. Variation: *Hektor.*

HENRY *(German)* Ruler of the house. Like Harry, another previously unpopular name in recent decades, Henry is one of the more popular choices around. Famous Henrys include Henry L. Mencken, Henry James, and Henry Longfellow. But perhaps an unconscious influence for the name's increasing popularity is Henry David Thoreau, who seems to be in the environmental news on a regular basis all over the country, which is pretty good considering that he's been dead for more than a hundred years. Variations: *Henery, Henri, Henrik, Henrique, Henryk.*

HERBERT *(German)* Shining army. Variations: *Heibert, Herb, Herbie.*

HERMAN *(German)* Army man. Herman Munster and Herman Melville, the author of Moby Dick, are among the most famous recipients of the name. Variations: *Hermann, Hermon.*

HERNANDO *(Spanish)* Brave traveler.

HOWARD *(English)* Observer. Last name. Howard isn't widely used in the United States today, but earlier in the century it was chosen with great frequency in Britain because people felt that it had a decidedly aristocratic feel. Howard is a saint as well as, and perhaps most famously remembered, an eccentric billionaire by the name of Hughes. It's not clear why this name went out of fashion after being one of the top twenty names for boys from the late nineteenth century through to the 1950s. Variation: *Howie.*

HUGH *(English)* Intelligent. Some famous Hughs include Hugh Hefner, actor Hugh Grant, and Hugh Downs. Variations: *Hew, Huey, Hughes, Hughie, Huw.*

HUNTER *(English)* Hunter. Although by definition the name Hunter sounds refined and mannered, parents may consider that writer Hunter Thompson has earned a reputation as a maverick.

Slightly Daring Choices

HADLEY *(English)* Meadow of heather. Variations: *Hadlea, Hadlee, Hadleigh, Hadly, Headley, Hedley, Hedly.*

HADRIAN *(Scandinavian: Swedish)* Black earth.

HADRIEL *(Hebrew)* God's glory.

HAGAN *(Irish)* Home ruler. Variations: *Hagen, Haggan.*

HALDAN *(Scandinavian)* Half Danish. Variations: *Haldane, Halden.*

HALE *(English)* Healthy. Variation: *Haley.*

HALEN *(Scandinavian: Swedish)* Hall.

HALIL *(Turkish)* Good friend.

HALIM *(Arabic)* Gentle.

HALSEY *(English)* The island that belongs to Hal. Variations: *Hallsey, Hallsy, Halsy.*

HALSTEN *(Scandinavian)* Rock and stone. Halston is perhaps best known as the last name of a designer who was famous in the '70s. Though some image-conscious parents may have chosen the name for their sons born then, it is an unusual choice today. Variations: *Hallstein, Hallsten, Hallston, Halston.*

Boys' Names from the Old Testament

The names of the books of the Old Testament have provided a wealth of names for Jewish and Christian parents alike to ponder for their baby boys. Joshua, Samuel, Joel, Malachi, and Daniel are just a few of the names that represent centuries of history and respect for the past. Here are some more examples of the many Old Testament options:

ABEL: *Adam's son*
ABRAHAM: *First Israelite called by God*
ADAM: *First man, husband of Eve*
ASHER: *Son of Jacob and Zilpah*
BENJAMIN: *Son of Jacob and Rachel*
DANIEL: *Prophet*
DAVID: *Second King of Israel, great-grandson of Boaz and Ruth*
ELEAZAR: *Aaron's son*
ELIJAH: *Prophet; traveled to heaven in a chariot of fire*
GIDEON: *Hero of the Israelites*
ISAAC: *Son of Abraham and Sarah; Rebecca's husband*
JACOB: *Son of Isaac and Rebecca*
JAPHETH: *Son of Noah*
JONAH: *Prophet swallowed by large fish*
JOSEPH: *Son of Jacob and Rachel*
LEVI: *Son of Jacob and Leah*
MORDECAI: *Uncle of Esther*
NATHAN: *Prophet*
NOAH: *Builder of the ark*
SAMUEL: *Prophet*
SETH: *Adam's son*
SOLOMON: *third King of Israel, son of David and Bathsheba*
URIAH: *Husband of Bathsheba*

HAMAL *(Arabic)* Lamb.

HAMID *(Arabic)* Greatly praised. Derivative of Mohammed. Variations: *Hammad, Hammed.*

HAMILL *(English)* Scarred. Variations: *Hamel, Hamell, Hamil, Hammill.*

HAMLIN *(German)* One who loves to stay at home. Variations: *Hamelin, Hamlen, Hamlyn.*

HAMMET *(English)* Village. Variations: *Hammett, Hammond.*

HAMUND *(Scandinavian)* Mythological figure.

HANNES *(Scandinavian)* God is good. Variation of John. Variations: *Haensel, Hannu, Hans, Hansel, Hansl.*

HANSON *(Scandinavian)* Son of Hans. Variations: *Hansen, Hanssen, Hansson.*

HARDEN *(English)* Valley of rabbits. Variation: *Hardin.*

HAREL *(Hebrew)* Mountain of God.

HARI *(Hindu)* Tawny. Some people may think this is another way to spell Harry, but it is the name for the Hindu sun god; a Sikh guru from the seventeenth century also claimed this name.

HARLAN *(English)* Army land. Variations: *Harland, Harlen, Harlenn, Harlin, Harlyn, Harlynn.*

HARLOW *(English)* Meadow of the hares.

HARPER *(English)* Harp player. Harper is a great name for parents who are looking for an androgynous last name as first name that hasn't gotten around much and possesses no negative connotations. Harper is also used as a girls' name.

HAVEN *(English)* Sanctuary. Variation: *Havin.*

HAWTHORN *(English)* Where hawthorns grow. Variation: *Hawthorne.*

HAYES *(English)* Hedges. Variation: *Hays.*

HAYWARD *(English)* Protector of hedged area.

HENLEY *(English)* High meadow. Last name.

HILLARD *(German)* Tough soldier. Variations: *Hilliard, Hillier, Hillyer.*

HILLEL *(Hebrew)* Highly praised. Jewish families are choosing this name more frequently for their sons. Hillel was the name of one of the first great Talmudic scholars.

HILTON *(English)* Town on a hill. Variation: *Hylton.*

HOGAN *(Irish)* Youth.

HOLDEN *(English)* Hollow valley. Holden Caulfield from *Catcher in the Rye* is one of the most famous literary characters of all time. Fans of this book might consider naming their son Holden.

HOLLIS *(English)* Near the holly trees.

HOUGHTON *(English)* Town on the cliff.

HOUSTON *(English)* Town on the hill.

HUDSON *(English)* Son of Hugh.

HUNTLEY *(English)* Meadow of the hunter. Variations: *Huntlea, Huntlee, Huntleigh, Huntly.*

HYDE *(English)* Measure of land in England in the Middle Ages.

Living on the Edge

HABIB *(Arabic)* Dear.

HADAD *(Arabic)* The Syrian god of virility.

HADWIN *(English)* Friend in war. Variations: *Hadwinn, Hadwyn, Hadwynne.*

HAGLEY *(English)* Surrounded by hedges. Variations: *Haglea, Haglee, Hagleigh, Haig.*

HAIDAR *(Arabic)* Lion.

HAKEEM *(Arabic)* Wise. Hakeem is common in Muslim countries, as it is one of the ninety-nine qualities of Allah that are detailed in the Koran, but it is becoming more popular here, particularly among African-American and Muslim families. Variations: *Hakem, Hakim.*

HALBERT *(English)* Bright hero. Variation: *Halburt.*

HALYARD *(Scandinavian)* Defender of the rock. Variations: *Hallvard, Hallvor, Halvor, Halvar.*

HAMISH *(Scottish)* He who removes. Hamish, which is appearing more frequently among parents who want their son's name to convey an Arabic feel—even though it originates in Scotland—also has its roots in Yiddish, where it means comfortable.

HAMLET *(English)* Village. Unless you are a die-hard Shakespeare fan, it might not be a good idea to name your son this.

HANAN *(Hebrew)* God is good.

HANDEL *(German)* God is good.

HANDLEY *(English)* Clearing in the woods. Variations: *Handlea, Handleigh, Hanley.*

HANNIBAL *(English)* Unknown definition. Parents would be smart to steer clear from naming their child Hannibal, unless you want your child to be associated with the serial killer Dr. Hannibal Lecter from *Silence of the Lambs.*

HARAL *(Scottish)* Leader of the army. Variation: *Arailt.*

HARB *(Arabic)* War.

HARBIN *(French)* Little bright warrior.

HARISH *(Hindu)* Lord. Variation: *Haresh.*

HARITH *(Arabic)* Plowman. Variation: *Harithah.*

HARKIN *(Irish)* Dark red. Variation: *Harkan, Harken.*

HARLEY *(English)* Rabbit pasture. Variations: *Arlea, Arleigh, Arley, Harlea, Harlee, Harleiah, Harly.*

HARTMAN *(German)* Hard man. Variation: *Hartmann.*

HARTWELL *(English)* Well where stags drink. Variations: *Harwell, Harwill.*

HASAD *(Turkish)* Harvest.

HASANT *(African: Swahili)* Handsome. Variations: *Hasan, Hasin, Hassan, Hassani, Husani.*

Jewish Names

In America today, the names that Jewish families select for their children are often determined by the form of Judaism that they follow. Orthodox Jews tend to select exact Biblical names for their sons and daughters. Reform and nonpracticing Jews often pick names that are more Americanized, although sometimes they will give their child a traditionally Jewish middle name.

One thing that both Orthodox and Reform Jews have in common in this country, however, is that they consider the naming of a new baby to be the perfect way to honor a deceased relative. Orthodox Jews tend to recycle the same names; Reform Jews often choose a more modern name that starts with the same letter as the relative's name. For instance, instead of choosing Sidney or Stanley for a new baby, they'll use Sam.

Sephardic Jews from Western Europe and the Middle East tend to use a naming practice that is prevalent in Egypt: They name their newborn babies after older relatives who are still alive. They believe this will add years to the adult's life while enhancing the baby's.

HASHIM *(Arabic)* Destroyer of evil. Variation: *Hasheem.*

HASIN *(Hindu)* Laughing.

HASKEL *(Hebrew)* Wisdom. Variations: *Chaskel, Haskell, Heskel.*

HASLETT *(English)* Land of hazel trees. Variation: *Hazlitt.*

HASSEL *(English)* From Hassall, the witches' corner. Variations: *Hassal, Hassall, Hassell.*

HASTIN *(Hindu)* Elephant.

HEINRICH *(German)* Ruler of the estate. Variation of Henry. Variations: *Heinrick, Heinrik, Henrik, Henrique, Henryk.*

HELMUT *(French)* Warrior. Helmut Kohl, Helmut Newton, and Helmut Lang have made this name visible, but it tends not to be too popular in this country.

HENDERSON *(English)* Son of Henry. Last name.

HERCULES *(Greek)* Zeus's son. Variations: *Herakles, Hercule.*

HERMES *(Greek)* Mythological messenger of the Greek gods.

HEVEL *(Hebrew)* Breath.

HEWITT *(English)* Last name.

HIDEAKI *(Japanese)* Wise.

HIDEO *(Japanese)* Superb.

HILARY *(Greek)* Happy. Before it became popular as a girls' name, Hilary was used for boys. Variations: *Hilaire, Hilarie, Hillary, Hillery.*

HILMAR *(Scandinavian)* Renowned nobleman.

HIMESH *(Hindu)* Snow king.

HIPPOCRATES *(Greek)* The father of medicine.

HIRAM *(Hebrew)* Most noble man. Variations: *Hirom, Hyrum.*

HIROSHI *(Japanese)* Generous.

HIRSH *(Hebrew)* Deer. Variations: *Hersch, Herschel, Hersh, Hershel, Hersz, Hertz, Hertzel, Herz, Herzl, Heschel, Hesh, Hirsch, Hirschel.*

HISHAM *(Arabic)* Generosity. Variation: *Hishim.*

HOBSON *(English)* Son of Robert. Hobson is a very refined name—the sort that might be good to select if you want your son to be a butler when he grows up.

HODIAH *(Hebrew)* God is great. Variations: *Hodia, Hodiya.*

HOKU *(Hawaiian)* Star.

HOLLEB *(Polish)* Dovelike. Variations: *Hollub, Holub.*

HOMER *(Greek)* Hostage. Homer is a noble name, unfortunately today associated as much with the father on the *Simpsons* as with the great epic poet of the third century

Items are due on the dates listed below:

Title: The complete book of baby names : the mos
t names,
Author: Bolton, Lesley.
Item ID: 0000620523829
Date due: 5/1/2019,23:59

Title: Baby names your child can live with
Author: Shaw, Lisa.
Item ID: 0000617801568
Date due: 5/1/2019,23:59

Euclid Public Library

Total Items: 2
Date Printed: 4/10/2019 5:22:37 PM

who penned the *Odyssey*. Variations: *Homere, Homeros, Homerus, Omer.*

HORACE *(Latin)* Old Roman clan name. Neither Horace nor its variant, Horatio, has ever been a wildly popular name. But Horatio actually has a bit of potential these days, as its illustrious past shows: Navy hero (Nelson), composers (Palmer), and aircraft pioneer (Phillips). Variations: *Horacio, Horatio.*

HORTON *(English)* Gray town. Think Dr. Seuss here. Variation: *Horten.*

HOWIN *(Chinese)* A swallow.

HOYT *(Irish)* Spirit.

HUBERT *(German)* Bright mind. Variations: *Hubbard, Hube, Huber, Huberto, Huey, Hugh, Hughes, Hugo, Uberto.*

HULBERT *(German)* Shining grace.

HUMBERT *(German)* Famous giant. Variations: *Humberto, Umberto.*

HUMPHREY *(English)* Peaceful. Humphrey has been most popular as a last name, but as a first name, it conjures up an image of a shaggy-haired happy kid running around the backyard. Then, of course, there's the adult version of Humphrey, as personified by the suave actor Humphrey Bogart. Variations: *Humfredo, Humfrey, Humfrid, Humfried, Humphery, Humphry.*

HURST *(English)* Grove of trees. Variation: *Hearst.*

HUSSEIN *(Arabic)* Little beauty. Variations: *Husain, Husein.*

HUXLEY *(English)* Hugh's meadow. Variations: *Hux, Huxlea, Huxlee, Huxleigh, Huxly.*

HYATT *(English)* High gate.

Tried and True Classics

IAN *(Scottish)* God is good. Ian is perhaps the most quintessentially British name you could give a boy. Ian Fleming is the writer who penned all of the James Bond stories, which could be the reason why Ian and England are so intertwined in our American minds. Ian hit its peak in both Britain and the United States in the mid-'60s. Variations: *Ean, Iain, Iancu, Ianos.*

IBRAHIM *(Arabic)* Father of many. Variation of Abraham.

IRA *(Hebrew)* Observant. Famous Iras include Ira Gershwin, brother of George, and Ira Allen, brother of Ethan.

IRVIN *(Scottish)* Beautiful. Variation: *Irvine.*

IRVING *(English)* Sea friend. Though Irving is not as popular as some other names that seem to be making a comeback these days, there is no doubt that it is being selected more in the '90s than it was ten or twenty years ago. Famous Irvings include Irving Berlin, Irving Stone, Irving Thalberg, and Irving Wallace. Variation: *Irv.*

ISAAC *(Hebrew)* Laughter. One way it's obvious that people have become more aware and proud of their ethnic heritage is by choosing names that have clear connections to their backgrounds. Isaac is a great example of this trend, as it is beginning to appear with greater frequency at synagogues and playgrounds alike. Isaacs who have made a name for themselves include Isaac Stern, Isaac Asimov, Isaac Hayes, and Isaac Bashevis Singer. Variations: *Isaak, Isak, Itzak, Ixaka, Izaak.*

ISAIAH *(Hebrew)* God helps me. Variations: *Isa, Isaia, Isia, Isiah, Issiah.*

IVAN *(Czech)* God is good. Variations: *Ivanchik, Ivanek, Ivano, Ivas.*

Slightly Daring Choices

ICARUS *(Greek)* Greek mythological figure who flew too close to the sun; his wings, attached to his body with wax, fell off and he plummeted to earth.

IKAIA *(Hawaiian)* God is my savior. Variation: *Isaia.*

IKALE *(Polynesian)* Eagle.

IKANI *(Polynesian)* Small, hot-headed child.

IKE *(English)* Short for Isaac, it has sometimes stood alone as an independent name. Variations: *Ikey, Ikie.*

ILIAS *(Greek)* The Lord is my God. Greek version of Elijah. Variation: *Ilia.*

ILYA *(Russian)* Nickname for Elias, which has become its own name. Variation: *Ilja.*

IMAD *(Arabic)* Support, pillar.

INGRAM *(English)* Raven. Variations: *Ingraham, Ingrim.*

INIGO *(Spanish)* From Ignatius. The movie *The Princess Bride* made this name visible by one of its unforgettable characters, Inigo Montoya.

INIKO *(African: Nigerian)* Hard times.

ISIDORE *(Greek)* Gift from Isis. Variations: *Isador, Isadore, Izzy.*

ISRAEL *(Hebrew)* Struggle with God. The country. Israel has been given to both Jewish boys and African-Americans in the last few decades. Variation: *Yisrael.*

IVES *(English)* Yew wood; archer. Variations: *Ivo, Ivon, Yves.*

IVORY *(African-American)* Ivory.

Living on the Edge

IAGO *(Italian)* He who grabs by the heel. Iago was an evil character in Shakespeare's play *Othello*, but the name is perhaps best known today as that of the parrot in the Walt Disney film *Aladdin*.

IAKEPA *(Hawaiian)* Hawaiian version of Jasper. Variations: *Iasepa, Kakapa, Kasapa.*

IAKONA *(Hawaiian)* To heal. Variation: *Iasona.*

IALEKA *(Hawaiian)* Descendant. Variation: *Iareda.*

IARFHLAITH *(Irish)* Tributary lord. Variation: *Jarlath.*

IBN-MUSTAPHA *(Arabic)* Son of the Mustapha.

ICHABOD *(Hebrew)* The glory is no more. Most associate this name with the schoolmaster from Washington Irving's story "The Legend of Sleepy Hollow." Variations: *Ikabod, Ikavod.*

ICHIRO *(Japanese)* First son.

IDI *(African: Swahili)* Born during the Idd festival.

IDRIS *(Welsh)* Impulsive.

IDWAL *(Welsh)* Lord + wall.

IEKE *(Hawaiian)* Wealth. Variation: *Iese.*

IELEMIA *(Hawaiian)* God will lift up. Variation: *Ieremia.*

IESTYN *(Welsh)* Moral.

IFOR *(Welsh)* Archer.

IGASHO *(Native American)* Traveler.

IGNAAS *(Scandinavian)* Fire.

IGNATIUS *(English)* Fervent; on fire. Personalities with this name are Iggy Pop and Ignatz the mouse in the cartoon strip *Krazy Kat*. Historically, Ignatius was a martyr in the Catholic church as well as the name of several saints. Variations: *Iggy, Ignac, Ignace, Ignacek, Ignacio, Ignatious, Ignatz, Ignaz, Ignazio, Inigo, Nacek, Nacicek.*

IGOR *(Russian)* Russian version of the Norwegian name Ingeborg, the guardian of the Norse god of peace.

IHAB *(Arabic)* Present.
IHSAN *(Arabic)* Benevolence.
IISHIM *(Hindu)* Spring.
IKAAKA *(Hawaiian)* Laughter. Variations: *Aikake, Isaaka.*
IKAIKALANI *(Hawaiian)* Spiritual power.
IKAMALOHI *(Polynesian)* Fish.
IKENAKI *(Hawaiian)* Fire.
ILLINGWORTH *(English)* Town in Britain.
ILLTUD *(Welsh)* Land of many people. Variation: *Illtyd.*
ILOM *(African: Nigerian)* I have enemies.
IL-SUNG *(Korean)* Superior.
IMAROGBE *(African: Nigerian)* Child born to a good family.
IMRAN *(Arabic)* Host.
IMRICH *(Czech)* Strength at home. Variation: *Imrus.*
INAR *(English)* Individual.
INCE *(Hungarian)* Innocent.
INCENCIO *(Spanish)* White one.
INEK *(Polish)* Boar friend.
INEN TOXXOUKE *(Native American: Nez Perce)* Echo.
INGEMAR *(Scandinavian)* Son of Ing, Norwegian god of peace. The most famous person with this name is director Ingmar Bergman. Variations: *Ingamar, Inge, Ingmar.*
INGER *(Scandinavian)* Ing's army. Variation: *Ingar.*
INGHAM *(English)* Area in Britain.
INGVAR *(Scandinavian)* Protector of Ing, the Norwegian god of peace.
INKPADUTA *(Native American: Sioux)* Chief of the Wahpekute Dakota tribe.
INNES *(Scottish)* Island. Variations: *Inness, Innis, Inniss.*
INNOCENZIO *(Italian)* Innocent. Variations: *Inocencio, Inocente.*
INOKE *(Polynesian)* Devoted.
INOKENE *(Hawaiian)* Innocent.
INTEUS *(Native American)* Unashamed.
IOAKIM *(Russian)* God will build.

IOELA *(Hawaiian)* God is Lord.

IOKEPA *(Hawaiian)* God will increase. Variations: *Iokewe, Iosepa.*

IOKIA *(Hawaiian)* God heals.

IOKINA *(Hawaiian)* God will develop. Variation: *Wakina.*

IOKUA *(Hawaiian)* God helps.

ION *(Irish)* God is good.

IONA *(Hawaiian)* Dove.

IONAKANA *(Hawaiian)* God will give. Variation: *Ionatana.*

IONGI *(Polynesian)* Young.

IORWERTH *(Welsh)* Handsome lord. Variation: *Yorath.*

IPPAKNESS WAYHAYKEN *(Native American: Nez Perce)* Mirror necklace.

IPYANA *(African: Tanzanian)* Grace.

IRAM *(English)* Shining.

IRATEBA *(Native American: Mojave)* Pretty bird. Variations: *Arateva, Yaratev.*

IROMAGAJA *(Native American: Sioux)* Crying. Variation: *Iromagaju.*

ISAM *(Arabic)* To pledge.

ISAS *(Japanese)* Valuable.

ISHA *(Hindu)* Lord.

ISHAAN *(Hindu)* Sun. Variation: *Ishan.*

ISHAM *(English)* Area in Britain.

ISHAQ *(Arabic)* Laughter.

ISHARA *(Hindu)* Sign.

ISHIEYO NISSI *(Native American: Cheyenne)* Two moons. Variation: *Ishaynishus.*

ISHMAEL *(Hebrew)* God will hear. Variations: *Ismael, Ismail, Yishmael.*

ISHNA WITCA *(Native American: Sioux)* Single man.

ISI *(Japanese)* Rock.

ISIKELI *(Polynesian)* God is strong.

ISKANDAR *(Arabic)* Protector. Variation: *Iskander.*

ISKEMU *(Native American)* Stream.
ISLWYN *(Welsh)* Grove.
ISMAH *(Arabic)* God listens. Variation: *Ismatl.*
ISMAT *(Arabic)* Protector.
ISOROKU *(Japanese)* Fifty-six.
ISSA *(African: Swahili)* Protection.

Eastern European Boys' Names

If you grew up in the '60, '70s, or even '80s, names like Natasha and Boris conjure up images of Bulwinkle cartoons. However, there is much more to be said for Eastern European names: Countries such as Russia, Poland, and Czechoslovakia have produced many striking names that have a rich, earthy sound to them.

Many boys' names that originate in Eastern Europe contain "-slav" as a suffix; in Polish, it turns to "-slaw." They both mean glorious. For instance, Miroslaw means a glorious peace, and Vaslav translates into glorious riches. Of course, not all Slavic names use this suffix—take Pavel, for instance, as well as Slavic versions of Anglicized names we're familiar with, such as Tomas and Filip.

Here are some other popular Eastern European (Russian) boys' names:

ALEXI
DMITRI
FEODOR
IGOR
IVAN
KONSTANTIN
NICOLAI
OLEG
VLADIMIR
YURI

ISTU *(Native American)* Pine sap.
ISTVÁN *(Hungarian)* Crown. Variation: *Isti.*

ITHEL *(Welsh)* Charitable lord.

ITZA-CHO *(Native American: Apache)* Eagle.

IUKEKINI *(Hawaiian)* Righteous.

IUKINI *(Hawaiian)* Well born. Variation: *Iuaini.*

IYAPO *(African: Nigerian)* Tribulation.

IYE *(Native American)* Smoke.

IZZ ALDIN *(Arabic)* Power of faith. Variations: *Izz Alden, Izz Eddin.*

IVOR *(Scandinavian: Norwegian)* Norwegian god. Variations: *Ivar, Iver.*

Tried and True Classics

JACKSON *(English)* Son of Jack. Variation: *Jakson.*

JACOB *(Hebrew)* Supplanter or heel. Jacob first appears in the Book of Genesis in the Bible; Jacob was the youngest son of Isaac and Rebecca. It is very popular among parents these days, possibly because it displays a sense of forthrightness and openness. No upper-crust pretentions here. Perhaps the most famous literary Jacob was created by Charles Dickens in *A Christmas Carol.* Variations: *Jaco, Jacobus, Jacoby, Jacquet, Jakab, Jake, Jakie, Jakiv, Jakob, Jakov, Jakub, Jakubek, Kiva, Kivi.*

JACY *(Native American)* Moon. Variation: *Jace.*

JAMAL *(Arabic)* Handsome. Variations: *Gamal, Gamil, Jamaal, Jamahl, Jamall, Jameel, Jamel, Jamell, Jamil, Jamill, Jammal.*

JAMES *(English)* He who replaces. Variation of Jacob. James—by itself and in its many incarnations—has never really gone out of style. It can be formal or casual, and a boy with the name of James will either love it or prefer one of the more informal versions. Later on, however, having the option to be called James as an adult adds to the respect the name possesses. Famous Jameses include James Taylor, James Stewart, James Cagney, James Mason, and Jimi Hendrix. Variations: *Jacques, Jaime, Jaimey, Jaimie, Jaimito, Jamey, Jamie, Jayme, Jaymes, Jaymie, Jim, Jimi, Jimmey, Jimmie, Jimmy.*

JAMESON *(English)* Son of James. Variations: *Jamieson, Jamison.*

JARED *(Hebrew)* Descend. Jared, with its many variants, has been very popular since the mid-'60s, when it first began to appear with some regularity. Jared, however, was around as a common name in Puritan America, although it fell into a kind of black hole. Variations: *Jarad, Jarid, Jarod, Jarrad, Jarred, Jerad, Jered, Jerod, Jerrad, Jerrod, Jerryd, Yarden, Yared.*

JASON *(Hebrew)* God is my salvation. Jason Priestley, Jason Robards, and a variety of other TV and Hollywood stars combined to turn Jason into one of the hottest names of the '70s and '80s. Names that start with the letter "J" constitute a sizable percentage of names today, and when Jason first began to catch on, it represented a fresh new approach to "J" names. Today, Jason is still popular, but it can border on overuse in some areas of the country; selecting a form of Jason with a different spelling will help your son to stand apart. Variations: *Jace, Jacen, Jaison, Jase, Jasen, Jayce, Jaycen, Jaysen, Jayson.*

JAVIER *(Spanish)* Homeowner. Variation of Xavier.

JAY *(French)* Blue jay. Jay Gould, Jay Leno, and the wealthy Jay Gatsby from F. Scott Fitzgerald's novel *The Great Gatsby* are just three of the famous men with this name who have pierced the public consciousness. Parents like Jay as a choice for their sons because it's a simple name, yet still conveys a bit of a sophisticated image, probably from the Gatsby connection. Variations: *Jae, Jai, Jave, Jaye, Jeays, Jeyes.*

JEAN *(French)* He replaces. French version of John. Variations: *Jean-Francois, Jean-Michel, Jean-Phillipe, Jeannot.*

JEFFERSON *(English)* Son of Jeffrey.

JEFFREY *(German)* Peace. Jeffrey was one of the most popular names in the United States in the 1970s, but like many names that are strongly tied with a particular point in time, it is declining in popularity today. When parents do choose it, they tend to select one of its more unusual spellings. Jeffrey and its variations beginning with "G" have been extremely popular throughout Europe for most of the previous millennium. Variations: *Geoff, Geoffrey, Geoffry, Giotfredo, Jeff, Jefferies, Jeffery, Jeffries, Jeffry, Jefry.*

JEREMY *(Hebrew)* The Lord exalts. From Jeremiah. Jeremy has been a popular name among American parents in the last couple of decades. Famous Jeremys include actor Jeremy Irons and a frog named Jeremy Fisher in one of Beatrix Potter's books. However, like its counterpart Jason, Jeremy has become a bit too popular for some, who decide to opt for one of the many variants available. Variations: *Jem, Jemmie, Jemmy, Jeramee, Jeramey, Jeramie, Jere, Jereme, Jeremey, Jeremi, Jeremia, Jeremias, Jeremie, Jerimiah, Jeromy, Jerr, Jerrie, Jerry.*

JERMAINE *(German)* German. Variations: *Jermain, Jermane, Jermayne.*

JEROME *(Latin)* Sacred name. Name of a saint. Variations: *Jeron, Jerone, Jerrome.*

JESSE *(Hebrew)* God exists. Jesse Jackson, Jesse James, and Jesse Owens are the most popular people with this name, and even though it has been thought of more as a girls' name in recent years, at its peak in the '70s, it was extremely popular for boys. Jesse is great for all ages: little kids, teenagers, young fathers, and even grandfathers. Jesse has staying power, and is hip to boot. Variations: *Jesiah, Jess, Jessey, Jessie, Jessy.*

JOEL *(Hebrew)* God is Lord.

JOHN *(Hebrew)* God is good. If you count all of the variations, spellings, and language usages around the world, it's possible that more boys are named John than any other name. John cuts across all categories: in religion, there's John the Baptist and St. John the Divine; in movies, it seemed for a while in the 1950s, there was no other name to give to the lead male character (Johnny Angel, Johnny Guitar, Johnny Cool); and in entertainment, there's John Wayne, Johnny Carson, Johnny Depp, and Johnny Cash, and then Johnny Weissmuller—an Olympic gold medalist swimmer in 1924. With this prestige and a wide variety of Johns to choose from, it's a good bet that John in one or more of its forms will never be out of style. Variations: *Jack, Jackie, Jacky, Joao, Jock, Jockel, Jocko, Johan, Johann, Johannes, Johnie, Johnnie, Johnny, Jon, Jonam, Jone, Jonelis, Jonnie, Jonny, Jonukas, Jonutis, Jovan, Jovanus, Jovi, Jovin, Jovito, Jovon, Juan, Juanito.*

JOHNSON *(English)* Son of John. Variations: *Johnston, Jonson.*

JONAH *(Hebrew)* Dove. Biblical book. Variations: *Jonas, Yonah, Yonas, Yunus.*

JONATHAN *(Hebrew)* Gift from God. In the Bible, Jonathan was King Saul's oldest son and was best known as King David's best friend. Parents have liked Jonathan because it is based on a classic name—John—but is more distinctive. Robert Wagner's mystery-loving Jonathan Hart on the '80s TV show *Hart to Hart* has probably contributed to today's image of Jonathan as warm, intelligent, and sexy. Other Jonathans include Jonathan Winters and Jonathan Swift. Variations: *Johnathan, Johnathen, Johnathon, Jon, Jonathen, Jonathon, Jonnie, Jonny, Jonothon.*

JORDAN *(Hebrew)* To descend. Jordan is a unisex name as well as an occasional last name, which has helped to make it as popular as it is. During the Crusades, the name caught on when soldiers brought water from the River Jordan back home with them to baptize their children. Variations: *Jorden, Jordy, Jori, Jorrin.*

JORGE *(Spanish)* Farmer. Variation: *Jorgen.*

JOSEPH *(Hebrew)* God will increase. Perhaps the best-known Joseph is the Biblical carpenter who was Mary's husband and Jesus' earthly father. This fact, and its many varieties in America and around the world, may be the reason the name has never fallen out of style. Amazingly enough, Joseph has been on the top ten list of boys' names in New York for almost a hundred years, longer than any other name for either boys or girls. Famous Josephs have included Franz Joseph Haydn, Mormon founder Joseph Smith, and novelist Joseph Conrad. Variations: *Jodi, Jodie, Jody, Jose, Josecito, Josef, Joselito, Josephe, Josephus, Josip.*

JOSHUA *(Hebrew)* God is my salvation. Joshua was the leader of the Jews after Moses, and a book in the Bible is named for him. However, Joshua has only started to become popular since the 1960s, although other Biblical names have been used for centuries. Variations: *Josh, Joshuah.*

JUDE *(Hebrew)* Praise God. Variations: *Juda, Judah, Judas, Judd, Judson.*

JULIAN *(Latin)* Version of Julius. Saint. Variations: *Julien, Julion, Julyan.*

JULIUS *(Latin)* Young. Roman clan name. Variations: *Giulio, Julio.*

JUSTIN *(Latin)* Just. Variations: *Justen, Justino, Justo, Juston, Justus, Justyn.*

Slightly Daring Choices

JABIR *(Arabic)* Comforter.

JACINTO *(Spanish)* Hyacinth. Variations: *Ciacintho, Clacinto, Jacindo.*

JADON *(Hebrew)* God has heard. Variations: *Jacdon, Jaden, Jaydon.*

JADRIEN *(African-American)* Combination of Jay and Adrien.

JAEGAR *(German)* Hunger.

JAEL *(Hebrew)* To ascend.

JAGGER *(English)* To haul something.

JAIRUS *(Hebrew)* God clarifies.

JALEN *(African-American)* Calm.

JAMAINE *(Arabic)* German.

JAMAR *(African-American)* Newly created. Variations: *Jamarr, Jemar, Jimar.*

JAN *(Czech)* God is good. Variations: *Janco, Jancsi, Jando, Janecek, Janek, Janik, Janika, Jankiel, Janne, Jano, Janos, Jenda.*

JANSON *(Scandinavian)* Son of Jan. Variations: *Jansen, Jantzen, Janzen.*

JANUS *(English)* Born in January. Roman god.

JARAH *(Hebrew)* Sweet.

JAREB *(Hebrew)* He struggles. Variations: *Jarib, Yarev, Yariv.*

JAREK *(Czech)* Spring. Variations: *Jariusz, Jariuszek, Jarousek.*

JARELL *(African-American)* Newly created. Variations: *Jarel, Jarrel, Jarrell, Jarul.*

JARETH *(African-American)* Newly created. Variations: *Jarreth, Jerth.*

JARON *(Hebrew)* To shout. Variations: *Gerron, Jaran, Jaren, Jarin, Jarran, Jarren, Jarron, Jeran, Jeren, Jeron, Jerrin, Jerron.*

JARRETT *(English)* Brave with a spear. Variations: *Jarret, Jarrete.*

JARVIS *(German)* Honorable. Variation: *Jervis.*

JASPER *(English)* Wealthy one. Variation: *Jaspar.*

JAVAN *(English)* Son of the Biblical Japheth. Variations: *Javin, Javon.*

JAVAS *(Hindu)* Fast.

JAVON *(African-American)* Newly created. Variations: *Javonne, Jevon.*

JELANI *(African: Nigerian)* Strong. Variations: *Jalani, Jehlani.*

JENDA *(Czech)* God is good.

JENKIN *(Flemish)* Little John. Variations: *Jenkins, Jenkyn, Jenkyns.*

JENSI *(Hungarian)* Well born. Variations: *Jenci, Jens.*

JERIAH *(Hebrew)* God sees.

JERNEY *(Slavic)* Unknown definition.

JERRELL *(African-American)* Newly created. Variations: *Gerrell, Jarell, Jarrel, Jarrell, Jeriel, Jerriel, Jerul.*

JERRICK *(African-American)* Newly created. Variations: *Jerick, Jerrie.*

JERVIS *(English)* Unknown definition. Variation: *Gervase.*

JERZY *(Polish)* Farmer. Variation: *Jersey.*

JETT *(English)* Airplane.

JEVIN *(African-American)* Unknown definition. Variation: *Jevon.*

JIVAN *(Hindu)* Life. Variation: *Jivin.*

JOACHIM *(Hebrew)* God will determine. Variations: *Joaquim, Joaquin.*

Living on the Edge

JABBAR *(Hindu)* One who comforts.

JABEZ *(Hebrew)* Born in pain. Because this name ends in a "z," I always thought it was Spanish. However, it shows up on the gravestones in many old cemeteries, a testament to its Puritan roots in this country. Variations: *Jabes, Jabesh, Jabus.*

JABIN *(Hebrew)* God has created.

JABIR *(Arabic)* Healer. Variations: *Gabir, Gabr, Jabbar, Jabr.*

JAFAR *(Arabic)* River. Variations: *Gafar, Jafari.*

JAHAN *(Arabic)* World.

JAKEEM *(Arabic)* Noble.

JAKUB *(Czech)* Supplanter. Variations: *Jakoubek, Kuba, Kubes, Kubicek.*

JAL *(Gypsy)* Wanderer.

JAPHETH *(Hebrew)* He increases. Japheth was the oldest son of Noah. Variation: *Japhet.*

JARMAN *(German)* German. Variation: *Jerman.*

JAZON *(Polish)* Healer.

JEDIDIAH *(Hebrew)* Beloved of God. Variations: *Jed, Jedd, Jedediah, Jedidia, Yedidia, Yedidiah, Yedidya.*

JESUS *(Hebrew)* The Lord is my salvation.
JETHRO *(Hebrew)* Fame. Variation: *Jeth.*
JEX *(English)* Unknown definition.
JIRO *(Japanese)* Second son.
JOAB *(Hebrew)* Praise the Lord. Variation: *Jobe.*
JOAH *(Hebrew)* God is his brother.
JOB *(Hebrew)* Oppressed. Variations: *Joab, Jobe, Joby.*
JONTE *(African-American)* Newly created. Variations: *Johatay, Johate, Jontae.*
JOSHA *(Hindu)* Satisfaction.
JOSIAH *(Hebrew)* God supports. Variations: *Josia, Josias, Josua.*
JUMAH *(African: Swahili)* Born on Friday. Variation: *Juma.*
JUNIOR *(English)* Young.
JURGEN *(German)* Farmer. Variation of George.

Tried and True Classics

KAREEM *(Arabic)* Generous. In this country, basketball star Kareem Abdul-Jabbar is the most famous man around with this name today. Its definition, generous, is one of the ninety-nine qualities ascribed to God in the Koran. Variations: *Karim, Karime.*

KARL *(German)* Man. Variations: *Karlen, Karlens, Karlin.*

KEITH *(Scottish)* Forest. Keith was cool in the '70s when both a Rolling Stone and a Partridge had the name.

KENNEDY *(Irish)* Helmet head; ugly head. In the '60s, Kennedy was a name given to boys to honor the esteemed family from Massachusetts. Today, the name is also used for girls—for example, MTV had a VJ named Kennedy. Variations: *Canaday, Canady, Kenneday.*

KENNETH *(Irish)* Handsome; sprung from fire. Helped along by the macho image of Barbie's boyfriend Ken, this name was the epitome of masculinity through the '50s and '60s. However, it also conjures up images of medieval England and the Knights of the Round Table due to its appearance in a novel by Sir Walter Scott. Variations: *Ken, Kendall, Kenney, Kennie, Kennith, Kenny, Kenyon.*

KEVIN *(Irish)* Handsome. Some famous Kevins are actors Kevin Kline, Kevin Bacon, and Kevin Costner. Their reputations belie the fact that the name originated with a saint in the seventh century A.D. who headed a monastery in Dublin. Even today, however, Saint Kevin is the patron saint of Dublin. Variations: *Kavan, Kev, Kevan, Keven, Kevon, Kevyn.*

KIRK *(Scandinavian: Norwegian)* Church. Kirk was once an extremely appealing name, owing to the success of Michael's father, Kirk Douglas. Variations: *Kerk, Kirke.*

Most Popular Boys' Names from the 1970s

Although after the late '60s hit, more unusual names gained steam, during the 1970s, parents-to-be primarily continued to choose solid and traditional names, at least when it came to boys. Safe but common Biblical names—like David and John—were also big.

1. Michael
2. Robert
3. David
4. James
5. John
6. Jeffrey
7. Steven
8. Christopher
9. Brian
10. Mark
11. William
12. Eric
13. Kevin
14. Scott
15. Joseph
16. Daniel
17. Thomas
18. Anthony
19. Richard
20. Charles
21. Kenneth
22. Matthew
23. Jason
24. Paul
25. Timothy
26. Sean
27. Gregory
28. Ronald
29. Todd
30. Edward
31. Derek
32. Keith
33. Patrick
34. Darryl
35. Dennis
36. Andrew
37. Donald
38. Gary
39. Allen
40. Douglas
41. George
42. Marcus
43. Raymond
44. Peter
45. Gerald
46. Frank
47. Jonathan
48. Lawrence
49. Aaron
50. Phillip

KYLE *(Scottish)* Narrow land. Although Kyle is also a popular choice for girls these days, the name for boys has made it into the top twenty most popular names of the '90s. In Hebrew, it means crowned with laurel. Since the name is so newly popular, expect it to be prominent for the next five to ten years. Variations: *Kiel, Kile, Ky, Kyele, Kyler.*

Slightly Daring Choices

KACEY *(English)* He announces peace. Nickname for Casimir. Variation: *Kasey.*

KADAR *(Arabic)* Powerful. Variations: *Kade, Kedar.*

KADE *(Gaelic)* Swamp.

KADIN *(Arabic)* Friend. Variation: *Kadeen.*

KAELAN *(Gaelic)* Powerful soldier. Variations: *Kalan, Kalen, Kalin.*

KAEMON *(Japanese)* Right-handed.

KAHIL *(Turkish)* Young. Kahil is a name that is popular in many different countries, not just Turkey. In Hebrew, it means perfect; in Greece, it means beautiful. Up until the 1970s the form of the name we had most often seen was Cahil, the English version of this name. However, African-American families have made this name more popular in the United States. Variations: *Cahil, Kahlil, Kaleel, Khaleel, Khalil.*

KAI *(Hawaiian)* Sea.

KAISER *(Bulgarian)* Hairy.

KAJ *(Greek)* Earth.

KALA *(Hindu)* Black.

KALANI *(Polynesian)* Gallon.

KALE *(Hawaiian)* Man. Variations: *Kalolo, Karolo.*

KALEA *(Hawaiian)* Joy.

KALIL *(Arabic)* Good friend. Variation: *Kailil.*

KALINO *(Hawaiian)* Brilliant.

KAMAL *(Arabic)* Perfect. Like many of the other Arabic and Turkish names for boys that begin with "K," Kamal is becoming more popular in this country, especially among African-American families. Variations: *Kameel, Kamil.*

KANA *(Hawaiian)* God is my judge. Variations: *Dana, Daniela, Dano, Kaniela.*

KANE *(Welsh)* Beautiful; (Japanese) Golden. In America, Kane is becoming more popular for both boys and girls. One very hot variation has been introduced by superstar actor, Keanu Reeves. Variations: *Kain, Kaine, Kayne, Keanu.*

KASIM *(Arabic)* Divided. Variation: *Kaseem.*

KASIMIR *(Slavic)* He announces peace.

KASS *(German)* Blackbird. Variations: *Kasch, Kase.*

KAYIN *(African: Nigerian)* Famous.

KEANE *(English)* Sharp. Variations: *Kean, Keen, Keene.*

KEARN *(Irish)* Dark. Variation: *Kern.*

KEARNEY *(Irish)* The winner. Variations: *Karney, Karny, Kearny.*

KEATON *(English)* Hawk nest. Variations: *Keeton, Keiton, Keyton.*

KEEFE *(Irish)* Beloved. Variations: *Keefer, Keifer.*

KEEGAN *(Irish)* Small and passionate. Besides being a perfect name for a little boy who's always getting into trouble, Keegan is also considered to be the astrological sign of fire, which includes Sagittarius, Leo, and Aries. Variations: *Kagen, Keagan, Keegen, Kegan.*

KEENAN *(Irish)* Small and old. Variations: *Keenen, Keenon, Kenan, Kienan, Kienen.*

KELBY *(German)* A farm by a spring. Variations: *Kelbey, Kelbie, Kellby.*

KELL *(English)* Spring.

KELLY *(Irish)* Warrior. Not too long ago, Kelly was a name given in equal measure to both boys and girls. But today, a boy with the name of Kelly is a rare thing indeed. Variations: *Kelley, Kellie.*

KELSEY *(English)* Island. Frasier star Kelsey Grammer is the most well-known actor with this name. Variations: *Kelsie, Kelsy.*

KELTON *(English)* Town of ships.

KELVIN *(English)* Name of a Scottish River. Variations: *Keloun, Kelvan, Kelven, Kelvyn.*

KEMAL *(Turkish)* Honor.

KEMP *(English)* Fighter.

KENAN *(Hebrew)* To attain. Variation: *Cainan.*

KENDALL *(English)* Last name. Valley of the River Kent. Variations: *Kendal, Kendell.*

KENDRICK *(English)* Royal hero. Variations: *Kendricks, Kendrik, Kendryck.*

KENLEY *(English)* Meadow of the king. Variations: *Kenlea, Kenlee, Kenleigh, Kenlie, Kenly.*

KENT *(English)* County in England.

KENYA *(African-American)* African country.

KERRY *(Irish)* County in Ireland. Variations: *Kerrey, Kerrie.*

KIEFER *(German)* Barrel maker. Not a very popular name but it belongs to famous actor Kiefer Sutherland. Variation: *Keefer.*

KIERAN *(Irish)* Dark. Variations: *Keiran, Keiren, Keiron, Kieron, Kyran.*

KILEY *(English)* Narrow land.

KILLIAN *(Irish)* Conflict. Though Killian in itself is a noble name, I venture a guess to say that most people today in this country who name their boys Killian do so after the famous brew. Variations: *Kilian, Killie, Killy.*

KIMBALL *(English)* Leader in war. Variations: *Kim, Kimbal, Kimbell, Kimble.*

KINCAID *(Celtic)* Leader in war.

KINGSTON *(English)* Town of the king. Variation: *Kinston.*

KIPP *(English)* Hill with a sharp peak. Variations: *Kip, Kipper, Kippie, Kippy.*

KIRAN *(Hindu)* Ray of light.

KIRBY *(English)* Village of the church. Variations: *Kerbey, Kerbi, Kerbie, Kirbey, Kirbie.*

KLAUS *(German)* Victorious people. Short for Nicholas. Variations: *Claes, Claus, Clause, Klaas, Klaes.*

KOREN *(Hebrew)* Shining.

KORT *(Scandinavian)* Wise counselor.

KWAN *(Korean)* Powerful.

KYAN *(African-American)* Variation of Ryan.

Living on the Edge

KADEEM *(Arabic)* Servant.

KADIR *(Arabic)* Green. Variation: *Kadeer.*

KADO *(Japanese)* Entrance.

KAHO *(Polynesian)* Arrow.

KAIHAU *(Polynesian)* Leader.

KAILAHI *(Polynesian)* To gorge.

KAKANA *(Hawaiian)* Powerful.

KALECHI *(African: Nigerian)* Praise God.

KALEO *(Hawaiian)* One voice.

KALHANA *(Hindu)* Name of twelfth-century poet.

KALIQ *(Arabic)* Artistic.

KALU *(Hindu)* Name of founder of the Sikh religion.

KAMAU *(African: Kenyan)* Warrior.

KAMBAN *(Hindu)* Twelfth-century poet.

KANALE *(Hawaiian)* Hawaiian version of Stanley. Variation: *Sanale.*

KANG *(Chinese)* Healthy.

KANGI *(Native American: Sioux)* Raven. Variation: *Kangee.*

KANIEL *(Hebrew)* Reed. Variations: *Kan, Kani, Kanny.*

KANJI *(Japanese)* Tin.

KANTU *(Hindu)* Happy.

KAPILA *(Hindu)* Monkey.

KARIF *(Arabic)* Born in the fall. Variation: *Kareef.*

KARIO *(African-American)* Variation of Mario.

KARNEY *(Irish)* The winner. Variations: *Carney, Carny, Karny.*

KARR *(Scandinavian)* Swamp.

KASEKO *(African: Zimbabwean)* To tease.

KASI *(Hindu)* Bright.

KASIB *(Arabic)* Fertile. Variation: *Kaseeb.*

KASIYA *(African: Malawian)* Trip.

KASPAR *(Persian)* Protector of wealth. Variation: *Kasper.*

KAY *(Welsh)* Joy.

KAYAM *(Hebrew)* Stable.

KEAZIAH *(African-American)* Cassia.

KEB *(Egyptian)* Egyptian god.

KEDAR *(Hindu)* God of mountains.

KEDEM *(Hebrew)* Old.

KEFIR *(Hebrew)* Lion cub.

KEIR *(Irish)* Dark-skinned; swarthy. Variations: *Keiron, Kerr, Kieran, Kieron.*

KEMUEL *(Hebrew)* To help God.

KENELM *(English)* Brave helmet.

KENJI *(Japanese)* Second son.

KENWARD *(English)* Brave protector.

KENWAY *(English)* Brave fighter.

KERMIT *(Irish)* Free of jealousy. This name is undoubtedly associated with the famous green frog; however, there are some brave parents who are forging ahead and naming their baby boys after the *Sesame Street* muppet.

Strange but True Names

We've all known people who have names that are just, well, not the prettiest or most handsome names around. However, these names—like Helga, Chumley, Bertha, and other names from decades past—don't usually sound mellifluous to us in the present due to years and years of association and the ways in which each generation regards the most common names of their time. Here, however, we're not just talking about changing times. These names are just plain strange—and funny.

WINDSOR CASTLE
GROANER DIGGER
ZACHARY ZZZRA *(last in the phone book)*
REVEREND CHRISTIAN CHURCH
LAVENDER SIDEBOTTOM
JORDAN RIVER
STONE WALL
MINERAL WATERS

First, you laugh. Then your next though is, "What the heck were those parents thinking?" And so there really is a lesson to be learned amid all this ridiculousness: Think long and hard before choosing your child's name, and don't just think of the first or middle name—consider those choices with your last name as well!

KERSEN *(Indonesian)* Cherry.

KERWIN *(Irish)* Dark. Variations: *Kerwen, Kerwinn, Kerwyn, Kirwin.*

KES *(English)* Falcon.

KESTER *(English)* One who carries Christ in his heart. Variation of Christopher.

KIDD *(English)* Young goat.

KIM *(Vietnamese)* Gold.

KING *(English)* King.

KINGSLEY *(English)* Meadow of the King. If it weren't for the actor Ben Kingsley or for the novelist Kingsley Amis, most parents-to-be would not be aware of the possibility of using Kingsley for their sons. Variations: *Kingslea, Kingslie, Kingsly.*

KINNARD *(Irish)* Top of the hill. Variation: *Kinnaird.*

KIRIL *(Greek)* The Lord. Variations: *Kirillos, Kyril.*

KIRKLEY *(English)* Church meadow. Variations: *Kirklea, Kirklee, Kirklie, Kirkly.*

KLEMENS *(Polish)* Mild; compassionate. Variation: *Klement.*

KNIGHT *(English)* Unknown definition. Last name.

KNOX *(English)* Hills.

KNUTE *(Scandinavian: Danish)* Knot.

KOJI *(Japanese)* Child.

KOJO *(African: Ghanian)* Born on Monday.

KONA *(Hawaiian)* Leader of the world. Variation: *Dona.*

KONG *(Chinese)* Glorious or sky.

KONO *(Native American: Miwok)* Squirrel with a pine nut.

KONTAR *(African: Ghanian)* Only child.

KOPANO *(African: Botswana)* Union.

KORB *(German)* Basket.

KORESH *(Hebrew)* To dig. Variations: *Choreish, Choresh.*

KORNEL *(Czech)* Horn. Variations: *Kornek, Nelek.*

KOSTI *(Scandinavian: Finnish)* Staff of God.

KUBA *(Czech)* One who replaces. Variation of Jacob. Variation: *Kubo.*

KUMAR *(Hindu)* Son.

Tried and True

LARRY *(English)* Originally a nickname for Lawrence, but it's recently been considered a stand-alone name. Variations: *Larrie, Lary.*

LARS *(Scandinavian)* Crowned with laurel. Variation: *Larse.*

LAWRENCE *(English)* Crowned with laurel. The name Lawrence has been popular with great regularity since it first emerged in the third century A.D.; Saint Lawrence was a martyr. Throughout the ages, this name has made regular appearances in the work of Shakespeare and in other literature, including *Lawrence of Arabia.* Lawrence was a very popular name in the '40s and '50s, but even back then parents were actively considering variations of the name, which is how we ended up with Lorne Green, Lorne Michaels, and Lorenzo Lamas. Today, parents are once again choosing the name Lawrence for their sons. Variations: *Larry, Laurance, Laurence, Laurencio, Laurens, Laurent, Laurenz, Laurie, Lauris, Laurus, Lawrance, Lawrey, Lawrie, Lawry, Loren, Lorence, Lorencz, Lorens, Lorenzo, Lorin, Lorry, Lowrance.*

LEE *(English)* Meadow. It seems that the name Lee has always been hugely popular, both as a first and last name and as a good name for both boys and girls. Today, parents who see the simple spelling of Lee as a bit too run-of-the-mill are frequently choosing Leigh. Or, more frequently, they are tacking it on to the end of another boys' name, creating names like Lynnlee and Huntleigh. Lee Marvin, Lee Iaccoca, and even Lee Harvey Oswald have all contributed to the visibility of this name. Variation: *Leigh.*

LEIF *(Scandinavian: Norwegian)* Beloved. Leif is a great choice for parents who like the name Lee but who need something a little bit more exciting. Famous Leifs have included Leif Garrett and Leaf Phoenix, brother of the late River. Variations: *Leaf, Lief.*

LEIGHTON *(English)* Town by the meadow. Variations: *Layton, Leyton.*

LEO *(Latin)* Protect. Variations: *Leokau, Leontios, Leopold.*

LEON *(French)* Lion. Variations: *Leo, Leonas, Leone, Leonek, Leonidas, Leosko.*

LEONARD *(German)* Bold as a lion. Leonard owes most of its present visibility to popular culture. Leonardo is one of the Mutant Ninja Turtles, a group of hugely popular cartoon characters. The young actor Leonardo di Caprio has had leading roles in several recent movies, including *What's Eating Gilbert Grape?* and *Romeo and Juliet*. In fact, given the name's positive and somewhat exotic connotations, Leonard might be making a comeback. Nevertheless, several men who were named Leonard promptly gave up the name once they got into the entertainment field, including Tony Randall and Roy Rogers. Variations: *Len, Lenard, Lennard, Lenny, Leonardo, Leonek, Leonhard, Leonhards, Leonid, Leontes, Lienard, Linek, Lon, Lonnie, Lonny.*

LEROY *(French)* The king. Variations: *Le Roy, LeeRoy, Leeroy, LeRoi, Leroi, LeRoy.*

LESTER *(English)* Last name. Area in Britain, Leicester. Like its cousin Leslie, Lester has gone way out of fashion. The most famous Lester in recent years has been the character Les Nessman on the old sitcom *WKRP in Cincinnati*. Variation: *Les.*

LIONEL *(Latin)* Little lion. Variations: *Leonel, Lionell, Lionello, Lonell, Lonnell.*

LLOYD *(Welsh)* Gray or sacred. Variation: *Loyd.*

LOGAN *(Irish)* Hollow in a meadow. Logan is one of those names that manages to convey a wealth of different connotations, all of them positive. What comes to mind? Swift, smart, sexy, and just a bit intriguing.

LOUIS *(French)* Famous warrior. Louis is an old and highly esteemed French name. Dating from the sixth century A.D., Louis has been the name of no fewer than eighteen kings in France and great jazz trumpeter Louis Armstrong. Today, Louis is on the verge of making a comeback. It is that kind of traditional yet nonboring name that might just appeal to parents today. Variations: *Lew, Lewe, Lotario, Lothair, Lothar, Lothario, Lou, Luigi, Luis.*

LUCAS *(English)* Based on an area in southern Italy (Luca). It is a very popular name today, partially because it makes a great name for a little boy toddling around and a teenager who grows six inches a year as well as for a sensitive, handsome adult who you'd be proud to call your son. Luke, another version of the name, is also very popular, though it seems to be on the downswing while Lucas has not yet peaked. Variations: *Loukas, Luc, Lukas, Luke.*

LUTHER *(German)* Famous warrior. Luther has been popular in the past as a middle name, probably owing to Martin Luther King. The visibility of singer Luther Vandross however, may make this name more popular as a first name in the next few years.

LYLE *(French)* The island. Lyle is one of those wonderful, lazy names that conjures up long summer afternoons on the porch when it's too hot to do anything but drink a glass of lemonade. Singer Lyle Lovett only encourages this image and probably also the name's usage in coming years. Variations: *Lisle, Ly, Lyall, Lyell, Lysle.*

Slightly Daring Choices

LACHLAN *(Scottish)* Hostile. Variation: *Lachlann.*

LACY *(French)* Unknown definition. Variation: *Lacey.*

LADAN *(Hebrew)* Witness.

LAEL *(Hebrew)* Belongs to God.

LAFAYETTE *(French)* Last name.

LAIRD *(Scottish)* Leader of the land.

LAMAR *(Latin)* The sea. In German, the name Lamar also means having lots of land. Variations: *Lamarr, Lemar, Lemarr.*

LAMBERT *(German)* Bright land. Variations: *Lambard, Lampard; (Scandinavian)* Famous land. Variation: *Lammert.*

LAMOND *(African-American)* Variation of Lamont. Other variations: *La Mond, La Monde, Lammond.*

LAMONT *(Scandinavian)* Lawyer. Variation: *Lamonte, Lamond.*

LANCELOT *(French)* Servant. This famous Knight of the Roundtable's nickname Lance is more common. Variations: *Lance, Lancelott, Launcelot.*

LANDER *(English)* Landlord. Variations: *Landers, Landor.*

LANDON *(English)* Grassy meadow. The name Landon is a great name for a boy with literary aspirations. Variations: *Landan, Landen, Landin.*

LANDRY *(English)* Leader.

LANE *(English)* One who lives near the lane. Variations: *Laine, Layne.*

LANG *(Norse)* Tall. Variation: *Lange.*

LANGDON *(English)* Long hill. Variation: *Langden.*

LANGSTON *(English)* Long town. Variations: *Langsden, Langsdon.*

LARKIN *(Irish)* Cruel. Larkin is another one of those androgynous last-name names that is, as of now, pretty underutilized, which makes it a great choice for parents who want to give their little boys a name that's different but not that different.

LARON *(French)* Thief.

LASAIRIAN *(Irish)* Flame. Variations: *Laisrian, Laserian.*

LASZLO *(Hungarian)* Famous leader. Variations: *Laslo, Lazuli.*

LAWSON *(English)* Son of Lawrence.

LEANDER *(Greek)* Lion man. Variations: *Leandre, Leandro, Leandros.*

LEITH *(Scottish)* Broad river.

LELAND *(English)* Meadow land.

LEN *(Native American: Hopi)* Flute.

LENNON *(Irish)* Cape.

LENNOX *(Scottish)* Many elm trees. Depending upon how you spell this name, it could have the feel of fine china—Lenox—or of a bull in a china shop—Lennox. Variation: *Lenox.*

LENSAR *(Gypsy)* With his parents. Variation: *Lendar.*

LERON *(Hebrew)* My song. Variations: *Lerone, Liron, Lirone, Lyron.*

LEWY *(Irish)* Unknown definition. Variation: *Lughaidh.*

LEX *(English)* Lex, a shortened version of Alexander, has turned into an independent name all its own. It is also the name of Superman's nemesis, Lex Luthor.

LEYLAND *(English)* Uncultivated land.

LINCOLN *(English)* Town by a pool. Variations: *Linc, Link.*

LINDELL *(English)* Valley of the linden trees. Variations: *Lindall, Lindel, Lyndall, Lyndell.*

LINLEY *(English)* Meadow of linden trees. Variations: *Linlea, Linlee, Linleigh, Linly.*

LINTON *(English)* Town of linden trees. Variations: *Lintonn, Lynton, Lyntonn.*

LIRON *(Hebrew)* My song. Variation: *Lyron.*

LOCKE *(English)* Fort. Variations: *Lock, Lockwood.*

LOMAN *(Irish)* Little bare one; (Serbian) Delicate.

LOMAS *(English)* Unknown definition. Last name.

LOMBARD *(Latin)* Long beard.

LON *(Irish)* Brutal. Variations: *Lonnie, Lonny.*

LORCAN *(Irish)* Little fierce one.

LORNE *(Scottish)* Area in Scotland. Variation: *Lorn.*

LUCIUS *(Latin)* Light. Variations: *Luca, Lucan, Lucca, Luce, Lucian, Luciano, Lucias, Lucien, Lucio.*

LYNDEN *(English)* Hill with lime trees. Variations: *Linden, Lyndon, Lynne.*

LYNTON *(English)* Town with lime trees. Variation: *Linton.*

LYSANDER *(Greek)* Liberator. Variation: *Lisandro.*

Living on the Edge

LA VONN *(African-American)* The small one. Variations: *La Vaun, La Voun.*

LADD *(English)* Young man. Variations: *Lad, Laddey, Laddie, Laddy.*

LAIS *(East Indian)* Lion.

LAKE *(English)* Body of water.

LAL *(Hindu)* Lovely.

LALLO *(Native American: Kiowa)* Little boy.

LANGWORTH *(English)* Long paddock.

LANI *(Hawaiian)* Sky.

LANTY *(Irish)* Servant of St. Secundus. Variations: *Laughun, Leachlainn, Lochlainn, Lochlann.*

LAPHONSO *(African-American)* Noble. Variations: *Lafonso, LaPhonso.*

LATEEF *(Arabic)* Gentle. Variation: *Latif.*

LATHROP *(English)* Farm with barns. Variations: *Lathe, Lay.*

LATIMER *(English)* Interpreter. Variation: *Latymer.*

LAVAN *(Hebrew)* White.

Celebrities' Real Names

Hollywood has really shaped the way we perceive celebrity names. Especially in times past, there were plenty of celebrities whose given names weren't the most alluring. Take a peak at the transformations:

BEFORE	AFTER
Allen Stewart Konigsberg	Woody Allen
Bernice Frankel	Beatrice Arthur
Charles Buchinsky	Charles Bronson
Frederick Austerlitz	Fred Astaire
Betty Joan Perske	Lauren Bacall
Edna Rae Gillooly	Ellen Burstyn
Maurice Joseph Micklewhite	Michael Caine
Frances Gumm	Judy Garland
Anthonio Dominick Benedetto	Tony Bennett
Dino Paul Crocetti	Dean Martin
Cherilyn Sarkisian	Cher
Vincent Furnier	Alice Cooper
Doris Kappelhoff	Doris Day
Pauline Matthews	Kiki Dee
Gary Hartpence	Gary Hart
Joseph Levitch	Jerry Lewis
Marvin Lee Aday	Meat Loaf
Lew Alcindor	Kareem Abdul-Jabbar
Walter Palahnuik	Jack Palance
Bobby Moore	Ahmad Rashad
Raquel Tejada	Raquel Welch

LAVI *(Hebrew)* Lion.

LAWLER *(Irish)* One who mutters. Variations: *Lawlor, Lollar, Loller.*

LAZARUS *(Hebrew)* God's help. Variations: *Eleazer, Laza, Lazare, Lazaro, Lazzro.*

LE SONN *(African-American)* Newly created.

LEBEN *(Hebrew)* Life.

LEIBEL *(Hebrew)* My lion. Variation: *Leib.*

LEOPOLD *(German)* Brave people. Variations: *Leo, Leupold.*

LESLIE *(Scottish)* Low meadow. One famous Leslie who held onto his name is the actor Leslie Howard; one who let go of it was Bob Hope. He had to or else he would have been known as Less Hope! Variations: *Les, Leslea, Lesley, Lesly, Lezly.*

LEVERETT *(French)* Baby rabbit. Variations: *Lev, Leveret, Leverit, Leveritt.*

LEVI *(Hebrew)* Attached. Variations: *Levey, Levin, Levon, Levy.*

LEWIN *(English)* Beloved friend.

LINDBERG *(German)* Mountain of linden trees.

LINDSAY *(English)* Island of linden trees. This name is primarily a girls' name with the exception of Fleetwood Mac singer Lindsey Buckingham. Variations: *Lindsee, Lindsey, Lindsy, Linsay, Linsey, Lyndsay, Lyndsey.*

LINFORD *(English)* Ford of linden trees. Variation: *Lynford.*

LINFRED *(German)* Gentle peace.

LINUS *(Greek)* Flax. This Peanuts character's name is not very popular in America.

LIVINGSTON *(English)* Leif's settlement. Singer Livingston Taylor is perhaps the best-known Livingston around. The name itself is rarely used, but presents a good choice for parents who are looking for a name that is distinctive and just a bit different, but still commands respect. Variation: *Livingstone.*

LLEWELLYN *(Welsh)* Lionlike. Variations: *Lewellen, Lewellin, Llewelin, Llewelleyn.*

LOCHAN *(Hindu)* Eyes.

LORD *(English)* Lord.

LORIMER *(Latin)* Harness maker. Variation: *Lorrimer.*

LORING *(German)* Son of a famous soldier. Variation: *Lorring.*

LOT *(Hebrew)* Concealed.

LOUDON *(German)* A low valley. Variations: *Louden, Lowden, Lowdon.*

LOVELL *(English)* Last name. Variation: *Lovel.*

LOWELL *(English)* Young wolf. Variation: *Lowel.*

LUDGER *(Scandinavian)* People with spear.

LUDWIG *(German)* Famous soldier. It may have worked for Beethoven, but not in the 21st century.

LUISTER *(African)* One who listens.

LUNDY *(Scottish)* Child born on Monday.

LUNN *(Irish)* Strong; warlike. Variations: *Lon, Lonn.*

Tried and True Classics

MADISON *(English)* Son of the mighty warrior. Whether it's an avenue, a president, or a baby name, Madison is an up-and-comer, for both girls and boys. Variations: *Maddie, Maddison, Maddy, Madisson.*

MALCOLM *(English)* A servant. Its burgeoning popularity has probably been helped along by Malcolm X, Malcolm-Jamal Warner from the Cosby show, and even the late publisher Malcolm Forbes. Variations: *Malcolum, Malcom, Malkolm.*

MARCUS *(Latin)* Warlike. Variations: *Marco, Marcos.*

MARIO *(Italian)* Roman clan name.

MARK *(English)* Warlike. The most famous Marks are Mark Antony, Saint Mark, the writer Samuel Clemens, who is known by his pen name, Mark Twain, and Olympic swimmer Mark Spitz. Today, parents who are partial to the name tend to choose one of the variations listed here and not its original incarnation. Variations: *Marc, Marco, Marko, Markos.*

MARLON *(French)* Little hawk. Legendary actor Marlon Brando made this name very cool in his time, and today, famous Marlons include singer Marlon Jackson and actor/comedien Marlon Wayans. Variation: *Marlin.*

MARSHALL *(French)* One who cares for horses. Because it conveys such an in-charge tone, perhaps people in the military will prefer it for their kids, but for the rest of us, expect it to be quite an unusual choice. Variations: *Marschal, Marsh, Marshal.*

MARTIN *(Latin)* Warlike. Martin was always much more popular as a last name than a first name, except of course in the case of the Rev. Martin Luther King, Jr., who ironically was first christened with the name Michael. The feminine forms of Martin—Martina and Martine—seem to be more popular today than the male version. Most parents who use the name for their sons today tend to use it as a middle name. Variations: *Mart, Martan, Martel, Marten, Martey, Martie, Martinas, Martiniano, Martinka, Martino, Martinos, Martins, Marto, Marton, Marty, Martyn, Mertin.*

MARVIN *(English)* Mariner. Variations: *Marv, Marvyn.*

MATTHEW *(Hebrew)* Gift of the Lord. Matthew has been a very popular name, both 2,000 years ago and today. Matthew is a more interesting name than many of the other traditional Biblical names, for instance, John and James, but it is also immensely helped by the multitudes of attractive Hollywood men with the name. There's Matthew Broderick, Matthew Modine, and Matt Dillon. And if Matthew doesn't strike your fancy, there are many variations for you to choose from to inject a little spice into your son's name. Variations: *Mateo, Mateus, Mathe, Mathew, Mathia, Mathias, Mathieu, Matias, Matt, Matteo, Matthaus, Matthia, Matthias, Mattias, Matty.*

MAURICE *(Latin)* Dark-skinned. Variations: *Maurey, Mauricio, Maurie, Mauris, Maurise, Maurizio, Maury, Morey, Morice, Morie, Moris, Moriss, Morrice, Morrie, Morris, Morriss, Morry.*

MAXWELL *(Scottish)* Marcus's well. Twenty years ago who could have ever foreseen the vast popularity of the name Max today? Parents who are choosing this name for their sons invariably give them the full name of Maxwell but refer to them as Max. Variation: *Max.*

MELVIN *(Irish)* Great chief. Although other names have become popular today, even an actor with Mel Gibson's appeal doesn't seem to be popularizing this name—notice that he goes by the short form. Variations: *Malvin, Malvinn, Malvon, Malvonn, Mel, Melvern, Melvyn, Melwin, Melwinn.*

MICHAEL *(Hebrew)* Who is like God. Along with Mohammed and John, Michael could be one of the most popular boys' names in the world in any language. The reasons? Famous Michaels get lots of press, both good and bad, and as a result, the name is always out there. In addition, the name is liberally scattered through both the Old and New Testaments as well as throughout the Koran. Today's famous Michaels include Michael Millken, Michael J. Fox, Michael Jackson, Michael Jordan, and Michael Douglas, plus others with variations of the name: Mickey Rourke, Mickey Rooney, and Mick Jagger. Michael has been at the top of the names list in this country for over four decades. Variations: *Makis, Micah, Micha, Michail, Michak, Michal, Michalek, Michau, Micheal, Michel, Michele, Mick, Mickel, Mickey, Mickie, Micky, Miguel, Mihail, Mihailo, Mihkel, Mikaek, Mikael, Mikala, Mike, Mikelis, Mikey, Mikhail, Mikhalis, Mikhos, Mikkel, Mikko, Mischa, Misha, Mitch, Mitchel, Mitchell.*

MILES *(English)* Soldier. You can't go wrong with this name. Your son will also share this name with legendary jazz musician Miles Davis. Variations: *Milo, Myles.*

MILLER *(English)* One who mills grain.

MILO *(German)* Generous.

MILTON *(English)* Mill town.

MOHAMMED *(Arabic)* Greatly praised. If Michael is the most popular name in the United States and many European countries, then Mohammed and its numerous variations is probably the most popular name in Muslim countries, if not actually the world. Mohammed is the name of the prophet of Islam, and the popularity of the name could possibly be explained by an old Muslim proverb: If you have a hundred sons, give them all the name Mohammed. The name is also becoming hugely popular among African-Americans. The most famous recent bearer of this name, obviously, is the great fighter Mohammed Ali. Variations: *Ahmad, Amad, Amed, Hamdrem, Hamdum, Hamid, Hammad, Hammed, Humayd, Mahmed, Mahmoud, Mahmud, Mehemet, Mehmet, Mohamad, Mohamed, Mohamet, Mohammad, Muhammad.*

MONTEL *(English)* Unknown definition. As with his counterpart named Arsenio, talk-show host Montel Williams probably provided most Americans with their first exposure to his name. However, as is the case with any unusual name that is exposed by a celebrity, you should be on the lookout for a rash of Montels over the next few years.

MONTGOMERY *(English)* Rich man's mountain. Variations: *Monte, Montgomerie, Monty.*

MORGAN *(Welsh)* Great and bright. Variations: *Morgen, Morrgan.*

MURRAY *(Scottish)* Mariner. Murray is another one of those great last names as first names that is perfectly posed for rejuvenation. Somewhat common during the '40s and '50s, Murray seems to be less popular these days. Variations: *Murrey, Murry.*

Slightly Daring Choices

MAC *(Scottish)* Son of. Variation: *Mack.*

MACADAM *(Scottish)* Son of Adam. Variations: *MacAdam, McAdam.*

MACALLISTER *(Irish)* Son of Alistair. Variations: *MacAlister, McAlister, McAllister.*

MACAULAY *(Scottish)* Son of the moral one. Child star Macaulay Culkin brought this name to the mainstream but it still hasn't become too popular.

MACKENZIE *(Irish)* Son of a wise leader. Variations: *Mack, MacKenzie, Mackey, Mackie, McKenzie.*

MACY *(French)* Matthew's estate. Variation: *Macey.*

MADDOX *(Welsh)* Generous. Variations: *Maddock, Madock, Madox.*

Famous Male Characters from Film and Literature

Certainly, kids named Rhett in the '40s were named as a result of Americans who just went crazy over *Gone with the Wind*. Today, Americans continue to be exposed to a variety of new and unusual names because of fictional characters. From Shakespeare to soap operas, there are a wealth of characters for parents-to-be to ponder.

Here's just a sampling:

DIRK PITT: *character in Tom Clancy novels*
FORREST GUMP: *title character from the movie*
HEATHCLIFF LINTON: Wuthering Heights' *tortured protagonist*
JIM STARK: Rebel Without a Cause
LUKE SKYWALKER: Star Wars' *Jedi hero*
TOM SAWYER: *well-know mischief-maker from Mark Twain's novels*
WILLIAM WALLACE: *Scottish leader in* Braveheart
IAGO, HAMLET, ROMEO, PROSPERO, and BENEDICK: *Just a few of the many male characters from Shakespeare's plays*
ARTHUR, LANCELOT, GALAHAD, and MERLIN: *Medieval names from Authurian legend*
MICKEY, DONALD, SEBASTIAN, SIMBA, and NEMO: *male Disney characters (just steer clear of Goofy!)*

MAGEE *(Irish)* Son of Hugh. Variations: *MacGee, McGee.*
MAGUIRE *(Irish)* Son of the beige man. Variations: *MacGuire, McGuire, McGwire.*
MAITLAND *(English)* Town in Britain.

MAKARY *(Polish)* Blessed.

MAKYA *(Native American: Hopi)* One who hunts for eagles.

MALACHI *(Hebrew)* Messenger. Malachi was both a book in the Bible and the name of an Irish saint. As such, you wouldn't expect it to appear with any great frequency today, but this very old-fashioned name is suddenly becoming very popular. Variations: *Malachai, Malachie, Malachy, Malechy.*

MALIK *(Hindu)* King. Variations: *Maliq, Mallik.*

MALIN *(English)* Little strong warrior. Variations: *Mallin, Mallon.*

MALKAM *(Hebrew)* God is their king. Variations: *Malcam, Malcham.*

MALONEY *(Irish)* Regular churchgoer. Variations: *Malone, Malony.*

MANDEL *(German)* Almond. Variation: *Mandell.*

MANDER *(Gypsy)* From me.

MANLEY *(English)* Man's meadow. Variations: *Manlea, Manleigh, Manly.*

MANNING *(English)* Son of a man.

MARCELLUS *(Latin)* Young warrior. Variations: *Marceau, Marcel, Marcelin, Marcello.*

MARCH *(English)* One who lives by a border.

MARDEN *(English)* Valley with a pool.

MAREK *(Czech)* Warlike. Variations: *Marecek, Mares, Marik, Marousek.*

MARION *(French)* Bitter; defiant.

MARLEY *(English)* Meadow near a lake. Variations: *Marlea, Marleigh, Marly.*

MARLOW *(English)* Hill near a lake. Variation: *Marlowe.*

MARQUIS *(African-American)* Nobleman. Variations: *Markeece, Markeese, Markese, Marques, Marqui, Marquise.*

MARSDEN *(English)* Swampy valley. Variation: *Marsdon.*

MASLIN *(French)* Little twin. Variations: *Maslen, Masling.*

MASON *(French)* Stone carver or worker. Variations: *Mace, Masson.*

MATTAN *(Hebrew)* Gift. Variations: *Matan, Matena, Maton, Mattun.*

MAYER *(Latin)* Larger. Variations: *Mayor, Meier, Meir, Meirer, Meuer, Myer.*

MAYNARD *(English)* Hard strength. Variations: *Maynhard, Meinhard, Menard.*

MEAD *(English)* Meadow. Variations: *Meade, Meed.*

MELDON *(English)* Mill on a hill. Variation: *Melden.*

MERCER *(English)* Shopkeeper. Variation: *Merce.*

MERRICK *(English)* Dark-skinned. Variation: *Merryck.*

MERRILL *(English)* Bright as the sea. Masculine version of Murie. Variations: *Meril, Merill, Merrel, Merrell, Merril, Meryl.*

MONROE *(Irish)* Red marsh. Variations: *Monro, Munro, Munroe.*

MORAY *(Scottish)* Last name.

MORDECAI *(Hebrew)* Name commonly given to boys born during Purim. Variations: *Mordche, Mordechai, Mordi, Motche.*

MORELAND *(English)* Uncultivated land. Variations: *Moorland, Morland.*

MORI *(Hebrew)* My guide. Variations: *Morie, Moriel.*

MORLEY *(English)* Meadow on a moor. Variations: *Moorley, Moorly, Morlee, Morleigh, Morly, Morrley.*

MORRISON *(English)* Son of Morris. Variation: *Morrisson.*

MORSE *(English)* Son of Maurice.

MORVEN *(Scottish)* Big mountain peak.

MUNIM *(Arabic)* Charitable.

MURDOCH *(Scottish)* Sailor. Variations: *Murdo, Murdock, Murtagh.*

MURPHY *(Irish)* Sea fighter.

MYERS *(English)* One who lives in a swamp. Variation: *Myer.*

Living on the Edge

MAALIN *(Hindu)* Wreath.

MACBRIDE *(Irish)* Son of Saint Brigid. Variations: *Macbryde, McBride.*

MACCABEE *(Hebrew)* Hammer. Variations: *Macabee, Makabi.*

MACDONALD *(Scottish)* Son of Donald. The Macdonalds were a powerful Scottish clan. Variations: *MacDonald, McDonald.*

MACGOWAN *(Irish)* Son of the blacksmith. Variations: *MacGowan, Magowan, McGowan.*

MACHIR *(Hebrew)* Commerce.

MACKINLEY *(Irish)* Learned ruler. Variations: *MacKinley, McKinley.*

MACON *(English)* City in Georgia.

MAHIR *(Arabic)* Capable.

MAKIMO *(Hawaiian)* Great.

MALKI *(Hebrew)* My king.

MALKIAH *(Hebrew)* God is my king. Variations: *Malkia, Malkiya, Malkiyahu.*

MALLORY *(French)* Sad. Variations: *Mallery, Mallorie, Malory.*

MANDALA *(African: Malawian)* Flowers.

MANFRED *(English)* Man of peace. Variations: *Manafred, Manafryd, Manfrid, Manfried, Mannfred, Mannfryd.*

MANSEL *(English)* In a clergyman's house. Variation: *Mansell.*

MANSFIELD *(English)* Field by a river.

MANSUR *(Arabic)* Divine assistance. Variation: *Mansour.*

MANTON *(English)* Man's town. Variations: *Mannton, Manten.*

MARID *(Arabic)* Defiant.

MARSTON *(English)* Town by a marsh.

MARWAN *(Arabic)* Unknown definition.

MATAIO *(Hawaiian)* Gift from God. Variation: *Makaio.*

MATANIAH *(Hebrew)* Gift from God. Variations: *Matania, Matanya, Matitia, Matitiah, Matityah, Matityahu, Mattaniah, Mattathias, Matya.*

MATEJ *(Czech)* Gift from God. Variations: *Mata, Matejek, Matejicek, Matejik, Matousek, Matyas, Matys, Matysek.*

MATENI *(Polynesian)* Warrior.

MATHER *(English)* Mighty army.

MATOK *(Hebrew)* Sweet.

MAUI *(Hawaiian)* God who discovered fire.

MAVERICK *(American)* Nonconformist. Even with the *Top Gun* reference, this one won't cut it. Cool enough for Tom Cruise but not your kid, unless his best friend's name is Goose.

MAXIMILIAN *(Latin)* Greatest. Variations: *Maksim, Maksimka, Maksum, Massimiliano, Massimo, Max, Maxi, Maxie, Maxim, Maxime, Maximilano, Maximiliano, Maximillian, Maximino, Maximo, Maximos, Maxy.*

MAYFIELD *(English)* Strong man's field.

MAYHEW *(French)* Gift from the Lord. Variation of Matthew.

MEHITABEL *(Hebrew)* God benefits. Mehitabel, another Biblical name, is perhaps best known as one of the characters in the book *Archy and Mehitabel* by the author Don Marquis; Archy was a cockroach and Mehitabel was a cat.

MEHTAR *(East Indian)* Prince.

MEIR *(Hebrew)* Bright one. Variations: *Mayer, Meyer, Myer.*

MELBOURNE *(English)* City in Australia. Variations: *Melborn, Melburn, Milbourne, Milburn, Millburn, Millburne.*

MELVILLE *(English)* Mill town.

MENDEL *(Hebrew)* Wisdom. Variations: *Mendeley, Mendell.*

MERLIN *(English)* Falcon. Merlin actually originated as a name for girls, but the name gradually gravitated to common use for males. While actress Merle Oberon is the most famous female of this name, the name and its variations are mostly claimed by male celebrities: Merle Haggard and Merlin Olsen. Variations: *Marlin, Marlon, Merle, Merlen, Merlinn, Merlyn, Merlynn.*

MERRIPEN *(Gypsy)* Life.

MERRITT *(English)* Small and famous. Variations: *Merit, Meritt, Merrett.*

MERVIN *(Welsh)* Sea hill. Variations: *Mervyn, Murvin, Murvyn.*

MEYER *(German)* Farmer. Variation: *Mayer.*

MIKASI *(Native American: Omaha)* Coyote.

MIKOLAS *(Czech)* Victorious people. Variation: *Mikuls.*

MILAN *(Slavic)* Beloved.

MILLARD *(English)* Guard of the mill.

MILLS *(English)* The mills.

MODRED *(English)* Brave adviser. Variation: *Mordred.*

MOHAN *(Hindu)* Enchanting.

MORAN *(Hebrew)* Guide.

MORTIMER *(French)* Still water. If Walt Disney had gone along with his first choice and named his mouse Mortimer instead of Mickey, there would be a lot more Mortimers around today. Variations: *Mort, Mortmer, Mortym.*

MORTON *(English)* Town by a moor. Variation: *Morten.*

MOSES *(Hebrew)* Arrived by water. Variations: *Moise, Moises, Moisey, Mose, Mosese, Mosha, Moshe, Moss, Moyse, Moze, Mozes.*

MURIEL *(Irish)* Bright as the sea.

MUSAD *(Arabic)* Lucky. Variations: *Misid, Musaed.*

MUSTAPHA *(Arabic)* Chosen. Variation: *Mustafa.*

MYRON *(Greek)* Aromatic oil. Variations: *Miron, Myreon.*

Tried and True Classics

NATHAN *(Hebrew)* Gift from God. The real name of the late, great comedian George Burns was Nathan, and though the name might seem really stodgy or old-fashioned, it is actually very popular today. Not only is it in the top hundred boys' names of the 1990s, but it was also in the top hundred list back in George Burns's day. Nathan was the name of a prophet who appeared in the Old Testament Book of II Samuel, and it's been around ever since. Nathan is a pretty common name in Great Britain and Australia, as well as in the United States. Famous Nathans who kept their names include Nathanial Hawthorne and Nat King Cole. Variations: *Nat, Natan, Nataniele, Nate, Nathanial, Nathaniel, Nathen, Nathon, Natt, Natty.*

NEIL *(Irish)* Champion. Neil is an easygoing name that has always been independent; its original spelling is Niall. Famous Neils include Neil Simon, Neil Sedaka, and Neil Young. Variations: *Neal, Neale, Neall, Nealle, Nealon, Neile, Neill, Neille, Neils, Nels, Niadh, Nial, Niall, Nialle, Niel, Niels, Nigel, Niles, Nilo.*

NELSON *(English)* Son of Neil. The former vice-president Nelson Rockefeller probably didn't have the effect of enhancing the popularity of the name Nelson, but it is beginning to gain some ground these days. Other Nelsons include Nelson Mandela and singer Nelson Eddy. Variations: *Nealson, Neilson, Nilson, Nilsson.*

NICHOLAS *(Greek)* People of victory. Nicholas has been hot for about the last two decades. Nicholas was first mentioned in the Book of Acts, and the Biblical figure was followed by Saint Nicholas, who is considered to be the patron saint of children (and eventually transmogrified into Santa Claus). Why is Nicholas so popular? It just sounds like a folksy, friendly name that will serve a boy well from toddlerhood all the way through to grampahood. Whether it's little Nicky or Grampa Nick, Nicholas fits no matter what the age. Famous Nicholases, besides Santa Claus, include the protagonist of *Nicholas Nickleby* by Dickens and Nicholson Baker. Though some feel the name is too popular, most parents who choose the name for their sons won't agree. Variations: *Nic, Niccolo, Nichol, Nick, Nickolas, Nickolaus, Nicky, Nicol, Nicolaas, Nicolai, Nicolas, Nikita, Nikki, Nikky, Niklas, Niklos, Niko, Nikolai, Nikolais, Nikolas, Nikolaus, Nikolo, Nikolos, Nikos, Nikula.*

NIGEL *(Irish)* Champion. Variation of Neil. Variations: *Nigal, Nigiel, Nigil.*

NOAH *(Hebrew)* Rest. Every little kid knows who Noah is, and so do an increasing number of parents who are choosing this name for their baby boys. Variations: *Noach, Noak, Noe, Noi, Noy.*

NOEL *(French)* Christmas. Variations: *Natal, Natale, Nowel, Nowell.*

NOLAN *(Irish)* Little proud one. Variations: *Noland, Nolen, Nolin, Nollan, Nuallan.*

NORMAN *(English)* Northerner. The name Norman originated from the French tribe in Normandy that is most famous for invading England in the year 1066. Famous Normans include writer Norman Mailer and clergyman Norman Vincent Peale. Variations: *Norm, Normand, Normando, Normen, Normie.*

Slightly Daring Choices

NADIM *(Hindu)* Friend. Variation: *Nadeem.*

NALDO *(Spanish)* Good advice.

African Names

The wide variety of cultures from the African continent as well as the many individual countries means that there are a huge number of names to choose from if you want your son or daughter to exhibit a bit of African heritage in his name.

In Kenya, some tribes choose several names for the babies born to a family. The first name a baby receives is called a birth name, and is usually picked by a maternal grandmother or grandfather of the baby. About a month and a half later, the baby gets another, more permanent name, which the child's parents or father's parents get to choose.

In Ghana, parents participate in a naming ceremony where the whole tribe takes part. The ceremony occurs a week after the child is born, and the baby's father selects a name, most often taking it from an elderly, dignified relative. In Nigeria, a name is frequently given that is descriptive of the conditions of the birth itself; this name is referred to as an oraku. The child also receives a name that is known as an oriki, or another name that projects the parents' wishes for the child. You may want to adapt this tradition, making your child's first name the equivalent of an oriki, and the middle name an oraku.

NALIN *(Hindu)* Lotus.
NAMID *(Native American)* Star dancer.
NAMIL *(Arabic)* To achieve.

NAMIR *(Hebrew)* Leopard.

NANDAN *(Hindu)* Happiness.

NAREN *(Hindu)* Superior man.

NAVARRO *(Spanish)* Land. Variation: *Navarre.*

NAVIN *(Hindu)* New.

NEMO *(Greek)* One from Heaven. Before this name was of Disney fame, it was the name of the famous literary character Captain Nemo.

NEPTUNE *(Latin)* Roman god of the sea.

NERO *(Latin)* Strong. Variations: *Neron, Nerone.*

NESBIT *(English)* Curve in the road. Variations: *Naisbit, Naisbitt, Nesbitt, Nisbet, Nisbett.*

NESTOR *(Greek)* Traveler.

NEVADA *(Spanish)* Snow-covered. Like the names of other western states and cities, Nevada is catching on among parents who are looking for something different for their sons.

NEVILLE *(French)* New town. Variations: *Nevil, Nevile, Nevill, Nevyle.*

NEVIN *(Irish)* Holy. Variations: *Nev, Nevan, Nevins, Niven.*

NEWLIN *(Welsh)* New pond. Variations: *Newlun, Newlyn.*

NIAZ *(Hindu)* Gift.

NOAM *(Hebrew)* Delight.

NOCONA *(Native American: Comanche)* Wanderer. Variation: *Nokoni.*

NODIN *(Native American)* The wind. Variation: *Noton.*

NOE *(Polish)* Quiet.

NORRIS *(English)* Northerner. Alternative spellings: *Noris, Norreys, Norrie, Norriss, Norry.*

NORTHROP *(English)* Northern farm. Variation: *Northrup.*

NORTON *(English)* Northern town.

NORVAL *(Scottish)* Northern village. Variations: *Norvil, Norvill, Norville, Norvylle.*

NORVELL *(English)* North well. Variation: *Norvel.*

NYE *(Welsh)* Honor.

Living on the Edge

NABIL *(Arabic)* Noble.
NAGATAKA *(Japanese)* Childhood obligation.
NAGID *(Hebrew)* Leader. Variation: *Nageed.*
NAHELE *(Hawaiian)* Forest.
NAIJA *(African: Ugandan)* Next-born.
NAIM *(Arabic)* Happy. Variation: *Naeem.*
NAIRNE *(Scottish)* River. Variation: *Nairn.*
NAJIB *(Arabic)* Smart. Variations: *Nagib, Najeeb.*
NAM *(Vietnamese)* South.
NAOMHAN *(Irish)* Little holy one. Variation: *Nevan.*
NAPOLEON *(Greek)* Lion of the woodland dell.
NARAIN *(Hindu)* The Hindu god Vishnu.
NARAYANA *(Hindu)* Man.
NARCISSUS *(Greek)* Daffodil. Variation: *Narcisse.*
NARD *(Persian)* Chess game.
NARESH *(Hindu)* Ruler of men.
NASHOBA *(Native American: Choctaw)* Wolf. Variation: *Neshoba.*
NASR *(Arabic)* Victory. Variations: *Nasser, Nassor.*
NAV *(Hungarian)* Name.
NAVEED *(Hindu)* Good thoughts.
NAYLAND *(English)* Island resident.
NECHEMYA *(Hebrew)* God's comfort. Who would have ever thought that Jeremiah would become popular? Nechemya could be headed in the same direction if there are enough parents out there who take the first step. Variations: *Nechemia, Nechemiah, Nehemiah.*
NEDAVIAH *(Hebrew)* Charity of the Lord. Variations: *Nedabiah, Nedavia, Nedavya.*
NEEL *(Hindu)* Blue. Variations: *Neelendra, Neelmani.*
NEGASI *(Ethiopian)* He will become royalty.

NEPER *(Spanish)* New city.

NETANIAH *(Hebrew)* Gift of Jehovah. Variations: *Netania, Netanya, Nethaniah.*

NETO *(Spanish)* Earnest one.

NEWELL *(English)* New hall. Variations: *Newall, Newel, Newhall.*

NIBAW *(Native American)* To stand up.

NICABAR *(Spanish)* To steal.

NICODEMUS *(Greek)* Jewish leader.

NIEN *(Vietnamese)* Year.

NIGAN *(Native American)* In the lead.

NILI *(Hebrew)* Israel's glory.

NIMROD *(Hebrew)* Rebel.

NINIAN *(Scottish)* Unknown definition.

NIPTON *(English)* Another name for the Isle of Wight.

NIRAM *(Hebrew)* Fertile meadow.

NIRVAN *(Hindu)* Bliss.

NISAN *(Hebrew)* Miracle. Variation: *Nissan.*

NISHAD *(Hindu)* Seventh note of a scale.

NITIS *(Native American)* Good friend. Variation: *Netis.*

NIUTEI *(Polynesian)* Coconut tree.

NIXON *(English)* Son of Nicholas.

NIZAR *(Arabic)* Unknown definition.

NOADIAH *(Hebrew)* Meeting with God. Variations: *Noadia, Noadya.*

NOBLE *(Latin)* Well bred.

NOELANI *(Hawaiian)* Heavenly rain.

NOHEA *(Hawaiian)* Handsome.

NORBERT *(German)* Famous northerner. Variation: *Norberto.*

NORTHCLIFF *(English)* Northern cliff. Variations: *Northcliffe, Northclyff, Northclyffe.*

NORVIN *(English)* Northern friend. Variations: *Norvyn, Norwin, Norwinn, Norwyn, Norwynn.*

NORWARD *(English)* Guardian of the north.

NORWOOD *(English)* Northern woods.
NOY *(Hebrew)* Beauty.
NUMA *(Arabic)* Kindness. Masculine form of Naomi.
NUMAIR *(Arabic)* Panther.
NUNCIO *(Italian)* Messenger. Variation: *Nunzio.*

Tried and True Classics

OLIVER *(Latin)* Olive tree. Variations: *Oliverio, Olivero, Olivier, Olivor, Olley, Ollie, Olliver, Ollivor.*

OMAR *(Arabic)* The first son or most high follower of the prophet. Omar Sharif, General Omar Bradley, and poet Omar Khayyam have all lent exposure to this name. Despite the lack of a public figure with this name today, some parents are beginning to consider this name for their own sons. Variations: *Omarr, Omer.*

ORLANDO *(Italian)* Famous land. Variations: *Ordando, Orland, Orlande, Orlo.*

ORSON *(Latin)* Bearlike. Orson Welles—whose real first name was George—put this name on the map. Today the name seems to be making a comeback, probably in deference to the late great actor from *Citizen Kane.* Variations: *Orsen, Orsin, Orsini, Orsino.*

OSCAR *(English)* Divine spear. Back when Oscar the Grouch first arrived on the scene, Jack Klugman was starring as Oscar Madison in *The Odd Couple.* The reputations that both of these Oscars had back then tended to discourage parents from choosing the name for their own kids. Today, however, Oscar is considered cool, and actually a way to poke fun at our earlier associations with the name. The great success of Steven Spielberg's movie *Schindler's List,* about Oskar Schindler, will probably do a lot to enhance the name. Other famous Oscars have included Oscar Wilde, Oscar Hammerstein, and Oscar de la Renta. Variations: *Oskar, Osker, Ossie.*

OTIS *(English)* Son of Otto.

OTTO *(German)* Wealthy. Otto is so out on a limb that there are some people who consider it a cutting-edge name to give their sons. Otto is popular all over the world, including in Hungary, Germany, Sweden, and Russia. Variations: *Odo, Otello, Othello, Otho, Othon, Oto, Ottomar.*

OWEN *(Welsh)* Well born. Owen could easily be considered a second cousin to the name Evan. Some parents consider Owen a better name than Evan these days, since the latter is a bit overused. Variations: *Owain, Owin.*

Slightly Daring Choices

OAKES *(English)* Near oak trees. Variations: *Oak, Ochs.*

OAKLEY *(English)* Meadow of oak trees. Variations: *Oaklee, Oakleigh, Oakly.*

OBERON *(German)* Noble and bearlike. Variations: *Auberon, Auberron.*

OCEAN *(English)* Ocean. Variation: *Oceanus.*

ODELL *(English)* Forested hill. Variations: *Ode, Odey, Odi, Odie.*

ODIN *(Scandinavian)* One-eyed Norse god.

ODINAN *(African)* Fifteenth child.

ODION *(African: Nigerian)* First-born of twins.

OLERY *(French)* Leader.

ONAN *(Turkish)* Wealthy.

ONANI *(African)* A glance.

ORAN *(Irish)* Green. Variations: *Orin, Orran, Orren, Orrin.*

ORBAN *(Hungarian)* Urbanite.

OREN *(Hebrew)* Ash tree. Variations: *Orin, Orrin.*

ORION *(Greek)* Son of fire or light; sunrise. Mythological son of Poseidon.

ORMAN *(German)* Sailor. Variations: *Ormand, Ormond, Ormonde.*

The Most Popular Boys' Names from the 1980s

When it comes to names, as with many other things in life, what goes around always comes around. Look at the top boys' names of the 1950s, and you'll see that the top fifty names from the 1980s are almost a carbon copy of the names from that decade.

1. Michael
2. Christopher
3. Matthew
4. David
5. Jason
6. Daniel
7. Robert
8. Eric
9. Brian
10. Joseph
11. Ryan
12. James
13. Steven
14. John
15. Jeffrey
16. Adam
17. Justin
18. Andrew
19. Mark
20. Nicholas
21. William
22. Jonathan
23. Brandon
24. Thomas
25. Joshua
26. Scott
27. Paul
28. Kevin
29. Anthony
30. Richard
31. Sean
32. Charles
33. Aaron
34. Bradley
35. Timothy
36. Benjamin
37. Patrick
38. Jeremy
39. Derek
40. Gregory
41. Kenneth
42. Philip
43. Alexander
44. Donald
45. Edward
46. Kyle
47. Nathan
48. Jesse
49. Ronald
50. Carl

ORON *(Hebrew)* Light.

ORRICK *(English)* Old oak tree. Variation: *Orric.*

OSBORN *(English)* Divine bear. Variations: *Osborne, Osbourn, Osbourne, Osburn, Osburne.*

OSGOOD *(English)* Divine and good. Variations: *Oz, Ozzi, Ozzie, Ozzy.*

OSHEA *(Hebrew)* Helped by God. Variation: *Oshaya.*

OSILEANI *(Polynesian)* Speaks up.

OSMAN *(Polish)* God protects.

OSMAR *(English)* Divine and marvelous.

OSMOND *(English)* Divine protector. Variations: *Osman, Osmand, Osmonde, Osmund, Osmunde.*

OSRED *(English)* Divine adviser.

OSRIC *(English)* Divine ruler. Variation: *Osrick.*

OSTEN *(Latin)* Esteemed. Variations: *Ostin, Ostyn.*

OSWALD *(English)* Divine power. Variations: *Ossie, Osvald, Oswaldo, Oswall, Oswell.*

OSWIN *(English)* Divine friend. Variations: *Osvin, Oswinn, Oswyn, Oswynn.*

OZ *(Hebrew)* Power. Unless he is a wizard, don't choose this one.

Living on the Edge

OBA *(African: Nigerian)* King.

OBADIAH *(Hebrew)* Servant of God. Obadiah has the potential to catch on among parents who would like to give their baby boys a name from the Bible that is just a bit different. One of its nicknames, Obie, is close to Opie, the character played by an extremely young Ron Howard back in the wholesome days of TV sitcoms. Variations: *Obadias, Obe, Obed, Obediah, Obie, Ovadiach, Ovadiah.*

OBASI *(African: Nigerian)* Honoring God.

OBATAIYE *(African: Nigerian)* King of the world.

OBAYANA *(African: Nigerian)* The king warms himself at the fire.

OBERT *(German)* Wealthy and brilliant.

OBI *(African: Nigerian)* Heart.

OCTAVIUS *(Latin)* Eighth child. Variations: *Octave, Octavian, Octavien, Octavio, Octavo, Ottavio.*

ODAKOTA *(Native American: Sioux)* Friends.

ODHRAN *(Irish)* Pale green. Variations: *Odran, Oran.*

ODISSAN *(African)* Thirteenth son.

ODOLF *(German)* Wealthy wolf. Variation: *Odolff.*

ODYSSEUS *(Greek)* One of the leaders of the Trojan War.

OGANO *(Japanese)* Deer pasture.

OGDEN *(English)* Valley of oak trees. Variations: *Ogdan, Ogdon.*

OISIN *(Irish)* Young deer. Variations: *Ossian, Ossin.*

OISTIN *(Irish)* Respected.

OKELLO *(African: Ugandan)* Born after twins.

OKEMOS *(Native American)* Small chief.

OKO *(African: Nigerian)* The god Ogun.

OLADELE *(African: Nigerian)* We are honored at home.

OLAF *(Scandinavian)* Forefather. Olaf is a very common name in Norway. There have been many other ethnic names that have become part of the American culture, but Olaf doesn't seem as if it will ever totally fit in. And so despite its esteemed background—Olaf served as the name of no fewer than five Norwegian kings—it may not be an up-and-comer here in the United States. Variations: *Olaff, Olav, Olave, Olen, Olin, Olof, Olov, Olyn.*

OLAFEMI *(African: Nigerian)* Fortunate.

OLDRICH *(Czech)* Noble king. Variations: *Olda, Oldra, Oldrisek, Olecek, Olik, Olin, Olouvsek.*

Muslim Boys' Names

The Koran is the holy book of the Islamic faith, which was founded by the prophet Mohammed in 610 A.D. As a result, many Muslim boys are given the name Mohammed. Some believe that it is the most popular name in the world, with close to one thousand variations.

Other names from the Koran for boys are frequently derived from the ninety-nine beneficial qualities of God that are written in the Muslim holy book: Hakeem and Nasser, which respectively translate to wise and victorious, are two such names. It is difficult to find any Muslim name that does not have a positive spin to it, and for boys, this includes choices such as Nadir (precious) and Baha (magnificent).

Following are some other common Muslim names for boys:

ABDUL	**HUSSEIN**	**RAHMAN**
ALIM	**JAMAL**	**SALIH**
AMIR	**KADIR**	**SHARIF**
CEMAL	**KAMAL**	**TAHIR**
DEKEL	**KHALID**	**YASIR**
FADIL	**MAHMUD**	**ZAIM**
HABIB	**MOHAMMAD**	
HALIM	**NUMAIR**	

OLEG *(Russian)* Holy. The chance of Oleg's reaching the top-hundred names list in this country is just a little less remote than the chances for Olaf, primarily because of Oleg's association with the designer Oleg Cassini. Variation: *Olezka.*

OLIWA *(Hawaiian)* Olive.

OLNEY *(English)* Town in Britain.

OMANAND *(Hindu)* Joy from a meditation chant.

OMRI *(Hebrew)* Servant of God.

ONSLOW *(English)* Fan's hill. Variation: *Ounslow.*

ONUR *(Turkish)* Dignity.

ORESTES *(Greek)* Mountain. Variations: *Aresty, Oreste.*

ORUNJAN *(African: Nigerian)* God of the noontime sun.

ORVILLE *(French)* Golden town. Variations: *Orv, Orval, Orvell, Orvelle, Orvil.*

ORVIN *(English)* Friend with a spear. Variations: *Orwin, Orwynn.*

OSAKWE *(African: Nigerian)* God agrees.

OSBERT *(English)* Divine and bright.

OSCEOLA *(Native American: Creek)* Black drink.

OSEI *(African: Ghanian)* Noble.

OTHNIEL *(Hebrew)* Lion of God. Variation: *Otniel.*

OTOKAR *(Czech)* One who watches his wealth.

OTSKAI *(Native American: Nez Perce)* Leaving.

OTTAH *(African: Nigerian)* Skinny boy.

OURAY *(Native American: Ute)* Arrow.

OVED *(Hebrew)* Worshiper. Variation: *Obed.*

OXFORD *(English)* Oxen crossing a river.

OZNI *(Hebrew)* To listen.

OZURU *(Japanese)* Stork.

Tried and True Classics

PARKER *(English)* Park keeper. Though actress Parker Posey has recently leapt onto the Hollywood scene with a great flourish, Parker actually started out as a popular boys' name during the 1800s in this country. The most famous male Parker was of course Parker Stevenson, who played in the *Hardy Boys* TV show. Variations: *Park, Parke, Parkes, Parks.*

PATRICK *(Irish)* Noble man. Saint Patrick, the patron saint of Ireland, has been popular all over the world for the last two centuries. There are a slew of famous Patricks in this country, including Pat Boone, Patrick O'Neil, Patrick Ewing, and Patrick Swayze. Parents who like the name but who want something just a little bit different for their own sons are choosing one of the many variations of the name. Variations: *Paddey, Paddie, Paddy, Padraic, Padraig, Padruig, Pat, Patek, Patric, Patrice, Patricio, Patricius, Patrik, Patrizio, Patrizius, Patryk.*

PAUL *(Latin)* Small. Famous Pauls include Beatle Paul McCartney, singer Paul Anka, and Revolutionary War hero Paul Revere. Variations: *Pablo, Pal, Pali, Palika, Pall, Paolo, Pasha, Pashenka, Pashka, Paska, Paulin, Paulino, Paulis, Paulo, Pauls, Paulus, Pauly, Pavel, Pavils, Pavlicek, Pavlik, Pavlo, Pavlousek, Pawel, Pawl, Pol, Poul.*

PERCIVAL *(French)* Pierce the valley. Variation: *Perceval.*

PERCY *(French)* Valley prisoner. Variations: *Pearce, Pearcey, Pearcy, Percey.*

PERRY *(English)* Traveler.

PETER *(Greek)* Rock. Peter is a common, friendly name that seems to be one of the oldest names around. It appears in the Bible as a saint's name, in a much-loved children's book, and in nursery rhymes—Peter Rabbit, Peter Piper—as well as onstage and in the movies: consider Peter O'Toole, Peter Sellers, and Peter Ustinov. Though it was popular as a Biblical name up until the sixteenth century, Peter fell out of favor until almost the early part of the twentieth century in both the United States and Europe. Peter has never been a trendy name; it's rock-solid like its definition. Variations: *Pearce, Pears, Pearson, Pearsson, Peat, Peder, Pedro, Peers, Peet, Peeter, Peirce, Petey, Petie, Petras, Petro, Petronio, Petros, Petter, Pierce, Piero, Pierre, Pierrot, Pierrson, Piers, Pierson, Piet, Pieter, Pietro, Piotr, Pyotr.*

PHILIP *(Greek)* Lover of horses. In recent times, Philip has a bit of a regal feel to it, owing to Britain's Prince Philip. Philip was also one of the original twelve apostles in the Bible, and though the name was pretty popular in this country in the '60s, it seems that Philip is more common as a last name these days. The name Philip strikes many people as an exclusively French name; however, it is found in the languages of most European countries. Besides the prince, the Philip that many Americans are most familiar with is Phil Donahue. Variations: *Felipe, Felipino, Fil, Filib, Filip, Filipo, Filippo, Fillipek, Fillipp, Fillips, Phil, Philippe, Phill, Phillip, Phillipe, Phillipos, Phillipp, Phillippe, Phillips, Pilib, Pippy.*

PRESTON *(English)* Priest's town. Preston seems to be one of those names that has great potential, but it still retains a bit of prissiness that keeps many parents from considering it for their sons.

Slightly Daring Choices

PADGET *(English)* Young assistant. Variations: *Padgett, Paget, Pagett.*

PAGE *(French)* Intern. Variation: *Paige.*

PAGIEL *(Hebrew)* Worships God.

PALMER *(English)* Carrying palm branches. Palmer is one of those mild-mannered last names that is quickly catching on as a popular first name for both boys and girls. Look for Palmer to make gentle inroads into the top hundred names for boys. Variations: *Pallmer, Palmar.*

PARIS *(Greek)* The city. Variation: *Parris.*

PARLAN *(Scottish)* Farmer.

PARNELL *(French)* Little Peter. Variations: *Parkin, Parnel, Parrnell.*

PARR *(English)* Castle park. Variations: *Parrey, Parrie.*

PARRY *(Welsh)* Son of Harry.

PASCAL *(French)* Easter child. Variations: *Pascale, Pascalle, Paschal, Pascoe, Pascow, Pasqual, Pasquale.*

PATTIN *(Gypsy)* A leaf.

PATTON *(English)* Soldier's town. Variations: *Paten, Patin, Paton, Patten, Pattin.*

PAYNE *(Latin)* Countryman. Variation: *Paine.*

PEARSON *(English)* Son of Piers. Variation: *Pierson.*

PELHAM *(English)* Region in Britain.

PELL *(English)* Parchment paper.

PENN *(English)* Enclosure. Variation: *Pen.*

PEPIN *(German)* One who perseveres. Variations: *Pepi, Peppi, Peppie, Peppy.*

PERKIN *(English)* Little Peter. Variations: *Perkins, Perkyn.*

PEYTON *(English)* Soldier's estate. Variation: *Payton.*

PHELAN *(Irish)* Wolf.

PHINEAS *(Hebrew)* Oracle. Variation: *Pinchas.*

PHOENIX *(Greek)* Immortal. Variation: *Phenix.*

PILAR *(Spanish)* Pillar.

PIRAN *(English)* Unknown definition. Variations: *Peran, Pieran.*

PIRRO *(Greek)* Red hair.

PLACIDO *(Spanish)* Peaceful. Singer Placido Domingo has added some degree of visibility to this name, and it might make the short list for parents who are looking for specifically Italian names for their sons. Variations: *Placid, Placidus, Placyd, Placydo.*

PLATT *(French)* Flat land. Variation: *Platte.*

POCANO *(Native American: Pueblo)* Spirits coming.

PONCE *(Spanish)* Fifth. Explorer Ponce de Leon was the only famous person to have this name.

PORTER *(Latin)* Gatekeeper.

POWELL *(English)* Last name. General Colin Powell has brought this name to the forefront. There's no telling what the future for Powell as a first name will be if the general ever decides to return to politics, but I'd venture a guess to say that more parents would consider it for a possible first name for their sons. Variation: *Powel.*

PRAVIN *(Hindu)* Capable.

PRESCOTT *(English)* Priest's cottage. Variations: *Prescot, Prestcot, Prestcott.*

PRESLEY *(English)* Priest's meadow. Variations: *Presleigh, Presly, Pressley, Prestley, Priestley, Priestly.*

PRICE *(Welsh)* The son of an ardent man. Variation: *Pryce.*

PRINCE *(Latin)* Prince. Variations: *Prinz, Prinze.*

PRYOR *(Latin)* Leader of the monastery. Variation: *Prior.*

Living on the Edge

PAAHANA *(Hawaiian)* Busy.

PACO *(Spanish)* Diminutive of Francisco. Variations: *Pacorro, Paquito.*

PADDY *(Irish)* Nickname for Patrick. Variations: *Paddey, Paddie.*

PAHKATOS *(Native American: Nez Perce)* Five cuts.

PAINTER *(English)* Painter.
PAKELIKA *(Hawaiian)* Nobleman.
PAKI *(South African)* Witness.
PAL *(Gypsy)* Brother.
PALAKI *(Polynesian)* Black. Variations: *Palefu, Peleki.*
PALANI *(Hawaiian)* Frenchman. Variation: *Farani.*
PALAUNI *(Polynesian)* Brown.
PALLATON *(Native American)* Fighter. Variations: *Palladin, Pallaten.*
PANAS *(Greek)* Immortal.
PANCHO *(Spanish)* Frenchman. Variation: *Panchito.*
PANOS *(Greek)* Rock.
PANTNI *(Hindu)* Name of the developer of Sanskrit.
PAPIANO *(Hawaiian)* Hawaiian version of Fabian. Variation: *Fabiano.*
PARRISH *(English)* County; church area. Variation: *Parish.*
PARVAIZ *(Hindu)* Happy. Variations: *Parvez, Parviz, Parwiz.*
PATABSU *(Native American)* Fire ant.
PATAMON *(Native American)* Raging man.
PATANJAU *(Hindu)* Fallen palm tree.
PATWIN *(Native American)* Man.
PAXTON *(English)* Peaceful town. Variations: *Packston, Pax, Paxon, Paxten.*
PAYAT *(Native American)* He is coming. Variations: *Pay, Payatt.*
PAZ *(Spanish)* Peace.
PEADAR *(Irish)* Rock. Variation: *Peadair.*
PEDAHEL *(Hebrew)* God redeems. Variation: *Pedael.*
PEDAT *(Hebrew)* Atonement.
PEKELO *(Hawaiian)* Stone. Variation: *Peka.*
PELAGIOS *(Greek)* From the sea.
PELEKE *(Hawaiian)* Wise counselor. Variation: *Ferede.*
PEMBROKE *(Irish)* Cliff. Variation: *Pembrook.*
PENEKIKO *(Hawaiian)* Blessed. Variations: *Benedito, Beni, Peni.*
PENLEY *(English)* Fenced meadow. Variations: *Penlea, Penleigh,*

Penly, Pennlea, Pennleigh, Pennley.

PENMINA *(Hawaiian)* Hawaiian version of Benjamin. Variation: *Beniamina.*

PERACH *(Hebrew)* Flower. Variation: *Perah.*

PERACHIAH *(Hebrew)* God's flower. Variations: *Perachia, Perachya.*

PEREGRINE *(Latin)* Falcon. Variations: *Peregrin, Peregryn.*

PERETZ *(Hebrew)* Spring forward. Variations: *Perez, Pharez.*

PERICLES *(Greek)* Name of famous Greek orator.

PESACH *(Hebrew)* Spared. The name for Passover. Variation: *Pessach.*

PESEKAVA *(Polynesian)* Song about kava.

PEVERELL *(French)* Piper. Variations: *Peverall, Peverel, Peveril.*

PEWLIN *(Welsh)* Small. Variation: *Peulan.*

PEZI *(Native American: Sioux)* Grass.

PHARAOH *(Egyptian)* King. Variation: *Pharoah.*

PHELPS *(English)* Son of Philip.

PHILANDER *(Greek)* Loves men.

PHILEMON *(Greek)* Kiss.

PHILO *(Greek)* Loving.

PICKFORD *(English)* Ford at a peak.

PIERCY *(English)* Pierced hedge. Variation: *Piercey.*

PILA *(Hawaiian)* Hawaiian version of Bill.

PINO *(Italian)* God will add.

PINON *(Native American)* Constellation.

PIO *(Latin)* Pious. Variation: *Pius.*

PITNEY *(English)* Island of a headstrong man. Variation: *Pittney.*

PITT *(English)* Ditch.

PIZI *(Native American: Sioux)* Man in the middle.

PLATO *(Greek)* Broad-shouldered. Variation: *Platon.*

PODALADALTE *(Native American: Kiowa)* Snake head.

POHDLOHK *(Native American: Kiowa)* Old wolf.

POLLARD *(English)* Bald. Variations: *Poll, Pollerd, Pollurd.*

The Most Popular Boys' Names from the 1990s

You'll find names on this list that appear in every previous decade. Perhaps parents were looking back to simpler times and choosing names from the years we perceive as easier to live in. Boys' names for the '90s are also heavy in Biblical influence—think Daniel, Matthew, and John.

1. Michael
2. Christopher
3. Matthew
4. Joshua
5. Andrew
6. Daniel
7. Justin
8. David
9. Ryan
10. John
11. Steven
12. Robert
13. James
14. Nicholas
15. Joseph
16. Brian
17. Jonathan
18. Kyle
19. Sean
20. William
21. Brandon
22. Eric
23. Zachary
24. Thomas
25. Anthony
26. Kevin
27. Adam
28. Tyler
29. Jacob
30. Jeffrey
31. Jason
32. Timothy
33. Benjamin
34. Corey
35. Aaron
36. Mark
37. Alexander
38. Richard
39. Cody
40. Jeremy
41. Nathan
42. Travis
43. Derek
44. Jared
45. Patrick
46. Scott
47. Charles
48. Dustin
49. Jordan
50. Jesse

POLLUX *(Greek)* Crown. Variations: *Pol, Pollack, Polloch, Pollock.*

POMEROY *(French)* Apple orchard. Variations: *Pommeray, Pommeroy.*

PONTUS *(Greek)* God of the sea.

PORFIRIO *(Greek)* Purple stone. Variations: *Porphirios, Prophyrios.*

POSOA *(Polynesian)* Flirting.

POV *(Gypsy)* Ground or mud.

POWA *(Native American)* Rich.

PREM *(Hindu)* Love.

PREMYSL *(Czech)* First. Variations: *Myslik, Premek, Premousek.*

PRENTICE *(English)* Apprentice. Variations: *Pren, Prent, Prentis, Prentiss.*

PREWITT *(French)* Brave little one. Variations: *Prewett, Prewit, Pruitt.*

PRIMO *(Italian)* First son. Variations: *Preemo, Premo.*

PROCTOR *(Latin)* Official. Variations: *Prockter, Procter.*

PROKOP *(Czech)* Very progressive.

PROSPER *(Latin)* Fortunate. Variation: *Prospero.*

PURVIS *(English)* Purveyor. Variations: *Purves, Purviss.*

PUTNAM *(English)* One who lives near a pond.

Tried and True Classics

QUENTIN *(Latin)* Fifth. Names with "x"s and "z"s in them seem to be pretty popular right now and you would expect the same thing to be true of names with "q"s in them. Quentin is probably the leading candidate for the most common name that begins with a "Q," especially since actor and director Quentin Tarantino hit the bigtime with his movie *Pulp Fiction.* Variations: *Quent, Quenten, Quenton, Quint, Quinten, Quintin, Quinton, Quito.*

QUINCY *(French)* The estate of the fifth son. Famous Quincys in recent years include the composer and singer Quincy Jones as well as the TV medical examiner Quincy played by actor Jack Klugman. Variation: *Quincey.*

Slightly Daring Choices

QUILLAN *(Irish)* Cub. Variation: *Quillen.*

QUINLAN *(Irish)* Strong man. Variations: *Quindlen, Quinley, Quinlin, Quinly.*

QUINN *(Irish)* Wise. Variation: *Quin.*

QUIRIN *(English)* A magic spell.

Living on the Edge

QABIL *(Arabic)* Able.

QAMAR *(Arabic)* Moon.

QASIM *(Arabic)* Provider.

QING-NAN *(Chinese)* The younger generation.

QUADREES *(African-American)* Four. Variations: *Kwadrees, Quadrhys.*

QUAN VAN *(Vietnamese)* Authorized.

QUANAH *(Native American: Comanche)* Aromatic.

QUANG THIEU *(Vietnamese)* Smart.

QUED *(Native American: Kiowa)* Decorated robe.

QUENNELL *(French)* Oak tree. Variation: *Quennel.*

QUIGLEY *(Irish)* One with messy hair.

QUIMBY *(Norse)* A woman's house. Variations: *Quenby, Quim, Quin, Quinby.*

QUINTO *(Spanish)* Home ruler. Variation: *Quiqui.*

QUIRINUS *(Latin)* Roman god of war.

QUNNOUNE *(Native American: Narragansett)* Tall.

QUON *(Chinese)* Bright.

QUSAY *(Arabic)* Distant. Variation: *Qussay.*

Tried and True Classics

RALPH *(English)* Wolf counselor. Ralph Kramden is probably the first Ralph that comes to mind for most of us because reruns of *The Honeymooners* have been influential for decades. Variations: *Ralphie, Raoul, Raul, Raulas, Raulo, Rolf, Rolph.*

RANDOLPH *(English)* Wolf with a shield. One of the variations for Randolph, Randy, has become more popular as a given name than the original. Variations: *Randal, Randall, Randel, Randell, Randey, Randie, Randil, Randle, Randol, Randolf, Randy.*

RAOUL *(French)* Variation of Ralph. Variation: *Raul.*

RAPHAEL *(Hebrew)* God has healed. Contrary to popular opinion, Raphael is not a variation of Ralph, but a name that has stood on its own ever since Biblical times. One famous Raphael was the great painter; however, most kids and parents these days are more familiar with Raphael, the Teenage Mutant Ninja Turtle. Variations: *Rafael, Rafel, Rafello, Raffaello.*

RAY *(English)* Royal. Variations: *Rayce, Raydell, Rayder, Raydon, Rayford, Raylen, Raynell.*

RAYMOND *(German)* Counselor and protector. Raymond began to catch on in the United States only in the mid-nineteenth century, before becoming one of the most popular names for boys in 1900. Famous Rays include Raymond Burr, the character that Dustin Hoffman played in the movie *Rainman*, Raymond Chandler, and Raymond Carver. Variations: *Raimondo, Raimund, Raimunde, Raimundo, Rajmund, Ramon, Ramond, Ramone, Ray, Rayment, Raymonde, Raymondo, Raymund, Raymunde, Raymundo, Reimond.*

Famous Male Authors and Artists

Some parents name their babies after famous writers or artists in the hopes of increasing their chances of turning into budding Picassos or Hemingways. Is it wishful thinking? Who knows, but just remember that a young star who's appeared in a number of successful movies might turn people from thinking of your Leonardo as a "da Vinci" to a "DiCaprio."

CLAUDE MONET
DAVID HOCKNEY
EDGAR ALLAN POE
GABRIEL GARCIA MARQUEZ
GEOFFREY CHAUCER
GUSTAVE KLIMT
HERMAN MELVILLE
MAURICE SENDAK
NATHANIEL HAWTHORNE
PABLO PICASSO
SALVADOR DALI
WALT WHITMAN

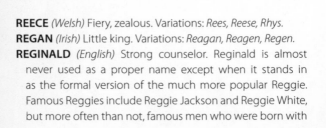

REECE *(Welsh)* Fiery, zealous. Variations: *Rees, Reese, Rhys.*

REGAN *(Irish)* Little king. Variations: *Reagan, Reagen, Regen.*

REGINALD *(English)* Strong counselor. Reginald is almost never used as a proper name except when it stands in as the formal version of the much more popular Reggie. Famous Reggies include Reggie Jackson and Reggie White, but more often than not, famous men who were born with the name Reggie or Reginald have changed their names for ones they consider more suitable—like Rex Harrison and Elton John. Variations: *Reg, Reggie, Reginalt.*

RENÉ *(French)* Reborn. Variations: *Renat, Renato, Renatus, Renne, Rennie, Renny.*

REUBEN *(Hebrew)* Behold a son. Most people consider the name Reuben only in the context of a heaping corned beef sandwich. However, Reuben is showing signs of bubbling up—recent *American Idol* winner Ruben Studdard has brought the name back into the public eye. Parents who are looking for a name with tradition and spirit will be glad to know the Biblical Reuben founded one of the tribes of Israel. Who knows if this name will catch on? Think of the singer Ruben Blades and the Partridge family manager named Reuben Kincaid. Variations: *Reuban, Reubin, Reuven, Reuvin, Rube, Ruben, Rubin, Rubu.*

REYNOLD *(English)* Powerful adviser. Variations: *Ranald, Renald, Renaldo, Renauld, Renault, Reynaldo, Reynaldos, Reynolds, Rinaldo.*

RICHARD *(German)* Strong ruler. For much of this century, the name Richard gave the impression of a noble Englishman who was sent to this country to teach us some manners. This impression is probably due to the vast influx of noted British actors who began to make their way to Hollywood around the middle of the century. These men include Richard Burton, Richard Chamberlain, Richard Attenborough, and Richard Todd, among others. In the mid-1970s, however, Richard took a nosedive on the popularity charts of new baby boys, the same time that Richard M. Nixon left office. Variations: *Dic, Dick, Dickie, Dicky, Ricard, Ricardo, Riccardo, Ricciardo, Rich, Richardo, Richards, Richart, Richerd, Richi, Richie, Rick, Rickard, Rickert, Rickey, Rickie, Ricky, Rico, Rihards, Riki, Riks, Riocard, Riqui, Risa, Ritch, Ritchard, Ritcherd, Ritchie, Ritchy, Rostik, Rostislav, Rostya, Ryszard.*

ROBERT *(English)* Bright fame. Robert is one of the most popular names in the world, especially here in the United States. It has endless variations in every language, and one theory holds that so many men were named Robert from the time of the Middle Ages up until today that many variants were necessary so that people could distinguish one Robert from another. Famous Roberts include Robert Kennedy, Robbie Robertson, Robert Taylor, Robert Wagner, Robert Young, Robert Redford, and Robert de Niro. Variations: *Bob, Bobbey, Bobbie, Bobby, Riobard, Rob, Robb, Robbi, Robbie, Robbin, Robby, Robbyn, Rober, Robers, Roberto, Roberts, Robi, Robin, Robinet, Robyn, Rubert, Ruberto, Rudbert, Ruperto, Ruprecht.*

RODERICK *(German)* Famous ruler. Actor Roddy McDowell and singer Rod Stewart have brought attention to this name, but Rod and Roderick have always been more popular in Britain than in this country. Variations: *Rod, Rodd, Roddie, Roddy, Roderic, Roderich, Roderigo, Rodique, Rodrich, Rodrick, Rodrigo, Rodrique, Rurich, Rurik.*

RODNEY *(English)* Island clearing. Variations: *Rodnee, Rodnie, Rodny.*

ROGER *(German)* Renowned spearman. There have been plenty of famous Rogers throughout the last couple of decades, including Roger Moore, Roger Daltree, and even Roger Rabbit. Variations: *Rodger, Rogelio, Rogerio, Rogerios, Rogers, Ruggerio, Ruggero, Rutger, Ruttger.*

ROLAND *(German)* Famous land. Shakespeare used the name Roland in his play *As You Like It*, and in three others. In Britain today a variation of Roland—Rollo—is very popular right now; here in the United States, Rollo is a type of chocolate candy. Variations: *Rolle, Rolli, Rollie, Rollin, Rollins, Rollo, Rollon, Rolly, Rolo, Rolon, Row, Rowe, Rowland, Rowlands, Rowlandson.*

Famous Composers

Classical music offers a rich variety of names that any parent today can use to gain inspiration. You might not think this is such a cool idea, but just look at Eddie Van Halen's son, who's named Wolfgang, after Mozart. There are also many American composers from whom you could choose a suitable name for your child: Samuel Barber, Aaron Copland, Charles Ives, Amy Beach, and Virgil Thomson are just a few.

Following is a sampling of others:

ANTON DVOŘÁK
BENJAMIN BRITTEN
CAMILLE SAINT-SAENS
CLARA SCHUMANN
CLAUDIO MONTEVERDI
DOMENICO SCARLATTI
ENRIQUE GRANADOS
FRANÇOIS COUPERIN
FRANZ SCHUBERT
JEAN SIBELIUS
JULES MASSENET
KARL CZERNY
ORLANDO GIBBONS
RALPH VAUGHAN WILLIAMS
SERGEI RACHMANINOFF
THOMAS TALLIS

ROMAN *(Latin)* One from Rome. Variations: *Romain, Romano, Romanos, Romulo, Romulos, Romulus.*

RONALD *(English)* Powerful adviser. As American politics go, so, frequently, go popular baby names. This certainly was the case with the growing visibility of Ronald in the early '80s. Variations: *Ranald, Ron, Ronn, Ronney, Ronni, Ronnie, Ronny.*

RORY *(Irish)* Red. Rory is hot, hot, hot. Rory is such a spirited name that many parents are choosing it for their sons. Variations: *Ruaidri, Ruairi, Ruaraidh.*

ROY *(Irish)* Red. Roy was a very popular boys' name in the '50s because of the cowboy singer Roy Rogers. In these days when parents prefer a baby name with lots of possibilities, Roy presents only one: *Roy.* Variation: Roi.

RUDOLPH *(German)* Famous wolf. There are some famous men out there with this name, including former New York City Mayor Rudy Giuliani and Russian ballet dancer Rudolph Nureyev. If you really love this name, however, just be prepared that your kid's peers might tease him plenty and ask him where his red nose is. Variations: *Rodolfo, Rodolph, Rodolphe, Rolf, Rolfe, Rolle, Rollo, Rolph, Rolphe, Rudey, Rudi, Rudie, Rudolf, Rudolfo, Rudolpho, Rudolphus, Rudy.*

RUPERT *(German)* Bright fame. British actor Rupert Everett bears this name but it is not too common in America. Variation of Robert. Variations: *Ruperto, Ruprecht.*

RUSH *(English)* Red-haired.

RUSSELL *(French)* Red-haired. This name is making a comeback probably because of Russell Crowe. Variations: *Rus, Russ, Russel.*

RUSTY *(French)* Red-haired. Variation: *Rustie.*

RYAN *(Irish)* Last name. The growth in popularity of Ryan seemed to coincide with both the celebrity of Ryan O'Neill and American women's desire for the sensitive American man. Ryan is not a name you'd think of for a bully. But again, a big reason for its popularity is that it is an Irish name and a last name all rolled into one, and most names today that fit this description can count on some degree of popularity. Variations: *Ryne, Ryon, Ryun.*

Slightly Daring Choices

RADCLIFF *(English)* Red cliff. The name Radcliff has a tweedy, uppercrust sound to it. Mothers who might choose Radcliff may be thinking about their alma mater, Radcliffe. Variations: *Radcliffe, Radclyffe.*

RADEK *(Czech)* Famous ruler. Variations: *Radacek, Radan, Radik, Radko, Radouvsek, Radovs.*

RADFORD *(English)* Red ford or ford with reeds. Variations: *Rad, Radd, Radferd, Radfurd, Redford.*

RADIMIR *(Czech)* Happy and famous. Variations: *Radim, Radomir.*

RADLEY *(English)* Red meadow. Variations: *Radlea, Radlee, Radleigh, Radly.*

RADMAN *(Slavic)* Joy.

RADNOR *(English)* Red shore.

RAFFERTY *(Irish)* Prosperous. Variations: *Rafe, Rafer, Raferty, Raff, Raffarty, Raffer, Raffi, Raffy.*

RAGNAR *(Norse)* Power. Variations: *Rainer, Rainier, Rayner, Raynor.*

RAIDEN *(Japanese)* God of thunder.

RAINI *(Native American)* A god.

RALEIGH *(English)* Deer meadow. Variations: *Rawleigh, Rawley, Rawly.*

RALSTON *(English)* Ralph's town.

RAMIRO *(Portuguese)* Great judge. Variation: *Ramirez.*

RAMSAY *(English)* Island of rams. Variations: *Ramsey, Ramsy.*

RAND *(English)* Fighter.

RANIER *(English)* Mighty army.

RANON *(Hebrew)* Joyful song.

RANSLEY *(English)* Raven meadow. Variations: *Ransleigh, Ransly.*

RASHAD *(Arabic)* Moral work. Variation: *Rashid.*

RASMUS *(Greek)* Beloved.

RAVI *(Hindu)* Sun. Variation: *Ravee.*

RAWLINS *(French)* Last name. Variations: *Rawlinson, Rawson.*

RAYBURN *(English)* Brook for deer. Variations: *Rayborn, Raybourne, Rayburne.*

READ *(English)* Red-haired. Variations: *Reade, Reed, Reid, Reide, Reyd.*

READING *(English)* Son of the red-haired one. Variations: *Redding, Reeding, Reiding.*

REDMOND *(Irish)* Counselor. Variation of Raymond. Variations: *Radmond, Radmund, Redmund.*

REEVE *(English)* Bailiff. Variations: *Reave, Reeves.*

REMY *(French)* From Rheims, a town in central France. Variations: *Remee, Remi, Remie, Remmy.*

RENAUD *(French)* Powerful.

RENDOR *(Hungarian)* Policeman.

RENNY *(Irish)* Small and mighty.

RENTON *(English)* Deer habitat.

RENZO *(Italian)* Laurel. Diminutive form of Lorenzo.

REX *(Latin)* King.

REY *(Spanish)* King. Variation: *Reyes.*

REYNARD *(French)* Fox. Variation: *Renard.*

RHETT *(Welsh)* Fiery. Variation: *Rhys.*

RHODES *(Greek)* Island of roses. Variations: *Rhoades, Rhodas, Rodas.*

RIDER *(English)* Horseman. Variations: *Ridder, Ryder.*

Male Figures from Greek Mythology

Greek gods have been the recipients of some of the most mellifluous names around. Here are just some of the many Greek gods and other mythological figures:

ADONIS: *God of beauty*
APOLLO: *God of war*
ARES: *God of war*
ATLAS: *Held the world on his shoulders*
CRONOS: *God of harvests; father of Zeus*
EROS: *God of love*
HELIOS: *God of the sun*
HEPHAESTUS: *God of fire*
HERMES: *Messenger for the gods*
ORION: *God of the hunt*
PAN: *God of shepherds*
PONTUS: *God of the sea*
THANATOS: *God of death*
TRITON: *God of the sea*
ZEUS: *King of the gods*

RIDGLEY *(English)* Meadow on a ridge. Variations: *Ridgeleigh, Ridgeley, Ridglea, Ridglee, Ridgleigh.*

RIDLEY *(English)* Red meadow. Variations: *Riddley, Ridlea, Ridleigh, Ridly.*

RIGEL *(Arabic)* Foot.

RILEY *(Irish)* Brave. Riley seems to be a good candidate for becoming more popular as a name for boys in the United

States, since it is Irish and is traditionally thought of as a last name. Variations: *Reilly, Ryley.*

RIMON *(Hebrew)* Pomegranate.

RING *(English)* Ring.

RINGO *(Japanese)* Apple. Beatles fanatics will most likely be the only ones who choose this name for their sons.

RIO *(Spanish)* River. Variation: *Reo.*

RIORDAN *(Irish)* Minstrel. Variations: *Rearden, Reardon.*

RIP *(Dutch)* Ripe.

RIPLEY *(English)* Shouting man's meadow. Variations: *Ripleigh, Riply, Ripp.*

RISHON *(Hebrew)* First.

RISLEY *(English)* Meadow with shrubs. Variations: *Rislea, Rislee, Risleigh, Risly.*

RISTON *(English)* Town near shrubs.

RITTER *(German)* Knight.

ROALD *(German)* Famous leader.

ROARK *(Irish)* Mighty. Variations: *Roarke, Rorke, Rourke.*

ROBINSON *(English)* Son of Robert. Variations: *Robbinson, Robeson, Robson, Robynson.*

ROCCO *(Italian)* Rest. Variations: *Rock, Rockie, Rocky.*

ROCK *(English)* Rock. Variations: *Rockford, Rockie, Rocky.*

RODMAN *(English)* Famous man.

ROGAN *(Irish)* Redhead.

ROHAN *(Irish)* Red.

ROMANY *(Gypsy)* Gypsy.

ROMEO *(Italian)* Pilgrim visiting Rome.

RONAN *(Irish)* Little seal.

RONEL *(Hebrew)* Song of God.

RONI *(Hebrew)* Joyful.

ROONEY *(Irish)* Red-haired. Variations: *Roone, Roonie, Roony.*

ROPER *(English)* Maker of rope.

ROSCOE *(Scandinavian)* Deer forest.

ROSLIN *(Scottish)* Small redheaded child. Variations: *Roslyn,*

Rosselin, Rosslyn.

ROSS *(Scottish)* Cape. Variations: *Rosse, Rossie, Rossy.*

ROTH *(German)* Red.

ROWAN *(Irish)* Red. Variation: *Rowen.*

ROWLEY *(English)* Unevenly cleared meadow. Variations: *Rowlea, Rowlee, Rowleigh, Rowlie, Rowly.*

ROYAL *(French)* Royal. Variation: *Royall.*

ROYCE *(American)* Roy's son. Variations: *Roice, Royse.*

Living on the Edge

RABBI *(Hebrew)* My master.

RABI *(Arabic)* Breeze.

RABY *(Scottish)* Famous and bright. Variations: *Rab, Rabbie, Rabi.*

RACHIM *(Hebrew)* Compassion. Variations: *Racham, Rachmiel, Raham, Rahim.*

RAD *(Arabic)* Thunder.

RADBORNE *(English)* Red stream. Variations: *Rad, Radborn, Radbourn, Radbourne, Radburn, Radburne, Radd.*

RADHI *(East African)* Goodwill.

RAFAT *(Arabic)* Merciful.

RAFIQ *(Hindu)* Friend. Variations: *Rafee, Rafi, Rafiki.*

RAHIM *(Hindu)* Compassionate.

RAJAB *(Arabic)* Seventh month. Variation: *Ragab.*

RAMADAN *(Arabic)* Ninth month of the Muslim year.

RANCE *(African)* Borrower. Variations: *Rancel, Rancell, Ransel, Ransell.*

RANGER *(French)* Protector of the forest. Variations: *Rainger, Range.*

RANIT *(Hebrew)* Song. Variation: *Ronit.*

RANKIN *(English)* Shield.

RANSFORD *(English)* Raven ford.

RANSOM *(English)* Son of the protector. Variations: *Ransome, Ranson.*

RAPIER *(French)* As strong as a sword.

RASHID *(Turkish)* Righteous. Variations: *Rasheed, Rasheid, Rasheyd.*

RAWDON *(English)* Craggy hill.

RAZI *(Hebrew)* My secret. Variations: *Raz, Raziel.*

REGIN *(Scandinavian)* Judgment.

REMINGTON *(English)* Family of ravens. Variations: *Rem, Remee, Remi, Remie, Remmy.*

REMUS *(Latin)* Swift.

RENFRED *(English)* Strong peace.

REXFORD *(English)* King's ford.

RIDGE *(English)* Ridge. Variation: *Rigg.*

RIDGEWAY *(English)* Road on a ridge.

RIYAD *(Arabic)* Garden. Variation: *Riyadh.*

ROCHESTER *(English)* Stone fortress.

ROOSEVELT *(Dutch)* Field of roses.

ROSARIO *(Portuguese)* The rosary.

ROSWELL *(English)* Rose spring.

ROUSSE *(French)* Red-haired.

ROVER *(English)* Wanderer.

ROXBURY *(English)* Town of the rook.

ROYSTON *(English)* Last name. Variation: *Roystan.*

ROZEN *(Hebrew)* Leader.

RUDD *(English)* Ruddy skin.

RUDYARD *(English)* Red paddock.

RUFORD *(English)* Red ford. Variation: *Rufford.*

RUFUS *(Latin)* Red-haired. Variations: *Ruffus, Rufo, Rufous.*

RUGBY *(English)* Rook fortress.

RURIK *(Scandinavian)* Famous king. Variations: *Roar, Rorek, Roth, Rothrekr.*

RUSHFORD *(English)* Ford with rushes.

RUSKIN *(French)* Child with red hair.

RUTHERFORD *(English)* Cattle crossing. Variation: *Rutherfurd.*

RUTLAND *(Norse)* Red land.

RUTLEY *(English)* Red meadow.

RYCROFT *(English)* Field of rye. Variation: *Ryecroft.*

RYE *(Polish)* Strong ruler.

RYLAND *(English)* Land of rye. Variation: *Ryeland.*

Tried and True Classics

SALVATORE *(Latin)* Savior. Variations: *Sal, Salvador, Salvator.*

SAMSON *(Hebrew)* Sun. Variations: *Sampson, Sanson, Sansone.*

SAMUEL *(Hebrew)* God listens. Though Samuel has tended to be somewhat popular over the last 100 years or so, it seems that it has fallen in and out of favor. Right now, Sam is popular, perhaps owing to the success of playwright Sam Shepard and the history of the TV show *Cheers*, in which Sam Malone tended bar. Sam is a just-another-guy name that should continue to be popular through the rest of this decade and beyond. Variations: *Sam, Sammie, Sammy, Samouel, Samuele, Samuello.*

SAUL *(Hebrew)* Asked for. If the parents of Beatle Paul McCartney had given their son the original name of Paul the Apostle, then all those girls back in the '60s would have been yelling "Saul! Saul!" Novelist Saul Bellow is probably the most famous celebrity with this name.

SCOTT *(English)* One from Scotland. Scott has always been an all-American name, belying its roots. Famous Scotts from the States include F. Scott Fitzgerald and Francis Scott Key, for whom Fitzgerald was named. Variations: *Scot, Scottie, Scotto, Scotty.*

SEAN *(Irish)* God is good. Variation of John. Sean is also a popular girls' name, albeit with different spellings, most frequently Shawn. Today, Sean is still a pretty hip name for babies—perhaps actors Sean Penn and Sean Connery have something to do with it. Variations: *Seann, Shaine, Shane, Shaughn, Shaun, Shawn, Shayn, Shayne.*

Top Boys' Names of 2000

1. Jacob
2. Michael
3. Matthew
4. Joshua
5. Christopher
6. Nicholas
7. Andrew
8. Joseph
9. Daniel
10. Tyler
11. William
12. Ryan
13. Brandon
14. John
15. Zachary
16. David
17. Anthony
18. James
19. Justin
20. Alexander
21. Jonathan
22. Christian
23. Austin
24. Dylan
25. Ethan
26. Benjamin
27. Noah
28. Samuel
29. Robert
30. Kevin
31. Nathan
32. Cameron
33. Thomas
34. Hunter
35. Jordan
36. Kyle
37. Caleb
38. Jason
39. Logan
40. Aaron
41. Eric
42. Gabriel
43. Brian
44. Luis
45. Adam
46. Jack
47. Juan
48. Isaiah
49. Connor
50. Steven

SEBASTIAN *(Latin)* One from Sebastia, an ancient Roman city. Like Sean, Sebastian is a really cool name, although it doesn't get one-tenth of the play today that Sean does. This is changing, however; the name does seem to be popping up with greater frequency. Variations: *Seb, Sebastien, Sebbie.*

SETH *(Hebrew)* To appoint. Of the popular names today, Seth is unusual because it really has no nicknames or variations. Perhaps the sound of the name is still distinctive enough. Seth was the third son of Adam and Eve and was born after the death of his older siblings, Cain and Abel. It's interesting to note that in the past, the name Seth was frequently given to a newborn son after his parents had already lost a child. Today, Seth has no morbid association. It's just a neat name.

SEYMOUR *(French)* From St. Maur, a village in France. Variations: *Seamor, Seamore, Seamour, Si, Sy.*

SHELBY *(English)* Village on the ledge. Shelby seems to be a name with real possibilities, an acceptable alternative to an outdated name like Sheldon. However, as a name that begins with the letters "Sh," it may continue to be used more for girls than for boys. Variations: *Shelbey, Shelbie.*

SIDNEY *(English)* One from Sidney, a town in France. Sidney was once quite the aristocratic name; however, a slow and gradual adoption of the name by girls (with a "y" in place of the "i") has made this name a rarity for young boys today. Variations: *Sid, Siddie, Sidon, Sidonio, Syd, Sydney.*

SIMON *(Hebrew)* God hears. Simon is gaining ground today among parents who see an almost French distinction in the name. Variations: *Simeon, Simion, Simm, Simms, Simone, Symms, Symon.*

SINCLAIR *(French)* Town in France. Variations: *Sinclare, Synclair.*

SOLOMON *(Hebrew)* Peaceable. One of the most obviously Old Testament names around, Solomon seems to be making headway among parents who are looking for a Biblical name that is also somewhat hip. Variations: *Salamen, Salamon, Salamun, Salaun, Salman, Salmon, Salom, Salomo, Salomon, Salomone, Selim, Shelomoh, Shlomo, Sol, Solaman, Sollie, Solly, Soloman, Solomo, Solomonas, Solomone.*

Top Boys' Names of 2001

1. Jacob
2. Michael
3. Nicholas
4. Matthew
5. Joshua
6. Andrew
7. Joseph
8. Christopher
9. Anthony
10. Dylan
11. Tyler
12. John
13. Daniel
14. Zachary
15. Alexander
16. Brandon
17. Jonathan
18. William
19. Christian
20. Cameron
21. Ethan
22. Ryan
23. Justin
24. David
25. Benjamin
26. Austin
27. Nathan
28. James
29. Logan
30. Eric
31. Samuel
32. Hunter
33. Noah
34. Brian
35. Thomas
36. Connor
37. Caleb
38. Robert
39. Kevin
40. Jose
41. Kyle
42. Sean
43. Luis
44. Jason
45. Elijah
46. Gabriel
47. Aaron
48. Devin
49. Steven
50. Jordan

SONNY *(English)* Son. Variation: *Sonnie.*

SPENCER *(English)* Seller of goods. Spencer is on the upswing in this country, and not only because actor Spencer Tracy continues to permeate the American consciousness through his movies with Katharine Hepburn, which are frequently rerun on cable channels. But the simple fact of the matter is that this name is just real cool. Variations: *Spence, Spense, Spenser.*

STANLEY *(English)* Stony meadow. Back in its day—which was around the middle of the nineteenth century—Stanley was quite a noble name. The most famous Stanley we know is the comic actor Stan Laurel, the better half of Laurel and Hardy. Variations: *Stan, Stanlea, Stanlee, Stanleigh, Stanly.*

STEPHEN *(Greek)* Crowned. Stephen holds the distinction of being the name of the first Christian on record; and its history has served as a built-in boost in any country where Christianity is practiced. The different variations of the name each provide clearly distinct feels. For instance, Steve Garvey and Steve McQueen have a somewhat swaggering personality, while Stephen Sondheim, Stephen King, and Steven Spielberg convey a more artistic image. The less formal version "Stevie" is claimed by two well-known musicians: Stevie Wonder and Stevie Ray Vaughan. Nowadays, Stephen with a "ph" is used less often than Steven with a "v." Though the name is not as popular as it once was, it is still used with some regularity, and it will be with us for quite some time. Variations: *Stefan, Stefano, Stefanos, Stefans, Steffan, Steffel, Steffen, Stefos, Stepa, Stepan, Stepanek, Stepek, Stephan, Stephane, Stephanos, Stephanus, Stephens, Stephenson, Stepka, Stepousek, Stevan, Steve, Steven, Stevenson, Stevie.*

STEWART *(English)* Steward. Variations: *Stew, Steward, Stu, Stuart.*

SYLVESTER *(Latin)* Forested. From Sylvester Stallone to Sylvester the Cat all the way to Sylvester the disco singer from the '70s, this name is a veritable grab-bag of images and associations. Variations: *Silvester, Silvestre, Silvestro, Sly.*

Slightly Daring Choices

SABIN *(Latin)* The name of an ancient Roman clan. Variations: *Sabine, Sabino.*

SABIR *(Arabic)* Patient. Variation: *Sabri.*

SADLER *(English)* Saddle maker. Variation: *Saddler.*

SAFFORD *(English)* River crossing at the willows.

SAKARIA *(Scandinavian)* God remembers. Variation of Zachariah. Variations: *Sakari, Sakarias.*

SALTON *(English)* Town in the willows.

SAMIR *(Arabic)* Entertainer.

SANDFORD *(English)* Sandy crossing. Variations: *Sandfurd, Sanford.*

SANTIAGO *(Spanish)* Saint.

SANTO *(Spanish)* Holy. Variation: *Santos.*

SAWYER *(English)* Woodworker. Variations: *Sayer, Sayers, Sayre, Sayres.*

SCANLON *(Irish)* Little trapper. Variations: *Scanlan, Scanlen.*

SCULLY *(Irish)* Town crier.

SEAMUS *(Irish)* He who supplants. Variation of James. Variation: *Shamus.*

SEATON *(English)* Town by the sea. Variations: *Seeton, Seton.*

SEDGWICK *(English)* Sword place. Variations: *Sedgewick, Sedgewyck, Sedgwyck.*

SEGEL *(English)* Treasure. Variations: *Seagel, Segell.*

SELAH *(Hebrew)* Song.

SELBY *(English)* Manor in the village. Variation: *Shelby.*

SERENO *(Latin)* Calm.

SERGE *(Latin)* Servant. Variations: *Serg, Sergei, Sergey, Sergi, Sergie, Sergio, Sergius.*

SHANAHAN *(Irish)* Wise one.

SHANLEY *(Irish)* Small and ancient. Variations: *Shanleigh, Shannleigh, Shannley.*

SHANNON *(Irish)* Old. Shannon was once solely a name for boys, but sometime in the early 1940s, parents began to choose it for their girls as well. Today, Shannon appears much more frequently among girls than boys, perhaps helped along by the proliferation of girls' names that begin with "Sh." Variations: *Shannan, Shannen.*

SHARIF *(Hindu)* Respected. Variations: *Shareef, Shereef, Sherif.*

SHAW *(English)* Grove of trees.

SHEA *(English)* Requested. Variations: *Shae, Shai, Shaye.*

SHEEHAN *(Irish)* Calm.

SHELDON *(English)* Steep valley. Variations: *Shelden, Sheldin.*

SHELLEY *(English)* Meadow on a ledge. Variation: *Shelly.*

SHELTON *(English)* Town on a ledge.

SHERIDAN *(Irish)* Wild man. Variations: *Sheredan, Sheridon, Sherridan.*

SHILOH *(Hebrew)* Gift from God. Variation: *Shilo.*

SIEGFRID *(German)* Victory and peace. Variations: *Siegfried, Sigfredo, Sigfrido, Sigfroi, Sigifredo, Sigvard.*

SIGMUND *(German)* Victory shield. Variations: *Siegmund, Sigmond.*

SILVA *(Latin)* Forest. Variations: *Silas, Silvain, Silvan, Silvano, Silvanus, Silvio, Sylas, Sylvain, Sylvan, Sylvanus.*

SIMA *(Hebrew)* Treasure.

SIMPSON *(English)* Son of Simon. Variation: *Simson.*

SKIP *(Scandinavian)* Boss of a ship. Variations: *Skipp, Skipper, Skippie, Skippy.*

SLADE *(English)* Valley. Variations: *Slaide, Slayde.*

SLANE *(Czech)* Salty.

SLOAN *(Irish)* Soldier. Variation: *Sloane.*

SMITH *(English)* Blacksmith. Variations: *Smitty, Smyth, Smythe.*

SOREN *(Scandinavian)* Apart.

SPALDING *(English)* Divided field. Before the famed monologuist Spalding Gray first became well known in the '80s, the common association most of us had with the name

Spalding had to do with a tennis ball. Variation: *Spaulding.*

STANBURY *(English)* Fort made of stone. Variations: *Stanberry, Stanbery.*

STANFORD *(English)* Stony ford. Variations: *Stamford, Stan, Standford.*

STANISLAUS *(Polish)* Glorious camp. Variations: *Stach, Stanislao, Stanislas, Stanislau, Stanislus, Stanislav, Stanislaw, Stas, Stash, Stashko, Stashko, Stasio.*

STANTON *(English)* Stony town. Variations: *Stanten, Staunton.*

STARR *(English)* Star.

STEADMAN *(English)* One who lives on a farm. Variations: *Steadmann, Stedman.*

STEELE *(English)* One who resists. Variation: *Steel.*

STEIN *(German)* Stone. Variation: *Steen.*

STERLING *(English)* First-class. Variation: *Stirling.*

STOCKWELL *(English)* Spring with tree stumps.

STODDARD *(English)* Protector of horses.

STORM *(English)* Storm. Most people who meet the celebrated weathercaster from New York named Storm Field figure that his name is a joke. But Storm is his real name, given to him by his weathercaster father, Frank Field.

STRATFORD *(English)* River crossing near a street.

STROM *(German)* River.

STYLES *(English)* Stile, or stairs that go over a wall.

SULLIVAN *(Irish)* Black-eyed. With its last name origins and Irish roots, the stage is set for Sullivan to become more popularly used. Variations: *Sullavan, Sullevan, Sulliven.*

SULLY *(English)* Southern meadow. Variations: *Sulleigh, Sulley.*

SUTHERLAND *(Scandinavian)* Southern land. Variation: *Southerland.*

SWAIN *(English)* Herdsman or knight's attendant.

SWEENEY *(Irish)* Small hero. Variation: *Sweeny.*

Top Boys' Names of 2002

1. Jacob
2. Michael
3. Matthew
4. Joshua
5. Nicholas
6. Christopher
7. Joseph
8. Ethan
9. Andrew
10. Daniel
11. William
12. Anthony
13. Jonathan
14. Zachary
15. David
16. Tyler
17. Christian
18. John
19. Alexander
20. Ryan
21. Dylan
22. Brandon
23. James
24. Brian
25. Justin
26. Caleb
27. Austin
28. Samuel
29. José
30. Benjamin
31. Nathan
32. Kevin
33. Logan
34. Cameron
35. Eric
36. Gabriel
37. Robert
38. Noah
39. Thomas
40. Jordan
41. Aidan
42. Hunter
43. Connor
44. Jason
45. Jaden
46. Sean
47. Elijah
48. Kyle
49. Stephen
50. Jackson

Living on the Edge

SABER *(French)* Sword. Variation: *Sabre.*

SADDAM *(Arabic)* Unknown definition. In the wake of the present-day political turmoil, the name Saddam has to be among the rarest names to appear on birth certificates in this country.

SAID *(Arabic)* Happy. Variations: *Saeed, Saied, Saiyid, Sayeed, Sayid, Syed.*

SAMOSET *(Native American: Algonquin)* He who walks a lot. Variation: *Samaset.*

SANCHO *(Latin)* Sacred. Variation: *Sauncho.*

SARGENT *(French)* Officer. Variations: *Sarge, Sergeant.*

SAVILLE *(French)* Town of willows. Variations: *Savil, Savile, Savill, Savilla, Savylle.*

SAWNEY *(Scottish)* Protector of men. Variations: *Sawnie, Sawny.*

SAXON *(English)* Sword. Variations: *Saxe, Saxen.*

SEELEY *(English)* Blessed.

SEFTON *(English)* Town in the rushes.

SENIOR *(French)* Lord.

SERAPHIM *(Greek)* The angels; (Hebrew) Zealous. Variations: *Serafin, Serafino, Seraphimus.*

SEWARD *(English)* Protector of the sea. Variation: *Sewerd.*

SHADRACH *(Hebrew)* Unknown definition. Variations: *Shad, Shadrack.*

SHALOM *(Hebrew)* Peace. Variation: *Sholom.*

SHEPHERD *(English)* Sheepherder. Variations: *Shep, Shepard, Shephard, Shepp, Sheppard, Shepperd.*

SHERLOCK *(English)* Bright hair. Variations: *Sherlocke, Shurlock.*

SHERMAN *(English)* One who cuts cloth. Variations: *Scherman, Schermann, Shermann.*

SHERWIN *(English)* Bright friend. Variations: *Sherwind, Sherwinn, Sherwyn, Sherwynne.*

SHIVA *(Hindu)* Fortunate. Variations: *Sheo, Shiv, Sib, Siva.*

SHLOMO *(Hebrew)* Peace.

SIVAN *(Hebrew)* Ninth month of the Jewish year.

SNOWDEN *(English)* Snowy mountain. Variation: *Snowdon.*

SOMERTON *(English)* Summer town. Variations: *Somervile, Somerville.*

SPEAR *(English)* Man with a spear. Variations: *Speare, Spears, Speer, Speers, Spiers.*

STACY *(Greek)* Fertile. Variation: *Stacey.*

STANDISH *(English)* Stony park.

STRUTHERS *(Irish)* Brook.

Tried and True Classics

TAYLOR *(English)* Tailor. Taylor is really gaining ground for both boys and girls in this country but there are signs that it will soon become the sole property of girls. Boys will have to switch to Tyler or another popular last name as first name that begins with "T." Variations: *Tailer, Tailor, Tayler, Taylour.*

TERENCE *(Latin)* Roman clan name. Twenty and thirty years ago, boys called Terry had Terence as their real names. Today, Terence has become somewhat of a relic since parents have been brave enough to name their sons Terry from the start. Terry is yet another instance of a name that started out being exclusively male, crossed over to become popular for both boys and girls, and then in the end, began to be associated almost exclusively with girls. Variations: *Tarrance, Terencio, Terrance, Terrence, Terrey, Terri, Terry.*

THEODORE *(Greek)* Gift from God. Variations: *Teador, Ted, Tedd, Teddey, Teddie, Teddy, Tedor, Teodor, Teodoro, Theo, Theodor.*

THOMAS *(Aramaic)* Twin. Saint Thomas was the impetus for this name as it started to become popular around the time of the Middle Ages. Today, Thomas is popular all over the world, and is one of the names that parents in this country are looking to in order to instill a sense of history and tradition in their own sons. Variations: *Tam, Tameas, Thom, Thoma, Thompson, Thomson, Thumas, Thumo, Tom, Tomas, Tomaso, Tomasso, Tomaz, Tomcio, Tomek, Tomelis, Tomi, Tomie, Tomislaw, Tomm, Tommy, Tomsen, Tomson, Toomas, Tuomas, Tuomo.*

TIMOTHY *(Greek)* Honoring God. Any name that rhymes with Jimmy—like Timmy does—is a great name for a kid.

Variations: *Tim, Timmothy, Timmy, Timo, Timofeo, Timon, Timoteo, Timothe, Timotheo, Timotheus, Timothey, Tymmothy, Tymothy.*

TOBIAS *(Hebrew)* God is good. Variations: *Tobe, Tobey, Tobia, Tobiah, Tobie, Tobin, Toby.*

TODD *(English)* Fox. Variation: *Tod.*

TONY *(Latin)* Nickname for Anthony that has evolved into its own freestanding name. Variations: *Toney, Tonie.*

TRAVIS *(French)* Toll-taker. No one knows for sure why this name has suddenly become popular in the last ten or fifteen years, except for the fact that it is a last name that begins with the letter "T," which accounts for many of the newly popular boys' names. Travis sounds like it originates in Britain, but it is actually French; it appears infrequently in Britain. One famous celebrity with the name is Travis Tritt. Variations: *Traver, Travers, Travus, Travys.*

TRENT *(Latin)* Rushing waters. Variations: *Trenten, Trentin, Trenton.*

TREVOR *(Welsh)* Large homestead. Since Trevor seems to be cut from the same cloth as Travis, you'd think it would be nearly as popular. This is not the case, however, so feel free to use it and think of it as unique. Variations: *Trefor, Trev, Trevar, Trever, Trevis.*

TREY *(English)* Three.

TRISTAN *(Welsh)* Famous Welsh folklore character. Variations: *Tris, Tristam.*

TYLER *(English)* Tile maker. Tyler was an extremely popular name in the '90s for both boys and girls, though it was more widely used for boys. If you already had a child in nursery school in the '90s, there's a good chance that one or more of the boys in your child's class was named Tyler. Parents liked the name because it was both formal and casual. Variations: *Ty, Tylar.*

TYRONE *(Irish)* Land of Owen. Variations: *Tiron, Tirone, Ty, Tyron.*

TYSON *(English)* Firebrand. Variations: *Tieson, Tison, Tysen.*

Top Boys' Names of 2003

1. Jacob
2. Aidan
3. Ethan
4. Matthew
5. Nicholas
6. Joshua
7. Ryan
8. Michael
9. Zachary
10. Tyler
11. Dylan
12. Andrew
13. Connor
14. Jack
15. Christopher
16. Caleb
17. Alexander
18. Logan
19. Jaden
20. Nathan
21. Noah
22. Joseph
23. Benjamin
24. Daniel
25. William
26. Anthony
27. Cameron
28. James
29. Austin
30. Jackson
31. Justin
32. Brandon
33. John
34. David
35. Sean
36. Gavin
37. Evan
38. Christian
39. Caden
40. Alex
41. Samuel
42. Gabriel
43. Hunter
44. Thomas
45. Luke
46. Braydon
47. Jordan
48. Jonathan
49. Kyle
50. Elijah

Slightly Daring Choices

TAB *(German)* Brilliant. Variation: *Tabb.*

TAD *(Welsh)* Father. Variation: *Tadd.*

TAI *(Vietnamese)* Skill.

TAJ *(Hindu)* Crown.

TAKODA *(Native American: Sioux)* Friends.

TALBOT *(English)* Last name. Variations: *Talbert, Talbott, Tallbot, Tallbott.*

TALE *(African: Botswana)* Green.

TALIB *(Arabic)* Searcher.

TALIESIN *(Welsh)* Radiant brow. Variation: *Taltesin.*

TALOR *(Hebrew)* Morning dew.

TANNER *(English)* One who tans leather. There are a slew of last names beginning with "T" that are currently very popular for use as first names for boys. Tanner is one of a group that includes Tucker, Taylor, and Travis. Variations: *Tan, Tanier, Tann, Tanney, Tannie, Tanny.*

TATE *(English)* Happy. Variations: *Tait, Taitt, Tayte.*

TAVOR *(Hebrew)* Unlucky. Variation: *Tabor.*

TENNESEE *(Native American: Cherokee)* The state.

TENNYSON *(English)* Son of Dennis. Variations: *Tenney, Tennie, Tenny.*

TERRILL *(German)* Follower of Thor. Variations: *Terrall, Terrel, Terrell, Terryl, Terryll, Tirrell, Tyrrell.*

TESHER *(Hebrew)* Donation.

TEVIN *(African-American)* Variation of Kevin.

TEX *(American)* Nickname for Texas.

THADDEUS *(Aramaic)* Brave. Variations: *Taddeo, Tadeo, Tadio, Thad, Thaddaus.*

THAI *(Vietnamese)* Many.

THANE *(English)* Warrior. Variations: *Thain, Thaine, Thayn, Thayne.*

THATCHER *(English)* Roof thatcher. Variations: *Thacher, Thatch, Thaxter.*

THERON *(Greek)* Hunter.

THOR *(Scandinavian: Norwegian)* Thunder. No matter which version of Thor you choose for your son, you are choosing one of the most popular names in Denmark. It's a powerful name and should continue to become more popular in the United States. Variations: *Tor, Torr.*

THORNE *(English)* Thorn. Variation: *Thorn.*

THURSTON *(Scandinavian)* Thor's stone. Variations: *Thorstan, Thorstein, Thorsteinn, Thorsten, Thurstain, Thurstan, Thursten, Torstein, Torsten, Torston.*

TIERNAN *(Irish)* Little lord. Variations: *Tierney, Tighearnach, Tighearnan.*

TITO *(Spanish)* To honor.

TITUS *(Greek)* Of the giants. Variations: *Tito, Titos.*

TIVON *(Hebrew)* Lover of nature.

TOMLIN *(English)* Little twin. Variation: *Tomlinson.*

TORGER *(Scandinavian)* Thor's spear. Variations: *Terje, Torgeir.*

TORIN *(Irish)* Chief.

TORIO *(Japanese)* Bird's tail.

TORRANCE *(Irish)* Little hills. Variations: *Torin, Torrence, Torrey, Torrin, Torry.*

TOWNSEND *(English)* Town's end.

TRACY *(French)* Area in France. Variations: *Trace, Tracey, Treacy.*

TRAYTON *(English)* Town near trees.

TREMAIN *(Celtic)* Stone house. Variations: *Tremaine, Tremayne.*

TROY *(Irish)* Soldier. Variations: *Troi, Troye.*

TRUMAN *(English)* Loyal one. Variations: *Trueman, Trumaine, Trumann.*

TUCKER *(English)* One who works with cloth.

TUDOR *(Welsh)* Royal dynasty.

TULLY *(Irish)* Peaceful. Variations: *Tull, Tulley, Tullie.*

TURNER *(English)* Woodworker.

TWAIN *(English)* Split in two. Variations: *Twaine, Twayn.*

TY *(American)* Unknown definition. Variation: *Tye.*

TYNAN *(Irish)* Dark.

TYRELL *(Latin)* Roman clan name. Variations: *Terrell, Tirell, Tyrrell.*

Living on the Edge

TAGGART *(Irish)* Son of a priest.

TAHOMA *(Native American: Navajo)* Shoreline. Variation: *Tohoma.*

TAMMANY *(From Thomas)* Twin. Variation: *Tamanend.*

TANAKI *(Polynesian)* Keep score.

TANI *(Japanese)* Valley.

TANK *(Polynesian)* God of the sky.

TARLETON *(English)* Thor's town.

TARRANT *(Welsh)* Thunder. Variation: *Tarrent.*

TAVISH *(Irish)* Twin. Variations: *Tavis, Tevis.*

TAWNO *(Gypsy)* Small.

TAYIB *(Arabic)* Good.

TEARLACH *(Scottish)* Man.

TELEK *(Polish)* Ironworker.

TELEM *(Hebrew)* Furrow.

TELFORD *(French)* One who works with iron. Variations: *Telfer, Telfor, Telfour.*

TEMPEST *(French)* Storm.

TEMPLE *(English)* Temple.

TEMPLETON *(English)* Town near the temple. Variations: *Temple, Templeten.*

TENDOY *(Native American: Bannock)* To climb. Variation: *Tendoi.*

TENNANT *(English)* Tenant. Variations: *Tenant, Tennent.*

TERACH *(Hebrew)* Goat. Variations: *Tera, Terah.*

TET *(Vietnamese)* Festival.

TEVA *(Hebrew)* Nature.

TEVITA *(Polynesian)* Cherished.

THAW *(English)* Melt.

THEMBA *(South African)* Hope.

THEOBALD *(German)* Brave people. Variations: *Thebaud, Thebault, Thibault, Thibaut, Tibold, Tiebold.*

THEODORIC *(German)* Leader of the people. Variation: *Thierry.*

THESEUS *(Greek)* Ancient mythological figure.

THIASSI *(Scandinavian)* Ancient mythological figure. Variations: *Thiazi, Thjazi.*

THORALD *(Scandinavian: Norwegian)* One who follows Thor. Variations: *Thorold, Torald.*

THORLEY *(English)* Thor's meadow. Variations: *Thorlea, Thorlee, Thorleigh, Thorly, Torley.*

THORNLEY *(English)* Thorny meadow. Variations: *Thornlea, Thornleigh, Thornly.*

THORNTON *(English)* Thorny town. Author Thornton Wilder is the most notable person with this name.

THURLOW *(English)* Thor's hill.

TIARNACH *(Irish)* Godly. Variation: *Tighearnach.*

TIBOR *(Slavic)* Sacred place. Variations: *Tiebout, Tybald, Tybalt, Tybault.*

TOAL *(Irish)* Strong people. Variations: *Tuathal, Tully.*

TOBAR *(Gypsy)* Road.

TONG *(Vietnamese)* Aromatic.

TORAO *(Japanese)* Tiger.

TORD *(Scandinavian)* Peace of Thor.

TSELA *(Native American: Navajo)* Stars lying down.

TUAN *(Vietnamese)* Unimportant.

TYDEUS *(Greek)* Ancient mythological figure.

TYEE *(Native American)* Chief.

TYKE *(Native American)* Captain.
TWYFORD *(English)* Place where rivers converge.
TYMON *(Greek)* Praise the Lord.

Tried and True Classics

ULYSSES *(Latin)* Wrathful. Variation of Odysseus. Variations: *Ulises, Ulisse.*

UMBERTO *(Italian)* Famous German. Variation of Humbert.

Slightly Daring Choices

UDAY *(Hindu)* To show up. Variation: *Udayan.*

UDELL *(English)* Yew grove. Variations: *Dell, Eudel, Udall, Udel.*

ULAN *(African)* First-born of twins.

ULEKI *(Hawaiian)* Hawaiian version of Ulysses. Variation: *Ulesi.*

ULF *(Scandinavian)* Wolf. Variation: *Ulv.*

ULL *(Scandinavian)* Glory.

ULMER *(English)* Famous wolf. Variations: *Ullmar, Ulmar.*

ULRIC *(German)* Wolf power; (Scandinavian) Noble ruler. Variations: *Ulrich, Ulrick, Ulrik, Ulrike.*

UMAR *(Arabic)* To bloom.

UMED *(Hindu)* Desire.

UPTON *(English)* Hill town.

UPWOOD *(English)* Forest on a hill.

URBAN *(Latin)* Man from the city. Though rural parents-to-be would probably never consider this name for their baby boys, Urban is slowly catching on as a hip, sophisticated name for parents who are looking for a name that's just a bit different. There were a number of popes who went by the name Urban, but the name never really made inroads in this country until very recently. Variations: *Urbain, Urbaine, Urbane, Urbano, Urbanus, Urvan.*

URI *(Hebrew)* God's light. Variations: *Uria, Uriah, Urias, Urie, Uriel.*

URIAN *(Greek)* Heaven.

URIEN *(Welsh)* Privileged birth.

URSAN *(Latin)* Bear. Variation: *Urson.*

URVIL *(Hindu)* The sea.

USENI *(African: Malawian)* Tell me.

USI *(African: Malawian)* Smoke.

USTIN *(Russian)* Just.

Living on the Edge

UALTAR *(Irish)* Ruler of the army. Variations: *Uaitcir, Ualteir.*

UANG *(Chinese)* Great.

UATA *(Polynesian)* Army leader. Variation: *Uate.*

UBADAH *(Arabic)* He who serves God.

UCHECHI *(African: Nigerian)* God's will.

UDOLF *(English)* Wealthy wolf. Variations: *Udolfo, Udolph.*

UGO *(Italian)* Intellect.

UHILA *(Polynesian)* Lightning.

UHUBITU *(Native American)* Dirty water.

UILLEOG *(Irish)* Small protector. Variations: *Uilleac, Uillioc.*

UINSEANN *(Irish)* One who conquers. Variation: *Uinsionn.*

UJALA *(Hindu)* Shining. Variation: *Ujaala.*

ULBRECHT *(German)* Grandeur.

UMI *(African: Malawian)* Life.

UNADUTI *(Native American: Cherokee)* Wooly head.

UNER *(Turkish)* Famous.

UNIKA *(African: Malawian)* To shine.

UNKAS *(Native American: Mohegan)* Fox. Variations: *Uncas, Wonkas.*

UNWIN *(English)* Enemy. Variations: *Unwinn, Unwyn.*

URJASZ *(Polish)* God is light.

USAMA *(Arabic)* Lion. Variation: *Usamah.*

UTATCI *(Native American)* Bear scratching.

UTHMAN *(Arabic)* Bird. Variations: *Othman, Usman.*

UTTAM *(Hindu)* Best.

UZIAH *(Hebrew)* God is my strength. Variations: *Uzia, Uziya, Uzziah.*

UZIEL *(Hebrew)* Powerful. Variation: *Uzziel.*

UZOMA *(African: Nigerian)* Born on a trip.

Tried and True Classics

VAUGHN *(Welsh)* Small. Perhaps the most famous man with the name Vaughn was the British composer Ralph Vaughan Williams. Even though the name is of Welsh origin, in the middle of this century, the name was much more popular in the United States than overseas. It's a great name, and not used nearly enough today. Variation: *Vaughan.*

VERNON *(French)* Alder tree. Variations: *Vern, Verne.*

VICTOR *(Latin)* Conqueror. Owing to its definition, Victor was one of the most popular names during the time of the Romans. It fell out of favor throughout most of the Middle Ages, until it became popular in Britain again in the early part of this century. In this country, two famous Victors were Victor Borge and Victor Mature. Variations: *Vic, Vick, Victoir, Victorien, Victorino, Victorio, Viktor, Vitenka, Vitor, Vittore, Vittorio, Vittorios.*

VINCENT *(Latin)* To conquer. Vincent has been a popular name throughout the ages, however today, some people equate Vincent solely with the nicknames Vinnie and Vince. Famous Vincents have included Vincent Price and Vincent van Gogh. Variations: *Vikent, Vikenti, Vikesha, Vin, Vince, Vincente, Vincenz, Vincenzio, Vincenzo, Vinci, Vinco, Vinn, Vinnie, Vinny.*

VIRGIL *(Latin)* Roman clan name. Variations: *Vergil, Virgilio.*

VITO *(Latin)* Alive. Variations: *Vital, Vitale, Vitalis.*

VLADIMIR *(Slavic)* Famous prince. Variations: *Vlad, Vladamir, Vladimeer, Vladko, Vladlen.*

Slightly Daring Choices

VACHEL *(French)* Small cow. Variation: *Vachell.*
VADIN *(Hindu)* Educated orator.
VAIL *(English)* From the valley; city in Colorado. Variations: *Vaile, Vale, Vayle.*

Top Boys' Names of 2004

1.	Jacob	11.	Zachary
2.	Aidan	12.	Andrew
3.	Ethan	13.	Dylan
4.	Ryan	14.	Jack
5.	Matthew	15.	Jayden
6.	Michael	16.	Logan
7.	Tyler	17.	Caden
8.	Joshua	18.	Caleb
9.	Nicholas	19.	Alexander
10.	Connor	20.	Nathan

VAINO *(Scandinavian: Finnish)* Wagon builder.
VALA *(Polynesian)* Loincloth.
VALDEMAR *(German)* Famous leader.
VALENTINE *(Latin)* Strong. Variations: *Val, Valentin, Valentino, Valentyn.*
VALERIAN *(Latin)* Healthy. Variations: *Valerie, Valerien, Valerio, Valery, Valeryan.*
VALI *(Scandinavian)* Ancient mythological figure.
VALIN *(Hindu)* Mighty soldier. Valin is a variation of the name Balin, a very British name. In the Hindu religion, however, Valin is the monkey king. Variations: *Valen, Valyn.*
VANCE *(English)* Swampland. Variations: *Van, Vancelo, Vann.*

VANDAN *(Hindu)* Salvation.

VANYA *(Russian)* God is good. Variation of John. Variations: *Vanek, Vanka.*

VARDEN *(French)* Green mountains. Variations: *Vardon, Verden, Verdon, Verdun.*

VAREN *(Hindu)* Superior.

VARICK *(German)* Defending ruler. Variation: *Varrick.*

VARIL *(Hindu)* Water.

VARTAN *(Armenian)* Rose.

VASANT *(Hindu)* Spring.

VASIL *(Czech)* Kingly. Form of Basil. Variations: *Vasile, Vasilek, Vasili, Vasilios, Vasilis, Vasilos, Vasily, Vassily.*

VASIN *(Hindu)* Leader.

VIDOR *(Hungarian)* Happy.

VILA *(Czech)* From William, Will + helmet. Variations: *Vilek, Vilem, Vilhelm, Vili, Viliam, Vilko, Ville, Vilmos.*

VILMOS *(German)* Steady soldier.

VINAY *(Hindu)* Courteous.

VINE *(English)* One who works in a vineyard.

VINSON *(English)* Son of Vincent.

VON *(Scandinavian)* Hope.

Living on the Edge

VALMIKI *(Hindu)* Ant hill.

VALU *(Polynesian)* Eight.

VAN *(Dutch)* Sometimes used as prefix to a surname, it can also stand alone as a first name.

VANDA *(Lithuanian)* Ruling people. Variation: *Vandele.*

VANDYKE *(Dutch)* From the dyke. Variation: *Van Dyck.*

VANNEVAR *(English)* Unknown definition.

VANSLOW *(English)* Unknown definition. Variations: *Vansalo, Vanselow, Vanslaw.*

VARDHAMMA *(Hindu)* Growth. Variation: *Vardhaman.*

VARESH *(Hindu)* God is superior.

VARUN *(Hindu)* God of water. Variations: *Varin, Varoon.*

VASU *(Hindu)* Prosperous.

VATSYAYANA *(Hindu)* The author of the *Kama Sutra.*

VEA *(Polynesian)* Chief. Variations: *Veamalohi, Veatama.*

VEASNA *(Cambodian)* Lucky.

VELESLAV *(Czech)* Great glory. Variations: *Vela, Velek,Velousek.*

VELTRY *(African-American)* Unknown definition.

VENCEL *(Hungarian)* Wreath.

VENCESLAV *(Czech)* Glorious government.

VENEDICT *(Russian)* Blessed. Variation of Benedict. Variations: *Venedikt, Venka, Venya.*

VERDUN *(French)* City in France. Variations: *Verden, Verdon.*

VERE *(French)* Area in France.

VERED *(Hebrew)* Rose.

VERLIE *(French)* Town in France. Variation: *Verley.*

VERLIN *(American)* Spring. Variations: *Verle, Verlon.*

VERRILL *(French)* Loyal. Variations: *Verill, Verrall, Verrell, Verroll, Veryl.*

VIDA *(English)* Beloved.

VIDAR *(Scandinavian)* Ancient mythological figure.

VIDKUN *(Scandinavian)* Vast experience.

VIET *(Vietnamese)* Destroy.

VIHS *(Hindu)* Increase.

VIJAY *(Hindu)* Victory. Variations: *Bijay, Vijen, Vijun.*

VIJAYENDRA *(Hindu)* Victorious god of the sky. Variation: *Vijendra.*

VILIAMI *(Polynesian)* Protector.

VILJO *(Scandinavian: Finnish)* Guardian.

VILOK *(Hindu)* To see.

VIMAL *(Hindu)* Pure.
VINOD *(Hindu)* Fun.
VITALIS *(Latin)* Life.
VITUS *(French)* Forest. Variation: *Vitya.*
VIVEK *(Hindu)* Wisdom. Variations: *Vivekanand, Vivekananda.*
VIVIAN *(Latin)* Full of life.
VLADISLAV *(Czech)* Glorious ruler. Variation: *Ladislav.*
VLADLEN *(Russian)* Vladimir + Lenin.
VLAS *(Russian)* One who stammers.
VOJTECH *(Czech)* Comforting soldier. Variations: *Vojta, Vojtek, Vojtresek.*
VOLKER *(German)* Protector of the people.
VOLNEY *(German)* Spirit of the people.
VOLYA *(Russian)* Ruler of the people. Variation of Walter. Variations: *Vova, Vovka.*
VOSHON *(African-American)* God's grace.
VUI *(Vietnamese)* Cheerful.

Tried and True Classics

WADE *(English)* To cross a river. Wade is one of those short, compact names that seem to command respect without inviting teasing. Margaret Mitchell used the name in her novel *Gone with the Wind.*

WALDEN *(English)* Forested valley. Walden is an attractive choice for parents today, because it falls into the category of nature names as well as last name as first name. Some parents will choose it out of deference to Henry David Thoreau and Walden Pond, while others will select it because of its fine upstanding manner and tone. Variation: *Waldon.*

WALTER *(German)* Ruler of the people. Though to some ears Walter may sound a bit outdated, it seems to be rapidly gaining ground among parents-to-be as a name that is at once dignified and folksy. Though obviously the name isn't used as frequently as it was in the '30s and '40s, the far-reaching reputation of journalist Walter Cronkite has given this name a moral, honest feel. Other famous Walters include Walter Pidgeon, Walt Disney, and poet Walt Whitman. Variations: *Walt, Walther, Waltr, Watkin.*

WARREN *(German)* Protector friend. Actor Warren Beatty has injected the name with a reputation of sex appeal and worldliness. Another famous American Warren was the president Warren Harding. Variations: *Warrin, Warriner.*

WAYNE *(English)* Wagon maker. Version of Wainwright. Variations: *Wain, Wainwright, Wayn, Waynwright.*

WESLEY *(English)* Western meadow. Wesley first gained prominence as a religious last name, as two brothers, John and Charles Wesley, were the founders of the Methodist Church in England. Parents who belonged to the church soon began to use the brothers' last name for their newborn sons' first names as a tribute to them. Today, Wesley is not among the most popular of names, but it could definitely be a sleeper. Variations: *Wes, Wesly, Wessley, Westleigh, Westley.*

WILBUR *(German)* Brilliant. Variations: *Wilber, Wilbert, Wilburt, Willbur.*

WILLIAM *(German)* Constant protector. William is one of the most popular names throughout English-speaking countries. There are a slew of famous Williams, including Prince William, William Shakespeare, Billy Idol, Willem Dafoe, Will Smith, William Faulkner, William Holden, and Willem de Kooning; four American presidents, several kings, and plenty of knights. William is as popular today in this country as it was in the 1040s in Europe. Although there are myriad variations of the name, the traditional William is most common as both a given name and the everyday name that parents use to refer to their sons. Variations: *Bill, Billie, Billy, Guillaume, Guillaums, Guillermo, Vas, Vasilak, Vasilious, Vaska, Vassos, Vila, Vildo, Vilek, Vilem, Vilhelm, Vili, Viliam, Vilkl, Ville, Vilmos, Vilous, Will, Willem, Willi, Williamson, Willie, Willil, Willis, Willy, Wilson, Wilhelm.*

WILSON *(English)* Son of Will. Variation: *Willson.*

WINSTON *(English)* Friend's town. Variations: *Winsten, Winstone, Winstonn, Winton, Wynstan, Wynston.*

WOLFGANG *(German)* Wolf fight. Wolfgang Puck—the famous chef—has brought new visibility to this name. Wolf and Wolfie are great nicknames for this name.

WYATT *(French)* Little fighter. Name your child this, and it will most likely conjure images of cowboy Wyatt Erp. Variations: *Wiatt, Wyat.*

Slightly Daring Choices

WADLEY *(English)* Meadow near a river crossing. Variations: *Wadleigh, Wadly.*

WADSWORTH *(English)* Village near a river crossing. Variation: *Waddsworth.*

WAGNER *(German)* Wagon maker. Variation: *Waggoner.*

WAITE *(English)* Watchman. Variations: *Waits, Wayte.*

WAKEFIELD *(English)* Damp field. Variation: *Wake.*

WAKELEY *(English)* Damp meadow. Variations: *Wakelea, Wakeleigh, Wakely.*

WALCOTT *(English)* Cottage by the wall. Variations: *Wallcot, Wallcott, Wolcott.*

WALDEMAR *(German)* Name of a famous ruler.

WALDO *(German)* Strong.

WALFORD *(English)* River crossing.

WALFRED *(German)* Peaceful ruler.

WALKER *(English)* One who walks on cloth. Last name.

WALLACE *(Scottish)* One from Wales. Variations: *Wallach, Wallie, Wallis, Wally, Walsh, Welch, Welsh.*

WALTON *(English)* Walled town.

WARD *(English)* Observer. Variations: *Warde, Warden, Worden.*

WARDELL *(English)* Watchman's hill.

WARDLEY *(English)* Watchman's meadow. Variations: *Wardlea, Wardleigh.*

WARE *(English)* Observant.

WARWICK *(English)* House near a dam. Variations: *Warick, Warrick.*

WATSON *(English)* Son of Walter.

WAVERLY *(English)* Meadow of aspen trees. Variations: *Waverlee, Waverleigh, Waverley.*

WAYLON *(English)* Roadside land. Variations: *Way, Waylan, Wayland, Waylen, Waylin.*

WELBORNE *(English)* Spring-fed river. Variations: *Welborn, Welbourne, Welburn, Wellborn, Wellbourn, Wellburn.*

WELDON *(English)* Well near a hill. Variations: *Welden, Welldon.*

WELFORD *(English)* Well near a river crossing. Variation: *Wellford.*

WELLINGTON *(English)* Temple in a clearing. There's Beef Wellington and the Duke of Wellington—not to be confused with Duke Ellington.

WELLS *(English)* Source of water.

WELTON *(English)* Well for a town.

WENDELL *(German)* Wanderer. Variations: *Wendel, Wendle.*

WENDICE *(African-American)* Unknown definition.

WENTWORTH *(English)* White man's town.

WERNER *(German)* Defending army. Variations: *Warner, Wernher.*

WESTCOTT *(English)* Western cottage. Variations: *Wescot, Wescott, Westcot.*

WESTON *(English)* Western town. Variations: *Westen, Westin.*

WETHERBY *(English)* Farm of male sheep, known as wether. Variations: *Weatherbey, Weatherbie, Weatherby, Wetherbey, Wetherbie.*

WETHERELL *(English)* Sheep corner. Variations: *Weatherell, Weatherill, Wetherill, Wethrill.*

WETHERLY *(English)* Sheep meadow. Variations: *Weatherley, Weatherly, Wetherleigh, Wetherley.*

WHALLEY *(English)* Forest by a hill. Variation: *Whallie.*

WHARTON *(English)* Town on a river bank. Clearly some alums from the Wharton Business School in Philadelphia might want to name their sons Wharton because, after all, the skills acquired with the education at the famous business school are going to come in handy when it comes to supporting said baby. Though Wharton is more commonly used as a last name, it is beginning to show signs of acknowledgment as a first name. Variation: *Warton.*

WHEATLEY *(English)* Wheat field. Variations: *Wheatlea, Wheatleigh, Wheatlie, Wheatly.*

WHEATON *(English)* Town of wheat.

WHITFORD *(English)* White ford.

WHITLEY *(English)* White meadow.

WHITLOCK *(English)* White-haired one.

WHITMAN *(English)* White-haired man.

WHITMORE *(English)* White moor. Variations: *Whitmoor, Whittemore, Witmore, Wittemore.*

WHITNEY *(English)* White island.

WHITTAKER *(English)* White field. Variations: *Whitacker, Whitaker.*

WILDON *(English)* Wild valley.

WILEY *(English)* Water meadow. Variations: *Willey, Wylie.*

WILFORD *(English)* River crossing by willow trees.

WILFRED *(English)* Purposeful peace. Variations: *Wilfredo, Wilfrid, Wilfried, Wilfryd.*

WILKINSON *(English)* Son of little Will. Variations: *Wilkes, Wilkie, Wilkins, Willkins, Willkinson.*

WILLIAMSON *(English)* Son of William. Variations: *Willey, Willi, Willie, Willis, Wylie.*

WILLOUGHBY *(English)* Willow tree farm. Variations: *Willoughbey, Willoughbie.*

WILMER *(German)* Resolute fame. Variations: *Willimar, Willmer, Wylmer.*

WILTON *(English)* Town with a well. Variations: *Wilt, Wylton.*

WINDHAM *(English)* Friend of the town. Variations: *Win, Winn, Wyndham, Wynne.*

WINDSOR *(English)* From Windsor. Variation: *Wyndsor.*

WINFIELD *(English)* Friend's field. Variations: *Winnfield, Wynfield, Wynnfield.*

WINFRED *(English)* Peaceful friend.

WINSLOW *(English)* Friend's hill.

WINTHROP *(English)* Friend's village.

WOLCOTT *(English)* Wolf's cottage.

WRIGHT *(English)* Carpenter.

Popular Celebrity Names: Boys

Celebrities have always been trendsetters, and Hollywood stars are no exception. Many people are so inspired by the beauty, glamour, machismo, or comedic talent of certain entertainers that they hope their children could draw those qualities from taking on their name alone. Other times, certain entertainers might bring unfamiliar names to light. The following list of actors have turned their names into household words—literally—by inspiring new parents:

ANDY GARCIA
ANTHONY HOPKINS
ANTONIO BANDERAS
BILLY ZANE
BRAD PITT
BUD ABBOTT
CHRISTOPHER REEVE
CLINT EASTWOOD
DANNY DEVITO
DEAN CAIN
DENNIS QUAID
DENZEL WASHINGTON
EDDIE MURPHY
GABRIEL BRYNE
HARRY HAMLIN
HARVEY KEITEL
JACK NICHOLSON
JAMES DEAN
JIMMY SMITS
JOHNNY DEPP
KEANU REEVES
KEVIN COSTNER
KYLE MCLACHLAN
LENNY BRUCE
LOU DIAMOND PHILLIPS
MACAULAY CULKIN
MATT DILLON
MEL GIBSON
RALPH MACCHIO
ROBERT DOWNEY, JR.
SAMMY DAVIS, JR.
STEVEN SEAGAL
WESLEY SNIPES
WILLIAM BALDWIN

WYCLIFF *(English)* White cliff. Musician Wyclef Jean has brought attention to this more unusual name. Variations: *Wycliffe, Wyclef.*

WYNDHAM *(English)* Town near the path. Variation: *Windham.*

WYNN *(English)* Friend. Variations: *Win, Winn, Wynne.*

Living on the Edge

WABAN *(Native American)* Easterly wind.

WACHIRU *(African: Kenyan)* Son of a lawmaker.

WAHIB *(Arabic)* To give.

WAIL *(Arabic)* One who returns to Allah.

WAKEMAN *(English)* Watchman.

WALDRON *(German)* Strong raven.

WALENA *(Hawaiian)* Hawaiian version of Warren.

WALERIAN *(Polish)* Strong. Variation: *Waleran.*

WALID *(Arabic)* Newborn. Variation: *Waleed.*

WALKARA *(Native American: Ute)* Yellow. Variation: *Wakara.*

WALLER *(English)* Wall maker.

WALWORTH *(English)* Walled farm.

WALWYN *(English)* Welsh friend. Variations: *Walwin, Walwinn, Walwynn, Walwynne.*

WANETA *(Native American: Sioux)* He who charges another.

WANJOHI *(African: Kenyan)* Brewer.

WANONCE *(Native American: Sioux)* Place of attack.

WAPASHA *(Native American: Sioux)* Red leaf. Variations: *Wabasha, Wapusha.*

WAPI *(Native American)* Lucky.

WARBURTON *(English)* Old fortress.

WARFIELD *(English)* Field by the weir (a device placed in a river to catch fish).

WARFORD *(English)* River crossing by the weir.

WARLEY *(English)* Meadow by the weir.

WASHAKIE *(Native American: Shoshone)* Gourd.

WASHBURN *(English)* Flooded river.

WASHINGTON *(English)* Town of smart men.

WEBLEY *(English)* Weaver's meadow. Variations: *Webbley, Webbly, Webly.*

WEBSTER *(English)* Weaver. Variations: *Web, Webb, Weber.*

WEI-QUO *(Chinese)* Leader of a nation.

WEKESA *(African: Kenyan)* Born during the harvest.

WELBY *(English)* Waterside farm. Variations: *Welbey, Welbie, Wellbey, Wellby.*

WEN *(Armenian)* Born in winter.

WENUTU *(Native American)* Sky clearing.

WESH *(Gypsy)* Forest.

WESTBROOK *(English)* Western stream. Variations: *Wesbrook, West, Westbrooke.*

WESTBY *(English)* Western farm.

WHEELER *(English)* Wheel maker.

WHISTLER *(English)* Occupational name: *whistler or piper.*

WHITBY *(English)* Farm with white walls. Variations: *Whitbey, Whitbie.*

WHITCOMB *(English)* White valley. Variation: *Whitcombe.*

WHITELAW *(English)* White hill. Variation: *Whitlaw.*

WHITFIELD *(English)* White field.

WICHADO *(Native American)* Compliant.

WICKHAM *(English)* Village paddock.

WIKOLI *(Hawaiian)* Hawaiian version of Victor. Variation: *Vitori.*

WILU *(Native American)* Chicken hawk warbling.

WINGATE *(English)* Winding gate.

WINGI *(Native American)* Willing.

WINWARD *(English)* My brother's forest.

WIT *(Polish)* Life.

WOJTEK *(Polish)* Soldier of consolation. Variation: *Wojteczek.*

WOLFE *(English)* Wolf. Variations: *Wolf, Woolf.*

WOODFORD *(English)* River crossing in the forest. Variation: *Woodforde.*

WOODROW *(English)* Row in the woods. Variations: *Wood, Woody.*

WOODVILLE *(English)* Forest town.

WOODWARD *(English)* Protector of the forest. Variation: *Woodard.*

WORTH *(English)* Enclosed farm.

WORTHY *(English)* Enclosure. Variations: *Worthey, Worthington.*

WUHAUTYAH *(Native American: Nez Perce)* Blowing wind.

WUIRTON *(Native American)* Thrive.

WULITON *(Native American)* To succeed.

WUNAND *(Native American)* God is good.

WUYI *(Native American)* Flying turkey vulture.

WYBERT *(English)* Brilliant at war.

WYNONO *(Native American)* First-born son.

Tried and True Classics

XAVIER *(English)* New house. In a game of word association, the name Xavier will bring one of two reactions to most people's minds. It will either be the Cuban musician Xavier Cugat or, if they grew up in Catholic school, the ubiquitous Saint Francis Xavier. Although first names with an "x" in them are pretty popular these days, most parents like the letter to be in the middle of the name somewhere and not announcing its presence right up front. Xavier also makes a great middle name. Variations: *Saverio, Xaver.*

Slightly Daring Choices

XANTHUS *(Greek)* Blond. Variation: *Xanthos.*
XAYVION *(African-American)* The new house. Variations: *Savion, Sayveon, Sayvion, Xavion, Xayveon, Zayvion.*
XENOS *(Greek)* Guest. Variations: *Xeno, Zenos.*

Living on the Edge

XENOPHON *(Greek)* Alien voice.
XERXES *(Persian)* Ruler.
XIAOPING *(Chinese)* Small bottle.
XIMEN *(Spanish)* Obedient. Variations: *Ximenes, Ximon, Ximun.*
XING-FU *(Chinese)* Happiness.
XI-WANG *(Chinese)* Desire.
XYLON *(Greek)* One who lives in the forest.

Tried and True Classics

YALE *(English)* Up on the hill.

YOSEF *(Hebrew)* God increases. Variations: *Yoseff, Yosif, Yousef, Yusef, Yusif, Yusuf, Yuzef.*

YOSHI *(Japanese)* Quiet.

YUL *(Chinese)* Past the horizon.

YULE *(English)* Christmas.

YURI *(Russian)* Farmer.

YUSUF *(Arabic)* God will increase. Variations: *Youssef, Yousuf, Yusef, Yusif, Yussef.*

YVES *(French)* Yew wood. Designer Yves St. Laurent brings glamour and fashion to this high-class French name, though its definition points to lowlier pursuits. Yvonne, the feminine version of Yves, has always been more popular than the male form of the name. Variation: *Yvon.*

Slightly Daring Choices

YADIN *(Hebrew)* God will judge. Variation: *Yadon.*

YAKAR *(Hebrew)* Dear. Variation: *Yakir.*

YAKIM *(Hebrew)* God develops. Variation: *Jakim.*

YAMAL *(Hindu)* One of a twin.

YAMIN *(Hebrew)* Right hand. Variation: *Jamin.*

YANA *(Hebrew)* He answers. Variations: *Janai, Jannai, Yan, Yannai.*

YANCY *(Native American)* Englishman. Variations: *Yance, Yancey, Yantsey.*

YANKA *(Russian)* God is good.

YANNIS *(Greek)* God is good. Variation of John. Variations: *Yannakis, Yanni, Yiannis.*

YARDAN *(Arabic)* King.

YARDLEY *(English)* Enclosed meadow. Variations: *Yardlea, Yardlee, Yardleigh, Yardly.*

YARIN *(Hebrew)* To understand.

YERED *(Hebrew)* To come down. Variation: *Jered.*

YERIEL *(Hebrew)* Founded by God. Variation: *Jeriel.*

YERIK *(Russian)* God is exalted. Variation of Jeremiah. Variation: *Yeremey.*

YORK *(English)* Yew tree. Variations: *Yorick, Yorke, Yorrick.*

YUMA *(Native American)* Son of the chief.

YUNIS *(Arabic)* Dove. Variations: *Younis, Yunus.*

YUSHUA *(Arabic)* God's help.

YUSTYN *(Russian)* Just.

Living on the Edge

YAAKOV *(Hebrew)* Supplanter or heel. Variation: *Yankov.*

YAAR *(Hebrew)* Forest.

YADID *(Hebrew)* Beloved.

YAFEU *(African: Ghanian)* Bold.

YAHOLO *(Native American: Creek)* One who hollers.

YAHYA *(Arabic)* God is good. Variation: *Yihya.*

YAIR *(Hebrew)* God will teach. Variation: *Jair.*

YAKECEN *(Native American)* Song from the sky.

YAKEZ *(Native American)* Heaven.

YANOACH *(Hebrew)* Rest.

YAPHET *(Hebrew)* Attractive. Variations: *Japhet, Japheth, Yapheth.*

YAQUB *(Arabic)* To grab by the heel. Variation: *Yaqoob.*

YARB *(Gypsy)* Herb.

YASAHIRO *(Japanese)* Peaceful.

YASH *(Hindu)* Famous.

YASHASKAR *(Hindu)* One who brings fame.

YASUO *(Japanese)* Calm.

YASAR *(Arabic)* Wealth. Variations: *Yaser, Yasir, Yasser, Yassir.*

YASIN *(Arabic)* Prophet.

YATES *(English)* Gates. Variation: *Yeats.*

YAZID *(African: Swahili)* To increase.

YE *(Chinese)* Universe.

YECHEZKEL *(Hebrew)* God strengthens. Variations: *Chaskel, Chatzkel, Keskel.*

YEHOSHUA *(Hebrew)* God is salvation. Variation: *Yeshua.*

YEHOYAKIM *(Hebrew)* God will establish. Variations: *Jehoiakim, Yehoiakim, Yoyakim.*

YEHUDI *(Hebrew)* A man from Judah; someone who is Jewish. The virtuoso violinist Yehudi Menuhin has made many Americans familiar with this name. Variations: *Yechudi, Yechudil, Yehuda, Yehudah.*

YELUTCI *(Native American)* Quiet bear.

YEMON *(Japanese)* Guardian.

YEN *(Vietnamese)* Calm.

YEOMAN *(English)* Servant.

YESHAYAHU *(Hebrew)* God saves. Variation: *Yeshaya.*

YEVGENYI *(Russian)* Well born.

YIRMEYAHU *(Hebrew)* God will restore.

YISHACHAR *(Hebrew)* Reward. Variations: *Issachar, Sachar, Yisaschar.*

YISRAEL *(Hebrew)* Israel.

YITRO *(Hebrew)* Plenty. Variation: *Yitran.*

YITZCHAK *(Hebrew)* Laughter. Both Yitzchak Rabin and Itzak Perlman have made us aware of this name. Variations: *Itzhak, Yitzhak.*

YMIR *(Scandinavian)* Ancient mythological figure.

YO *(Chinese)* Bright.

YONATAN *(Hebrew)* Gift from God.
YONG *(Chinese)* Brave.
YONG-SUN *(Korean)* Courage.
YOOMTIS KUNNIN *(Native American: Nez Perce)* Grizzly bear blanket.
YORATH *(English)* Worthy god. Variations: *Iolo, Iorwerth.*
YOSHA *(Hebrew)* Wisdom.
YOTIMO *(Native American)* Bee flying to its hive.
YOTTOKO *(Native American)* Mud from the river.
YOUKIOMA *(Native American: Hopi)* Flawless. Variations: *Youkeoma, Yukeoma, Yukioma.*
YOUNG-JA *(Korean)* Forever stable.
YOUNG-JAE *(Korean)* Forever prosperous.
YOUNG-NAM *(Korean)* Forever south.
YOUNG-SOO *(Korean)* Forever rich.
YUAN *(Chinese)* Round.
YUCEL *(Turkish)* Noble.
YUKIKO *(Japanese)* Snow. Variations: *Yuki, Yukio.*
YURCHIK *(Russian)* Farmer. Variation of George. Variations: *Yura, Yuri, Yurik, Yurko, Yurli, Yury.*
YUTU *(Native American)* Coyote hunting.
YUVAL *(Hebrew)* Brook. Variation: *Jubal.*

Tried and True Classic

ZACHARIAH *(Hebrew)* The Lord has remembered. Zachariah and its many variations is one of the more popular names around today, probably because it has that Biblical connotation as well as the trendy lightning-rod letter "Z." Little Zacharys are all over the place these days. Variations: *Zacaria, Zacarias, Zach, Zacharia, Zacharias, Zacharie, Zachary, Zachery, Zack, Zackariah, Zackerias, Zackery, Zak, Zakarias, Zakarie, Zako, Zeke.*

ZEKE *(Hebrew)* The strength of God. Zeke got its start as a nickname for Ezekiel, and gradually came into its own as an independent name. For parents who like this name, it may be best to use the original as a given name, so your son can have some variety.

Slightly Daring Choices

ZAFAR *(Arabic)* To win. Variation: *Zafir.*

ZAHID *(Arabic)* Strict.

ZAHIR *(Hebrew)* Bright. Variations: *Zaheer, Zahur.*

ZAHUR *(Arabic)* Flower.

ZAIDE *(Hebrew)* Older.

ZAIM *(Arabic)* General.

ZAKAI *(Hebrew)* Pure. Variations: *Zaki, Zakkai.*

ZAKUR *(Hebrew)* Masculine. Variation: *Zaccur.*

ZALE *(Greek)* Strength from the sea. Variation: *Zayle.*

Ethnic Variations

As Americans continue to travel to all corners of the globe, and as more people from other countries are living and working in the United States, we will be exposed to an increasingly wide community of people. This will continue to be reflected in the names we choose for our kids.

If you want to give your baby a name that sounds a bit exotic, but is really just a variation of a traditional name, you might consider another version of the name from a particular nationality. For instance, the Spanish variation of William is Guillermo, while Paul becomes Pavel in Polish or Paolo in Italian. Likewise, Jane is Juana in Spanish; Jana in Hungarian.

Of course, you could also pick a name from your own ethnic background that doesn't necessarily correspond with any American equivalent—Welsh and Irish names are currently popular, as well as a wealth of names from many African countries. And there's certainly no reason why you couldn't select a name from another ethnic group that you share no roots with, just because you like the name!

As previously "exotic" names are used more and more in the United States, they'll start to become part of the American mainstream, and thirty years from now, they might actually be commonplace.

ZALMAN *(Hebrew)* Peaceful.

ZAMIEL *(German)* God has heard. Variation of Samuel.

ZAMIR *(Hebrew)* Song.

ZAN *(Hebrew)* Well fed.

ZANE *(English)* God is good. Variation of John. Zane is a great name with the potential to become even bigger than Zachary. The recent popularity of this name can be traced to the writer Zane Grey, who chose it as a suitable substitute for his real name, Pearl. In fact, he took the name from one of his great-grandfathers, Ebenezer Zane, who founded the town of Zanesville in Ohio. Variations: *Zain, Zayne.*

ZAREB *(African)* Guardian.

ZARED *(Hebrew)* Trap.

ZAREK *(Polish)* May God protect the king.

ZAVAD *(Hebrew)* Present. Variation: *Zabad.*

ZAVDIEL *(Hebrew)* Gift from God. Variations: *Zabdiel, Zebedee.*

ZAYD *(Arabic)* To increase. Variations: *Zaid, Zayed, Ziyad.*

ZAYN *(Arabic)* Beauty.

ZELIG *(Hebrew)* Holy.

ZELIMIR *(Slavic)* Desires peace.

ZENAS *(Greek)* Generous. Variations: *Zeno, Zenon.*

ZENDA *(Czech)* Well born.

ZERACH *(Hebrew)* Light. Variations: *Zerachia, Zerachya, Zerah.*

ZEREM *(Hebrew)* Stream.

ZERIKA *(Hebrew)* Rainshower.

ZERO *(Arabic)* Worthless.

ZESIRO *(African: Ugandan)* First-born of twins.

ZEVID *(Hebrew)* Present.

ZIA *(Hebrew)* Unknown definition.

ZIMRAN *(Hebrew)* Sacred.

ZIMRI *(Hebrew)* Valuable.

ZINAN *(Japanese)* Second son.

ZINDEL *(Hebrew)* Protector of mankind. Variation of Alexander. A lot of kids might think that the name Zindel is actually pretty cool, due to the fact that a popular children's author is named Paul Zindel. An advantage of this name is that if your kid decides that later on he doesn't care for it, he can go to its original root, Alexander, and select another one of that name's many variations. Variation: *Zindil.*

ZION *(Hebrew)* Guarded land.

ZIVAN *(Czech)* Alive. Variations: *Zivanek, Zivek, Zivko.*

ZIVEN *(Slavic)* Lively. Variations: *Ziv, Zivon.*

ZIYA *(Arabic)* Light. Variation: *Zia.*

ZIYAD *(Arabic)* To increase.

ZORYA *(Slavic)* Star.

ZURIEL *(Hebrew)* The Lord is my rock.

Living on the Edge

ZACCHEUS *(Hebrew)* Pure.

ZAHAVI *(Hebrew)* Gold.

ZAKARIYYA *(Arabic)* God knows.

ZAKI *(Arabic)* Smart.

ZBIGNIEW *(Polish)* To get rid of anger. Variation: *Zbyszko.*

ZBYHNEV *(Czech)* Rid of anger. Variations: *Zbyna, Zbynek, Zbysek.*

ZDENEK *(Czech)* God of wine. Variations: *Zdenecek, Zdenko, Zdenousek, Zdicek.*

ZDESLAV *(Czech)* Glory is here. Variations: *Zdik, Zdisek, Zdislav.*

ZDZISLAW *(Polish)* Glory is here. Variations: *Zdzich, Zdziech, Zdziesz, Zdzieszko, Zdzis, Zdzisiek.*

ZEBADIAH *(Hebrew)* Gift from God. Variations: *Zeb, Zebediah.*

ZEBULON *(Hebrew)* To exalt. Variations: *Zebulen, Zebulun.*

Asian Boys' Names

In an ancient country like China, it's to be expected that the practice of naming babies reflects they ways people honor their heritage, specific cultural facets, or even old superstitions. For instance, Chinese parents often decide to give a boy a run-of-the-mill name so that the evil spirits will pass him by—because his name is so boring.

Boys in Japan are frequently named for their position in the birth order in their family, or after their parents' desire that their sons live a long life: Chi, which means thousand in Japanese, is one such name.

ZEDEKIAH *(Hebrew)* God is just. Variations: *Tzedekia, Tzidkiya, Zed, Zedechiah, Zedekia, Zedekias.*

ZEEMAN *(Dutch)* Seaman.

ZE'EV *(Hebrew)* Wolf.

ZEHARIAH *(Hebrew)* Light of God. Variations: *Zeharia, Zeharya.*

ZEHEB *(Turkish)* Gold.

ZEKI *(Turkish)* Smart.

ZEMARIAH *(Hebrew)* Song. Variations: *Zemaria, Zemarya.*

ZEPHANIAH *(Hebrew)* Protection. Variations: *Zeph, Zephan.*

ZEPHYRUS *(Greek)* West wind.

ZETHUS *(Greek)* Son of Zeus who built the great stone wall around the town of Thebes, which was named for his wife.

ZEUS *(Greek)* Living. King of the gods. Variations: *Zeno, Zenon, Zinon.*

ZEVACH *(Hebrew)* Sacrifice. Variation: *Zevachia, Zevachtah, Zevachya, Zevah.*

ZEVADIAH *(Hebrew)* God bestows. Variations: *Zevadia, Zevadya.*

ZEVULUN *(Hebrew)* House. Variations: *Zebulon, Zebulun, Zevul.*

ZHONG *(Chinese)* Second brother.

ZHU *(Chinese)* Wish.

ZHUANG *(Chinese)* Strong.

ZIKOMO *(African: Malawian)* Thank you.

ZIMRAAN *(Arabic)* Celebrated.

ZIPKIYAH *(Native American: Kiowa)* Big bow. Variations: *Zipkoeete, Zipkoheta.*

ZITKADUTA *(Native American: Sioux)* Red bird.

ZITOMER *(Czech)* To live in fame. Variations: *Zitek, Zitousek.*

ZIV *(Hebrew)* To shine. Variations: *Zivan, Zivi.*

ZLATAN *(Czech)* Golden. Variations: *Zlatek, Zlaticek, Zlatik, Zlatko, Zlatousek.*

ZOLTIN *(Hungarian)* Life. Variation: *Zoltan.*

ZOMEIR *(Hebrew)* One who prunes trees. Variation: *Zomer.*

ZOTOM *(Native American: Kiowa)* One who bites.

ZOWIE *(Greek)* Life.

ZUBERI *(African: Swahili)* Strong.

ZUHAYR *(Arabic)* Young flowers. Variation: *Zuhair.*

ZWI *(Scandinavian)* Gazelle.

ZYA TIMENNA *(Native American: Nez Perce)* Heartless.

ZYGMUNT *(Polish)* Victorious protection.

Part 2

GIRLS' NAMES

Tried and True Classics

ABIGAIL *(Hebrew)* Father's joy. Abigail is one of those wonderful girls' names that conjure up image of colonial days in America. In the Bible, Abigail was the name of King David's wife, but in this country more people are familiar with the name through the advice columnist Abigail Van Buren (more commonly known as Dear Abby). Variations: *Abagael, Abagail, Abagale, Abbey, Abbi, Abbie, Abbigael, Abbigail, Abbigale, Abby, Abbye, Abbygael, Abbygail, Abbygale, Abigale, Abigayle, Avigail.*

ADA *(German)* Though it can be a derivative of Adelaide, in German the name Ada means a woman who comes from aristocracy. Variations: *Adamine, Adaminna, Addie, Mina, Minna.*

ADELAIDE *(English)* Like Abigail, this once-unpopular name that dates from early America is making a comeback as Americans turn to more solid, traditional, albeit just-a-bit different names for their babies. Also like Abigail, Adelaide has a bevy of variations: *Adal, Adala, Adalaid, Adalaide, Adalee, Adali, Adalie, Adalley, Addal, Adele, Adelia, Adelice, Adelicia, Adeline, Adelis, Adell, Adella, Adelle, Della, Edeline, Eline.*

ADRIANE *(German)* Black earth. Adriane should appeal to parents who are looking for a pretty name that stands out. Variations: *Adriana, Adriane, Adrianna, Adriannah, Adrianne, Adrien, Adriena, Adrienah, Adrienne.*

AGATHA *(Greek)* Good. Agatha is the patron saint of firefighters and nurses, but except for fans of mystery writer Agatha Christie, most new parents will crinkle up their noses at the suggestion of using this name for their young daughters. Of course, this situation could change, but someone has to be first. Variations: *Aga, Agace, Agacia, Agafia, Agasha, Agata, Agate, Agathe, Agathi, Agatta, Ageneti, Aggi, Aggie, Aggy, Akeneki.*

AGNES *(Greek)* Virginal, chaste. Though Agnes is rarely chosen by parents-to-be today, a century ago it was one of the most popular names in this country. Variations: *Agnella, Agnesa, Agnesca, Agnese, Agnesina, Agneska, Agness, Agnessa, Agneta, Agneti, Agnetta, Agnola, Agnolah, Agnolla, Agnolle, Nesa, Ness, Nessa, Nessi, Nessia, Nessie, Nessy, Nesta, Senga, Ynes, Ynesita, Ynez.*

AIDAN *(Irish)* Fire. Aidan is an androgynous name, though it's more common for boys than girls. If girls continue to appropriate this name, however, look for Aidan almost exclusively as a girls' name within twenty years. Variations: *Aidana, Aydana, Edana.*

AISHA *(Arabic)* Life. This has become a popular name in the last two decades for African-American girls and for those who follow Islam, since Aisha was Mohammed's favorite wife. Variations: *Aishah, Aisia, Aisiah, Asha, Ashah, Ashia, Ashiah, Asia, Asiah, Ayeesa, Ayeesah, Ayeesha, Ayeeshah, Ayeisa.*

ALEXANDRA *(Greek)* One who defends. Feminine version of Alexander. Alexandra and its many variations have always seemed to have an elitist, upper-crust aura to them. The name has been long associated with the royalty, including Great Britain's Queen Victoria, whose real name was Alexandrina, and Princess Alexandra of Denmark. Variations: *Alejandrina, Aleka, Aleksasha, Aleksey, Aleksi, Alesia, Aleska, Alessandra, Alessa, Alessi, Alex, Alexa, Alexanderia, Alexanderina, Alexena, Alexene, Alexi, Alexia, Alexie, Alexina, Alexiou, Alexis.*

ALICE *(English)* Noble. Originally a variation of the name Adelaide, Alice came into its own as a popular name in the '40s and '50s. Variations: *Alis, Alles, Allice, Allyce, Alyce.*

ALICIA *(English, Hispanic, Swedish)* Truthful. Alicia and its variations are very popular today among parents who want lush, beautiful names for their daughters. Variations: *Alesha, Alesia, Alisha, Alissa, Alycia, Alysha, Alyshia, Alysia, Ilysha.*

ALISA *(Hebrew)* Happiness. Although there isn't really much difference between Alicia and Alisa just from the look of it, the origins of these two names are notably different. Christian parents tend to prefer Alicia while Jewish parents clearly favor Alisa, because its origins are in the Hebrew language. Variations: *Alisah, Alisanne, Alissa, Alissah, Aliza, Allisa, Allisah, Allissa, Allissah, Allyea, Allysah, Alyssa, Alyssah.*

ALLISON *(German)* Diminutive version of Alice. Today, the name Allison has a most interesting distinction. It is the second most popular name that mothers who have completed four years of college and beyond choose for their daughters. Variations: *Alisann, Alisanne, Alison, Alisoun, Alisun, Allcen, Allcenne, Allicen, Allicenne, Allie, Allisann, Allisanne, Allisoun, Ally, Allysann, Allysanne, Allyson, Alyeann, Alysanne, Alyson.*

ALTHEA *(Greek)* With the potential to heal. Althea is a breathy, feminine name. The most famous example was the great tennis player of the '50s, Althea Gibson. Variations: *Altha, Althaia, Altheta, Althia.*

AMANDA *(Latin)* Loved. Amanda is a very popular name these days, possibly because it has a bit of the patrician air to it, but also because one of its variations—Mandy—is such a casual, approachable name. Variations: *Amandi, Amandie, Amandine, Amandy, Amata, Manda, Mandaline, Mandee, Mandi, Mandie, Mandy.*

AMBER *(English)* Semiprecious stone. Variations: *Ambar, Amberetta, Amberly, Ambur.*

AMELIA *(Latin)* Hardworking. The female avatrix Amelia Earhart was perhaps the most famous example of this name; however, Amelia also has a traditional, early-American kind of sound to it. Variations: *Amalea, Amalie, Amelcia, Ameldy, Amelie, Amelina, Amelinda, Amelita, Amella.*

AMY *(English)* Loved. Author Louisa May Alcott was the first to use the name Amy in a popular work of fiction in this country. In the '70s, Amy was a popular name, but it fell out of favor in the '80s. Today, it's back with a vengeance. Variations: *Aimee, Aimie, Amada, Amata, Ami, Amice, Amie, Amil.*

ANASTASIA *(Greek)* Resurrection. Anastasia is a wonderfully romantic name that is a natural should you want your daughter to study ballet, visit Russia, or tend an organic garden in the country. Variations: *Anastace, Anastacia, Anastacie, Anastase, Anastasie, Anastasija, Anastasiya, Anastassia, Anastatia, Anastazia, Anastice, Anastyce.*

ANDREA *(Latin)* Womanly. Feminine version of Andrew. Andrea has regularly appeared in the top fifty names for girls since the 1950s; however, today, the name is more commonly used in one of its more exotic variations, especially the name Andie, after the actress Andie MacDowell. Variations: *Andera, Andra, Andreana, Andree, Andreea, Andrene, Andrette, Andria, Andriana, Andrianna, Andrienne, Andrietta, Andrina, Andrine.*

ANGELA *(Greek)* Messenger of God, angel. Actresses Angela Lansbury, Angie Dickenson, and Anjelica Huston have given us three different variations of the name. Variations: *Aingeal, Ange, Angel, Angele, Angelene, Angelia, Angelica, Angelika, Angelina, Angeline, Angelique, Angelita, Angie, Angiola, Anjelica, Anngilla.*

ANN *(English)* Grace. Ann, along with its many variations, was one of the most commonly used names—as either a first or middle name—until the craze for unusual names first hit in the late 1960s. It's interesting that the two major spellings—Ann and Anne—have gone back and forth in popularity. For instance, from 1900 to 1950, Ann was the most popular form. However, in 1950, after Princess Anne was named, that version became more popular than Ann, ten times over. Variations: *Ana, Anita, Anitra, Anitte, Anna, Annah, Anne, Annie, Annita, Annitra, Annitta, Hannah, Hannelore.*

ANNABELLE *(English)* Lovable. Variations: *Anabel, Anabele, Anabell, Anabelle, Annabel, Annabell.*

ANNAMARIE *(English)* Ann + Marie. It was once very popular to take the "Plain Jane" name Ann and combine it with other girls' names to create something that was just a bit more beautiful than either of the words by themselves. Especially when the version of Ann is Anna, the resulting names are particularly romantic and roll off the tongue. Variations of the "Ann +" combo include: *Annalie, Annalisa, Annamae, Annamaria, Annamarie, Annamay, Anneliese, Annelise, Annelle, Annemae, Annemarie, Annetta, Annette.*

ANTOINETTE *(French)* Priceless. Feminine version of Anthony. Antoinette and its variants are very beautiful names. Perhaps the most famous woman with this name was the notorious French ruler Marie Antoinette. Variations: *Antonella, Antonetta, Antonette, Antonia, Antonie, Antonieta, Antonietta, Antonina, Antonine, Tonelle, Tonette, Toney, Toni, Tonia, Tonie, Tony.*

APRIL *(English)* Named for the month. Variations: *Abrial, Abril, Aprilete, Aprilette, Aprili, Aprille, Apryl, Averil, Avril.*

ARIEL *(Hebrew)* Lioness of God. The name Ariel burst onto the scene in the early '90s when the Disney movie *The Little Mermaid* hit. Ariel was previously known as a water sprite as well as a male sprite in Shakespeare's *Tempest*. Ariel also appears as the title of one of Sylvia Plath's works, and these various sources provide a wide array of inspiration. Variations: *Aeriel, Aeriela, Ari, Ariela, Ariella, Arielle, Ariellel.*

ARLENE *(English)* Pledge. Back in the '40s and '50s, Arlene was one of the more popular names for girls, perhaps owing to actresses Arlene Francis and Arlene Dahl. Today, because of this earlier association, the name will strike most parents as dated. Variations: *Arleen, Arlie, Arliene, Arlina, Arline, Arlise, Arlys.*

ASHLEY *(English)* Ash tree. Ashley started out as a boys' name, with Ashley Wilkes from *Gone with the Wind* popularizing it. But from that point on, Ashley seemed destined to be a girls' name, possibly because of the sensitivity of the Margaret Mitchell character. Naming a boy Ashley might not be the best idea, since Ashley is about the most popular girls' name in the United States. Variations: *Ashely, Ashla, Ashlan, Ashlea, Ashlee, Ashleigh, Ashlie, Ashly, Ashton.*

ASTRID *(Scandinavian)* Godlike beauty and strength. Astrid is a great alternative to another Norwegian name for girls that is used in this country, Ingrid. Astrid, however, has a softer feel to it and more parents should consider it. Variations: *Astrud, Astryd.*

The Most Popular Girls' Names from the 1940s

It's telling that during the serious period of war in the 1940s, it's difficult to find more than the top ten names of the times. Although a slew of more popular names sprouted in the late 1940s and 1950s at the start of the Baby Boom—perhaps reflecting the increased sense of optimism and newfound personal freedom of the times—during the early 1940s, the range of popular baby names was quite limited.

1. Mary
2. Maria
3. Linda
4. Barbara
5. Patricia
6. Betty
7. Sandra
8. Carolyn
9. Gloria
10. Martha

AUDREY *(English)* Nobility and strength. Of course, the late actress Audrey Hepburn was responsible for making this name a popular choice through the end of the 1950s. Today, it's not as popular, but it's one of those great old-fashioned names that is due for a comeback. Variations: *Audey, Audi, Audie, Audra, Audre, Audree, Audreen, Audri, Audria, Audrie, Audry, Audrye, Audy.*

AVA *(English)* Birdlike. Like Audrey, the name Ava is permanently connected with one actress: Ava Gardner. Variations: *Aualee, Avah, Avelyn, Avia, Aviana, Aviance, Avilina, Avis, Aviva.*

Slightly Daring Choices

AALIYAH *(African-American)* To rise. The late singer Aaliyah Haughton has made this name more famous.

ACADIA *(Native American: Micmac)* Village.

ADALIA *(Hebrew)* God as protector.

ADINA *(Hebrew)* Gentle, delicate. Variations: *Adeana, Adin, Adine.*

ADONIA *(Greek)* Beauty. It is also a festival held after the annual harvest. Feminine name for the Greek god Adonis.

ADORA *(Latin)* Much adored. Variations: *Adoree, Adoria, Adorlee, Dora, Dori, Dorie, Dorrie.*

ADRIA *(Latin)* Dark; from the sea. Feminine version of Adrian. Variations: *Adrea, Adreea, Adria, Adriah.*

AFRICA *(African-American)* The continent. Variation: *Afrika.*

AIDA *(Arabic)* Reward; also an opera by the Italian composer Guiseppe Verdi.

AINSLEY *(Scottish)* A meadow. Variations: *Ainslee, Ainsleigh, Ainslie, Ansley, Aynslee, Aynsley.*

ALAIA *(Arabic)* Virtuous.

ALANA *(Hawaiian)* To float. Variations: *Alaina, Alani, Alanna, Alayne, Alene, Alenne, Allane.*

ALEGRIA *(Spanish)* Joy. Variations: *Alegra, Allegria.*

ALFREDA *(English)* Counselor of elves. Feminine version of Alfred. Variations: *Alfre, Alfredah, Alfredda, Alfreeda, Alfrieda, Alfryda, Allfrieda, Allfry, Allfryda, Elfre, Elfrea, Elfrida, Elfrieda Elva, Freda, Freddi, Freddie, Freddy, Fredi, Fredy, Freeda, Freedah, Frieda, Friedah, Fryda, Frydah.*

ALINA *(Russian)* Nobility; light. Variations: *Aleen, Aleena, Alenah, Aline, Alline, Allyna, Alyna, Alynah, Alyne, Leena, Leenah, Lena, Lenah, Lina, Lyna, Lynah.*

ALMEDA *(Latin)* Determined; destined for success. Variations: *Allmeda, Allmedah, Allmeta, Almedah, Almeta, Almetah, Almida, Almidah, Almita.*

ALMOND *(English)* Nut.

AMARA *(Greek)* Lovely, immortal girl. Variations: *Amarande, Amaranta, Amarante, Amarantha, Amarinda, Amarra, Amarrinda, Mara, Marra.*

AMARIS *(Hebrew)* Covenant of God. Variations: *Amaria, Amariah.*

AMAYA *(Japanese)* Night rain.

AMETHYST *(English)* Violet quartz stone.

ANAIS *(Hebrew)* Gracious.

ANYA *(Latvian)* Grace of God. Variation: *Anyuta.*

ARABELLA *(English)* In prayer. Variations: *Arabel, Arabela, Arbell, Arbella, Bel, Bella, Belle, Orabella, Orbella.*

ARDEN *(Latin)* Excited.

ARELLA *(Hebrew)* Angel. Variation: *Arela.*

ARIA *(Italian)* Melody.

ARIANA *(Welsh)* Silver. Variations: *Ariane, Arianie, Arianna, Arianne.*

ARISTA *(Greek)* Harvest.

ASHANTI *(African-American)* Ashanti is a name used to

commemorate a part of western Africa from which American slaves were captured. Variations: *Ashaunta, Ashuntae.*

ASIA *(English)* Named after the continent.

ASPEN *(English)* Tree. Aspen is a city in the western United States, which is all that some place names need to become popular as names for boys and girls.

ATHENA *(Greek)* Goddess of wisdom. Variation: *Athene.*

AUBREY *(English)* Counselor of elves.

AUGUSTA *(Latin)* Majestic. Feminine version of August and Augustus. Variations: *Agusta, Augustia, Augustina, Augustine, Augustyna, Augustyne, Austina, Austine, Austyna, Austyne.*

AURORA *(Latin)* Roman goddess of dawn. Variation: *Aurore.*

AUTUMN *(American)* The fall season.

AVALON *(Gaelic)* Island of apples.

AVERILL *(English)* April. Variations: *Avaril, Averil, Averilla, Averyl.*

AVERY *(English)* Elf advisor. Avery fits the baby-naming trends of the new millennium perfectly, since it is unisex as well as a last name.

AYANNA *(African-American)* Created as a variation of Anna. Variations: *Ayana, Ayania.*

AZARIA *(Hebrew)* Helped by God. Variations: *Azariah, Azelia.*

Creative Spelling

One way of ensuring that your child's name is unique is to take a common or classic name and then give it a new twist with an unusual spelling. It's not a bad idea, but be sure to think this plan through. People might see your child's name and inadvertently assume it's just a misspelling. This could mean that you and your child will spend lots of time correcting everyone!

Living on the Edge

ADELIZA *(English)* Created by combining Adelaide and Liza.

ADELPHA *(Greek)* Caring sister.

ADHITA *(Hindu)* Student.

ADOLPHA *(German)* Noble wolf. Feminine version of Adolph.

AGRIPPA *(Latin)* If you give your daughter this name, you should be sure that she was born feet first, because that's just what this name means. Variations: *Agrafina, Agrippina, Agrippine.*

AIDEEN *(Irish)* Unknown definition. Variations: *Adene, Etain.*

AIKO *(Japanese)* Little one.

AILA *(Scandinavian: Finnish)* Bright light. Variations: *Aile, Ailee, Ailey, Aili, Ailie, Ailis, Ailse.*

AKIVA *(Hebrew)* Shelter. Variations: *Kiba, Kibah, Kiva, Kivah.*

ALA *(Hawaiian)* Fragrant.

ALALA *(Greek)* In Greek mythology, Alala is the sister of Ares, the god of war.

ALARICE *(Greek)* Noble. Variation: *Alarica.*

ALITA *(Spanish)* Nobility.

AMANA *(Hebrew)* Loyal. Variations: *Amania, Amaniah, Amanya.*

AMOR *(Spanish)* Love. Variation: *Amorette.*

ANCI *(Hungarian)* Grace of God.

ANINA *(Hebrew)* Answer to a prayer.

ANTIGONE *(Greek)* The daughter of Oedipus and Jocasta.

ANWEN *(Welsh)* Fair, beautiful. Variation: *Anwyn.*

ARCELIA *(Spanish)* Treasure chest.

ARTHURINA *(Gaelic)* Rock; nobility. Variations: *Artheia, Arthelia, Arthene, Arthuretta, Arthurine, Artina, Artis, Artri.*

AVIS *(Latin)* Old Roman family name. Variation: *Avice.*

AZRA *(Hindu)* Virgin.

AZRIELA *(Hebrew)* God is my strength.

AZURA *(French)* Blue. Variations: *Azor, Azora, Azure, Azzura, Azzurra.*

Tried and True Classics

BAILEY *(English)* Bailiff. Bailey has become a popular name for both boys and girls in the last decade. Variations: *Bailee, Baylee, Bayley, Baylie.*

BAMBI *(Italian)* Child. Variations: *Bambie, Bambina, Bamby.*

BARBARA *(Greek)* Foreign. Barbara was once one of the most popular names for girls. However, its usage has dropped off dramatically as parents today associate the name with their parents' generation. Popular Barbaras have included Barbara Bush, Barbara Stanwyck, and Barbra Streisand. As part of its legacy, however, Barbara has left behind lots of variations on a theme: *Babb, Babbett, Babbette, Babe, Babett, Babette, Babita, Babs, Barb, Barbary, Barbe, Barbette, Barbey, Barbi, Barbie, Barbra, Barby, Basha, Basia, Vaoka, Varenka, Varina, Varinka, Varka, Varvara, Varya, Vava.*

BEATRICE *(Latin)* She brings joy. Beatrice was popularized through Dante's work *The Divine Comedy* and in the Shakespeare play *Much Ado about Nothing*, but the Beatrice that most American kids know is Beatrix Potter, who wrote the first stories about Peter Rabbit. Variations: *Bea, Beatrisa, Beatrise, Beatrix, Beatriz, Beattie, Bebe, Bee, Beitris, Beitriss.*

BELINDA *(English)* Dragon. Variation: *Belynda.*

BELLE *(French)* Beautiful. Variations: *Bela, Bell, Bella, Belva, Belloma.*

BERNADETTE *(French)* Brave as a bear. Feminine version of Bernard. Bernadette is a pretty name and should be used more often than it is. Actress Bernadette Peters is perhaps the most famous Bernadette around. Variations: *Berna, Bernadene, Bernadett, Bernadina, Bernadine, Bernarda, Bernardina, Bernardine, Bernetta, Bernette, Berni, Bernie, Bernita, Berny.*

BERNICE *(Greek)* She brings victory. Variations: *Bema, Beranice, Berenice, Bernelle, Bernetta, Bernette, Bernicia, Bernie, Bernyce.*

BERTHA *(German)* Bright. This name hit its peak in both the United States and Great Britain in the 1870s. Variations: *Berta, Berthe, Berti, Bertie, Bertilda, Bertilde, Bertina, Bertine, Bertuska, Bird, Birdie, Birdy, Birtha.*

BETHANY *(English)* House of poverty; a Biblical village near Jerusalem. As we all seem a bit Tiffanyed out, Bethany has been starting to appear a little bit more often as a close enough substitute. Variations: *Bethanee, Bethani, Bethanie, BethAnn, Bethann, Bethanne, Bethannie, Bethanny.*

BEVERLY *(English)* Beaver stream. Beverly is a perfect example of a name that was previously exclusive to men. Once it started to be given to girls, though, parents dropped it for their sons like a hot potato. Beverly was a more popular girls' name during the first half of this century than it is today. Variations: *Bev, Beverelle, Beverle, Beverlee, Beverley, Beverlie, Beverlye.*

BIANCA *(Italian)* White. Variations: *Beanka, Biancha, Bionca, Bionka, Blanca, Blancha.*

BILLIE *(English)* Constant protector. Feminine version of William. Billie Holiday, Billie Jean King, and even Michael Jackson's "Billie Jean" have all made this casual name an appealing choice for a daughter. Though it might cause some confusion in the classroom with a boy named Billy present, he'll grow up and out of the name while a girl so named will tend to hang onto Billie forever. Variations: *Billa, Billee, Billey, Billi, Billy.*

BLAIR *(English)* A flat piece of land. In the 1950s, Blair was a commonly used name for well-to-do boys training to fill their father's gray flannel suits. In the '70s and '80s, Blair was also used as a girls' name, although it still had that same aura. Variations: *Blaire, Blayre.*

BLANCHE *(English)* White. Variations: *Blanca, Blanch, Blancha, Blanka, Blanshe, Blenda.*

BOBBIE *(English)* Bright fame. Feminine version of Robert. Variations: *Bobbee, Bobbette, Bobbi, Bobby, Bobbye, Bobina.*

BONNIE *(English)* Good. Bonnie has been somewhat popular, gaining visibility through the movies *Gone with the Wind* and *Bonnie and Clyde*, and, of course, singer Bonnie Raitt. Variations: *Boni, Bonie, Bonne, Bonnebell, Bonnee, Bonni, Bonnibel, Bonnibell, Bonnibelle, Bonny.*

BRANDY *(English)* A liquor. Variations: *Brandais, Brande, Brandea, Brandee, Brandi, Brandice, Brandie, Brandye, Branndea.*

BREANA *(Celtic)* Strong. Feminine version of Brian. Variations: *Breann, Breanna, Breanne, Briana, Briane, Briann, Brianna, Brianne, Briona, Bryanna, Bryanne.*

BRENDA *(English)* On fire. Feminine version of Brendan. Comic-strip heroine Brenda Starr, and Brenda Walsh from *Beverly Hills 90210,* have both popularized this name. Variations: *Bren, Brendalynn, Brenn, Brennda, Brenndah.*

BRIDGET *(Irish)* Strength. Bridget sounds like a good Catholic-girl kind of name. Actress Meredith Baxter Birney played a Bridget in the '70s TV show *Bridget Loves Bernie*. Variations: *Birgit, Birgitt, Birgitte, Breeda, Brid, Bride, Bridgett, Bridgette, Bridgitte, Brigantia, Brighid, Brigid, Brigid, Brigida, Brigit, Brigitt, Brigitta, Brigitte, Brygida, Brygitka.*

BRITTANY *(English)* Feminine version of Britain. This is one of the most popular names for girls since the mid-1980s. From the '90s on, it appears that girls' names with three syllables that end in the letter "y" and have at least one "n" in them are destined for the top ten list. Brittany falls into this category. Variations: *Brinnee, Britany, Britney, Britni, Brittan, Brittaney, Brittani, Brittania, Brittanie, Brittannia, Britteny, Brittni, Brittnie, Brittny.*

BROOKE *(English)* One who lives by a brook. Actress and child model Brooke Shields started the trend of baby girls named Brooke back in the '70s. Variation: *Brook.*

BRYN *(Welsh)* Mountain. Variations: *Brinn, Brynn, Brynne.*

BUNNY *(English)* Good; also rabbit. Nickname for Bonnie. Variations: *Bunni, Bunnie.*

Name Your Location

Currently, it's a hot trend to name boys and girls after a place: a state, a town, a region of the country, a street, or even an alma mater. Take Montana, Cheyenne, Dakota, or Sierra. Of course, the last three are names for pickup trucks, but that hasn't seemed to deter parents from selecting them.

In the recent past, place names for girls have been drawn from Southern states such as the Carolinas, Florida, and Georgia. Although names that end with the letter "a" are more likely to be used for girls since a name that ends in "a" has a traditionally female association, this is not a hard and fast rule. And, since many other place names don't have any gender connotations attached to them, parents are choosing them for their sons and daughters. Some examples include:

ACTON: *Town in Britain*
CARINTHIS: *A region in Germany*
CLYDE: *River in Scotland*
DARYL: *Area in France*
ELBA: *Area in Italy*
FRASER: *Town in France*
JORDAN: *Country in the Middle East*
KAILASH: *A Himalayan mountain*
KERRY: *County in Ireland*

Name Your Location—continued

LOUVAIN: *A city in Belgium*
MONEKA: *Sioux for the Earth*
NEVADA: *Western U.S. state (Spanish origin)*
PAAZANI: *Hindu for the Ganges River*
SIDNEY: *City in Austrailia*
VAIL: *City in Colorado*

It's a good possibility any name that reflects pride in history will be different from the names of your child's classmates. Just be sure you're not choosing a name for the sake of being trendy, because your choice might seem awkward later on, if this fad passes.

Slightly Daring Choices

BANITA *(Hindu)* Woman.
BAPTISTA *(Latin)* One who baptizes. Variations: *Baptiste, Batista, Battista, Bautista.*
BARIAH *(Arabic)* To succeed.
BARRIE *(English)* Pointed object. Feminine version of Barry.
BASIA *(Hebrew)* Daughter of God. Variations: *Basha, Basya.*
BASILIA *(Greek)* Royal. Feminine version of Basil. Variations: *Basila, Basilea, Basilie.*
BASIMA *(Arabic)* To smile. Variations: *Basimah, Basma.*
BATHIA *(Hebrew)* Daughter of God. Variations: *Basha, Baspa, Batia, Batya, Bitya, Peshe, Pessel.*
BATHILDA *(German)* Female soldier. Variations: *Bathild, Bathilde, Berthilda, Berthilde.*

BELÉN *(Spanish)* Bethlehem.

BELIA *(Spanish)* Oath of God. Variations: *Belica, Belicia.*

BELITA *(Spanish)* Little beauty.

BENA *(Hebrew)* Wise.

BENEDETTA *(Italian)* Blessed. Feminine version of Benedict. Variations: *Benedicta, Benedicte, Benedikta, Benetta, Benita, Benni, Benoite.*

BENITA *(Latin)* God has blessed. Variations: *Bena, Benitri, Bennie, Binnie.*

BENTLEY *(English)* Meadow of grass. Variations: *Bentlea, Bentlee, Bentleigh, Bently.*

BERDINE *(Greek)* Bright maiden.

BERNITA *(African-American)* Variation of Bernard.

BERRY *(American)* Berry. Variation: *Berri, Berrie.*

BERYL *(Greek)* Green gemstone. Variations: *Beril, Berrill, Berry, Beryla, Beryle.*

BETHEL *(Hebrew)* Temple.

BETHESDA *(Hebrew)* Biblical place.

BETHIA *(Hebrew)* Daughter of Jehovah. Variations: *Betia, Bithia.*

BETULAH *(Hebrew)* Young woman. Variations: *Bethula, Bethulah, Betula.*

BEULAH *(Hebrew)* Married. Variations: *Bealah, Beula.*

BINA *(Hebrew)* Knowledge. Variations: *Bena, Binah, Byna.*

BINALI *(Hindu)* Musical instrument.

BIRDIE *(English)* Variations: *Bird, Birdey, Byrd, Byrdie.*

BLAINE *(Gaelic)* Thin.

BLAKE *(English)* Light or dark.

BLASIA *(Latin)* Stutterer. Variation: *Blaise.*

BLOSSOM *(English)* Flower. Blossom was given some exposure during the second half of the '80s when a TV show starred a teenager of the same name. Even though flower names are popular, Blossom still seems way too close to similar vintage hippie names to really catch on.

BLUEBELL *(English)* Flower. Variation: *Bluebelle.*
BLYTHE *(English)* Happy. Variations: *Blithe, Blyth.*
BONITA *(Spanish)* Pretty. Variations: *Bo, Boni, Bonie, Nita.*
BRADLEY *(English)* Wide meadow. Variations: *Bradlee, Bradleigh, Bradlie, Bradly.*
BRANCA *(Portuguese)* White.
BREE *(English)* Person from England. Variations: *Brea, Bria, Brielle.*
BRENNA *(English)* Raven; black hair.
BRETT *(Latin)* From Britain. Variation: *Brette.*
BRICE *(English)* Quick. Variation: *Bryce.*
BRIE *(Celtic)* Strong. From Brian.
BRIER *(French)* Heather. Variation: *Briar.*
BRINA *(Slavic)* Defender. Variations: *Breena, Brena, Brinna, Bryn, Bryna, Brynn, Brynna, Brynne.*
BRISA *(Spanish)* Beloved. Variations: *Breezy, Brisha, Brisia, Brissa, Briza, Bryssa.*
BRISEIS *(Greek)* Mythological queen of Lyrnessus, whom Achilles won in a war.

Living on the Edge

BACHIKO *(Japanese)* Happy child.
BAHATI *(African: Swahili)* Lucky.
BAHIRA *(Arabic)* Electric.
BAKA *(Hindu)* Crane. Variation: *Baca.*
BAKARA *(Hebrew)* To visit.
BAKUL *(Hindu)* Flower. Variation: *Bakula.*
BAKURA *(Hebrew)* Ripe. Variation: *Bikura.*
BALALA *(African)* You must eat much to grow.
BALBINA *(Italian)* Stutterer. Variation: *Balbine.*

BANAN *(Arabic)* Fingertips.
BANO *(Hindu)* Bride.
BARA *(Hebrew)* To choose. Variations: *Bari, Barra.*
BARIKA *(Arabic)* Bloom.
BARKAIT *(Hebrew)* Morning star. Variation: *Barkat.*
BARRAN *(Irish)* Little top.
BAYO *(African: Nigerian)* Happiness.
BEATA *(Latin)* Blessed. Variation: *Beate.*
BEATHA *(Irish)* Life. Variation: *Betha.*
BEBHINN *(Irish)* Sweet woman.
BECHIRA *(Hebrew)* Select.
BEDRISKA *(Czech)* Peaceful ruler.
BEHIRA *(Hebrew)* Bright light.
BENE *(African)* Born during market week.
BERA *(German)* Bear.
BERIT *(Scandinavian)* Brilliant.
BERURIA *(Hebrew)* Chosen by God.
BETA *(Czech)* Grace of God. Variations: *Betka, Betuska.*
BETI *(Gypsy)* Small.
BETUEL *(Hebrew)* Daughter of God. Variation: *Bethuel.*
BHAMINI *(Hindu)* Beautiful lady.
BHARATI *(Hindu)* Cared for.
BIAN *(Vietnamese)* Secretive.
BIBI *(Arabic)* Lady. Variations: *Bibiana, Bibianna, Bibianne, Bibyana.*
BIBIANE *(Latin)* Lively.
BICH *(Vietnamese)* Jewelry.
BIDELIA *(Irish)* Strong. Variations: *Bedilia, Biddy, Bidina.*
BIENVENIDA *(Spanish)* Welcome.
BINTI *(African)* Daughter.
BINYAMINA *(Hebrew)* Right hand.
BIRA *(Hebrew)* Fortress. Variations: *Biria, Biriya.*
BIRCIT *(Scandinavian: Norwegian)* Power. Variation: *Birgit.*
BITHIA *(Hebrew)* Daughter of God.

BITHRON *(Hebrew)* Daughter of song.
BITKI *(Turkish)* A type of plant.
BITTAN *(Scandinavian: Swedish)* Strength.
BLANCHEFLEUR *(French)* White flower.
BLANDA *(Latin)* Seductive. Variations: *Blandina, Blandine.*
BLATH *(Irish)* Flower. Variations: *Blaithm, Blathnaid, Blathnait.*
BLESSING *(English)* To sanctify.
BLIMA *(Hebrew)* Blossom. Variations: *Blimah, Blime.*
BLODWEN *(Welsh)* White flower. Variations: *Blodwyn, Blodyn.*
BLOM *(African)* Flower.
BLONDELLE *(French)* Blond one. Variations: *Blondell, Blondie, Blondy.*
BLUM *(Hebrew)* Flower. Variation: *Bluma.*
BLY *(Native American)* High.
BO *(Chinese)* Precious.
BODIL *(Scandinavian)* Battle. Variations: *Bothild, Botilda.*
BOGDANA *(Polish)* Gift from God. Variations: *Boana, Bocdana, Bogna, Bohdana, Bohdana, Bohna.*
BOLADE *(African: Nigerian)* Honor is here.
BOLANILE *(African: Nigerian)* Wealth in our house.
BONA *(Hebrew)* Builder.
BONFILIA *(Italian)* Good daughter.
BORGNY *(Scandinavian)* Newly fortified.
BOSKE *(Hungarian)* Lily.
BOUPHA *(Cambodian)* Flower.
BOZIDARA *(Czech)* Divine gift. Variations: *Boza, Bozena, Bozka.*
BRACHA *(Hebrew)* Blessing. Variation: *Brocha.*
BRECK *(Gaelic)* Freckled.
BRETISLAVA *(Czech)* Glorious noise. Variations: *Breeka, Breticka.*
BRIDE *(Irish)* Irish goddess of poetry and song.
BRIT *(Celtic)* Freckled.
BRITES *(Portuguese)* Strength.
BROÀA *(Czech)* She who wins.

BROÀISLAVA *(Czech)* Glorious armor. Variations: *Brana, Branislava, Branka, Brona, Bronicka, Bronka.*

BRONISLAWA *(Polish)* Glorious protection. Variation: *Bronya.*

BRONWYN *(Welsh)* Pure of breast. Variation: *Bronwen.*

BRUCIE *(French)* Thick brush. Feminine version of Bruce. Variations: *Brucina, Brucine.*

BRUNA *(Italian)* Having brown skin or brown hair. Feminine version of Bruno.

BRUNELLE *(French)* Little brown-haired girl. Variations: *Brunella, Brunetta, Brunette.*

BRUNHILDA *(German)* Armor-clad maiden who rides into battle. This name conjures up images of matronly cartoon characters like BroomHilda, the green-hued witch who was always falling for handsome blond men. Variations: *Brunhild, Brunhilde, Brunnhilda, Brunnhilde, Brynhild, Brynhilda.*

BRYONY *(English)* Vine. Variations: *Briony, Bronie, Bryonie.*

BUA *(Vietnamese)* Good-luck charm.

BUENA *(Spanish)* Very good.

BUNMI *(African: Nigerian)* My gift.

BUSEJE *(African: Malawian)* Ask me.

BUTHAYNA *(Arabic)* Pasture. Variations: *Busayna, Buthaynah.*

BYHALIA *(Native American: Choctaw)* White oak trees.

Tried and True Classics

CAITLIN *(Irish)* Pure. Caitlin, created by the combination of Katherine and Lynn, has become a very popular name. Caitlin first became widely known in the United States in the early '80s, and it probably zoomed onto the top ten lists because it was derived from a popular, familiar name that was spelled in a fashion that was exotic to American eyes. Variations: *Caitilin, Caitlan, Caitlion, Caitlon, Caitlyn, Caitlynne, Catlin, Kaitlin, Kaitlyn, Kaitlynn, Kaitlynne, Katelin, Katelynn.*

CALLISTA *(Greek)* Beautiful. Callista Flockhart who played Ally McBeal made this name more popular in the late '90s. Variations: *Cala, Calesta, Cali, Calissa, Calista, Calisto, Callie, Cally, Callysta, Calysta, Kala, Kallie.*

CAMILLE *(French)* Assistant in the church. The name Camille used to have an aura of despair about it based on the tragic figure played by Greta Garbo in the movie of the same name. Enough time has passed, however, to make the name an attractive choice for a daughter once again. Variations: *Cam, Cama, Camala, Cami, Camila, Camile, Camilia, Camilla, Cammi, Cammie, Cammy, Cammylle, Camyla, Kamila, Kamilka.*

CANDACE *(English)* Royal title used by Ethiopian queens; white. Candace has become more popular in the last ten years as several TV actresses with the name have starred in hit shows. Variations: *Candee, Candice, Candie, Candis, Candiss, Candy, Candyce, Kandace, Kandi, Kandice, Kandy, Kandyce.*

CARA *(Italian)* Dear. Variations: *Caralea, Caralee, Caralisa, Carella, Cari, Carita, Carra, Kara, Karah, Karry.*

CAREY *(Welsh)* Near a castle. Carey is also frequently used as a boys' name. Variations: *Caree, Carree.*

CARISSA *(Greek)* Refined. Variations: *Carisa, Carisse.*

CARLA *(Italian)* Woman. Feminine version of Carl. Variations: *Carli, Carlie, Carly, Carlye.*

CARNI *(Hebrew)* Horn. Variations: *Carna, Carney, Carnia, Carnie, Carniela, Carniella, Carniya, Carny, Karni, Karnia, Karniela, Karniella, Karniya.*

CAROL *(German)* Woman. Variations: *Carel, Carey, Cari, Carleen, Carlene, Carley, Carlin, Carlina, Carline, Carlita, Carlota, Carlotta, Carlyn, Carlynn, Caro, Carola, Carole, Carolee, Caroll, Carri, Carrie, Carroll, Carry, Caru, Cary, Caryl, Caryle, Caryll, Carylle, Kari, Karie, Karri, Karrie, Karry, Karrye.*

CAROLINE *(German)* Woman. Feminine version of Carl, as well as Charles in diminutive form. Caroline always sounded more regal than just plain Carol, which may explain why Caroline is used more commonly today. Though Caroline could have received the same fate as Carol, several highly visible Carolines have served to redeem the name. First there was Caroline Kennedy; then came Princess Caroline of Monaco. And some parents are adding yet another regal spin on the name with one of the following variations: *Carolenia, Carolin, Carolina, Carolyn, Carolynn, Carolynne, Karolin, Karolina, Karoline, Karolyn, Karolyna, Karolyne, Karolynn, Karolynne.*

CARON *(Welsh)* Love. An unusual way to spell the more common Karen. Variations: *Carren, Carrin, Carron, Carrone, Caryn, Carynn.*

CASEY *(Irish)* Observant. Also common as a boys' name. Out of all the boys' names that become popular as girls' names, Casey may actually be one of the few that remain popular in both camps. Casey is a great name to take a girl from babyhood all the way through life. It's also a classic name, and even though it's just recently become popular, it isn't likely to suffer from the same trendiness as Tiffany and Brittany. Variations: *Cacia, Casee, Casie, Cassie, Caycey, Caysey, Kacey, Kacia, Kasee, Kasie, Kaycey, Kaysey.*

Natural Names

With more and more people growing more environmentally and globally conscious these days, a number of names relate to the environment and multiculturalism—or sometimes, both.

In the case of an environmentally based name, parents of girls have much more to choose from. Many of the things that appear in nature—crystal, rose, heather—are traditionally associated with the feminine and are used as girls' names. But there are also some traditional, masculine-sounding names that originate from the natural world, including Clay, Rock, and Forrest.

Multiculturalism throws the door wide open for both sexes. Today, parents can look to a large variety of sources to name their children, including Japanese, Turkish, Greek, African, and Native American. And since many of these names in other languages describe nature, parents who want their baby's name to fulfill a variety of roles can easily be satisfied. For example, the girls' name Azami describes a thistle flower in Japanese, while Misu for boys means rippling water in the Miwok Indian language.

CASSANDRA *(Greek)* Protector. Ancient mythological figure. Cassandra is a lush name that seems to be gaining ground in all kinds of families. Variations: *Casandera, Casandra, Cass, Cassandre, Cassaundra, Casson, Cassondra, Kasandera, Kasandra, Kass, Kassandra, Kassandre, Kassaundra, Kassie, Kasson, Kassondra.*

CASSIDY *(Gaelic)* Clever. Variations: *Cassidey, Cassidi, Cassidie, Kasady, Kassidey, Kassidi, Kassidie, Kassidy.*

CATHERINE *(English)* Pure. Cathy-with-a-C has always been a bit more formal than Kathy-with-a-K. Famous Catherines include Katharine Hepburn, Saint Catherine of Alexandria, and the Catherine in the novel *Wuthering Heights.* Variations: *Catalina, Catarina, Catarine, Cateline, Catharin, Catharine, Catharyna, Catharyne, Cathe, Cathee, Cathelin, Cathelina, Cathelle, Catherin, Catherina, Cathi, Cathie, Cathy, Catrin, Catrina, Catrine, Catryna, Caty.*

CECELIA *(Latin)* Blind. Feminine version of Cecil. Paul Simon's song "Cecelia" probably did more to put this name on the map than the Catholic saint of the same name. Today, variations of Cecelia, especially Cecily, seem to be more popular than the original. Variations: *C'Ceal, Cacilia, Cecely, Ceci, Cecia, Cecile, Cecilie, Cecille, Cecilyn, Cecyle, Cecylia, Ceil, Cele, Celenia, Celia, Celie, Celina, Celinda, Celine, Celinna, Celle, Cesia, Cespa, Cicely, Cicilia, Cycyl, Sessaley, Seslia, Sessile, Sessilly, Sheelagh, Sheelah, Sheila, Sheilagh, Sheilah, Shela, Shelah, Shelia, Shiela, Sisely, Sissie, Sissy.*

CELESTE *(Latin)* Heaven. Celeste is a name that both looks great and sounds great but has never totally caught on. Parents who choose this name for their daughters will undoubtedly be complimented on their choice. Variations: *Cela, Celesse, Celesta, Celestia, Celestiel, Celestina, Celestine, Celestyn, Celestyna, Celinka, Celisse, Cesia, Inka, Selinka.*

CHANTAL *(French)* Rocky area. Variations: *Chantale, Chantalle, Chante, Chantele, Chantelle, Shanta, Shantae, Shantal, Shantalle, Shantay, Shante, Shanteigh, Shantel, Shantell, Shantella, Shantelle, Shontal, Shontalle, Shontelle.*

CHARITY *(Latin)* Dear. In the eighteenth century, Charity was one of the temperance names along with Prudence and Patience. It seems to be becoming more popular today; however, it will probably remain relatively rare. Variations:

Charita, Charitee, Charitey, Sharitee.

CHARLOTTE *(French)* Small beauty. Variant of Charles.

CHELSEA *(English)* Ship port. Currently a popular name: *it incorporates the aura of Great Britain plus it's the name of a particular place—a region of London and of New York.* President Clinton's daughter has given a huge boost to the visibility of this name. Variations: Chelsa, Chelsee, Chelsey, Chelsi, Chelsie, Chelsy.

CHER *(French)* Dear. Variations: *Chere, Cherey, Cheri, Cherice, Cherie, Cherise, Sheralynne, Shereen, Shereena, Sherena, Sherene, Sheri, Sherianne, Sherilin, Sherina, Sherralin, Sherrilyn, Sherry, Sherrylene, Sherryline, Sherrylyn, Sherylin, Sherylyn.*

CHERYL *(English)* Charity. Variations: *Cherill, Cherrill, Cherryl, Cheryle, Cheryll, Sherryll, Sheryl.*

CHLOE *(Greek)* Young blade of grass. Chloe is becoming a very popular name. Over the years, its major appearances have included many novels in the seventeenth century and, in the Bible, I Corinthians. In the '70s, Chloe began to appear with increasing frequency in Britain, and the name traveled over here in the early part of the '90s. Variations: *Clo, Cloe.*

CHRISTINE *(English)* Anointed one. Feminine version of Christian. Though Christine was the norm a couple of decades ago, today its variations reign. With their multiple syllables and varying endings, the variations hold much appeal for parents who are looking for a girls' name that is traditional yet still unusual. Famous Christine variations include actress Kirstie Alley, model Christie Brinkley, and actress Kirsten Dunst. Variations: *Chris, Chrissy, Christa, Christen, Christi, Christiana, Christiane, Christiann, Christianna, Christie, Christina, Christy, Teena, Teina, Tena, Tina, Tinah.*

CLARA *(English)* Bright. Clara seems to be a name from the old country that has the potential for becoming widely used today. Variations: *Clair, Claire, Clairette, Clairine, Clare, Claresta,*

Clareta, Clarette, Clarice, Clarie, Clarinda, Clarine, Claris, Clarisa, Clarissa, Clarisse, Clarita, Claryce, Clerissa, Clerisse, Cleryce, Clerysse, Klara, Klari, Klarice, Klarissa, Klaryce, Klaryssa.

CLAUDIA *(Latin)* Lame. Feminine version of Claude. Variations: *Claudelle, Claudette, Claudina, Claudine.*

COLETTE *(French)* Triumphant people. The French novelist who helped to bring this name into the public eye was actually using her last name for her pen name. Its origin is a variation of the name Nicolette. Variations: *Coletta, Collet, Collete, Collett.*

COLLEEN *(Gaelic)* Girl. Variations: *Coleen, Colene, Coline, Colline.*

CONSTANCE *(English)* Steady. Variations: *Connie, Constancia, Constancy, Constanta, Constantia, Constantina, Constanza.*

CONSUELA *(Spanish)* Consolation. Variation: *Consuelo.*

COREY *(Irish)* The hollow. Variations: *Cori, Corie, Corri, Corrie, Corry.*

CORINNE *(French)* The hollow. Variations: *Carine, Carinna, Carinne, Carynna, Corina, Corine, Corinna, Correna, Corrianne, Corrienne, Corrine, Corrinn, Korina, Korinne, Korrina.*

COURTNEY *(English)* Dweller in the court, or farm. In the late '80s, Courtney was one of the most popular names given to girls in this country and its popularity continued through the '90s. Variations: *Cortney, Courtenay, Courteney, Courtnie.*

CRYSTAL *(Latin)* Clear as ice; ice, gem. In the '80s, the name was widely popularized by Linda Evans's character, Krystle, on the TV show *Dynasty*, and back in the nineteenth century, in England, it actually had its start as a name for boys. Variations: *Christal, Cristalle, Cristel, Crystol, Kristal, Kristle, Kristol, Krystal, Krystalle, Krystel, Krystle.*

CYNTHIA *(Greek)* Goddess of the moon. Variations: *Cindi, Cindie, Cindy, Cinthia, Cintia, Cyndi, Cynth, Cynthie, Cyntia, Kynthia.*

Slightly Daring Choices

CADENCE *(Latin)* Rhythmic. Variations: *Cadena, Cadenza, Kadena, Kadence, Kadenza.*

CAILIN *(Scottish)* Triumphant people. Variations: *Caelan, Caileen, Cailyn, Calunn, Cauleen, Caulin.*

CALIDA *(Greek)* Most beautiful; (Spanish) Affectionate, warm. Variation: *Callida.*

CALLA *(Greek)* Lily.

CALLIOPE *(Greek)* Pretty muse. Variations: *Kalliope, Kallyope.*

CALLULA *(Latin)* Little beauty.

CAMELIA *(English)* Flower. Variations: *Camellia, Camilla, Kamelia.*

CANDRA *(Latin)* Radiant.

CAPRICE *(Italian)* On a whim. Variations: *Capriana, Capricia, Caprie, Kapri, Kaprice, Kapricia, Kaprisha.*

CAPUCINE *(French)* Cowl, collar. Variations: *Cappucine, Capucina.*

CARINA *(Italian)* Darling; (Scandinavian) Keel of a ship. Variations: *Carena, Cariana, Carin, Carinna, Karina.*

CARITA *(Italian)* Charity. Variation: *Caritta.*

CARMA *(Hebrew)* Orchard. Variations: *Carmania, Carmaniya, Carmel, Carmela, Carmeli, Carmen, Carmia, Carmiela, Carmit, Carmiya, Karmel, Karmela, Karmeli, Karmia, Karmit, Karmiya.*

CARSON *(Scottish)* Last name.

CASSIA *(Greek)* Cinnamon.

CASTALIA *(Greek)* Mythological nymph.

CERISE *(French)* Cherry. Variations: *Cherice, Cherise, Cherrise, Sarise, Sharise, Sherice, Sherise, Sheriz.*

CESARINA *(Latin)* Hairy. Feminine version of Cesar. Variations: *Cesarea, Cesarie, Cesarin.*

CHALINA *(Spanish)* A rose.

CHANDELLE *(African-American)* Candle. Variations: *Chan, Chandell, Shan, Shandell, Shandelle.*

CHANEL *(French)* This relatively new name was inspired by the French designer Coco Chanel. Variations: *Chanell, Chanelle, Channell, Channelle, Shanell, Shanelle, Shannelle.*

CHANIA *(Hebrew)* Camp. Variations: *Chaniya, Hania, Haniya.*

CHANNARY *(Cambodian)* Moon-faced girl.

CHANYA *(Hebrew)* God's grace. Variation: *Hanya.*

CHARLA *(English)* Man. Feminine version of Charles. Variations: *Charlaine, Charlayne, Charlena, Charlene, Charli, Charlie, Charline, Cherlene, Cherline, Sharlayne, Sharleen, Sharlene.*

CHARMAINE *(French)* Song. Variations: *Charmain, Charmane, Charmayne.*

CHASTITY *(Latin)* Purity. Variations: *Chasta, Chastina, Chastine.*

CHAVON *(Hebrew)* God is good. Variation: *Chavonne.*

CHERRY *(French)* Cherry; usually pronounced with a "sh" sound. Variations: *Chere, Cheree, Cherey, Cherida, Cherise, Cherita, Cherreu, Cherri, Cherrie.*

CHEYENNE *(Native American: Algonquin)* Specific tribe. Variations: *Cheyanna, Cheyanne, Chiana, Chianna.*

CHIARA *(Italian)* Clear.

CHINA *(English)* Country. Variations: *Chyna, Chynna.*

CIARA *(Irish)* Black. Variations: *Ceara, Ciarra, Ciera, Cierra.*

CIPRIANA *(Greek)* From Cyprus. Variations: *Cipriane, Ciprianna, Cypriana, Cyprienne.*

CLEMENTINE *(English)* Gentle. Variations: *Clementia, Clementina, Clemenza.*

CLEOPATRA *(Greek)* Technically, Cleopatra translates to mean her father's fame, but we think of her as the partner of Mark Antony. Variations: *Clea, Cleo.*

CLIO *(Greek)* One of the nine Greek muses. Clio is the muse of history.

CLOVER *(English)* Flower.

COLBY *(English)* Dark farm.

CONNOR *(Irish)* High desire. Though Connor is very popular for boys, any name that's this striking and this popular will make it over to the girls' side, and we can see that this is already happening.

Girls' Names from the New Testament

The New Testament is also full of female names. Female players in this part of the Bible include a number of Marys (most important being the Mother of Jesus), Elizabeth, and Martha.

Here are some other choices:

ANNA: *Prophetess who called Jesus the messiah*
BETHANY: *Village in the Book of Luke*
EUNICE: *Mother of Timothy*
JULIA: *Woman greeted by Paul in the Book of Romans*
MAGDALA: *Town of Mary Magdalene*
PHOEBE: *Woman in Book of Romans*
SALOME: *Stepdaughter of Herod Antipas*
TABITHA: *Woman in the Book of Acts*

CORAL *(English)* Coral. Variations: *Coryl, Koral.*
CORBY *(English)* Town in Britain.
CORDELIA *(English)* Heart. Variations: *Cordella, Cordelle.*
CORNELIA *(English)* Horn. Feminine version of Cornelius. Variations: *Cornela, Cornelie, Cornella, Neelia, Neely, Neelya, Nela, Nelia, Nila.*
COSETTE *(French)* Victorious army. Variation: *Cozette.*
CRESCENT *(French)* Shape. Variations: *Crescentia, Cressant, Cressent, Cressentia.*
CYRA *(Persian)* Sun.

CYRILLA *(Latin)* Godly. Feminine version of Cyril.
CZARINA *(Latin)* Empress.

Living on the Edge

CACHAY *(African-American)* Prestigious. Possibly derives from French word "cachet." Variations: *Cashay, Kachay, Kashay.*
CAILIDORA *(Greek)* Gift of beauty.
CALIDA *(Spanish)* Adoring.
CALTHA *(Latin)* Yellow flower. Variation: *Kaltha.*
CALVINA *(Latin)* Without hair. Feminine version of Calvin. Variation: *Calvine.*
CALYPSO *(Greek)* Girl in hiding; Greek nymph.
CAM *(Vietnamese)* Citrus.
CAMEO *(Italian)* A piece of profile jewelry. Variation: *Cammeo.*
CANDIDA *(Latin)* White. Variation: *Candide.*
CANTARA *(Arabic)* Small bridge.
CARINTHIA *(German)* A region in Germany.
CASILDA *(Latin)* House.
CELANDINE *(Greek)* Yellow flower.
CELOSIA *(Greek)* On fire.
CERELLA *(English)* In springtime. Variation: *Cerelia.*
CERES *(Latin)* Roman goddess of agriculture.
CHANTERELLE *(French)* Cup. Variation: *Chantrelle.*
CHANTOU *(Cambodian)* Flower.
CHARA *(Spanish)* Rose. Variation: *Charo.*
CHARDE *(Arabic)* One who leaves.
CHARMIAN *(Greek)* Joy.
CHARO *(Spanish)* Rose.

CHARRON *(African-American)* Flat land. Variations: *Char Ron, Charryn, Cheiron.*

CHARU *(Hindu)* Attractive.

CHASIA *(Hebrew)* Protected by God. Variations: *Chasya, Hasia, Hasya.*

CHASINA *(Hebrew)* Strong. Variation: *Hasina.*

CHAVA *(Hebrew)* Life. Variations: *Chabah, Chapka, Chaya, Hava, Haya.*

CHAVI *(English, Gypsy)* Daughter. Variation: *Chavali.*

CHAVIVA *(Hebrew)* Beloved.

CHEMDA *(Hebrew)* Charm. Variation: *Hemda.*

CHEMDIAH *(Hebrew)* God is my hope. Variations: *Chemdia, Chemdiya, Hemdia, Hemdiah.*

CHENIA *(Hebrew)* Grace of God. Variations: *Chen, Chenya, Hen, Henia, Henya.*

CHENOA *(Native American)* White dove. Variation: *Shonoa.*

CHICA *(Spanish)* Girl.

CHIDORI *(Japanese)* A bird.

CHIQUITA *(Spanish)* Little girl.

CHITA *(Italian)* Pearl.

CHLORIS *(Greek)* The goddess of vegetation.

CHULA *(Hebrew)* Musician.

CHUMA *(African)* Bead; (Hebrew) Heat. Variations: *Chumi, Huma, Humi.*

CHUMANI *(Native American: Sioux)* Dew.

CHUMINA *(Spanish)* God.

CIANNAIT *(Irish)* Ancient. Variation: *Ciannata.*

CLELIA *(Latin)* Glorious.

CLEMATIA *(Greek)* Vine.

CLEMATIS *(Greek)* Flower.

CLEVA *(English)* One who lives on a hill.

CLIANTHA *(Greek)* Flower. Variations: *Cleantha, Cleanthe, Clianthe.*

CLIODHNA *(Irish)* Unknown definition. Variations: *Clidna, Cliona.*

CLODAGH *(Irish)* A river.

CLORIS *(Latin)* White, pure. Variation: *Chloris.*

CLOTILDA *(German)* Famous in battle. Variations: *Clothilda, Clothilde, Clotilde.*

CLYMENE *(Greek)* Famous.

CLYTIE *(Greek)* Splendid. Variations: *Clyte, Clytia.*

COLANDA *(African-American)* Variation of Yolanda.

COLUMBINE *(Latin)* Dove. Variations: *Colombe, Columba, Columbia, Columbina.*

COMFORT *(English)* To comfort.

CONCEPCION *(Latin)* Conception. Variations: *Concetta, Concettina.*

CONCORDIA *(Greek)* The goddess of harmony.

CORINTHIA *(Greek)* Woman from Corinth.

CORVINA *(Latin)* A raven.

COSIMA *(Greek)* Order. Feminine version of Cosmo. Variation: *Cosma.*

CREIRWY *(Welsh)* Jewel.

CRESSIDA *(Greek)* Gold.

CRISPINA *(Latin)* Curly hair. Feminine version of Crispin.

CYANEA *(Greek)* Blue.

CYBELE *(Greek)* The goddess of the earth.

CYMA *(Greek)* Blossoming. Variation: *Syma.*

CYNARA *(Greek)* Artichoke. Variation: *Zinara.*

CYTHEREA *(Greek)* The goddess of love and beauty. Variation: *Cytheria.*

Tried and True Classics

DAISY *(English)* Flower. Variations: *Dacey, Dacia, Dacy, Daisey, Daisha, Daisi, Daisie, Daizy, Daysi, Deyci.*

DANA *(English)* From Denmark. Dana is quickly becoming popular among both boys and girls, but it is more common as a girls' name. Variations: *Daina, Danay, Danaye, Dane, Danee, Danet, Danna, Dayna, Denae.*

DANIELLE *(English)* God is my judge. Feminine version of Daniel. Variations: *Danee, Danela, Danele, DaNell, Danella, Danette, Daney, Dani, Dania, Danica, Danice, Danie, Daniela, Daniella, Danika, Danila, Danita, Danyelle.*

DAPHNE *(Greek)* Ancient mythological nymph who was transformed into a laurel tree. Variations: *Dafne, Daphney, Daphny.*

DARCI *(Irish)* Dark one. Variations: *D'Arcy, Darcee, Darcey, Darcie, Darcy, Darsi, Darsie.*

DARIA *(Greek)* Luxurious. Variations: *Darian, Darianna, Dariele, Darielle, Darienne, Darrelle.*

DARLENE *(English)* Darling. Variations: *Darla, Darleane, Darleen, Darleena, Darlena, Darlina, Darline.*

DARYL *(English)* Last name; area in France. Darryl is traditionally a boys' name; however, the popularity of the actress Daryl Hannah has probably helped to increase its appearance as a girls' name. Variations: *Darel, Darrel, Darrell, Darrelle, Darryl, Darrylene, Darrylin, Darryline, Darrylyn, Darylin, Daryline, Darylyne.*

DAWN *(English)* Sunrise, the dawn. Dawn was a really popular name in the late '60s and early '70s because, while it had the feel of many of the hippie names that were cool back then, it still had a long standing in British tradition. This fact made it more acceptable among parents who knew their daughters had to get along in the real world someday. Variations: *Dawna, Dawne, Dawnelle, Dawnetta, Dawnette, Dawnielle, Dawnika, Dawnn.*

DEANA *(English)* Valley. Feminine version of Dean. Variations: *Deane, Deanna, Deena, Dene, Denna.*

DEANNA *(English)* Ocean lover. Variations: *Deane, Deann, Deanne, Deeana, Deeann, Deeanna, Deena, Deona, Deondra, Deonna, Deonne.*

DEBORAH *(Hebrew)* Bee. Variations: *Deb, Debbi, Debbie, Debby, Debi, Debora, Deborrah, Debra, Debrah, Devora, Devorah, Devra.*

DEDE *(African)* First-born daughter.

DEEDEE *(Hebrew)* Cherished.

DEIDRE *(Irish)* Fear, anger. Variations: *Dedra, Deidra, Deirdra, Deirdre, Deirdrie, Diedre, Dierdre.*

DELILAH *(Hebrew)* Delicate. Delilah is perhaps best known as Samson's mistress in the Biblical Book of Judges, and as the title and subject of one of the singer Tom Jones's songs. But Delilah is a feminine, lilting name that should be used more often for girls born today. Variations: *Dalila, Delila.*

DELLA *(English)* In Italian, Della literally translates to "of the," but as an English name, it's also a form of Adelaide, which means "nobility."

DELTA *(Greek)* Delta is the fourth letter of the Greek alphabet, but it could also be a favorite name in the south because of geographic deltas prevalent in the region. Actress Delta Burke gave this name a boost in the TV show *Designing Women.*

DENISE *(French)* Wine goddess. Feminine version of Dennis. The name Denise has been around since the days of the Roman Empire, and it was used with some regularity through the early seventeenth century. Then it became virtually extinct until the 1950s, when, in the United States and overseas, it grew to be very visible. Many parents today, however, may feel that the name is too evocative of the '50s and '60s, when it appeared as high as number fifteen on the list of top girls' names. Variations: *Denese, Deni, Denice, Deniece, Denisha, Denize, Dennise, Denyce, Denys, Denys.*

DESDEMONA *(Greek)* Misery; also a Shakespearean character. Variation: *Desdemonia.*

DESIRÉE *(French)* Longing. This pretty, feminine name's roots stem from Puritanical times, when "Desire" was the basic name. Today, Desirée is being given to girls of all ethnic backgrounds. Variations: *Desarae, Desira, Desyre, Dezarae, Dezirae, Diseraye, Diziree, Dsaree.*

DIANA *(Latin)* Divine. Roman goddess of the moon and of hunting. Diana has always been a popular name, but it has been made more widespread in the last twenty years by such high-profile Dianas as Diana Nyad, Diane Keaton, and of course, Princess Diana. Variations: *Dee, Diahann, Dian, Diane, Dianna, Dianne, Didi, Dyan, Dyana.*

DINAH *(Hebrew)* God will judge. Variations: *Deena, Denora, Dina, Dinorah, Diondra, Dyna, Dynah.*

DIONNE *(Greek)* Dione is a Greek mythological figure. Dionne is also the feminine version of Dennis, which in turn is formed from the name of another Greek god, Dionysus, the god of wine. Famous Dionne's include singer Dionne Warwick. Variations: *Deonne, Dion, Diona, Dione, Dionia, Dionna, Dionysia.*

DIVINE *(English)* Beloved friend. Feminine version of David. Variations: *Divina, Divinia.*

DOLLY *(English)* Doll. Nickname for Dorothy. Dolly Madison and Dolly Parton are both examples of famous Dollys. Variations: *Doll, Dollee, Dolley, Dollie.*

DOLORES *(Spanish)* Sorrow. Variations: *Delores, Doloras, Doloris, Doloritas.*

DOMINIQUE *(French)* Lord. Feminine version of Dominick. The boys' name Dominick has been around since the thirteenth century; no one knows exactly when the feminine form of the name came into being. Currently it is gaining ground in popularity, and its peak seems to be a few years down the road. Variations: *Dominica, Dominika.*

DONNA *(Italian)* Woman of the home. The name Donna was at its peak of popularity in the '50s and '60s. The thing to do then was to combine Donna with other names, like Marie and Sue. Famous Donnas include Donna Reed, disco songstress Donna Summer, and fashion designer Donna Karan. Variations: *Dahna, Donielle, Donisha, Donetta, Donnalee, Donnalyn, DonnaMarie, Donni, Donnie, Donya.*

DORA *(Greek)* Present. Nickname for Theodora. Variations: *Doralia, Doralyn, Doralynn, Doreen, Dorelia, Dorelle, Dorena, Dorenne, Dorette, Dori, Dorie, Dorinda, Dorita, Doru.*

DOREEN *(Irish)* Gloomy. Variations: *Doireann, Dorene, Dorine, Dorinnia, Doryne.*

DORIAN *(Greek)* A region in Greece. Also used as a boys' name. Variations: *Doriana, Dorianne, Dorrian, Dorryen.*

DORIS *(Greek)* A region in Greece. Doris was the name of a Greek goddess. Actress Doris Day made this name famous. Variations: *Dorice, Dorisa, Dorlisa, Dorolice, Dorosia, Dorrie, Dorrys, Dorys, Doryse.*

DOROTHY *(Greek)* Gift from God. Variations: *Dollie, Dolly, Dorethea, Doro, Dorotea, Dorotha, Dorothea, Dorothee, Dorothia, Dorrit, Dortha, Dorthea, Dot, Dottie, Dotty.*

DORY *(French)* Yellow-haired girl. Variations: *Dori, Dorri, Dorrie, Dorry.*

DREW *(Greek)* Manly; wise. Diminutive of Andrew. Variation: *Dru.*

The Most Popular Girls' Names from the 1950s

Perhaps more so in the '50s than in any other decade, parents traveled the tried-and-true route when it came to selecting names for their babies:

1. Linda
2. Mary
3. Patricia
4. Susan
5. Deborah
6. Kathleen
7. Barbara
8. Nancy
9. Sharon
10. Karen
11. Carol
12. Sandra
13. Diane
14. Catherine
15. Christine
16. Cynthia
17. Donna
18. Judith
19. Margaret
20. Janice
21. Janet
22. Pamela
23. Gail
24. Cheryl
25. Suzanne
26. Marilyn
27. Brenda
28. Beverly
29. Carolyn
30. Ann
31. Shirley
32. Jacqueline
33. Joanne
34. Lynn
35. Marcia
36. Denise
37. Gloria
38. Joyce
39. Kathy
40. Elizabeth
41. Laura
42. Darlene
43. Theresa
44. Joan
45. Elaine
46. Michelle
47. Judy
48. Diana
49. Frances
50. Maureen

Slightly Daring Choices

DABORA *(Czech)* To fight far away. Variations: *Dalena, Dalenka.*

DACEY *(Irish)* From the south. Variations: *Dacee, Daci, Dacia, Dacie, Dacy, Daicee, Daicy.*

DAGMAR *(German)* Glory. Variations: *Daga, Daggi, Dagi, Dagmara.*

DAGNA *(Scandinavian)* New day. Variations: *Dagne, Dagney, Dagny.*

DAHLIA *(Scandinavian)* Flower. Variations: *Dahla, Dalia, Daliah.*

DAIYA *(Polish)* Present.

DAKOTA *(Native American)* State name; also used for boys. Dakota is currently hot, hot, hot, but that can only mean that by the end of the century the name will be on the wane. If you don't want to be seen as one who automatically goes along with the crowd, pick a state with a less popular name.

DALE *(English)* Valley. Variations: *Dael, Daelyn, Dahl, Dalena, Dalene, Dalenna Dayle, Dalina, Dallana, Daly.*

DALILA *(African: Swahili)* Gentle. Variations: *Dalia, Dalice.*

DALLAS *(English)* Town in Scotland. Dallas is also showing up as a boys' name. Variation: *Dallis.*

DALYA *(Hebrew)* Branch. Variations: *Dalia, Daliya.*

DAMIA *(Greek)* To tame.

DAMITA *(Spanish)* Princess.

DANAE *(Greek)* Ancient mythological figure.

DANIAH *(Hebrew)* God's judgment. Variations: *Dania, Daniya, Danya.*

DANICA *(Slavic)* Morning star. Variations: *Danika Dannika, Dannica.*

DARA *(Hebrew)* Wisdom. Variations: *Dahra, Dareen, Darice, Darissa, Darra, Darrah.*

DARBY *(English)* A place where deer graze. Darby can also be a boys' name.

DARYN *(Greek)* Present, gift. Variations: *Daryan, Darynne.*

DASHA *(Greek)* God's exhibition.

DAVIDA *(Scottish)* Cherished friend. Feminine version of David. Variations: *Daveen, Davene, Davia, Daviana, Daviane, Davianna, Davidine, Davina, Davine, Davinia, Davita, Davonna, Davy, Davynn.*

DAYANA *(Arabic)* Divine.

DEANDRA *(African-American)* Newly created name. Variations: *Deanda, Deandrea, Deandria, Deeandra, Dianda, Diandra, Diandre.*

DELANEY *(Irish)* Child of a competitor. Variations: *Delaina, Delaine, Delayna, Delayne.*

DELIA *(Greek)* Visible. Variations: *Del, Delise, Delya, Delys, Delyse.*

DELICIA *(Latin)* Delight. Variations: *Daleesha, Dalicia, Dalisia, Deleesha, Delesha, Delesia, Delice, Delisa, Delise, Delisha, Delisia, Delys, Delyse.*

DELORA *(Spanish)* From the ocean.

DELPHINE *(Greek)* A dolphin. Variations: *Delfina, Delphi, Delphina.*

DEMETRIA *(Greek)* From Demeter, the Greek goddess of agriculture. Though many of you have probably not heard the name Demetria before, you are likely to be familiar with the short version of this name through an actress who uses it: actress Demi Moore. Variations: *Demeter, Demetra, Demetris, Demi, Demitra, Demitras, Dimetria.*

DENA *(Native American)* Valley. Variations: *Denav, Dene, Deneen, Denia, Denica.*

DESNA *(American)* Newly created name; unknown definition. Variations: *Desne, Desney.*

DESTINY *(French)* Fate. Variations: *Destanee, Destina, Destine, Destinee, Destini, Destinie.*

DEVA *(Hindu)* Divine.

DEVANY *(Gaelic)* Dark-haired. Variations: *Davanfe, Devaney, Devenny, Devinee, Devony.*

DEVIN *(Irish)* Poet. Variations: *Deva, Devinne.*

DEVON *(English)* Region in southern England. Variations: *Devan, Devana, Devanna, Devona, Devondra, Devonna, Devonne, Devyn, Devynn.*

DIAMOND *(English)* Jewel. Also occasionally used as a boys' name. Variations: *Diamanda, Diamante, Diamonique, Diamontina.*

DIDO *(Greek)* Ancient mythological figure.

DIELLE *(French)* God. Variation: *Diella.*

DIMA *(Arabic)* Rain.

DINIA *(Hebrew)* Wisdom of God. Variation: *Dinya.*

DIVONAH *(Hebrew)* South. Variations: *Dimona, Dimonah, Divona.*

DOMINA *(Latin)* Woman. Variation: *Domini.*

DONA *(English)* Mighty. Feminine version of Donald. Variations: *Donella, Donelle, Donetta.*

DONELLE *(Irish)* Ruler of the world. Variation: *Donla.*

DORÉ *(French)* Ornate. Dore is pronounced with the "e" as an "a," and with the accent on the second syllable. Variations: *Doree, Doretta, Dorette.*

DRINA *(Greek)* Protector. Variations: *Dreena, Drena.*

DRUSILLA *(Latin)* In the Bible, Drusilla is the name of Herod's daughter. Variations: *Drewsila, Drucella, Drucie, Drucilla, Drucy, Druscilla.*

DULCIE *(Latin)* Sweet. Variations: *Delcina, Delcine, Delsine, Dulce, Dulcea, Dulci, Dulcia, Dulciana, Dulcibella, Dulcibelle, Dulcina, Dulcine, Dulcinea.*

DUSTINE *(English)* Dusty place. Feminine version of Dustin. Variations: *Dustee, Dusty.*

DYANI *(Native American)* Deer.

DYLANA *(Welsh)* Born of the sea. Feminine version of Dylan.

Living on the Edge

DAFFODIL *(French)* Flower. Variations: *Daffi, Daffie, Daffy.*

DAGANA *(Hebrew)* Grain. Variations: *Dagan, Dagania, Deganya.*

DAI *(Japanese)* Grand.

DALAL *(Arabic)* To flirt. Variation: *Dhelal.*

DALIT *(Hebrew)* Running water.

DALMACE *(Latin)* An area in Italy. Variations: *Dalma, Dalmassa, Dalmatia.*

DAMALIS *(Greek)* Calf. Variations: *Dainala, Damalas, Damali, Damalla.*

DAMARIS *(Greek)* Calf. Variations: *Damara, Damaress, Dameris, Dameryss, Damiris.*

DAMAYANT *(Hindu)* Flirt.

DANU *(Welsh)* The mother of the gods.

DANUTA *(Polish)* Given by God.

DARDA *(Hebrew)* Pearl of wisdom.

DAY *(English)* Day.

DECEMBRA *(Persian)* Ten times.

DECIMA *(Latin)* Tenth. Feminine version of the obscure male name Decimus.

DELJA *(Polish)* Daughter of the sea.

DELLE *(Hebrew)* Jar.

DELPHA *(Greek)* Derived from Philadelphia, brotherly love. Variations: *Delphe, Delphia.*

DELU *(African)* Delu is typically given to the first girl born after the first three children were boys.

DELWYN *(Welsh)* Pretty and blessed.

DELYTH *(Welsh)* Pretty myth.

DERENDA *(American)* Newly created name. Unknown definition. Variation: *Derinda.*

DERICA *(English)* Dear. Variations: *Dereka, Derrica.*

DERORA *(Hebrew)* Independence. Variations: *Derorice, Derorit.*

DERRY *(Irish)* Red-haired. Variations: *Deri, Derrie.*

DERYN *(Welsh)* Bird. Variations: *Derren, Derrin, Derrine, Derron, Deryn.*

DEVAL *(Hindu)* Divine. Variations: *Devanee, Devee, Devi, Devika.*

DEVI *(Hindu)* Goddess of power and destruction.

DEWANDA *(African-American)* Combination of De + Wanda.

DIANTHA *(Greek)* Divine flower. Variations: *Diandre, Dianthe, Dianthia.*

DILYS *(Welsh)* Faithful. Variations: *Dylis, Dyllis, Dylys.*

DINKA *(African)* Family.

DISA *(Scandinavian: Norwegian)* Sprite.

DITA *(Czech)* Wealth; also derivative of Edith, which means property in war. Variation: *Ditka.*

DIXIE *(French)* Tenth; also a last name. Variations: *Dix, Dixee.*

DIZA *(Hebrew)* Joy. Variations: *Ditza, Ditzah.*

DONDI *(African-American)* Unknown definition.

DONNAG *(Scottish)* World ruler. Variations: *Doileag, Dolag, Dollag.*

DONOMA *(Native American: Omaha)* Sun.

DORCAS *(Greek)* Gazelle. Variation: *Doreka.*

DORIT *(Hebrew)* Generation.

DUANA *(Irish)* Dark-skinned. Feminine version of Duane. Variations: *Duna, Dwana.*

DUDEE *(Gypsy)* A star.

DUENA *(Spanish)* Chaperone.

DUHA *(Arabic)* Unseen.

DULAREE *(Hindu)* Beloved daughter.

DUSANA *(Czech)* Spirit. Variations: *Dusa, Dusanka, Dusicka, Duska.*

DWYNWEN *(Welsh)* White wave.

DYMPNA *(Irish)* Dympna is the patron saint of the mentally ill. Variation: *Dymphna.*

DZIKO *(South African)* The world.

Tried and True Classics

EDITH *(English)* Prosperity in war. Is Edith finally beginning to overcome the frumpy image that was perpetuated by Jean Stapleton on the TV series *All in the Family*? It could happen, especially since American novelist Edith Wharton, a chronicler of high society, has become chic again. Variations: *Edie, Edita, Edithe, Edy, Edyth, Edytha, Edythe, Eydie, Eydith.*

EDNA *(Hebrew)* Pleasure. Variation: *Ednah.*

EILEEN *(Irish)* Shining, bright. Familiar version of Helen. Variations: *Aileen, Ailene, Alene, Aline, Ayleen, Eilean, Eilleen, Ilene.*

ELAINE *(French)* Bright, shining. Derivative of Helen. Elaine was popular as a girls' name in the 1950s, but has recently fallen out of favor. That is, until the popularity of TV's *Seinfeld* and the character Elaine. Variations: *Alayna, Alayne, Allaine, Elaina, Elana, Elane, Elanna, Elayn, Elayne, Eleana, Elena, Eleni Alaina, Ellaina, Ellaine, Ellane, Ellayne.*

ELEANOR *(English)* Mercy. Derivative of Helen. Eleanor comes across as a very commonsense, solid type of name. Eleanor Roosevelt is probably the most famous bearer of the name. Though it does seems to be picking up steam recently, Eleanor is not as popular as other traditional girls' names that are being resurrected today. Variations: *Eleanore, Elenore, Eleonora, Eleonore, Elinor, Ellinor.*

ELIZABETH *(Hebrew)* I pledge to God. As you can see by the numerous variations, if you were to add up all the derivatives of Elizabeth, you'd undoubtedly end up with the most popular girls' name in the world by far. And because of all these wonderful variations, few girls choose to go by the main root. Variations: *Alzbeta, Babette, Bess, Bessey, Bessi, Bessie, Bessy, Bet, Beta, Beth, Betina, Betine, Betka, Betsey, Betsi,*

Betsy, Bett, Betta, Bette, Betti, Bettina, Bettine, Betty, Betuska, Boski, Eilis, Elis, Elisa, Elisabet, Elisabeta, Elisabeth, Elisabetta, Elisabette, Elisaka, Elisauet, Elisaveta, Elise, Eliska, Elissa, Elisueta, Eliza, Elizabetta, Elizabette, Elliza, Elsa, Elsbet, Elsbeth, Elsbietka, Elschen, Else, Elsee, Elsi, Elsie, Elspet, Elspeth, Elyse, Elyssa, Elyza, Elzbieta, Elzunia, Isabel, Isabelita, Liazka, Lib, Libbee, Libbey, Libbi, Libbie, Libby, Libbye, Lieschen, Liese, Liesel, Lis, Lisa, Lisbet, Lisbete, Lisbeth, Lise, Lisenka, Lisettina, Lisveta, Liz, Liza, Lizabeth, Lizanka, Lizbeth, Lizka, Lizzi, Lizzie, Lizzy, Vetta, Yelisaveta, Yelizaueta, Yelizaveta, Ysabel, Zizi, ZsiZsi.

ELLA *(German)* All, total.

ELLEN *(English)* Variation of Helen that has become a full-fledged name in its own right. Today's Ellens include actresses Ellen Barkin and Ellen DeGeneres. Variations: *Elan, Elen, Elena, Eleni, Elenyl, Ellan, Ellene, Ellie, Ellon, Ellyn, Elyn, Lene, Wily.*

The Most Popular Girls' Names from the 1960s

Even though the '60s have a reputation as a freewheeling, anything-goes decade, as the following list shows, the top baby names were still pretty tame. After all, those Americans who were busy participating in the upheavals of the late '60s were not starting their families until the following decade.

1. Mary
2. Susan
3. Lisa
4. Karen
5. Linda
6. Deborah
7. Kimberly
8. Donna
9. Patricia
10. Cynthia

ELOISE *(French)* Wise. Variations: *Eloisa, Eloisia, Eloiza, Elouise.*

ELSA *(German)* Noble. Elsa is a pretty name that has long been popular in Scandinavian as well as Hispanic countries. The name appeared in one of Wagner's operas, *Lohengrin*, and today, there is CNN style maven Elsa Klensch. Variations: *Else, Elsie, Elsy.*

ELVIRA *(Spanish)* Area in Spain. Variations: *Elva, Elvera, Elvia, Elvirah, Elvire.*

ELYSIA *(Latin)* From the Elysium Fields, the mythical home of the blessed. Variations: *Eliese, Elise, Elisia, Elyse, Ileesia, Iline, Illsa, Ilyse, Ilysia.*

EMANUELA *(Hebrew)* God is with us. Feminine version of Emanuel. Variations: *Em, Emanuelle, Emmanuela, Emmanuelle, Emmie, Emmy.*

EMILY *(German)* Industrious. Emily is one of those names that automatically implies brains and beauty as well as a nod toward old-fashioned days. In a recent study, Emily was the name that was most often chosen for daughters of women who have completed college and have gone on to further their education. Variations: *Aimil, Amalea, Amalia, Amalie, Amelia, Amelie, Ameline, Amy, Eimile, Em, Ema, Emalee, Emalia, Emelda, Emelene, Emelia, Emelina, Emeline, Emelyn, Emelyne, Emera, Emi, Emie, Emila, Emile, Emilea, Emilia, Emilie, Emilka, Emlynne, Emma, Emmalee, Emmali, Emmaline, Emmalynn, Emele, Emmeline, Emmiline, Emylin, Emylynn, Emlyn.*

EMMA *(German)* Embracing all. A wonderful, Victorian-era name that conjures up images of long, wavy chestnut hair, blue eyes, and cotton petticoats. Variations: *Em, Emmi, Emmie, Emmy.*

ENID *(Welsh)* Life. Varations: *Eanid, Enidd, Enud, Enudd.*

ERICA *(Scandinavian)* Leader forever. Feminine version of Eric. Erica is big and has been at least since the early '70s. In addition to possessing its Scandinavian definition, Erica is also another name for the heather plant. Variations: *Air-*

ica, Airika, Ayrika, Enrica, Enricka, Enrika, Ericka, Erika, Errika, Eyrica.

ERIN *(Gaelic)* Nickname for Ireland; also used occasionally as a boys' name; translates to western island. The ironic thing about Erin is that it is primarily an Americanized version of Ireland; it is not to be found in Ireland at all. And since the trend today, in the United States, is to search for Irish names that are truly Irish, Erin just may be left out in the cold. Variations: *Erene, Ereni, Eri, Erina, Erinn, Eryn.*

ESMERELDA *(Spanish)* Emerald. Variations: *Emerant, Emeraude, Esma, Esmaralda, Esmarelda, Esmiralda, Esmirelda, Ezmeralda.*

ESPERANZA *(Spanish)* Hope. Variations: *Esperance, Esperantia.*

ESTELLE *(French)* Star. Variations: *Essie, Essy, Estee, Estela, Estelita, Estella, Estrelita, Estrella, Estrellita, Stelle.*

ESTHER *(Hebrew)* Star. Variations: *Essie, Essy, Esta, Ester, Etti, Ettie, Etty.*

ESTRELLA *(French)* Child of the stars. Variation: *Estrelle.*

ETHEL *(English)* Noble. Once upon a time, Ethel was a quite fashionable variation of such names as Ethelinda, Ethelberta, and Etheldreda. The singer and dancer Ethel Merman seems to have provided us with this name's last hurrah, because although Ethel Mertz, Lucy's sidekick, was a good egg, the name has left subsequent generations with the feeling that Ethel leaves much to be desired. Variations: *Ethelda, Etheline, Ethelyn, Ethelynne, Ethille, Ethlin, Ethyl.*

EUGENIA *(Greek)* Well born. Feminine version of Eugene. This is the name of the Duke and Duchess of York's second daughter. Variations: *Eugena, Eugenie, Eugina.*

EVA *(Hebrew)* Giver of life. Variations: *Ebba, Evaine, Evathia, Evchen, Eve, Evelina, Eveline, Evi, Evicka, Evike, Evita, Evka, Evonne, Evy, Ewa, Yeuka, Yeva.*

EVELYN *(French)* Hazelnut. Evelyn is a great example of a name that started out as a boys' name—but then parents started to appropriate it for their daughters, rendering the male version all but obsolete. Evelyn became popular in the first couple of decades of this century as a girls' name, and by that point the name had disappeared from general consideration as a boys' name. Variations: *Aveline, Eoelene, Eveline, Evelyne, Evelynn, Evelynne, Evlin, Evline, Evlun, Evlynn.*

Slightly Daring Choices

EARLENE *(English)* Leader. Feminine version of Earl. Variations: *Earla, Earleen, Earley, Earlie, Earlinda, Earline, Erlene, Erlina, Erline.*

EARTHA *(English)* Earth. Variations: *Erta, Ertha, Hertha.*

EASTER *(English)* Named for the holiday.

EBERTA *(German)* Bright.

EBONY *(African-American)* Black wood. Variations: *Ebbony, Eboney, Eboni, Ebonie.*

EDLYN *(English)* Small noble girl.

EDMONDA *(English)* Rich protector. Feminine version of Edmund.

EDRICE *(English)* Strong property owner. Feminine version of Edric. Variations: *Edris, Edryce, Edrys, Eidris, Eydris.*

EDWARDINE *(English)* Rich protector. Feminine version of Edward. Variations: *Edwarda, Edwardeen, Edwardene, Edwardyne.*

EDWIGE *(French)* Joyful war. For some parents who are tempted to use Edna as a name for their daughters but think it's still entirely out of the loop, Edwige may be a good alternative. Variations: *Edvig, Edwig, Hedwig, Hedwige, Yadwigo.*

EDWINA *(English)* Rich friend. Feminine version of Edwin. Variations: *Edween, Edweena, Edwena, Edwiena, Edwuna, Edwyna.*

EFFIE *(Greek)* Singing talk. Variations: *Eff, Effy, Ephie, Eppie, Euphemia, Euphemie, Euphie.*

EILAH *(Hebrew)* Oak tree. Variations: *Aila, Ailah, Ala, Alah, Ayla, Eila, Eilona, Ela, Elah, Elona, Eyla.*

EIRWEN *(Welsh)* Fair. Variation: *Eirwyn.*

EISA *(Scandinavian)* Ancient mythological figure.

ELA *(Hindu)* Intelligent woman; (Polish) Noble. Variations: *Elakshi, Elee, Eli, Elina, Elita.*

ELBERTA *(English)* Noble, shining. Feminine version of Elbert. Variations: *Elbertina, Elbertine, Elbie.*

ELDORA *(Spanish)* Coated by gold. Variations: *Eldoree, Eldoria, Eldoris.*

ELECTRA *(Greek)* Shining one. A mythological figure who had her brother kill their mother and her lover in revenge for their father's murder. Variation: *Elektra.*

ELERI *(Welsh)* Smooth.

ELIANA *(Hebrew)* God has answered my prayers. Variation: *Eliane*

ELIKA *(Hawaiian)* Forever ruler.

ELILI *(Polynesian)* Periwinkle.

ELIORA *(Hebrew)* God is light. Variation: *Eleora.*

ELITA *(Latin)* Chosen.

ELIVAH *(Hebrew)* God is able. Variation: *Eliava.*

ELLI *(Scandinavian)* Old age.

ELLICE *(Greek)* Noble. Feminine version of Elias. Variation: *Elyce.*

ELMA *(Greek)* Helmet; (Turkish) Apple. Feminine version of Elmo.

ELORA *(Hindu)* God gives the laurel to the winner. Variation: *Ellora.*

EMERA *(English)* Industrious.

EMERALD *(English)* A jewel.

ENRICA *(Italian)* Leader of the house. Feminine version of Henry. Variations: *Enrieta, Enriqueta.*

ERINA *(Hindu)* Speech. Variation: *Erisha.*

ERLINDA *(Hebrew)* Spirit.

ERNESTINA *(English)* Earnest. Variations: *Erna, Ernaline, Ernesta, Ernestine, Ernestyna.*

ERROLYN *(English)* Area in Britain. Feminine version of Errol.

ESETERA *(Hawaiian)* Star. Hawaiian version of Esther. Variations: *Ekekela, Eseta.*

ESHANA *(Hindu)* Desire.

ETHELINDA *(German)* Noble serpent. Variations: *Etheleen, Ethelena, Ethelende, Ethelina, Ethelind, Ethylinda.*

ETTA *(English)* Diminutive.

EUDORA *(Greek)* Altruistic gift. Variation: *Eudore.*

EUNICE *(Greek)* Victorious. Variations: *Euniss, Eunys.*

EURYDICE *(Greek)* Greek mythological figure; wife of Orpheus. Variation: *Euridice.*

EVANGELINE *(Greek)* Good news. Variations: *Evangelia, Evangelina, Evangeliste.*

EVANIA *(Greek)* Serene.

EZRELA *(Hebrew)* God is my strength.

Living on the Edge

EADOIN *(Irish)* She has lots of friends.

EALASAID *(Scottish)* God is my oath.

EALGA *(Irish)* Noble.

ECHO *(Greek)* Ancient mythological nymph.

EDA *(English)* Happy. Variations: *Edda, Edde, Ede.*

EDDA *(Scandinavian)* Ancient mythological figure.

EDDI *(English)* Protector of property. Feminine version of Edward. Variations: *Eddie, Eddy, Eddye.*

EDELINE *(German)* Noble.

Scandinavian Girls' Names

Although you'll readily recognize many of these popular Scandinavian names, some are more unfamiliar to our American culture. Here are some of the most popular Scandinavian girls' names:

ANNA
ASTRID
BERTA
BRITTA
CHRISTINA
DAGMAR
ELISABETH
ERNA
EVA
GRETE
HEIDE
INGA
INGRID
KARI
KARIN
MARGARETA
MERETE
SIANE
ULLA
ULRIKA

EDEN *(Hebrew)* Pleasure. Variations: *Eaden, Eadin, Edena, Edenia, Edana, Edin.*

EDIAH *(Hebrew)* Decoration for God. Variations: *Edia, Ediya, Edya, Edyah.*

EDINA *(English)* One from Edinburgh, capital of Scotland. Variations: *Edeena, Edena, Edyna.*

EGIDIA *(Scottish)* Young goat.

EGLAH *(Hebrew)* Cow. Variation: *Egla.*

EGLANTINE *(French)* Sweetbriar. Variations: *Eglantilne, Eglantyne.*

EGYPE *(English)* The country Egypt.

EHANI *(Hindu)* Desire. Variation: *Ehina.*

EHAWEE *(Native American: Sioux)* She laughs.

EIBHLIN *(Irish)* Shining, bright; derivative of Helen.

EIFIONA *(Welsh)* Area in Wales.

EILEITHYIA *(Greek)* The goddess of childbirth. Variation: *Ilithyia.*

EILUNED *(Welsh)* Idol.

EIRPNE *(Greek)* Peace.

EITHNE *(Irish)* Kernel. Variations: *Eithna, Ena, Enya, Ethenia, Ethna, Ethnah, Ethnea, Ethnee.*

EKELA *(Hawaiian)* Noble. Variation: *Etela.*

EKUA *(African: Ghanian)* Born on a Wednesday.

ELAMA *(Hebrew)* God's people.

ELAMMA *(Hindu)* Mother goddess. Variation: *Ellama.*

ELATA *(Latin)* Held in high esteem.

ELDREDA *(English)* Elderly counselor.

ELEELE *(Hawaiian)* Black eyes.

ELENOLA *(Hawaiian)* Bright. Variations: *Elenoa, Elenora, Elianora.*

ELEU *(Hawaiian)* Alive.

ELGA *(Slavic)* Holy.

ELI *(Scandinavian: Norwegian)* Light.

ELIEZRA *(Hebrew)* God is salvation.

ELK *(Hawaiian)* Black.

ELKANA *(Hebrew)* God has created. Variation: *Elkanah.*

ELKE *(German)* Noble. Variation: *Elka.*

ELUNED *(Welsh)* Shape. Variation: *Eiluned.*

ELVA *(English)* Variation of Olivia.

ELVINA *(English)* Elf friend. Feminine version of Alvin. Variations: *Elvie, Elvy, Elwina.*

EMUNA *(Hebrew)* Faithful.

ENA *(Irish)* Bright, shining. Possibly a derivative of Helen.

ENNIS *(Irish)* A town in western Ireland. Variation: *Inis.*

ENOLA *(Native American)* Unknown definition.

EOGHANIA *(Welsh)* Youth.

ERELA *(Hebrew)* Angel.

ERIANTHE *(Greek)* Lover of flowers.

ERIKO *(Japanese)* Child with a collar.

ERMINE *(French)* Weasel. Variations: *Ermina, Erminia, Erminie, Ermy.*

ERNA *(Scandinavian)* Capable.

ERWINA *(English)* Boar; friend. Feminine version of Erwin.

ERYL *(Welsh)* Observer.

ESHE *(African: Swahili)* Life.

ESI *(African: Ghanian)* Born on Sunday.

ESME *(French)* Esteemed. Variations: *Esma, Esmee.*

EUBH *(Scottish)* Life. Variation: *Eubha.*

Tried and True Classics

FABRIZIA *(Italian)* One who works with her hands. Variations: *Fabrice, Fabricia, Fabrienne, Fabritzia.*

FAITH *(English)* Faith. Faith was another one of the virtue names that the Puritans liked so much back in the seventeenth century, and it is one of the few that has survived to this day. Faith, along with Hope, sounds more practical and everyday than either Charity or Prudence. Variations: *Faithe, Faythe.*

FARRAH *(English)* Pleasant. Variations: *Fara, Farah, Farra.*

FATIMA *(Arabic)* The prophet Mohammed's favorite daughter. Though Fatima has long been used for girls in Muslim families overseas, it hasn't appeared in the United States much until recently. Devout Muslims in America are now beginning to flock toward this name, following the lead of their relatives in Saudi Arabia, Egypt, and India. Variations: *Fatimah, Fatma, Fatuma.*

FAY *(French)* Fairy. Diminutive of Faith. Variations: *Faye, Fayette.*

FELICIA *(Latin)* Happy; lucky. Feminine version of Felix. Variations of Felicia like Felice or Felicity are also delicate and feminine options. Felicity, in fact, is becoming more popular for girls these days since the successful *American Girl* book series features a girl from colonial times named Felicity. Variations: *Falecia, Falicia, Falicie, Falisha, Falishia, Felice, Feliciana, Felicidad, Felicienne, Felicita, Felicitas, Felicity, Felise, Felita, Feliz, Feliza.*

FIONA *(Irish)* Fair, white. Variations: *Fionna, Fionne.*

FLANNERY *(Irish)* Red hair.

FLAVIA *(Latin)* Yellow hair. Variations: *Flavie, Flaviere, Flavyere, Flayia.*

FLORA *(Latin)* Flower. Flora has potential to become popular in the United States, since it is one of the more popular names in other countries, including Sweden, Britain, Germany, and Russia. Variations: *Fiora, Fiore, Fiorentina, Fiorenza, Fiori, Fleur, Fleurette, Fleurine, Flo, Flor, Florance, Florann, Floranne, Flore, Florella, Florelle, Florence, Florencia, Florentia, Florentyna, Florenze, Floretta, Florette, Flori, Floria, Floriana, Florie, Floriese, Florina, Florinda, Florine, Floris, Florrie, Florry, Floss, Flossey, Flossie.*

FRANCES *(Latin)* One who is from France. Feminine version of Francis. Frances was a perennial favorite in England through the latter half of the nineteenth century, and in this country, it reached its peak by the time the Great Depression hit. Though it has been considered somewhat square from that time all the way up until the '80s, Frances is beginning to take off again among parents who are looking for a traditional and classy name for their daughters. Famous Franceses include actress Frances Farmer and Courtney Love's daughter Frances Bean. Variations: *Fan, Fancy, Fania, Fannee, Fanney, Fannie, Fanny, Fanya, Fran, Franca, Francee, Franceline, Francena, Francene, Francesca, Francetta, Francette, Francey, Franchesca, Francie, Francina, Francine, Francisca, Francoise, Frank, Frankie, Franni, Frannie, Franzetta, Franziska, Paquita.*

FRANÇOISE *(French)* Frenchman.

FREDA *(German)* Peaceful. Variations: *Freada, Freddi, Freddie, Freddy, Frederica, Frederique, Freeda, Freida, Frida, Frieda, Fritzi, Fryda.*

Slightly Daring Choices

FABIA *(Latin)* One who grows beans. Feminine version of Fabian. Variations: *Fabiana, Fabiane, Fabianna, Fabienne, Fabiola.*

FADILA *(Arabic)* Virtue. Variation: *Fadilah.*

FAIVA *(Polynesian)* Game.

FALINE *(Latin)* Catlike.

FALLON *(Irish)* Related to a leader. Variation: *Falon.*

FARICA *(German)* Leader of peace.

FARIDA *(Arabic)* Unique. Variations: *Faridah, Farideh.*

FARIHA *(Arabic)* Happy. Variation: *Farihah.*

FARREN *(English)* Last name. Variation: *Faren.*

FAWN *(French)* Young deer. Variations: *Faina, Fanya, Fauan, Faun, Faunia, Fawna, Fawne, Fawnia, Fawnya.*

FELORA *(Hawaiian)* Flower. Variations: *Felorena, Folora, Polola, Pololena.*

FENIA *(Scandinavian)* Ancient mythological figure. Variation: *Fenja.*

FEODORA *(Russian)* Gift from God. Feminine version of Theodore.

FERNANDA *(German)* Peace and courage; brave traveler. Feminine version of Ferdinand.

FIALA *(Czech)* Violet.

FIDELIA *(Hawaiian)* Faithful. Variations: *Fidela, Fidele, Fidelina, Fidelity, Fidelma, Pikelia.*

FILIA *(Greek)* Friendship.

FILIPPINA *(Italian)* Lover of horses. Feminine version of Philip. Variation: *Filippa.*

FINOLA *(Irish)* White shoulders. Variations: *Effie, Ella, Fenella, Finella, Fionnaghuala, Fionneuala, Fionnghuala, Fionnuala, Fionnula, Fionola, Fynella, Nuala.*

FIPE *(Polynesian)* Bright.

FISI *(Polynesian)* Blossom.
FLAMINIA *(Latin)* Priest.
FLANNA *(Irish)* Red hair.
FLORIDA *(Spanish)* Flowery.
FLORIMEL *(Latin)* Flower plus honey.
FLOWER *(English)* Flower.
FORTUNA *(Latin)* Roman goddess of luck. Variations: *Fortunata, Fortune.*

Living on the Edge

FABAYO *(African: Nigerian)* Fortunate birth.
FAHIMA *(Arabic)* Smart.
FAIDA *(Arabic)* Abundant. Variation: *Fayda.*
FALAKIKA *(Polynesian)* Mat.
FALDA *(Icelandic)* Folded wings.
FALZAH *(Arabic)* Triumphant.
FANCY *(French)* Engaged. Nickname for fianceé. Variations: *Fancey, Fancie.*
FANG *(Chinese)* Fragrant.
FANG HUA *(Chinese)* Fragrant flower.
FANUA *(Polynesian)* Land.
FAOILTIARNA *(Irish)* Lord of the wolves.
FARDOOS *(Arabic)* Utopia.
FAREWELL *(English)* Goodbye; beautiful spring.
FATHIYA *(Arabic)* Victorious.
FATIN *(Arabic)* Bewitching. Variations: *Fatina, Fatinah.*
FATUIMOANA *(Polynesian)* Wreaths.
FAUSTINE *(Latin)* Lucky. The feminine version of Faust. Variations: *Fausta, Fauste, Faustina.*

FAYINA *(Ukrainian)* Woman from France.

FAYOLA *(African: Nigerian)* Lucky.

FAYRUZ *(Arabic)* Turquoise.

FAYZA *(Arabic)* Winner. Variations: *Faiza, Faizah, Fawzia.*

FEDORA *(Greek)* Gift from God.

FEIDHELM *(Irish)* Unknown definition. Variations: *Fedelma, Fidelma.*

FEIGE *(Hebrew)* Bird. Variations: *Faga, Faiga, Faigel, Feiga, Feigel.*

FELDA *(German)* From the field.

FEMI *(African: Nigerian)* Love me.

FENG *(Chinese)* Chinese sweet gum.

FERNLEY *(English)* Valley of ferns. Variations: *Fern, Ferne, Fernlee, Fernleigh, Fernly.*

FETUU *(Polynesian)* Star.

FIAMMETTA *(Italian)* Sputtering flame. Variation: *Fia.*

FIDDA *(Arabic)* Silver. Variation: *Fizza.*

FIELIKI *(Polynesian)* Wanting to be clean.

FIFI *(French)* Nickname of Josephine. Variations: *Fifine, Fina.*

FIHAKI *(Polynesian)* Braid of flowers.

FIKRIYA *(Arabic)* To meditate.

FINEEVA *(Polynesian)* Gabby woman.

FINEONGO *(Polynesian)* Beautiful woman.

FOLA *(African: Nigerian)* Honorable.

FOLADE *(African: Nigerian)* She brings honor.

FOLAMI *(African: Nigerian)* Respect me.

FOLAYAN *(African: Nigerian)* Walking proudly.

FOLUKE *(African: Nigerian)* God's care.

FONTANE *(French)* Fountain.

FRANTISKA *(Czech)* Free woman. Variations: *Frana, Franka.*

FRAYDA *(Hebrew)* Happy. Variations: *Fradel, Frayde, Freida, Freide.*

FREYA *(Scandinavian: Swedish)* Noble lady. Variations: *Freja, Freyja, Froja.*

FRIGG *(Scandinavian)* Beloved. Variation: *Frigga.*

FUJI *(Japanese)* Wisteria. Variations: *Fujiko, Fujiyo.*

African-American Girls' Names

When you see a name in this book that is of African-American origin and the definition reads "newly created," chances are the name was formed by taking a familiar, existing name and then changing a few letters so that the new version rhymes with the original. Many times, with girls' names, the prefix "La-" is added to change a familiar name, as in the case of the following examples:

LAPAULA
LARITA
LASHANNON
LASHARON
LASHAUN
LASHEBA
LASHELL
LASHERRI
LASHONA
LATANIA
LATASHA
LATESHA
LATRECIA
LATRICE

FUJO *(African: Swahili)* Born to divorced parents.
FUKAYNA *(Arabic)* Knowledgeable.
FULANDE *(Hindu)* Flower. Variation: *Fulangi.*
FULLA *(Scandinavian)* Mythological fertility goddess.
FUSI *(Polynesian)* Bananas. Variation: *Fusileka.*
FUYU *(Japanese)* Winter. Variation: *Fuyuko.*

Tried and True Classics

GABRIELLE *(Hebrew)* Heroine of God. Feminine version of Gabriel. Tennis star Gabriella Sabatini has brought new life to this name in the United States and elsewhere. Gabrielle is a wonderfully cultured name that doesn't sound as haughty as some other girls' names that have a sophisticated ring to them. This is probably owing to one of its nicknames, Gaby, which sounds anything but elitist. Gabrielle has already shown signs of cracking the top fifty list of baby names for girls in the United States; this trend should continue. Variations: *Gabbi, Gabby, Gabi, Gabriela, Gabriell, Gabriella, Gaby.*

GAIL *(Hebrew)* My father rejoices. Gail started out as a nickname for Abigail, back in the '40s when traditionally American names started to seem a bit stodgy and old-fashioned. Variations: *Gael, Gaile, Gale, Gayle.*

GENEVIEVE *(French)* White; Celtic woman. Genevieve has tended to be a continental sophisticated name, undoubtedly helped along by actress Genevieve Bujold. It has never been used that frequently in this country, and therefore tends to have a neutral connotation with most people. It seems the name should be more popular than it is currently, and given our culture's fascination with Europe, this could happen. Variations: *Genavieve, Geneva, Geneve, Geneveeve, Genivieve, Gennie, Genny, Genovera, Genoveva, Gina, Janeva, Jenevieve.*

GEORGIA *(Latin)* Farmer. Feminine version of George. Variations: *Georgeann, Georgeanne, Georgeina, Georgena, Georgene, Georgetta, Georgette, Georgganne, Georgganne, Georgiana, Georgianne, Georgie, Georgienne, Georgina, Georgine, Giorgia,*

Giorgina, Giorgyna, Jorgina.

GERALDINE *(French)* One who rules with a spear. Feminine version of Gerald. Variations: *Ceraldina, Deraldene, Geralda, Geraldeen, Geralyn, Geralynne, Geri, Gerianna, Gerianne, Gerilynn, Geroldine, Gerry, Jeraldeen, Jeraldene, Jeraldine, Jeralee, Jere, Jeri, Jerilene, Jerrie, Jerrileen, Jerroldeen, Jerry.*

GERIANNE *(American)* Gerry + Anne.

GERMAINE *(French)* One from Germany. Variations: *Germain, Germana, Germane, Germayn, Germayne.*

GERTRUDE *(German)* With the strength of a spear. One famous Gertrude is feminist author Gertrude Stein. Variations: *Gertie, Gertina, Gertraud, Gertrud, Gertruda, Gerty, Truda, Trude, Trudey, Trudi, Trudie, Trudy, Trudye.*

GIA *(Italian)* Queen.

GIGI *(French)* Gigi is an independent name that evolved from Gilberte.

GILDA *(English)* Golden.

GILLIAN *(English)* Youthful. Variations: *Gilian, Gillan, Gillianne, Gillyanne.*

GINA *(Hebrew)* Garden; (Italian) Nickname for names such as Regina and Angelina; (Japanese) Silvery. Gina was one of the more popular exotic names in the United States during the '50s and '60s, which is probably solely due to the exposure of Italian actress Gina Lollobrigida. Back then, Gina was the epitome of foreign glamour and sophistication. Actress Geena Davis has popularized a new spelling of the name. Variations: *Geena, Gena, Ginat, Ginia.*

GINGER *(English)* The spice. Diminutive of Virginia.

GINNY *(English)* Diminutive of Virginia. Variations: *Ginney, Ginnie.*

GIOVANNA *(Italian)* God is good. Another feminization of John.

GISELLE *(English)* Oath; hostage. This is a picture-perfect name for a ballerina; *Giselle* is a ballet by Gautier. Variations:

Gelsi, Gelsy, Gisela, Gisele, Gisella, Gizela, Gizella.

GLADYS *(Welsh)* Lame. Form of Claudia. About a hundred years ago Gladys was considered the most exotic, sexy name to come down the pike in quite some time. Variations: *Gwladus, Gwladys.*

GLENDA *(Welsh)* Holy and good.

GLORIA *(Latin)* Glory. There have been lots of famous Glorias over the years: Gloria Steinem, Gloria Swanson, Gloria Vanderbilt, and Gloria Estefan. Variations: *Gloree, Glori, Glorie, Glorria, Glory.*

GRACE *(Latin)* Grace. Grace has been around since the Middle Ages, and it has never really gone out of style. Famous Graces include singer Grace Slick, Grace Jones, and the late Grace Kelly and Gracie Allen. Variations: *Engracie, Graca, Gracey, Graci, Gracia, Graciana, Gracie, Gracy, Gratia, Grazia, Graziella, Grazielle, Graziosa, Grazyna.*

GUADALUPE *(Spanish)* Valley of wolves.

GUINEVERE *(Welsh)* Fair; yielding. Variations: *Gaenor, Gayna, Gaynah, Gayner, Gaynor.*

GWENDOLYN *(Welsh)* Fair brow. Variations: *Guendolen, Guenna, Gwen, Gwenda, Gwendaline, Gwendia, Gwendolen, Gwendolene, Gwendolin, Gwendoline, Gwendolynn, Gwendolynne, Gwenette,Gwennie, Gwenn, Gwenna, Gwenny.*

GWYNETH *(Welsh)* Happiness. Both Gwyneth and Gwendolyn are popular now because people consider girls' names that begin with "Gw" exotic and sophisticated at the same time. But Gwyneth is probably the more popular owing to the actress Gwyneth Paltrow, the daughter of Blythe Danner. Variations: *Gwenith, Gwennyth, Gwenyth, Gwynith, Gwynn, Gwynna, Gwynne, Gwynneth.*

Slightly Daring Choices

GAIA *(Greek)* Earth. Variations: *Gaioa, Gaya.*

GALENA *(Greek)* Healer.

GALINA *(Russian)* Bright one or shining one. Variation of Helen.

GARNET *(English)* Jewel. Variations: *Garnetta, Garnette.*

GELILAH *(Hebrew)* Rolling hills. Variations: *Gelalia, Gelalya, Gelila, Gelilia, Geliliya.*

GELSEY *(English)* Last name.

GEMINI *(Greek)* Twin. Variations: *Gemella, Gemelle, Gemina, Geminine.*

GEMMA *(Irish)* Jewel; (Italian) Precious stone. Variation: *Gem.*

GENEA *(Phoenician)* The first inhabitants of Phoenicia.

GENESEE *(Native American: Iroquois)* Wonderful valley.

GENESIS *(Hebrew)* Beginning. Variations: *Genessa, Genisa, Genisia, Genisis, Jenessa.*

GENNA *(Arabic)* Small bird.

GEONA *(Hebrew)* Glorification. Variation: *Geonit.*

GIACINTA *(Italian)* Hyacinth.

GIALIA *(Italian)* Youthful. Feminine version of Giulio. Variations: *Giala, Gialiana, Gialietta.*

GIANNA *(Italian)* God is good. Feminine version of John. Variations: *Giancinthia, Gianetta, Gianina, Giannina, Giannine, Jacenda, Jacenta, Jacey, Jacie, Jacinda, Jacindia, Jacinna, Jacinta, Jacinth, Jacintha, Jacinthe, Jacinthia, Jacynth, Jacyntha, Jacynthe.*

GILBERTE *(French)* Shining pledge. Feminine version of Gilbert. Variations: *Gilberta, Gilbertina, Gilbertine, Gill, Gillie, Gilly.*

GILIAH *(Hebrew)* God's joy. Variations: *Gilia, Giliya, Giliyah.*

GILL *(English)* Downy.

GILSEY *(English)* Jasmine.

GITANA *(Spanish)* Gypsy. Variations: *Gitane, Gitanna.*

GLENNA *(Irish)* Narrow valley. Variations: *Glen, Glenn.*

GLENNETTE *(Scottish)* Narrow valley. Feminine version of Glenn.

GLENYS *(Welsh)* Holy. Variations: *Glenice, Glenis, Glenise, Glennis, Glennys, Glenyse, Glenyss, Glynis.*

GODIVA *(English)* Gift from God.

GOLDA *(English)* Golden. Variations: *Goldarina, Goldarine, Goldia, Goldie, Goldif, Goldina, Goldy.*

GYPSY *(English)* Wanderer.

Girls' Names from the Old Testament

The Old Testament is filled with stories of unique and interesting women, and a book of the Bible, Ruth, is even named after one. After thousands of years' worth of use, it's certain that many of these strong, meaningful names will always be classics that never go out of style.

ABIGAIL: *Wife of David*
ASENATH: *Wife of Joseph*
BATHSHEBA: *Wife of Uriah and then David*
DELILAH: *Mistress of Samson*
EVE: *First woman, wife of Adam*
HAGAR: *Mother of Ishmael*
LEAH: *First wife of Jacob*
NAOMI: *Mother-in-law of Ruth*
RACHEL: *Wife of Jacob; mother of Joseph and Benjamin*
REBECCA: *Wife of Isaac, mother of Jacob*
RUTH: *Wife of Mahlon*
SARAH: *Wife of Abraham*
TAMAR: *Daughter of David*
ZILPAH: *Mistress of Jacob*

Living on the Edge

GADA *(Hebrew)* Lucky.
GAENOR *(Welsh)* Fair; smooth.
GAETANA *(Italian)* Area in Italy. Variation: *Gaetane.*
GAFNA *(Hebrew)* Vine.
GALA *(Scandinavian)* Singer; celebration. Variation: *Galla.*
GALATEA *(Greek)* White as milk. Variation: *Galatee.*
GALI *(Hebrew)* Hill, mound. Variations: *Gal, Galice.*
GALIENA *(German)* High one. Variations: *Galiana, Galianna.*
GALILANI *(Native American: Cherokee)* Friendly.
GALYA *(Hebrew)* God has redeemed. Variations: *Galia, Gallia, Gallya.*
GAMBHIRA *(Hindu)* Noble.
GAMMA *(Greek)* Third letter of the alphabet.
GANESA *(Hindu)* Goddess of wisdom.
GANIT *(Hebrew)* Garden. Variations: *Gana, Ganice.*
GANYA *(Hebrew)* Garden of God.
GARDENIA *(English)* Flower.
GARI *(German)* Spear. Feminine version of Gary.
GARIMA *(Hindu)* Importance.
GARLAND *(French)* Wreath. Variations: *Garlanda, Garlande, Garlandera.*
GASHA *(Russian)* Good. Russian version of Agatha. Variation: *Gashka.*
GAURI *(Hindu)* White. Variations: *Gori, Gowri.*
GAVRILLA *(Hebrew)* Heroine.
GAY *(French)* Joyful. Variations: *Gae, Gai, Gaye.*
GAYORA *(Hebrew)* Valley of light.
GAZELLE *(Latin)* Gazelle; graceful. Variation: *Gazella.*
GAZIT *(Hebrew)* Smooth stone.
GEELA *(Hebrew)* Joy.

GEFEN *(Hebrew)* Vine. Variations: *Gafna, Gafnit, Gaphna, Geffen.*

GEFJUN *(Scandinavian)* She who gives wealth. Variations: *Gefion, Gefjon.*

GELYA *(Russian)* Messenger.

GERANIUM *(Latin)* Flower.

GERD *(Scandinavian)* Guarded. Variations: *Gard, Gerda.*

GERUSHAH *(Hebrew)* Banishment. Variation: *Gerusha.*

GERVAISE *(French)* Unknown definition.

GEVA *(Hebrew)* Hill.

GEVIRAH *(Hebrew)* Queen. Variation: *Gevira.*

GHADA *(Arabic)* Graceful. Variations: *Ghadah, Ghayda.*

GHADIR *(Arabic)* River.

GHALIYA *(Arabic)* Pleasant odor. Variation: *Ghaliyah.*

GHITA *(Greek)* Pearl.

GHUFRAN *(Arabic)* To forgive.

GIBORAH *(Hebrew)* Strong. Variation: *Gibora.*

GILADAH *(Hebrew)* Hill of testimony. Variations: *Galat, Geela, Gila, Gili, Gilia.*

GILANAH *(Hebrew)* Happy. Variation: *Gilana.*

GRAINNE *(Irish)* Goddess of grain. Variations: *Grainnia, Grania, Granna.*

GREER *(Scottish)* Observant. Feminine version of Gregory.

GRETNA *(Scottish)* Scottish village.

GRISELDA *(German)* Gray fighting maid. Variations: *Grizelda, Zelda.*

GUDRUN *(Scandinavian)* Fight. Variations: *Cudrin, Gudren, Gudrinn, Gudruna, Guro.*

GUIDA *(Italian)* Guide.

GUILLERMA *(Spanish)* Will + helmet. Feminine version of William.

GULL *(Scandinavian)* Gold.

GUNHILDA *(Scandinavian: Norwegian)* Woman warrior. Variations: *Gunda, Gunhilde, Gunilda, Gunilla, Gunnhilda.*

GURICE *(Hebrew)* Lion cub. Variation: *Gurit.*

GUSTAVA *(Scandinavian: Swedish)* Staff of the gods. Feminine version of Gustav. Variations: *Gusta, Gustha.*

GYANDA *(Hindu)* Learned.

Tried and True Classics

HANNAH *(Hebrew)* Grace. In the Bible, Hannah was mother of the prophet Samuel, but even he couldn't have foreseen how popular his mother's name would remain. Hannah was very popular in Britain in the seventeenth through nineteenth centuries, and also in this country in the colonial era, when Biblical names were the norm. Variations: *Hana, Hanah, Hanna, Hanne, Hannele, Hannelore, Hannie, Honna.*

HARPER *(English)* Harp player. Harper Lee, author of *To Kill a Mockingbird,* first popularized this traditional last-name-as-first-name for girls. Surprisingly, Harper hasn't made much progress on the most popular names list, but it should, since today it pushes all the right buttons.

HARRIET *(German)* Leader of the house. Feminine version of Harry. Variations: *Harrie, Harrietta, Harriette, Harriot, Harriott, Hatsie, Hatsy, Hattie, Hatty.*

HAYLEY *(English)* Meadow of hay. Hayley is an extremely popular name for girls, but few people know that the name actually originated when child actress Hayley Mills first burst onto the scene. Before her parents took her mother's middle name for their daughter's first name, Hayley—more commonly spelled Haley—was known only as a last name. Variations: *Hailee, Hailey, Haley, Halie, Halley, Halli, Hallie, Hally, Haylee, Hayleigh, Haylie.*

HAZEL *(English)* The name of a tree. Variations: *Hazal, Hazeline, Hazell, Hazelle, Hazle.*

HEATHER *(English)* Flower. In this country, Heather has been popular since the '70s, but it really didn't start to take hold until the movie *Heathers* came out in the mid-'80s. Its popularity in Britain preceded the name's vogue on these shores as it peaked in England during the '50s, and it appears as though the movie did nothing to enhance the name's image over there.

HEIDI *(German)* Noble. Variations: *Hedie, Heida, Heide, Heidie, Hydie.*

HELEN *(Greek)* Light. Helen has a lengthy track record. Helen was a pivotal figure in Greek mythology as the daughter of Zeus, as well as the real-life mother of emperor Constantine the Great back in the fourth century A.D. Since the early days of the United States, Helen has gone in and out of fashion, most often alternating with its close relative, Ellen. Though Helen was not too popular in the '70s and '80s in the United States, it appears to be one of those names that's just waiting to happen. Variations: *Hela, Hele, Helena, Helene, Hellen, Helli.*

HELGA *(Scandinavian: Norwegian)* Holy.

HELOISE *(French)* Famous in war. Variation: *Heloisa.*

HENRIETTA *(German)* Leader of the home. Feminine version of Henry. Variations: *Hattie, Hatty, Hendrika, Henka, Hennie, Henrie, Henrieta, Henriette, Henrika, Hetta, Hettie.*

HESTER *(Greek)* Star. Variation of Esther. Though Ester may be on the verge of a comeback in the United States, don't look for Hester to hit the top ten list anytime soon. Variations: *Hesther, Hestia.*

HILARY *(Latin)* Glad. For at least the next few decades, this name will be indelibly connected with President Clinton's wife. Variations: *Hilaria, Hilarie, Hillary, Hillery, Hilliary.*

HILDA *(German)* Battle woman. Variations: *Hilde, Hildie, Hildy, Hylda.*

HISA *(Japanese)* Everlasting. Many of the more popular names for Japanese girls and boys are meant to impart the hope for longevity to the person with the name. Hisa is one of these names. Superstitions are frequently involved in picking a name for your baby, and this ancient Japanese custom could very well catch on in this country. Hisa is a beautiful name, regardless of its meaning, which may encourage non-Japanese parents to choose it. Variations: *Hisae, Hisako, Hisayo.*

HOLLY *(English)* Plant. Though Holly has always been more popular in England than in the United States, it should pick up over here in coming years. First, it's a seasonal name that many parents choose for their daughters who are born close to Christmastime. Second, it's a plant name, and this category of names seems particularly poised to grow in usage in the years to come. And as a bonus, Holly Hunter is a talented, prolific actress, which never hurts when it comes to the popularity of a name. Variations: *Hollee, Holley, Holli, Hollie, Hollyann.*

HONEY *(English)* Sweetener; term of affection.

HOPE *(English)* Hope.

HORATIA *(English)* A Roman clan name. Feminine version of Horatio. Variation: *Horacia.*

Slightly Daring Choices

HADASSAH *(Hebrew)* Myrtle. Variations: *Hada, Hadas, Hadasa, Hadassa, Hodel.*

HADIL *(Arabic)* Cooing pigeon.

HADLEY *(English)* Meadow of heather. Variations: *Hadlea, Hadlee, Hadleigh.*

HADYA *(Arabic)* Guide. Variation: *Hadiya.*

HAJAR *(Arabic)* To abandon. Variation: *Hagir.*

HALA *(Arabic)* Ring of light around the moon. Variation: *Halah.*

Names That Go Either Way

In this book, you'll see many names listed that might cause you to pause and say, "I thought that was a girls' name"—or vice versa. Plenty of names go both ways. Certainly, some names derived from places, like city names, accomplish this feat, but there are many other examples, including the following:

BLAIR	**HALEY**	**STACY**
BLAKE	**KELLY**	**TAYLOR**
BRETT	**LESLIE**	**TERRY**
BRICE	**LINDSAY**	**TYLER**
CASEY	**MARION**	**WHITNEY**
DANA	**ROBIN**	
DREW	**SAM**	

Just be careful in this department—there often comes a point when the connotations of a so-called androgynous name begin to lean more to one side. Years down the road, you don't want your son to hold it against you for giving him a "girlie" name, or your daughter to complain because her name sounds too "boyish."

HALCYON *(Greek)* Peaceful. If you're a person who believes that we are our names, and you want no surprises in your daughter, Halcyon is a good choice. Variations: *Halcion, Halcione, Halcyone.*

HALDANA *(Scandinavian: Norwegian)* One who is half Scandinavian: *Danish.* Variation: Haldane.

HALIA *(Hawaiian)* Remembering a loved one.

HALIMA *(Arabic)* Gentle. Variation: *Halimah.*

HALINA *(Russian)* Shining one. Russian version of Helen.

HALONA *(Native American)* Good luck.

HANIA *(Hebrew)* Resting place. Variation: *Haniya.*

HANSA *(Hindu)* Swan. Variations: *Hansika, Hansila.*

HARA *(Hindu)* Tawny.

HARALDA *(Scandinavian: Norwegian)* Army power. Feminine version of Harold.

HARITA *(Hindu)* The wind.

HARLEY *(English)* Rabbit pasture. Variations: *Harleigh, Harlie, Harly.*

HARMONY *(Latin)* Harmony. Variations: *Harmonee, Harmoni, Harmonia, Harmonie.*

HATHOR *(Egyptian)* The goddess of love.

HAVEN *(English)* Refuge.

HEAVEN *(English)* Paradise.

HEDIAH *(Hebrew)* Echo of God. Variations: *Hedia, Hedya.*

HEDWIG *(German)* Struggle. Variations: *Hadvig, Hadwig, Hedvig, Hedviga, Hedvige, Hedwiga, Hedwige.*

HELMA *(German)* Helmet. Variations: *Hillma, Hilma.*

HELMINE *(German)* Constant protector. Feminine version of William.

HELSA *(Scandinavian: Danish)* Glory to God.

HEPHZIBAH *(Hebrew)* My delight is in her. Hephzibah is one of those great old Biblical names that the Puritans loved. It has all the ingredients to become more popular in this country, but I'm afraid that it's just a bit too offbeat for most parents to consider. Variations: *Hephsibah, Hephzabah, Hepzibah.*

HERA *(Greek)* The mythological queen of the goddesses and wife of Zeus.

HERMIA *(Greek)* The mythological messenger for the Greek gods. Feminine version of Hermes. Variations: *Herma, Hermaine, Hermina, Hermione.*

HERMOSA *(Spanish)* Beautiful.

HESPER *(Greek)* Evening star. Variations: *Hespera, Hesperia.*

HIMANI *(Hindu)* Snow-covered. Variation: *Heemani.*

HINDA *(Hindu)* Female deer. Variations: *Hindel, Hindelle, Hynda.*

HISANO *(Japanese)* Meadow.

HOLDA *(German)* Hidden. Variations: *Holde, Holle, Hulda.*

HOLLIS *(English)* Near the holly. Variation: *Holice.*

HONORA *(English)* Honorable woman. Variations: *Honner, Honnor, Honnour, Honor, Honorah, Honorata, Honore, Honoria, Honorine, Honour.*

HOSANNA *(Greek)* Cry of prayer. Variation: *Hosannie.*

HUBERTA *(German)* Intelligent. Feminine version of Hubert. Variation: *Huette.*

HUNTER *(English)* Hunter.

Living on the Edge

HA *(Vietnamese)* River.

HABIBA *(Arabic)* Cherished. Variations: *Habibah, Haviva.*

HACHI *(Native American: Seminole)* River.

HADI *(Arabic)* Calm.

HADIYA *(African: Swahili)* Religious leader. Variation: *Hadiyah.*

HAE-WON *(Korean)* Grace.

HAFSAH *(Arabic)* Wife of Mohammed. Variation: *Hafza.*

HAGAR *(Hebrew)* Forsaken. Variation: *Haggar.*

HAGIA *(Hebrew)* Joy. Variations: *Hagice, Hagit.*

HALIAKA *(Hawaiian)* Leader of the house. Hawaiian version of Harriet. Variations: *Hariaka, Hariata.*

HALIMEDA *(Greek)* Of the sea.

HALKU *(Hawaiian)* Flower.

HALOLANI *(Hawaiian)* Fly like a bird.
HAMA *(Japanese)* Beach. Variation: *Hamako.*
HAMIDA *(Arabic)* To praise. Variations: *Hameedah, Hamidah.*
HANA *(Japanese)* Flower. Variations: *Hanae, Hanako.*
HANAN *(Arabic)* Merciful.
HANG *(Vietnamese)* Full moon.
HANH *(Vietnamese)* Ethical.
HANI *(Hawaiian)* Move softly.
HANIFA *(Arabic)* Follower of Islam. Variations: *Haneefa, Hanifah.*
HANITA *(Hindu)* Grace.
HANIYYA *(Arabic)* Happy. Variation: *Haniyyah.*
HANSINE *(Scandinavian)* God is good.
HANTAYWEE *(Native American: Sioux)* Cedar maiden.
HAPPY *(English)* Glad.
HAQIKAH *(Arabic)* Truthful.
HARSHA *(Hindu)* Happiness. Variations: *Harshida, Harshika, Harshina.*
HARU *(Japanese)* Born in spring. Variations: *Harue, Haruko.*
HASANATI *(Arabic)* Good.
HASIKA *(Hindu)* Laughter.
HASNA *(Arabic)* Strong.
HATEYA *(Native American)* Push with the foot.
HATHSHIRA *(Arabic)* Seventh daughter.
HATSU *(Japanese)* First-born.
HAUKEA *(Hawaiian)* Snow.
HAULANI *(Hawaiian)* Royalty.
HAUMA *(Hindu)* Gentle. Variations: *Haleema, Halimah.*
HAYA *(Japanese)* Fast.
HEBE *(Greek)* The goddess of youth.
HEDDA *(English)* Warfare. Variations: *Heda, Heddi, Heddie, Hetta.*
HEDVIKA *(Czech)* War of strife.
HEDY *(Greek)* Wonderful. Variations: *Hedia, Hedyla.*
HEE-YOUNG *(Korean)* Pleasurable wealth.
HELEDD *(Welsh)* Unknown definition. Variation: *Hyledd.*

HELKI *(Native American)* Touch.
HELTU *(Native American)* Bear that's friendly to people.
HEMALI *(Hindu)* Golden.
HE-RAN *(Korean)* Graceful orchid.
HERLINDIS *(Scandinavian)* Gentle army.
HETA *(Native American)* Rabbit hunt.
HIBERNIA *(Latin)* Latin name for Ireland.
HIBISCUS *(Latin)* Flower.
HIDE *(Japanese)* Excellent. Variation: *Hideyo.*
HIILANI *(Hawaiian)* Carried by heaven.
HIKMAT *(Arabic)* Wise.
HILMA *(German)* Nickname for Wilhelmina.
HIND *(Arabic)* India, land of Hindus.

Tried and True Classics

IDA *(English)* Youth. Ida was a big name fifty to one hundred years ago, which brought forth the Gilbert and Sullivan opera *Princess Ida*, the gay '90s song "Ida, Sweet as Apple Cider," and the actress Ida Lupino. Although other names from that period are hot today, Ida has not made much of a comeback. Variations: *Idalene, Idalia, Idalina, Idaline, Idalya, Idalyne, Ide, Idell, Idella, Idelle, Idetta, Idette, Idia.*

IMOGEN *(Latin)* Last-born; innocent. The best-known celebrity with this name was Imogene Coca. There are small rumblings of an increase in usage of this name both here and in Great Britain. Variations: *Imogene, Imogenia, Imogine.*

INÉS *(Spanish)* Pure. Variation of Agnes. Variations: *Inesita, Inessa, Inetta, Inez, Ynes, Ynesita, Ynez.*

INGA *(Scandinavian)* In Norse mythology, god of fertility and peace. Variations: *Ingaar, Inge, Ingo, Ingvio.*

INGRID *(Scandinavian)* Beautiful. Of all the feminine names from Scandinavia that begin with "Ing," Ingrid is the most widely used owing to the renown of actress Ingrid Bergman. There was a flurry of activity surrounding the name back in the '50s and '60s, but it faded until just recently and is now beginning to show signs of strength again.

IRENE *(Greek)* Peace. Irene has a long and rich history. One Irene became a saint in the fourth century A.D. Even before that, Irene was one of the more popular names during the Roman Empire. Its popularity continued right until the middle of the twentieth century, when it suddenly seemed to run out of steam. Today, the many variations of the name are more common than the original root. Variations: *Arina,*

Arinka, Eirena, Eirene, Eirini, Erena, Erene, Ereni, Errena, Irayna, Ireen, Iren, Irena, Irenea, Irenee, Irenka, Irina, Irine, Irini, Irisha, Irka, Irusya, Iryna, Orina, Orya, Oryna, Reena, Reenie, Rina, Yarina, Yaryna.

IRIS *(Greek)* Flower. Greek goddess of the rainbow. Variations: *Irisa, Irisha.*

ISABEL *(Spanish)* Pledge of God. Version of Elizabeth. Though Isabel seems like it might be too ethnic or too old-fashioned to be popular, the truth is that it is one of the more popular names around and still growing. Actress Isabella Rossellini has helped to bring exposure to this name. Variations: *Isa, Isabeau, Isabelita, Isabella, Isabelle, Isobel, Issi, Issie, Issy, Izabel, Izabele, Izabella, Izabelle, Izebela, Ysabel.*

ISADORA *(Greek)* Gift from Isis. Feminine version of Isidore. Variation: *Isidora.*

IVANA *(Slavic)* God is good. Feminine version of Ivan. Variations: *Iva, Ivania, Ivanka, Ivanna, Ivannia.*

IVORY *(Latin)* Ivory. Ivory is as popular among African-American parents as is its counterpart, Ebony, though I think it might be too much to name twins Ebony and Ivory. Parents in many African-American families like the name Ivory because it shows pride in their heritage, whether it alludes to the substance itself or to Africa's Ivory coast. Variations: *Ivoreen, Ivorine.*

IVY *(English)* Plant. Variations: *Iva, Ivey, Ivie.*

Slightly Daring Choices

IDRA *(Hebrew)* Fig tree.

IDRIYA *(Hebrew)* Duck. Variation: *Idria.*

Eastern European Girls' Names

Just as Eastern European boys' names contain suffixes, the same goes for girls—"-slava" and "-slawa" (in Polish) are added to the end of names. These suffixes mean "glorious," and so, for example, the name Jaroslava means "glorious spring." Other popular Eastern European girls' names include:

BELA	**LUDMILLA**	**SOFIA**
GALINA	**MARINA**	**TATIANA**
IRINA	**NATALYA**	**YELENA**
LARISA	**OLGA**	

IGNACIA *(Latin)* On fire. Feminine version of Ignatius. Variations: *Ignatia, Ignazia, Iniga.*

IKIA *(Hebrew)* God helps me.

ILANA *(Hebrew)* Tree. Variations: *Elana, Elanit, Ilanit.*

ILONA *(Hungarian)* Pretty.

ILSE *(German)* Pledge of God. Variation of Elizabeth. Variations: *Ilsa, Ilsie.*

IMA *(Japanese)* Now. Variations: *Imae, Imako.*

IMALA *(Native American)* Discipline.

IMAN *(Arabic)* Faith.

IMANA *(African: Rwandan)* God of all.

IMARA *(African: Swahili)* Firm.

IMELDA *(Italian)* Embracing the fight. Variation: *Imalda.*

IMIN *(Arabic)* Conviction.

IMPERIA *(Latin)* Imperial.

INANNA *(Babylonian)* The goddess of war.

INAS *(Arabic)* Friendly. Variations: *Inaya, Inayah.*

INDIA *(English)* The country.

INDIGO *(Latin)* Dark blue.

INDIRA *(Hindu)* Beauty. The famous Indian prime minister, Indira Gandhi (1917–1984), is most well known for this name.

INDRA *(Hindu)* Supreme god; god of the sky.

INDRE *(French)* River.

INOA *(Hawaiian)* Chant.

INOCENCIA *(Spanish)* Innocence. Variations: *Inocenta, Inocentia.*

INOLA *(Native American: Cherokee)* Black fox.

IOLA *(Welsh)* Worthy god. Variation: *Iole.*

IOLANA *(Hawaiian)* Violet.

IONA *(Greek)* Scottish island.

IONE *(Greek)* Violet. Variations: *Ionia, Ionie.*

IRMA *(German)* Complete.

IRVETTE *(English)* Friend of the sea. Feminine version of Irving.

ISHA *(Hebrew)* Woman; (Hindu) Protector.

ISHANA *(Hindu)* Desire. Variation: *Ishani.*

ISHI *(Japanese)* Stone. Variations: *Ishie, Ishiko, Ishiyo, Shiko, Shiuo.*

ISIS *(Egyptian)* Goddess of ancient Egypt.

ISLA *(Scottish)* Name of a river in Scotland.

ISMAELA *(Hebrew)* God listens. Variations: *Isma, Mael, Maella.*

ISMAT *(Arabic)* To protect.

ISMENE *(Greek)* The daughter of Oedipus and Jocasta.

ISRA *(Arabic)* Night trip.

ISTVAN *(Greek)* Crowned with laurels.

ITALIA *(Latin)* From Italy. Variation: *Talia.*

ITIAH *(Hebrew)* God is here. Variations: *Itia, Itiel, Itil, Itiya.*

ITIDAL *(Arabic)* Middle of the road.

IULIA *(Hawaiian)* A Roman clan name that also means young. Hawaiian version of Julia. Variations: *Iuliana, Kulia, Kuliana.*

IUNIA *(Hawaiian)* Good victory. Variation: *Eunika.*

IUSITINA *(Hawaiian)* Righteous. Variation: *Iukikina.*

IVEREM *(African: Nigerian)* Good luck.

IVRIA *(Hebrew)* In Abraham's land. Variations: *Ivriah, Ivrit.*

Living on the Edge

IANEKE *(Hawaiian)* God is good. Variations: *Ianete, Iani.*

IANTHE *(Greek)* Flower. Variation: *Iantha.*

IBTIHAJ *(Arabic)* Happiness.

IBTISAM *(Arabic)* To smile. Variations: *Ebtissam, Essam, Ibtissam, Issam.*

ICHCHANI *(Hindu)* Queen of twelfth century.

IDAA *(Hindu)* Earth. Variation: *Ila.*

IDE *(Irish)* Thirst. Variation: *Ita.*

IDONY *(Scandinavian)* Goddess of spring. Variations: *Idonea, Idun, Itiunnr.*

IDOWU *(African: Nigerian)* First child born after twins.

IDUNA *(Scandinavian: Norwegian)* Beloved. Variation: *Idonia.*

IENIPA *(Hawaiian)* Fair lady.

IFAMA *(African: Nigerian)* All is well.

IFE *(African: Nigerian)* Love.

IFETAYO *(African: Nigerian)* Love is joyful.

IHAB *(Arabic)* To give.

IHSAN *(Arabic)* Benevolent. Variations: *Ihsana, Ihsanah.*

IKABELA *(Hawaiian)* Pledged to God. Variation: *Ikapela.*

IKU *(Japanese)* Nurturing. Variation: *Ikuko.*

IKUSEGHAN *(African: Nigerian)* Peace is better than war. Variation: *Ikusegham.*

ILESHA *(Hindu)* God of the earth.

ILIA *(English)* One who comes from the town of Troy, also known as Ilium.

ILIMA *(Hawaiian)* Flower.

ILKA *(Slavic)* Admirer.

ILMA *(English)* Variation of William.

IMMACULADA *(Spanish)* Innocent. Variation: *Immaculata.*

IMMOKALEE *(Native American: Cherokee)* Falling water.

IN *(Korean)* Mankind.

INA *(Greek)* Pure. Variation: *Ena.*

INAM *(Arabic)* Charitable. Variation: *Enam.*

INDRANEE *(Hindu)* Wife of Indra, the god of the sky. Variation: *Indrayani.*

INDU *(Hindu)* Moon.

INGEBORG *(Scandinavian)* Protector of Ing, Norwegian god of peace. Variations: *Ingaberg, Ingaborg, Ingeberg, Inger, Ingmar.*

INGEGERD *(Scandinavian)* Ing's fortress. Variations: *Ingegard, Ingjerd.*

INSHTATHEUMBA *(Native American: Omaha)* Bright eyes.

IOLANTHE *(English)* Violet.

IOSEPINE *(Hawaiian)* God adds. Variations: *Iokepina, Iokepine, Kepina.*

IPHIGENIA *(Greek)* Sacrifice. Variation: *Iphigenie.*

ISAMU *(Japanese)* Active.

ISATAS *(Native American)* Snow. Variation: *Istas.*

ISAURA *(Greek)* Ancient country in Asia. Variation: *Isaure.*

ISEULT *(Irish)* Ruler of the ice. Variations: *Hisolda, Isolda, Isolde, Ysenit, Ysolte.*

ISOKA *(African: Nigerian)* Gift from God. Variations: *Isoke, Soka.*

ITINSA *(Native American: Tlingit)* Waterfall.

ITO *(Japanese)* Fiber.

ITUHA *(Native American)* Oak tree.

IUANA *(Native American)* Wind blowing over a bubbling stream.

IWA *(Japanese)* Rock.

IWALANI *(Hawaiian)* Sea bird.

IYABO *(African: Nigerian)* Mother comes back.

IZDIHAR *(Arabic)* Blossoming.

IZEGBE *(African: Nigerian)* Long-awaited child. Variation: *Izebe.*

IZUSA *(Native American)* White stone.

Tried and True Classics

JACEY *(American)* Newly created, possibly from the letters "J" and "C." Variations: *Jace, Jacy.*

JACINTA *(Spanish)* Hyacinth. Feminine version of Jacinto. Variations: *Glacinda, Glacintha, Jacinda, Jacintha, Jacinthe, Jacinthia, Jacki, Jacky, Jacquetta, Jacqui, Jacquie, Jacynth, Jacyntha, Jacynthe.*

JACQUELINE *(French)* He who replaces. Feminine version of Jacob. Jacqueline's heritage is undoubtedly French, however, the late Jackie Kennedy Onassis's glamour and poise served to put an American spin on the name. Interestingly enough, although Jackie O is as loved as ever, the name Jacqueline is still not as popular as it was back in the '20s when it regularly hit the top fifty list. Variations: *Jacaline, Jacalyn, Jackalin, Jackalyn, Jackeline, Jackelyn, Jacketta, Jackette, Jacki, Jackie, Jacklin, Jacklyn, Jacky, Jaclyn, Jaclynn, Jacoba, Jacobette, Jacobina, Jacolyn, Jacqualine, Jacqualyn, Jacqualynn, Jacquelean, Jacquelene, Jacquelin, Jacquelyn, Jacquelyne, Jacquelynn, Jacquelynne, Jacqueta, Jacquetta, Jacquiline, Jacquline, Jacqulynn, Jaculine, Jakelyn, Jaqueline, Jaquelyn, Jaquith.*

JADE *(Spanish)* Jade stone. Variations: *Jada, Jadee, Jadira, Jady, Jaida, Jaide, Jayde, Jaydra.*

JAIMIE *(English)* One who replaces. Feminine version of James. Jaimie was first popularized as a great girls' name in the '70s because it conveys so much energy and fitness, and a bit of tomboyishness—yet a girl with this name wouldn't hesitate to get dressed up to go out to dinner. Variations: *Jaime, Jaimey, Jaimi, Jaimy, Jamee, Jami, Jamie, Jayme.*

JAN *(Hebrew)* God is good. Variations: *Jana, Janina, Janine, Jann, Janna.*

JANE *(English)* God's grace. Variations: *Janey, Janica, Janice, Janicia, Janie, Janiece, Janis, Janise, Jannice, Jannis, Jayne, Sheenagh, Sheenah, Sheina, Shena.*

JANESSA *(American)* Combination of Jan and Vanessa. Variations: *Janesse, Janissa, Jannessa, Jenessa.*

JANET *(English)* Diminutive of Jane. Janet could be seeing more activity in the baby name department these days owing to the popularity of singer Janet Jackson, however, the name hasn't really been in vogue in this country since the '60s, when Miss Jackson was born. Other famous Janets include Janet Gaynor, Janet Leigh, and Janet Reno. Janet became an independent name in its own right around the start of the 1800s, and since then has spawned a number of interesting variations. Variations: *Janeta, Janeth, Janett, Janetta, Janette, Jannet, Janneth, Jannetta, Jenet, Jenett, Jenetta, Jenette, Jennetta, Jennette, Joanet, Sinead, Siobahn, Sioban, Siobhan.*

JANINE *(English)* God is good. Feminine version of John. Variations: *Janina, Jannine, Jeneen, Jenine.*

JASMINE *(Persian)* Flower. If it wasn't for the great success of the animated Disney movie *Aladdin*, Jasmine would probably have been relegated to a footnote of popular flower names that first hit around the turn of the century. But Princess Jasmine—and, to a lesser extent, actress Jasmine Guy have revived this wonderfully feminine name, and it has not yet hit its peak the second time around. Variations: *Jasmeen, Jasmin, Jasmina, Jazmin, Jazmine, Jessamine, Jessamyn, Yasiman, Yasman, Yasmine.*

JEAN *(Scottish)* God is good. Feminine version of John. Variations: *Jeana, Jeanette, Jeanna, Jeanne, Jeannie, Jennette.*

JEMIMA *(Hebrew)* Dove. Variations: *Jamima, Jemimah, Jemmie, Jemmimah, Jemmy, Mima, Mimma.*

JENNA *(Arabic)* Little bird. Variations: *Jannarae, Jena, Jenesi, Jenn, Jennabel, Jennah, Jennalee, Jennalyn, Jennasee.*

JENNIFER *(Welsh)* White; smooth; soft. Actually Jennifer is a version of Guinevere. It is perhaps the best example of the kind of trendy names that exploded in popularity overnight in the mid-'70s all the way up to the early '90s before slowing down. In Britain, the name peaked earlier, hitting number six in 1950. Variations: *Genn, Gennifer, Genny, Ginnifer, Jen, Jena, Jenalee, Jenalyn, Jenarae, Jenene, Jenetta Jenita, Jennis, Jeni, Jenice, Jeniece, Jenifer, Jeniffer, Jenilee, Jenilynn, Jenise, Jenn, Jennessa, Jenni, Jennie, Jennika, Jennilyn, Jennyann, Jennylee, Jeny, Jinny.*

JERALYN *(American)* Combination of Jerry and Marilyn. Variations: *Jerelyn, Jerilyn, Jerilynn, Jerralyn, Jerrilyn.*

JESSICA *(Hebrew)* He sees. Like Jennifer, Jessica was a regular fixture on the baby name hit parade from the mid-'70s, and it's still popular. Currently, singer Jessica Simpson is keeping this name in the spotlight. It made its first appearance in the Bible in the Book of Genesis. Shakespeare also used the name in *The Merchant of Venice*, giving the name to the daughter of Shylock. Parents today who like the name but who don't want to be considered trendy are choosing other variations related to Jessica. Variations: *Jesica, Jess, Jessa, Jesse, Jesseca, Jessey, Jessi, Jessie, Jessika.*

JEWEL *(French)* Jewel. Variation: *Jewelle.*

JILL *(English)* Young. Shortened version of Jillian. Some famous Jills include actresses Jill Ireland and Jill St. John. Variations: *Gil, Gill, Gyl, Gyll, Jil, Jilli, Jillie, Jilly, Jyl, Jyll.*

JILLIAN *(English)* Young. Variations: *Gilli, Gillian, Gillie, Jilian, Jiliana, Jillana, Jilliana, Jillianne, Jilliyanne, Jillyan, Jillyanna.*

JOAN *(Hebrew)* God is good. Like many of its traditional counterparts, Joan has gone in and out of style over the course of many centuries. Extremely popular during the Middle Ages, it seemed to wane in the 1600s, until the first half of the twentieth century, when it became one of the most popular names around. No doubt actresses Joan Crawford,

Joan Bennett, and Joan Fontaine kept the name in the public eye. Variations: *Joani, Joanie, Joannie, Jonee, Joni.*

JOANNE *(English)* God is good. Variations: *Joana, Joanna, Joannah, Johanna, Johanne.*

JOCELYN *(English)* Unknown definition, possibly a combination of Joyce and Lynn. Variations: *Jocelin, Joceline, Jocelyne, Joci, Jocie, Josaline, Joscelin, Josceline, Joscelyn, Joseline, Joselyn, Joselyne, Josiline, Josline.*

JODI *(Hebrew)* Praised. Variations: *Jodie, Jody.*

JORDAN *(English)* To descend. The name Jordan has a very curious background: During the Crusades, Christians who returned home brought water from the Jordan River for the express purpose of baptizing their children. As a result, many of those children were named Jordan—the boys at least. The name really didn't start to catch on for girls until the 1980s. Today, alas, Jordan is beginning to show the signs of strain that many androgynous names go through: Parents are ceasing to consider the name for their sons. Variations: *Jordana, Jordon, Jordyn.*

JORGINA *(Hispanic)* Farmer.

JOSEPHINE *(Hebrew)* God will add. Feminine version of Joseph. Variations: *Jo, Joey, Jojo, Josefa, Josefina, Josefine, Josepha, Josephe, Josephene, Josephina, Josetta, Josette, Josey, Josi, Josie.*

JOY *(English)* Happiness. Variations: *Gioia, Joi, Joie, Joya, Joye.*

JOYCE *(Latin)* Joyous. Joyce actually started out as a boys' name. It was the name of a saint in the seventh century A.D. This usage continued occasionally until the late Middle Ages, but Joyce started to be regularly used only during the nineteenth century. During the flapper era, Joyce was the third most common name for girls, which lasted through the '50s. Variations: *Joice, Joyousa.*

JUDITH *(Hebrew)* Of Judah; admired, praised. Variations: *Jitka, Jucika, Judey, Judi, Judie, Judit, Judita, Judite, Juditha, Judithe, Judy, Judye, Jutka.*

Most Popular Girls' Names from the 1970s

Although boys' names were reasonably run-of-the-mill during the 1970s, girls' names strayed a bit more off the beaten path.

1. Michelle
2. Jennifer
3. Kimberly
4. Lisa
5. Tracy
6. Kelly
7. Nicole
8. Angela
9. Pamela
10. Christine
11. Dawn
12. Amy
13. Deborah
14. Karen
15. Julie
16. Mary
17. Laura
18. Stacey
19. Catherine
20. Lori
21. Tammy
22. Elizabeth
23. Shannon
24. Stephanie
25. Kristin
26. Heather
27. Susan
28. Sandra
29. Denise
30. Theresa
31. Christina
32. Tina
33. Cynthia
34. Melissa
35. Patricia
36. Renee
37. Cheryl
38. Sherry
39. Donna
40. Erica
41. Rachel
42. Sharon
43. Linda
44. Barbara
45. Jacqueline
46. Rhonda
47. Andrea
48. Rebecca
49. Wendy
50. Maria

JULIA *(Latin)* Young. Roman clan name. Julia is a name that, shall we say, has legs. It's popular all over the world and has been since women in ancient Rome gave the name to their babies in honor of the emperor Julius Caesar. In this century, Julia was popular from the years immediately following World War II throughout the mid-'70s, when it rested for about a decade until actress Julia Roberts burst onto the scene and made it very popular again. Parents seem to prefer Julia over the perkier Julie. Variations: *Giulia, Iulia, Jula, Julcia, Julee, Juley, Juli, Juliana, Juliane, Julianna, Julianne, Julica, Julie, Julina, Juline, Julinka, Juliska, Julissa, Julka, Yula, Yulinka, Yuliya, Yulka, Yulya.*

JULIET *(English)* Downy. Variations: *Julieta, Julietta, Juliette, Julita.*

JUNE *(English)* The month. Variations: *Junae, Junel, Junella, Junelle, Junette, Juno.*

JUSTINE *(French)* Just. Feminine version of Justin. Variation: *Justina.*

Slightly Daring Choices

JA *(Hawaiian)* Fiery.

JAAMINI *(Hindu)* Night.

JADWIGE *(Polish)* Safety in war. Variation: *Jadwiga.*

JAE *(Latin)* Jaybird. Variations: *Jaya, Jaylee, Jayleen, Jaylene, Jaylynn.*

JAEL *(Hebrew)* Mountain goat.

JAIRA *(Spanish)* God teaches.

JALA *(Arabic)* Clear.

JALEESA *(African-American)* Jay + Lisa. Variations: *Ja Leesa, Ja Lisa.*

JALINDA *(African-American)* Jay + Linda. Variation: *Jalynda.*

JAMAICA *(English)* The country.

JAMELIA *(Arabic)* Handsome. Feminine version of Jamal. Variations: *Jamell, Jamila.*

JAMILA *(Arabic)* Beautiful. Variations: *Gamila, Gamilah, Jameela, Jamilah, Jamilla, Jamillah, Jamille, Jamillia.*

JANAE *(Hebrew)* God answers. Variations: *Janai, Janais, Janay, Janaya, Janaye, Jannae, Jeanae, Jeanay, Jenae, Jenai, Jenay, Jenaya, Jenee, Jennae, Jennay.*

JANAN *(Arabic)* Spirited.

JANITA *(Scandinavian)* God is good. Variations: *Jaantje, Jannike, Jans, Jansje.*

JANY *(Hindu)* Fire.

JAPERA *(African: Zimbabwean)* Complete.

JARDENA *(Hebrew)* To descend. Feminine version of Jordan.

JARITA *(Hindu)* Mother.

JARMILA *(Czech)* One who loves spring.

JASWINDER *(Hindu)* The god of the sky's thunder.

JAVIERA *(Spanish)* Shining. Variations: *Javeera, Xaviera.*

JAY *(Latin)* Happy. Variations: *Jai, Jaie, Jaye.*

JAYA *(Hindu)* Victory. Variations: *Ja Wanti, Janatika, Jayamala, Jayanti, Jayashree, Jayna, Jayt.*

JAYLENE *(English)* Blue jay. Variations: *Jae, Jaye, Jayline, Jaynell.*

JAYNE *(Hindu)* Victorious.

JAZLYN *(American)* Combination of Jazz and Lynn. Variations: *Jasleen, Jaslyn, Jaslynn, Jazlynn, Jazzalyn, Jazzlyn.*

JELENA *(Russian)* Light.

JEM *(English)* Supplanter or heel.

JEMINA *(Hebrew)* Right-handed. Variations: *Jem, Jemi, Jemma, Jemmi, Jemmie, Jemmy, Mina.*

JEMMA *(English)* Plant bud.

JENA *(Hindu)* Patience.

JENELLE *(English)* Yielding. Version of Guinevere.

JENNICA *(English)* God is good. Variation: *Jenica.*

JEREMIA *(Hebrew)* The Lord is great. Feminine version of Jeremiah.

JERICA *(English)* Unknown definition. Variations: *Jerika, Jerrica, Jerrika.*

JERSEY *(English)* Place name.

JIANA *(American)* Unknown definition.

JIMENA *(Spanish)* Heard.

JINX *(Latin)* Spell. Variation: *Jynx.*

JIRINA *(Czech)* Farmer. Variation: *Jiruska.*

JISELLE *(American)* Allegiance.

JOBY *(Hebrew)* Persecuted. Feminine version of Job. Variations: *Jobi, Jobie.*

JODELLE *(French)* Last name. Variations: *Jo Dell, Jodell.*

JOELLE *(French)* God is Lord. Feminine version of Joel. Variations: *Joda, Joell, Joella, Joellen, Joellyn, Joely.*

JOLÁN *(Hungarian)* Purple flower.

JOLÁNTA *(Czech)* Violet. Variation: *Jolana.*

JOLENE *(American)* Jolene is a combination name, formed by using "Jo" and "lene," a popular suffix in the beginnings of the baby boom. As you can see, the variations in spelling tended to get very creative. Jolene is considered by some to be a contemporary version of Josephine. Variations: *Jolean, Joleen, Jolian, Jolin, Joline, Jolinn, Jolinne, Jolyn, Jolynn, Jolynne, Jolyon.*

JOLIE *(French)* Pretty. Variations: *Jolee, Joley, Joli, Joline, Joly.*

JONAVA *(African-American)* Unknown definition.

JONELLA *(English)* God is good to all. Variations: *Jonelle, Joni, Jonie, Jony.*

JONINA *(Hebrew)* Dove. Variations: *Jona, Jonati, Jonit, Yona, Yonit, Yonita.*

JONNA *(English)* God is good. Variation of John. Variations: *Jahnna, Johnna.*

JONQUIL *(English)* Flower. Variations: *Jonquila, Jonquille.*

JORA *(Hebrew)* Autumn rain. Variation: *Jorah.*

JUANA *(Spanish)* God is good. Feminine form of John. Variations: *Juanetta, Juanita.*

JULA *(Polish)* Downy.

JUMANA *(Arabic)* Pearl. Variation: *Jumanah.*

Living on the Edge

JAE-HWA *(Korean)* Very beautiful.

JAFFA *(Hebrew)* Beautiful. Feminine version of Yaffa. Variations: *Jaffi, Jaffice, Jaffit, Jafit.*

JAHA *(African: Swahili)* Dignity.

JALAJAA *(Hindu)* Lotus. Variation: *Jalitaa.*

JALANEELI *(Hindu)* Moss.

JANAKI *(Hindu)* Mother. Variation: *Janika.*

JARKA *(Czech)* Spring. Variations: *Jaruse, Jaruska.*

JARNSAXA *(Scandinavian)* Ancient mythological figure. Variation: *Iarnsaxa.*

JAROSLAVA *(Czech)* Glorious spring.

JATHIBIYYA *(Arabic)* Attractive. Variations: *Gathbiyya, Gathbiyyah, Gathibiyya, Gathibiyyah, Gazbiyya, Gazbiyyah, Jathbiyya, Jathbiyyah, Jathibiyyah.*

JAWAHIR *(Arabic)* Gem. Variation: *Gawahir.*

JENDAN *(African: Zimbabwean)* Thankful.

JENDAYA *(African: Zimbabwean)* To give thanks.

JETHRA *(Hebrew)* Plenty.

JETTE *(Scandinavian: Danish)* Black. Variation: *Jetta.*

JEZEBEL *(Hebrew)* Virginal. Variations: *Jez, Jezzie.*

JINDRISKA *(Czech)* Ruler at home. Variations: *Jindra, Jindrina, Jindruska.*

JIN-KYONG *(Korean)* Bright jewel.
JING-WEI *(Chinese)* Small bird.
JINNAT *(Hindu)* Heaven.
JOAKIMA *(Hebrew)* God will judge.
JOAQUINA *(Spanish)* Flower. Variation: *Joaquine.*
JOCASTA *(Greek)* Shining moon.
JOCOSA *(Latin)* Playful.
JODHA *(Hindu)* Sixteenth century Hindu woman.
JOKE *(Hawaiian)* Happy.
JOKLA *(African: Swahili)* Robe of adornment.
JOVITA *(Latin)* Gladden.
JOYITA *(Spanish)* Jewel.
JUABAI *(Hindu)* Mother of the founder of the Maratha confederacy in the seventeenth century.
JUH *(Hindu)* Flower.
JUMAPIU *(African: Kenyan)* Born on Sunday.
JUMOKE *(African: Nigerian)* Loved by all.
JUN *(Chinese)* Truth of life. Variation: *Junko.*
JUTKA *(Hungarian)* Praise God.
JYOTI *(Hindu)* Light of the moon. Variation: *Jyotsana.*

Tried and True Classics

KACI *(English)* He commands peace. Feminine version of Casimir. Variations: *Kacey, Kacia, Kacie, Kacy, Kaycee, Kayci.*

KAITLIN *(English)* Combination of Kate and Lynn. Variations: *Kaitlinn, Kaitlinne, Kaitlynn, Katelin, Katelyn, Katelynne.*

KALLI *(Greek)* Singing lark. Variations: *Cal, Calli, Callie, Colli, Kal, Kallie, Kallu, Kally.*

KALLISTA *(Greek)* Most beautiful. Variations: *Cala, Calesta, Calista, Callie, Cally, Kala, Kalesta, Kali, Kalie, Kalika, Kalista, Kalli, Kallie, Kally, Kallysta.*

KAMILA *(Arabic)* Perfect. You might think that Kamila is a variation of the name Camille, but it has totally different roots and definition. Of course, some parents have deliberately designed the name so that it is a variation of Camille, but in its original form, Kamila is Arabic through and through. Variations: *Kameela, Kamilah, Kamilla, Kamillah, Kamla.*

KARA *(Greek)* Dear. Kara started out life spelled the Italian way with a "C," but somehow it became more popular with a "K." In any case, Kara is both exotic and familiar and parents should start to consider it more. Variations: *Kaira, Karah, Karalee, Karalyn, Karalynn, Kari, Kariana, Karianna, Karianne, Karie, Karielle, Karrah, Karrie, Kary.*

KAREN *(Scandinavian)* Diminutive of Katerina. Variations: *Caren, Carin, Caryn, Karin, Karina, Karon, Kerena.*

KARMEN *(English)* Garden. Variation of Carmen. Variations: *Karmina, Karmine, Karmita.*

KATHERINE *(Greek)* Pure. Katherine and all of its derivatives have been popular since the days of its Greek origin, when it was known as Aikaterina. Some of the most famous Katherines in this country have been Katherine Hepburn and authors Katherine Anne Porter and Katherine Mansfield. Though many parents today are favoring the more Gaelic forms of the name—like Katriona and Caitriona—Katherine itself presents a good choice simply based on all the variations you can choose from later. Variations: *Caitriona, Caren, Caron, Caryn, Caye, Kaethe, Kai, Kaila, Kait, Kaitlin, Karen, Karena, Karin, Karina, Karine, Karon, Karyn, Karyna, Karynn, Kata, Kataleen, Katalin, Katalina, Katarina, Kate, Katee, Kateke, Katerina, Katerinka, Katey, Katharin, Katharina, Katharine, Katharyn, Kathereen, Katherin, Katherina, Kathey, Kathi, Kathie, Kathleen, Kathlyn, Kathlynn, Kathren, Kathrine, Kathryn, Kathryne, Kathy, Kati, Katia, Katica, Katie, Katina, Katrina, Katrine, Katriona, Katryna, Kattrina, Katushka, Katy, Karrin, Katya, Kay, Kisan, Kit, Kitti, Kittie, Kitty, Kotinka, Kotryna, Yekaterina.*

KAYLA *(English)* Pure. Variation of Katherine. Kayla may have started to become popular about the same time that the name Caleb started to appear more frequently for boys. Although in definition they are not closely related, they both share a lyrical but compact sound. Once Kayla hit the American consciousness, it hit big and spread like wildfire. Today, Kayla is solidly entrenched on the top ten list for girls' names, even though it was nowhere to be seen even ten years ago. Variations: *Kaela, Kaelee, Kaelene, Kaeli, Kaeleigh, Kaelie, Kaelin, Kaelyn, Kaila, Kailan, Kailee, Kaileen, Kailene, Kailey, Kailin, Kailynne, Kalan, Kalee, Kaleigh, Kalen, Kaley, Kalie, Kalin, Kalyn, Kayana, Kayanna, Kaye, Kaylan, Kaylea, Kayleen, Kayleigh, Kaylene, Kayley, Kayli, Kaylle.*

KELLY *(Irish)* Female soldier. Kelly has had multiple personalities over the last hundred years: first it was a last name, then many Irish and American parents chose it for their boys, and today it is almost exclusively a girls' name. Kelly was at its most popular in the '70s, and parents who have selected the name for their daughters since then have, more often than not, selected one of the name's expressive variations.

Variations: *Kealey, Kealy, Keeley, Keelie, Keellie, Keely, Keighley, Keiley, Keilly, Keily, Kellee, Kelley, Kellia, Kellie, Kellina, Kellisa.*

KELSEY *(English)* Island. Variations: *Kelcey, Kelci, Kelcie, Kelcy, Kellsie, Kelsa, Kelsea, Kelsee, Kelseigh, Kelsi, Kelsie, Kelsy.*

KENDALL *(English)* Valley of the River Tent. Last name. Variations: *Kendal, Kendel, Kendell.*

KENDRA *(English)* Origin unknown; possibly a combination of Kenneth and Sandra. Kendra first surfaced in the United States in the 1940s, and even though it sounds like it could have come from Great Britain, it didn't reach those shores until the later part of the '60s. Variations: *Kena, Kenadrea, Kendria, Kenna, Kindra, Kinna, Kyndra.*

KERRY *(Irish)* County in Ireland. Like its counterpart, Kelly, Kerry was once a very popular name in this country. However, it seems as though its variations and creative spellings have gotten the better of it, rendering the original form almost obsolete. Like Kelly, Kerry started out as a boys' name. Variations: *Kera, Keree, Keri, Keriana, Keriann, Kerianna, Kerianne, Kerra, Kerrey, Kerri, Kerrianne, Kerrie.*

KIMBERLY *(English)* King's meadow. Kimberly was a well-used name at the turn of the century for boys, since it was a town in South Africa and many men were fighting a war there. To commemorate the battles, parents named their sons after the town. By the 1940s, Kimberly had already begun to take root as a girls' name, and it turned into one of the most popular names in the '60s and '70s. Today, however, it appears less frequently both here and in Britain. Variations: *Kim, Kimba, Kimba Lee, Kimball, Kimber, Kimberlea, Kimberlee, Kimberlei, Kimberleigh, Kimberley, Kimberli, Kimberlie, Kimberlyn, Kimbley, Kimmi, Kimmie, Kymberlee.*

KIRSTEN *(Scandinavian)* Anointed. Feminine version of Christian. Kirsten and its variations have always seemed to be underused in this country, compared to their relatives Kristen and Christine. However, because it's been underused,

Kirsten is becoming more popular than its counterparts today. Also, the visibility of actress Kirsten Dunst doesn't hurt. Variations: *Keerstin, Kersten, Kersti, Kerstie, Kerstin, Kiersten, Kierstin, Kirsta, Kirsti, Kirstie, Kirstin, Kirstine, Kirsty, Kirstyn, Kirstynn, Kyrstin.*

KORA *(Greek)* Girl. Variations: *Cora, Corabel, Corabella, Corabelle, Corabellita, Corake, Coralyn, Corella, Corena, Coretta, Corey, Cori, Corie, Corilla, Corinna, Corinne, Corissa, Corlene, Corri, Corrie, Corrin, Corrissa, Corry, Cory, Coryn, Coryna, Corynn, Korabell, Koree, Koreen, Korella, Korenda, Korette, Korey, Korie, Korilla, Korissa, Korri, Korrie, Korrina, Korry, Kory, Korynna, Koryssa.*

KORINA *(English)* Maiden. Korina has been around in the United States and in Britain since the middle of the nineteenth century, but seems to have always been slightly on the sidelines. This should make it a good choice for parents today who are looking for something just a bit different. Variations: *Korinna, Korinne, Korrina.*

KYLIE *(Australian Aboriginal)* Boomerang. Variations: *Kye, Kyla, Kylene.*

KYRA *(Greek)* Lady. Variations: *Keera, Keira, Kira, Kyrene, Kyria.*

Slightly Daring Choices

KACIA *(African-American)* Unknown definition. Variations: *Kaisha, Kasha, Kasia.*

KADIAH *(Hebrew)* A pitcher. Variations: *Kadia, Kadya.*

KAI *(Japanese)* Forgiveness; (Hawaiian) Sea. Although most people haven't heard of Kai as the name for a girl, they may be familiar with it as a word, since it frequently occurs in many Hawaiian place names. Kai has just recently started to appear in the United States as a name for girls. This is a name that is on its way up overall. Variations: *Kaiko, Kaiyo.*

Asian Girls' Names

Asian girls are frequently named after plants or creatures in nature. In the Chinese culture, as in others, boys are more highly prized than girls, especially since the country's one-child-per-family rule.

Like Chinese parents, Japanese mothers and fathers tend to give their daughters prettier, more descriptive names than they give their sons, although perhaps for more benevolent reasons. Japanese girls are frequently given names that reflect the Japanese culture's more favorable attitude toward the fairer sex: Kazu, which translates to meek and loyal, is a favorite. Girls also receive names inspired by nature that also reflect the moral attitudes of the society: Miyuki, or pure snow, is one such example.

KALI *(Hindu)* Energy. Variation: *Kalli.*

KALILA *(Arabic)* Beloved. As you can see, Kalila has spawned a wide variety of variant spellings. It's used most often in Arabic countries in much the same way that we use Honey or Sweetie. It is a pretty name and not entirely unfamiliar, which makes it a good candidate for increased popularity in the United States. Variations: *Kaila, Kailey, Kaleela, Kaleigh, Kalie, Kalilla, Kaly, Kayle, Kaylee, Kayleen, Kayleigh, Kaylene, Kayley, Kaylie, Kaylil, Kylila.*

KALINA *(Polish)* Flower. Variations: *Kaleen, Kaleena, Kalena, Kalene.*

KALINDA *(Hindu)* The sun. Variation: *Kaleenda.*

KAMALI *(African: Zimbabwean)* Guardian angel of infants. Most Americans are familiar with the designer Norma Kamali but wouldn't be aware that this particularly attractive name could be the first name of their daughter.

KARIS *(Greek)* Grace.

KARISMA *(English)* Variation of Charisma.

KARISSA *(Greek)* Dear.

KARLENE *(Latvian)* Man. Feminine version of Charles. Variations: *Karleen, Karlen, Karlena, Karlina.*

KARMA *(Hindu)* Fate.

KARMEL *(Hebrew)* Garden of grapes. Variations: *Cami, Carmel, Carmia, Karmeli, Karmi, Karmia, Karmiel, Karmielle.*

KASINDA *(African)* Child born after twins.

KASMIRA *(Slavic)* Bringing peace. Feminine version of Casimir.

KEENA *(English)* Unknown definition.

KEESHA *(African-American)* Newly created. Variations: *Keisha, Keshia, Kiesha.*

KELA *(Hawaiian)* Valley. Variation: *Dela.*

KELDA *(Scandinavian)* Fountain or spring. Variation: *Kilde.*

KELILA *(Hebrew)* Crown. Variations: *Kaile, Kaille, Kalia, Kayla, Kayle, Kyle, Kylia.*

KELINA *(Hawaiian)* Moon goddess.

KENDA *(Native American)* Magic. Variations: *Kenada, Kenadi, Kendi, Kendie, Kendy, Kennda, Kenndi, Kenndie, Kenndy.*

KENISHA *(African-American)* Beautiful woman. Variations: *Keneisha, Keneshia, Kennesha.*

KENTON *(English)* Place name.

KENYA *(Hebrew)* African country.

KENZIE *(Scottish)* Light one.

KERANI *(Hindu)* Sacred bells. Variations: *Kera, Kerie, Kery.*

KEREM *(Hebrew)* Orchard.

KEREN *(Hebrew)* Animal horn. Variations: *Kerrin, Keryn.*

KERENSA *(Cornish)* Love. Variations: *Karensa, Karenza.*

KIANNAH *(American)* Variation of Hannah. Though most people in this country are familiar with Kia as the name of a car imported from Korea, increased exposure to the name—even as it is used to refer to a four-wheel-drive sports utility vehicle—should help it become more popular. Variations: *Kia, Kiana, Kianah, Kianna.*

KIARA *(American)* Unknown definition. Variations: *Keira, Kiarra, Kiera, Kierra.*

KIKI *(Spanish)* Nickname for Enriqueta.

KIKILIA *(Hawaiian)* Blind.

KILEY *(Gaelic)* Handsome. Variation: *Kilee.*

KILIA *(Hawaiian)* Heaven.

KINSEY *(English)* Family member.

KIRA *(Bulgarian)* Throne. Variations: *Kiran, Kirana, Kiri, Kirra.*

KIRAN *(Hindu)* Light. Variation: *Kirina.*

KIRBY *(English)* Farm near a church.

KIRI *(Hindu)* Amaranth. Variation: *Kirsi.*

KIRIAH *(Hebrew)* Village. Variations: *Kiria, Kirya.*

KIRIMA *(Intuit)* Hill.

KYLA *(Hebrew)* Crown.

KYLE *(Scottish)* Narrow land. Of course, by now, you can see the signs: This highly popular '90s name for boys has already started to develop a following among girls.

KYOKO *(Japanese)* Mirror.

KYRIE *(Irish)* Dark.

Living on the Edge

KALLIRROE *(Greek)* Beautiful stream. Variations: *Callirhoe, Callirhot, Calliroe, Callirrhoe, Callirroe, Callirrot.*
KAMA *(Hebrew)* Ripe.
KAME *(Japanese)* Tortoise. Variations: *Kameko, Kameyo.*
KAMEA *(Hawaiian)* Sole one.
KAMI *(Polynesian)* Love.
KANA *(Hindu)* Tiny. Variation: *Kanika.*
KANANI *(Hawaiian)* Beautiful.
KANARA *(Hebrew)* Canary. Variation: *Kanarit.*
KAPUA *(Hawaiian)* Flower.
KARENZA *(Scottish)* Love. Variations: *Kerensa, Kerenza.*
KARIDA *(Arabic)* Virginal.
KARIMA *(Arabic)* Noble. Variation: *Karimah.*
KARMIL *(Hebrew)* Red.
KARUNA *(Hindu)* Compassion.
KASA *(Native American)* Dress made of fur. Variations: *Kahsha, Kasha.*
KASI *(Hindu)* The holy city.
KATRIEL *(Hebrew)* Crowned by God.
KATSU *(Japanese)* Triumphant. Variation: *Katsuko.*
KATURA *(African: Zimbabwean)* Relief.
KAUILA *(Hawaiian)* Acclaimed woman.
KAULA *(Hawaiian)* Clairvoyant.
KAZU *(Japanese)* Obedient. Variation: *Kazuko.*
KELULA *(Yiddish)* Girlfriend.
KESAVA *(Hindu)* Lots of hair.
KESHET *(Hebrew)* Rainbow.
KESI *(African: Swahili)* Daughter with a difficult father.
KESIA *(African-American)* Favorite. Variation: *Keshia.*
KETI *(Polynesian)* Pure.
KETIFA *(Hebrew)* To pick. Variation: *Ketipha.*

KETINA *(Hebrew)* Girl.

KETURAH *(Hebrew)* Perfume. Variation: *Ketura.*

KETZIA *(Hebrew)* Tree bark. Variations: *Kazia, Kesiah, Ketzi, Ketziah, Kezi, Kezia, Keziah, Kissie, Kizzie, Kizzy.*

KEVINA *(Irish)* Handsome. Feminine version of Kevin. Variations: *Keva, Kevia, Kevyn.*

KEWANEE *(Native American: Potawatomi)* Prairie hen. Variation: *Kewaunee.*

KISA *(Russian)* Kitten. Variations: *Keesa, Kysa.*

KISHA *(African-American)* Newly created.

KISHANDA *(African-American)* Newly created.

KITA *(Japanese)* North.

KITRA *(Hebrew)* Wreath.

KIWA *(Japanese)* Born on the border. Variations: *Kiwako, Kiwayo.*

Tried and True Classics

LACEY *(French)* Last name. Some name experts consider Lacey to be the American version of Larissa. Lacey was a common French name in the nineteenth century. Variations: *Laci, Lacie, Lacy.*

LAKEISHA *(African-American)* Newly created. There are numerous ways to spell this name. Lakeisha can be traced to Ayesha, which many Muslim families choose for their daughters. Variations: *Lakecia, Lakeesha, Lakesha, Lakeshia, Laketia, Lakeysha, Lakeyshia, Lakicia, Lakiesha, Lakisha, Lakitia, Laquiesha, Laquiesha, Laquisha, Lekeesha, Lekeisha, Lekisha.*

LANA *(English)* Rock. Variation of Alanna. Lana Turner, of course, was probably the most famous Lana that Americans have known. By the way, her original name was Julia, just about the most popular name going today. Variations: *Lanae, Lanice, Lanna, Lannette.*

LARA *(English)* Famous. The song "Lara's Theme," from the romantic movie *Dr. Zhivago*, was probably the sole determining factor in a seeming surplus of baby girls named Lara after 1965. The trend didn't last that long, however; parents today are leaning more toward Larissa. Variations: *Laralaine, Laramae, Lari, Larina, Larinda, Larita.*

LATOYA *(African-American)* Newly created. The visibility—and some say, the notoriety—of LaToya Jackson has made her first name one of the more popular "La" names around. As her reputation continues to ebb and flow, it will be interesting to see how that affects the popularity of Latoya as a baby name. Variations: *Latoia, Latoyia, Latoyla.*

LAURA *(Latin)* Laurel. Laura has appeared in the top twenty-five list of girls' names since the mid-'70s. Laura can trace its roots back to the fourteenth century in Italy, when it was spelled Lora. Laura has been equally popular both in the United States and in Britain. Variations: *Larette, Laural, Laure, Laureana, Laurel, Lauren, Laurena, Lauret, Laureta, Lauretta, Laurette, Laurie, Laurin, Lauryn, Lora, Loren, Lorena, Loret, Loreta, Loretta, Lorette, Lori, Lorin, Lorita, Lorrie, Lorrin, Lorry, Loryn.*

LAVERNE *(French)* Springlike. Variations: *Lavern, Laverna, Lavyrn, Lavyrne.*

LEAH *(Hebrew)* Weary. Slowly but surely, Leah is starting to appear more frequently among baby girls born today, especially among Jewish families. Leah, in the Book of Genesis, was first used as a given name in sixteenth-century Puritan England. Variations: *Lea, Leia, Leigha, Lia, Liah.*

LEANNA *(Gaelic)* Flowering vine. Variations: *Leana, Leane, Leann, Leanne, Lee Ann, Lee Anne, Leeann, Leeanne, Leianna, Leigh Ann, Leighann, Leighanne, Liana, Liane, Lianne.*

LEANORE *(English)* Bright one. Variation of Helen. Variations: *Leanor, Leanora, Lenor, Lenora, Lenorah, Lenore, Leonara, Leonora, Leonore.*

LEIGH *(English)* Meadow. In its simpler spelling, Lee, this name has always been more popular for boys than for girls, but Leigh is beginning to gain a following. Variation: *Lee.*

LESLIE *(Scottish)* Low meadow. Leslie has had a rich and colorful history, adapted from its original use as a last name in one of Robert Burns's poems. Burns spelled it as Lesley, but when parents began to use the name for their boys, they used the spelling of Leslie. The name remained popular among both sexes and in both spellings up until the 1940s. Today, Leslie is primarily a girls' name, although neither spelling predominates. Variations: *Leslea, Leslee, Lesley, Lesli, Lesly, Lezlee, Lezley, Lezli, Lezlie.*

LIESL *(German)* Nickname for Elizabeth. Variations: *Leizl, Liesa, Liese, Liesel, Liezel, Lisel, Lisl, Lisle.*

LILA *(Hindu)* Dance of God.

LILLIAN *(English)* Lily + Ann. Variations: *Lileana, Lilian, Liliana, Lilias, Lilika, Lillia, Lillianne, Lillyan, Lillyanna, Lilyan.*

LILY *(Latin)* Flower. Variations: *Lili, Lilia, Lilie, Lilli, Lillie, Lillye, Lilye.*

Zeroing in on Your Choice

Some parents will glance at a name and know instantly that it's the perfect name for their baby. For others, however, the name game is a more complicated process of elimination. If you've already spent some serious time flipping through the pages of this book and have marked some of the names that sound particularly attractive to you, you need to figure out how to narrow things down to one final choice.

So how, exactly, should you do this? First off, write down all of the names that sound good to you, middle names included. Write down your last name, too. Your partner should do the same thing, but separately. This is a good way to compare and contrast your baby name preferences.

Once you've drawn up a list, say the full name out loud to see how it sounds. After all, your child will be called by his or her name countless times in life. You have to make sure that the first, middle, and last names go well together.

LINDA *(Spanish)* Pretty one. In the '60s and '70s, it seemed that there were always a couple of girls with this name in every classroom. This was to be expected, since back in the '50s, Linda was the name that replaced Mary as number one. When it is used today, the most frequent spelling is Lynda. Variations: *Lin, Linday, Linde, Lindee, Lindi, Lindie, Lindy, Linn, Lyn, Lynada, Lynadie, Lynda, Lynde, Lyndy, Lynn, Lynnda.*

LINDSAY *(English)* Island of linden trees. Perhaps Lindsay was the reason that Linda hasn't remained more popular, even though except for sharing a few letters, the names have nothing in common. Lindsay was mostly a boys' name until the "bionic woman"—played by Lindsay Wagner on TV in the '70s—helped to bring this name to the forefront. Lindsay and its variant spellings appeared on the top ten baby name lists in the '80s, but as with all very popular names, ten or fifteen years can make a huge difference in how the name is perceived. Variations: *Lindsaye, Lindsey, Lindsi, Lindsie, Lindsy, Linsay, Linsey, Linzey, Lyndsay, Lyndsey, Lynsay, Lynsey.*

LINETTE *(Welsh)* Idol. Variations: *Lanette, Linet, Linetta, Linnet, Linnetta, Linnette, Lynetta, Lynette, Lynnet, Lynnette.*

LING *(Chinese)* Delicate.

LIONA *(Hawaiian)* Roaring lion.

LISA *(English)* Pledged by oath to God. Version of Elizabeth. Though I don't particularly think of my own parents as being faithful to the trends of their day, the fact that they named me Lisa is testament to how attuned they really were. In terms of popularity, Lisa was number four on the baby name hit parade in 1970, and number twelve in 1980, but today parents are clearly preferring to use one of the other derivatives of Elizabeth such as Liza or Libby. Variations: *Leesa, Leeza, Leisa, Liesa, Liese, Lisanne, Lise, Liseta, Lisetta, Lisette, Lissa, Lissette, Liza, Lizana, Lizanne, Lizette.*

LOIS *(English)* Famous soldier. Feminine version of Louis.

LOLA *(Spanish)* Sorrow. Nickname for Dolores. Variations: *Loleta, Loletta, Lolita.*

LONI *(English)* Ready for battle. Feminine version of Alphonso. Variations: *Lona, Lonee, Lonie, Lonna, Lonnie.*

LORELEI *(German)* A rocky cliff on the Rhine River. Variations: *Loralee, Loralie, Loralyn, Lorilee, Lura, Lurette, Lurleen, Lurlene, Lurline.*

LORNA *(Scottish)* Area in Scotland. Variation: *Lorrna.*

LORRAINE *(French)* Area in France. There was only one Lorraine in my entire high school class of 250, and I never understood why this pretty French name wasn't used more often. *Saturday Night Live* actress Loraine Newman helped increase popularity for this name, but it has never really hit in the United States the way it has in England and Scotland. In Ireland, it was one of the most popular names for girls in the '70s. Variations: *Laraine, Lauraine, Laurraine, Lorain, Loraine, Lorayne, Lorine, Lorrayne.*

LUCY *(English)* Light. Feminine version of Lucius. Lucy is a great old name that has finally made the comeback that it deserves. Lucia, the root for all Lucy-related names, is in turn the feminine version of an ancient Roman family name. Variations: *Lucetta, Lucette, Lucia, Luciana, Lucie, Lucienne, Lucilla, Lucille, Lucina, Lucinda, Lucita.*

LYDIA *(Greek)* Woman from Lydia, a region in ancient Greece. Variations: *Lidi, Lidia, Lidie, Lidka, Likochka, Lydiah, Lydie.*

LYNN *(English)* Pretty. Diminutive of Linda. Lynn was one of the more widely used names in the '40s and '50s, both as a first and a middle name, but it had appeared in this country as early as the 1920s, when actress Lynn Fontanne first made the transition from stage to screen in the early talkies. Variations: *Lin, Lina, Linell, Linelle, Linn, Linne, Lyn, Lyndall, Lyndel, Lyndell, Lyndelle, Lynelie, Lynell, Lynna, Lynne, Lynnelle.*

Slightly Daring Choices

LADIVA *(African-American)* Newly created.

LADONNA *(African-American)* Variations: *Ladon, Ladonne, Ladonya.*

LADY *(English)* Noble title.

LAEL *(Hebrew)* From God.

LAINA *(English)* Road.

LAINE *(English)* Bright one. Variation of Helen. Variations: *Lainey, Lane, Layne.*

LAREINA *(Spanish)* The queen. Variations: *LaRayne, Lareine, Larena, Larraine.*

LARISSA *(Greek)* Happy. Though Lara and Larissa seem to be related, they actually are derived from different roots. Larissa first began to appear in the 1960s, as did Lara from the movie Dr. Zhivago, but today it is Larissa that is still around. Variations: *Laresa, Laressa, Larisa, Laryssa.*

LARITA *(African-American)* Newly created.

LARK *(English)* Bird.

LATASHA *(African-American)* Newly created. Latasha has shown up in the top fifty names for African-American girls since the mid-'80s. Variation: *Latashia.*

LAVINIA *(Latin)* Roman woman. Variations: *Lavena, Lavenia, Lavina, Laviner, Lavinie, Levina, Levinia, Livinia, Lovina.*

LEILA *(Arabic)* Night. Variations: *Laila, Layla, Leela, Leelah, Leilah, Leilia, Lela, Lelah, Lelia, Leyla, Lila, Lilah.*

LENA *(English)* Bright one. Variation of Helen. Variations: *Lenah, Lene, Leni, Lenia, Lina, Linah, Line.*

LEONA *(Latin)* Lion. Feminine version of Leon. Variations: *Leonia, Leonie, Leonine, Leonissa, Leontyne.*

LETA *(Latin)* Happy. Variation: *Lida.*

LEXA *(Czech)* Protector of man. Feminine version of Alexander. Lexa and its variations are starting to appear more widely today, probably owing to the existence of an "x" within the name. Though most parents are using this name as a pet name for the more formal Alexandra, a few are choosing it as their daughter's given name. Variations: *Lexi, Lexia, Lexie, Lexina, Lexine.*

LIA *(Hebrew)* Tired.

LIANA *(French)* Twist like a vine. Variations: *Li, Lia, Lian, Liane, Liann, Lianna, Lianne.*

LIBERTY *(English)* Freedom.

LIBYA *(African-American)* Country in North Africa.

LILAC *(English)* Flower.

LILITH *(Arabic)* Night demon. It's a good bet that few people would have heard of Lilith without the character Dr. Lilith Sternin, the psychiatrist played by actress Bebe Neuwirth on the TV shows *Cheers* and *Frasier.* Lilith is actually the name of the wife that Adam had before Eve. According to legend, Lilith didn't like having a man calling the shots, so she departed, turning herself into a demon instead. Variation: *Lillis.*

LOURDES *(French)* Area in France.

LOVE *(English)* Love. Variations: *Lovey, Lovi, Lovie.*

LUCINDA *(Latin)* Beautiful light.

LUCITA *(Spanish)* Light.

LUCKY *(English)* Fortunate. Variations: *Luckie, Luckye.*

LUCRETIA *(Latin)* Roman clan name. Variations: *Lucrece, Lucrecia, Lucreecia, Lucrezia.*

LUNA *(Latin)* Roman moon goddess. Variations: *Lunetta, Lunette, Lunneta.*

LUPE *(Spanish)* She-wolf.

LURA *(English)* Unknown definition.

LUSELA *(Native American)* Bear foot.

LYRIS *(Greek)* Lyre; a small harp. Variation: *Lyra.*

Living on the Edge

LAMIS *(Arabic)* Soft.

LAMONICA *(African-American)* Newly created.

LAMYA *(Arabic)* Dark lips. Variation: *Lama.*

LAN *(Vietnamese)* Flower. Variation: *Lang.*

LANI *(Hawaiian)* Sky.

LANTHA *(Greek)* Purple flower. Variations: *Lanthe, Lanthia, Lanthina.*

LATRINA *(African-American)* Newly created.

LAUDOMIA *(Italian)* Praise the house.

LAUFEIA *(Scandinavian)* Leafy island. Variation: *Laufey.*

LEALA *(French)* Loyal. Variations: *Lealia, Lealie, Leola.*

LEALIKI *(Polynesian)* Waves.

LEANDA *(English)* Lion man. Variations: *Leandra, Leodora, Leoine, Leoline, Leona, Leonanie, Leonelle, Leonette, Leonice, Leonissa.*

LECIA *(Latin)* Short for Alicia or Felicia. Variations: *Lecy, Lisha, Lishia.*

LEIKO *(Japanese)* Proud.

LENICE *(African-American)* Newly created. Variations: *La Neece, LaNiece, Laniece.*

LENIS *(Latin)* Smooth, silky.

LENKA *(Czech)* Light.

LENNA *(German)* The strength of a lion. Variations: *Lenda, Lennah.*

LEONARDA *(German)* Roar of the lion. Variations: *Lenda, Leonarde.*

LEONIE *(French)* Lioness. Variations: *Leona, Leonda, Leondra, Leondrea, Leonela.*

LIBE *(Hebrew)* Love. Variations: *Liba, Libbe, Libbeh, Libi, Libke, Libkeh, Lipke, Lipkeh.*

LIBENA *(Czech)* Love. Variations: *Liba, Libenka, Libuse, Libuska, Luba.*

LOSA *(Polynesian)* Rosa. Variations: *Losana, Lose.*

LOSAKI *(Polynesian)* To meet.

LOTA *(Hindu)* Cup.

LOTTA *(Scandinavian: Swedish)* Woman. Variations: *Lotie, Lotte, Lottey, Lotti, Lottie, Lotty.*

LOTUS *(Greek)* A fruit.

LUBORNIRA *(Czech)* Great love. Variations: *Luba, Lubena, Lubina, Lubinka, Lubka, Luboska.*

LUDMILA *(Czech)* Loving people. Variations: *Lidka, Lidmila, Lidunka, Liduse, Liduska, Ludmilla, Luduna, Lyudmila.*

Tried and True Classics

MABEL *(English)* Lovable. Variations: *Mabelle, Mable, Maybel, Maybell, Maybelle.*

MACKENZIE *(Irish)* Daughter of a wise leader.

MADELINE *(French)* From Magdalen. Most parents today are familiar with the *Madeline* books by the author Ludwig Bemelmans. The character that Cybill Shepherd played in the TV show *Moonlighting* in the 1980s named Maddie may be responsible for the small upward blip we see today connected with the name. Variations: *Mada, Madalaina, Maddalena, Maddi, Maddie, Madelaine, Madelayne, Madeleine, Madelena, Madelene, Madelina, Madge, Magda.*

MADISON *(English)* Last name.

MADONNA *(Latin)* My lady.

MAGDALENA *(Spanish)* Woman from Magdala, area in the Middle East. Variations: *Magdala, Magdalen, Magdalene.*

MAISIE *(Scottish)* Pearl. Diminutive of Margaret. Variations: *Maisey, Maisy, Maizie.*

MALLORY *(French)* Unfortunate. Actress Justine Bateman, who played the character Mallory in the TV show *Family Ties* back in the '80s, may have unwittingly provided the spark for the whole trend of using boys' names and/or last names as suitable, attractive names for girls. Though today the name is indelibly connected with that era as well as the show, there are hundreds of like-minded names that a parent could choose from. Variations: *Malloreigh, Mallorey, Mallorie, Malorey, Malori, Malorie, Malory.*

MANUELA *(Spanish)* God is among us. Feminine version of Emanuel. Variation: *Manuelita.*

MARCIA *(Latin)* Warlike. Feminine version of Mark. After *The*

Brady Bunch faded from our weekly Friday dose, only to reemerge in daily rerun heaven, most parents would shudder at the thought of naming their daughters after the eldest Brady goody-two-shoes. However, as everything old becomes new again, eventually, Marcia just may start to catch on among parents. Variations: *Marce, Marcee, Marcela, Marcelia, Marcella, Marcelle, Marcena, Marcene, Marcey, Marci, Marcie, Marcina, Marcy, Marsha.*

Popular Celebrity Names: Girls

For going on a century now, female stars have impressed us with their style, beauty, and poise—on screen and off. No surprise that a variety of actresses' names have influenced parents-to-be through the decades. Here are just a few of the names brought to public attention by the following stars:

ALICIA SILVERSTONE
ANDIE MACDOWELL
ANGELA BASSETT
BETTE DAVIS
CANDICE BERGEN
CLAIRE DANES
CYBILL SHEPHERD
DEMI MOORE
EMMA THOMPSON
GEENA DAVIS
GILDA RADNER
GLENN CLOSE
GOLDIE HAWN
HALLE BERRY
HOLLY HUNTER
INGRID BERGMAN
JENNIFER JASON LEIGH

MARGARET *(English)* Pearl. Margaret has very deep roots, reaching back to the third century when it was the name of a popular saint. Later on, in the eleventh century, it was so popular that it was known as the national Scottish female name. It was also very popular in England and the United States: Margaret was a consistent member of the top ten girls' names list for the better part of the first half of the twentieth century. Today, many parents are beginning to take a second look. Variations: *Greeta, Greetje, Grere, Gret, Greta, Gretal, Gretchen, Gretel, Grethal, Grethel, Gretje, Gretl, Gretta, Groer, Maggi, Maggie, Maggy, Mair, Maire, Mairi, Mairona, Margara, Margareta, Margarethe, Margarett, Margaretta, Margarette, Margarita, Margarite, Marge, Margeret, Margerey, Margery, Margrett, Marguerette, Marguerite, Marj, Marjorie, Meagan, Meaghan, Meaghen, Meg, Megan, Megen, Meggi, Meggie, Meggy, Meghan, Meghann, Peg, Pegeen, Pegg, Peggey, Peggi, Peggie, Peggy, Reet, Reeta, Reita, Rheeta, Riet, Rieta, Ritta.*

MARGAUX *(French)* The name of a champagne. Variations: *Margo, Margot.*

MARGI *(Hindu)* Direction.

MARIA *(Latin)* Variation of Mary. Variations: *Marea, Mariah, Marie, Marya.*

MARIAN *(French)* Combination of Mary and Ann. Variations: *Mariana, Mariane, Mariann, Marianna, Marianne, Marion, Marrian, Marrion, Mary Ann, Maryann, Maryanna, Maryon, Maryonn.*

MARIE *(French)* Variation of Mary. It's funny what difference a letter will make to determine the popularity of a given name. Marie is a perfect example. While some parents consider Mary too Catholic and Maria too Hispanic, it seems that Marie has found a middle ground. French in origin, Marie was the second most popular name in the United States during the 1920s, when flapper-era parents must have thought that it represented the best of Europe and everything it had to offer. Today in the United States, Marie is still used more frequently than Mary and Maria combined.

MARIETTA *(French)* Diminutive of Mary. Variation: *Mariette.*

MARILYN *(English)* Combination of Mary and Lynn. Variations: *Maralin, Maralynn, Marelyn, Marilee, Marilin, Marilynne, Marralynn, Marrilin, Marrilyn, Marylin, Marylyn.*

MARINA *(Latin)* From the sea. Variations: *Marena, Marinda, Marine, Marinna, Marna.*

MARIS *(Latin)* Star of the sea. Though many people consider the up-and-coming Maris and its variations to be derivatives of Mary, it actually comes from the Latin marine term *stella maris*, which means "star of the sea." Maris first started to appear in the United States in the 1920s, and some of the variations—Marissa, for example—began to pop up in the '50s, but it didn't take a real foothold until more recently. Actress Marisa Tomei has been responsible for providing most of the exposure. Variations: *Marieca, Marisa, Marise, Marish, Marisha, Marissa, Marisse, Meris, Merisa, Merissa.*

MARISOL *(Spanish)* Sunny sea.

MARLENE *(English)* Combination of Maria and Magdalene. Variations: *Marla, Marlaina, Marlaine, Marlana, Marlane, Marlayne, Marlea, Marlee, Marleen, Marleina, Marlena, Marley, Marlie, Marlina, Marlinda, Marline, Marlyn.*

MARLO *(English)* Last name. Variation: *Marlow.*

MARNI *(Hebrew)* To rejoice. Variations: *Marna, Marne, Marney, Marnia, Marnie, Marnina, Merina.*

MARTHA *(English)* Lady. In the '80s, young celebrities like actress Martha Plimpton and MTV VJ Martha Quinn brought this old-fashioned name into contemporary times. Variations: *Macia, Marit, Marite, Marlet, Mart, Marta, Martell, Marth, Marthe, Marthena, Marti, Martie, Martina, Martita, Martus, Martuska, Marty, Martyne, Martynne, Masia, Matti, Mattie.*

MARTINA *(Latin)* Warlike. Feminine version of Martin. Variation: *Martine.*

MARY *(Hebrew)* Bitterness. The Virgin Mary. Back in the Middle Ages, you could be tried for blasphemy if you chose the name Mary for your daughter; back then, it was considered too sacred to use for a mere mortal. Of course, once attitudes changed, Mary quickly grew to become one of the most popular names among English-speaking countries. Famous Marys of the past include Mary Pickford, Mary Poppins, and Mary Tyler Moore. Variations: *Maree, Marella, Marelle, Mari, Marial, Marieke, Mariel, Mariela, Mariele, Mariella, Marielle, Marika, Marike, Maryk, Maura, Moira, Moll, Mollee, Molley, Molli, Mollie, Molly, Mora, Moria, Moyra.*

MATILDA *(Old German)* Maiden in battle. Matilda is a wonderful, lyrical name that many American parents are finding to be a perfect match for their newborn daughters. It's expressive enough on its own, but the many different variations are also very distinctive. Variations: *Maddi, Maddie, Maddy, Mat, Matelda, Mathilda, Mathilde, Matilde, Mattie, Matty, Matusha, Matylda, Maud, Maude, Tila, Tilda, Tildie, Tildy, Tilley, Tilli, Tillie, Tilly, Tylda.*

MAUREEN *(Irish)* Variation of Mary. Maureen was a quintessentially Irish name that appeared to be equally popular in Ireland, Britain, and the United States, at least up until 1960, when it began to become used less frequently. Famous Maureens include Maureen O'Sullivan and Maureen O'Hara, both movie stars who seemed to go into retirement about the time the name began to fade. Variations: *Maurene, Maurine, Moreen, Morreen, Moureen.*

MAXINE *(English)* Greatest in excellence. Feminine version of Maximilian. Variations: *Maxeen, Maxene, Maxi, Maxie, Maxima, Maximina, Maxina.*

MAY *(English)* Calendar month. Back in the 1920s, it was all the rage to use months of the year as names for girls, although this exclusive group seemed to focus on springtime: April, May, and June. May was very popular in the United States in the post–Civil War years, and seems to be catching on among parents today. Variations: *Mae, Mai, Mayleen, Maylene.*

MAYA *(Hindu)* God's power. Variation: *Mya.*

MELANIE *(Greek)* Dark-skinned. Variations: *Mel, Mela, Melaine, Melana, Melane, Melani, Melaniya, Melanka, Melany, Melanya, Melashka, Melasya, Melenia, Melka, Mellanie, Mellie, Melloney, Mellony, Melly, Meloni, Melonie, Melony, Milena, Milya.*

MELINDA *(Latin)* Honey. Variations: *Malina, Malinda, Malinde, Mallie, Mally, Mel, Meleana, Melina, Melinde, Meline, Mellinda, Melynda, Mindi, Mindie, Mindy.*

MELISSA *(Greek)* Bee. Today Melissa hovers around the bottom half of the top twenty-five list. The name is destined to move up the ranks slightly, owing to the success and popularity of singer Melissa Etheridge and actress Melissa Gilbert. Melissa is an ancient name that was first popular during the early Roman Empire as it was the name of the woman who nursed the mighty goddess Juno when she was a baby. Variations: *Melisa, Melisande, Melisandra, Melisandre, Melissande, Melissandre, Melisse, Mellisa, Mellissa.*

MELODY *(Greek)* Song. Variations: *Melodee, Melodey, Melodia, Melodice, Melodie.*

MERCEDES *(Spanish)* Mercy. Though it might be assumed that any girl named Mercedes today would be directly inspired by the luxury car, the fact is that the car received its name from the Spanish version of one of the popular ways to refer to the Virgin Mary, Our Lady of the Mercies. Variations: *Merced, Mercede.*

MEREDITH *(Welsh)* Great leader. Variations: *Meredithe, Merideth, Meridith, Merridith.*

MERI *(Scandinavian: Finnish)* Ocean. Variation: *Meriata.*

MERRY *(English)* Happy. Variations: *Meri, Merri, Merrie, Merrilee, Merrily.*

MERYL *(English)* Bright as the sea. Actress Meryl Streep is an obvious reason why this name has become popular for girls since the early '80s. Nevertheless, parents today are more likely to choose one of the variations that sound androgynous and resemble a last name. Of course, these two trends are responsible for many of the new girls' names out there. Variations: *Merill, Merrall, Merrel, Merrell, Merrill, Meryle, Meryll.*

MIA *(Italian)* Mine.

MICHAELA *(Hebrew)* Who is like God. Feminine version of Michael. Variations: *Makaela, Micaela, Mical, Michael, Michaella, Michal, Michala, Mickaula, Micki, Mickie, Micky, Mikella, Mikelle, Mychaela.*

MICHELLE *(French)* Who is like the Lord. More common feminine version of Michael. Michelle has been one of the few names that has been in the top ten list since the 1960s. The song "Michelle" by the Beatles can take credit for some of this popularity, as well as Michelle Pfeiffer, who grabbed the torch in the mid-'80s. It is beginning to see a challenge by a close relative, Michaela, and its variations that sound more androgynous to the ear. Variations: *Michele, Nichelle.*

MILDRED *(English)* Tender strength. Variation: *Mildrid.*

MILLICENT *(German)* Born to power. In the '50s and '60s, Millie—short for Millicent—seemed to be the ubiquitous name of every next-door neighbor in TV-land. Today, however, Millicent seems feminine and unusual but not strange: it's ripe for adoption into the top names list of the '90s. Variations: *Melicent, Meliscent, Mellicent, Milley, Milli.*

MINNIE *(English)* Feminine diminutive of William. Variations: *Minni, Minny.*

MIRANDA *(Latin)* Admirable. Variations: *Maranda, Meranda, Mira, Myranda, Randa, Randee, Randene, Randey, Randi, Randie, Randy.*

MIRIAM *(Hebrew)* Bitter. Variations: *Maijii, Maikki, Mair, Maire, Mairi, Maircna, Mame, Mamie, Mamy, Manon, Masha, Mashenka, Mashka, Miliana, Mima, Mimi, Mimma, Mimmie, Miri, Miriama, Mirian, Mirriam, Mirrian, Miryam, Myriam.*

MISSY *(English)* Diminutive of Melissa.

MONA *(Irish)* Noble.

Famous Female Characters from Film and Literature

Some people give their babies names from current movies and books because they're trendy. Others believe, for some reason, that if they give their baby the name of a person that is close to their hearts—whether it's a character in a book they read as a child or a favorite movie they viewed as an adult—perhaps their baby will embody some positive trait of that beloved character. Here's a sampling of female characters' names:

BECKY THATCHER: *Tom Sawyer's spunky pal in Mark Twain's novels*
DOROTHY GALE: *heroine of* The Wizard of Oz
ELIZABETH BENNETT: Pride and Prejudice
JO MARCH: Little Women
LOIS LANE: Superman
MOLLY BLOOM: Ulysses
SCARLETT O'HARA: Gone with the Wind
CRESSIDA, JULIET, PORTIA, DESDEMONA, and OPHELIA: *Just a few of the many female characters from Shakespeare's plays*
GUINEVERE: *Queen of Arthurian legend*
MINNIE, DAISY, AURORA, ARIEL, JASMINE, and NALA: *female characters in Disney movies.*

MONICA *(Latin)* Adviser or nun. The name Monica has a lot of energy to it; this trait is perhaps best embodied by the tennis champion Monica Seles. On the other hand, one of its variations, Monique, always sounds sultry; it's one of the best French names that you could give your daughter. Today, Monique is most popular among African-American families, who have placed it in the top fifty list of names for their daughters. Variations: *Monika, Monique.*

MORGAN *(Welsh)* Great and bright. Though in the past, Morgan has been more widely known as both a last name and a name for boys, actress Morgan Fairchild provided great exposure for this name in the 1980s. Originally, the sister of King Arthur, Morgan Le Fay, helped to create some feminine allure to the name. Variations: *Morgana, Morganne, Morgen.*

MURIEL *(Irish)* Bright as the sea. Though Muriel was a popular name in Britain from approximately the 1870s through to the 1930s, it has faded away ever since then. In this country, it never really got a foothold to begin with. But that could all change owing to the success of the Australian movie *Muriel's Wedding*. Variations: *Muirgheal, Murial, Muriell, Murielle.*

MYRA *(Latin)* Scented oil. Feminine version of Myron. Variations: *Murah, Myria, Myriah.*

Slightly Daring Choices

MAB *(Irish, Gaelic)* Joy. Queen Mab is a legendary Irish fairy queen.

MACY *(English)* Last name.

MAEVE *(Irish)* Delicate.

MAGENA *(Native American)* New moon.

MAGNOLIA *(Latin)* Flower name.

MAHALA *(Hebrew)* Tenderness. The late singer Mahalia Jackson popularized this name. Variations: *Mahalah, Mahalia, Mahaliah, Mahalla, Mahelia, Mehalia.*

MAIA *(Greek)* Mother. Greek nymph.

MAIDA *(English)* Maiden. Variations: *Maidie, Mayda.*

MAIZA *(Arabic)* Discerning.

MALINA *(Hawaiian)* Peaceful.

MARA *(Hebrew)* Bitter. Variation: *Marah.*

MARABEL *(English)* Beautiful Mary. Variations: *Marabelle, Marable, Marbella.*

MARELLA *(English)* Combination of Mary and Elle. Variation: *Marelle.*

MARETTA *(English)* Defiant. Variation: *Marette.*

MARONA *(Hebrew)* Flock of sheep.

MAUVE *(French)* The mallow plant. Variation: *Malva.*

MAVIS *(French)* Thrush. Variation: *Mayvis.*

MENA *(Dutch)* Strength. Variation: *Menna.*

MENIA *(Scandinavian)* Ancient mythological figure. Variation: *Menja.*

MERCIA *(English)* Ancient British kingdom.

MERCY *(English)* Mercy. Variations: *Mercey, Merci, Mercia, Mercie, Mersey.*

MERIEL *(Gaelic)* Brilliant seas. Variations: *Merial, Meriol, Merrill.*

MERLE *(French)* Blackbird. Variations: *Merl, Merla, Merlin, Merlina, Merline, Merlyn.*

MESSINA *(Latin)* Middle.

MICINA *(Native American)* New moon.

MIDORI *(Japanese)* Green.

MILA *(Slavic)* Loved by the people.

MILENA *(Czech)* Grace. Variations: *Milada, Miladena, Miladka, Milana, Milanka, Milenka, Milka, Miluse, Miluska, Mlada, Mladena, Mladka, Mladuska.*

MILI *(Hebrew)* Virtuous.

MINA *(Native American: Sioux)* First daughter.

MIRABEL *(Latin)* Wonderful. Magazine editor Grace Mirabella has been a factor in the increasing number of parents who are looking toward Mirabel and its variations as a suitable first name for their daughters. Though it seems that every girls' name that ends in "bel" is rising on the popularity scale, Mirabel is probably the most melodious. Variations: *Mirabell, Mirabella, Mirabelle.*

MIRELLA *(Hebrew)* God speaks. Variations: *Mireille, Mirelle, Mireya, Myrelle.*

MIRENA *(Hawaiian)* Beloved. Variation: *Milena.*

MISTY *(English)* Mist.

MONDAY *(English)* Day of the week.

MONTANA *(Spanish)* Mountain.

MORA *(Spanish)* Blueberry.

MYLA *(English)* Merciful. Variations: *Milena, Myleen, Mylene.*

MYRNA *(Irish)* Beloved. Variations: *Merna, Mirna, Muirna.*

MYSTIQUE *(French)* Mysterious. Variations: *Mistique, Misty, Mystica.*

Living on the Edge

MADIA *(Arabic)* To praise. Variations: *Madiha, Madihah.*

MALKAH *(Hebrew)* Queen. Variations: *Malcah, Malka, Malkia, Malkiah, Malkie, Malkit, Malkiya.*

MALKIN *(German)* Battle maiden.

MANETTE *(French)* Defiant.

MANGENA *(Hebrew)* Song. Variation: *Mangina.*

MANSI *(Native American)* Picked flower. Variations: *Mancey, Manci, Mancie, Mancy, Mansey, Mansie, Mansy.*

MARIGOLD *(English)* Flower.

MARVEL *(French)* A marvel. Variations: *Marva, Marvela, Marvele, Marvella, Marvelle.*

MATTHEA *(Hebrew)* Gift from God. Feminine version of Matthew. Variations: *Mattea, Mathea, Mathia, Matthea, Matthia, Mattia.*

MAYSA *(Arabic)* Walk proudly. Variation: *Maisah.*

MEDINA *(Arabic)* City in Saudi Arabia.

MEDORA *(English)* Gift from mother.

MEHITABEL *(Hebrew)* Benefited by God. In the old Don Marquis stories, Mehitabel was the streetwise cat friend of Archy, the cockroach, who took it upon himself to tell their stories by hopping across typewriter keys. Though some people may associate Mehitabel with other ancient names of less repute, like Medusa, Mehitabel is a wonderfully unusual name. Variation: *Mehetabel.*

MELBA *(English)* Variation of Melbourne; city in Australia. Variations: *Mellba, Mellva, Melva.*

MELCIA *(Polish)* Ambitious.

MELIORA *(Latin)* Better.

MELISANDE *(French)* Powerful. Variations: *Melasandre, Mellisande.*

MELITA *(Greek)* Honey. Variations: *Malita, Meleta, Melitta.*

MILADA *(Czech)* My love. Variation: *Mila*

MINERVA *(Latin)* The Roman goddess of wisdom.

MINETTA *(English)* Feminine nickname of William; Will + helmet. Variations: *Minette, Minna.*

MING *(Chinese)* Tomorrow.

MIZELA *(English)* Unknown definition. Variations: *Marzalie, Masella, Mazala, Mazella, Mazila, Mesella, Messella, Mezillah, Mizella, Mizelle, Mizelli.*

MODESTY *(Latin)* Modesty. Variations: *Modesta, Modestia, Modestina, Modestine.*

MORAN *(Hebrew)* Teacher. Variation: *Moranit.*

MORELA *(Polish)* Apricot.

MORENA *(Portuguese)* Brunette. Variations: *Moreen, Morella.*

MORI *(Japanese)* Forest. Variations: *Moriko, Moriyo.*

MORIAH *(Hebrew)* The Lord is my teacher. Variations: *Moria, Morice, Moriel, Morit.*

MYRTLE *(English)* Plant. Variations: *Myrta, Myrtilla.*

Tried and True Classics

NADIA *(Russian)* Hope. Variations: *Nada, Nadeen, Nadene, Nadina, Nadine, Nadiya, Nadja, Nadya, Natka.*

NANCY *(Hebrew)* Grace. Though its origins are Hebrew, Nancy seems more like one of the quintessentially American names. Nancy's peak in the United States occurred in the 1950s, when it placed in the top ten. It had peaked in Britain twenty years earlier. Famous Nancys include former first lady Nancy Reagan, fictional detective Nancy Drew, and Olympic skater Nancy Kerrigan. Variations: *Nan, Nana, Nance, Nancee, Nancey, Nanci, Nancie, Nancsi, Nanette, Nann, Nanna, Nanncey, Nanncy, Nanni, Nannie, Nanny, Nanscey, Nansee, Nansey.*

NAOMI *(Hebrew)* Pleasant. Naomi seems poised for newfound popularity for several reasons. It's a pretty name, it has strong Biblical overtones that appeal to many parents today, and it is also being spread by the fame of singer Naomi Judd and British model Naomi Campbell. Variations: *Naoma, Naomia, Naomie, Neoma, Noami, Noemi, Noemie.*

NATALIE *(Latin)* Birthday. The name was very popular in Britain from the 1960s through the mid-'80s (when it hit number fifteen on the top twenty list). Natalie is quietly beginning to make more of a mark in this country. The entertainment industry has given us several Natalies: singers Natalie Cole and Natalie Merchant, and the late actress Natalie Wood. Variations: *Natala, Natalee, Natalene, Natalia, Natalina, Nataline, Natalka, Natalya, Natelie, Nathalia, Nathalie.*

NATASHA *(Russian)* Rebirth. Natasha is a name that has many exotic connotations associated with it. For most of us, the first Natasha we met was on the *Rocky and Bullwinkle* show. In the '70s and '80s, actress Natassja Kinski kept the name alive, and today it's Natasha Richardson who is the preeminent example. But leaving all that aside, Natasha is just a beautiful name for a girl and later a woman. Variations: *Nastasia, Nastassia, Nastassja, Nastassya, Nastasya, Natashia, Tashi, Tashia, Tasis, Tassa, Tassie.*

NELL *(English)* Light. Jodie Foster's movie entitled *Nell,* in which she played the main character, has brought this name with a Victorian flair into the American consciousness. Back around the turn of the century, when the name was first popular, the variation Nellie was more common than its root. Today, both should grow in popularity as both a first and middle name. Variations: *Nella, Nelley, Nelli, Nellie, Nelly.*

NICOLE *(English)* People of victory. Feminine version of Nicholas. In 1980, Nicole was the fourth most popular girls' name in the United States. Actress Nicole Kidman is, perhaps, the most well-known contemporary bearer of this name. Variations: *Nichol, Nichola, Nichole, Nicholle, Nicki, Nickola, Nickole, Nicola, Nicoleen, Nicolene, Nicoletta, Nicolette, Nicolina, Nicoline, Nicolla, Nicolle, Nikki, Nikola, Nikoletta, Nikolette.*

NINA *(Spanish)* Girl. (Hebrew) Grace of God. Nina is an ancient name that has been around for several millennia. In Babylonian mythology, Nina was the goddess of the seas, and in the Incan culture, Nina ruled over fire. In this country, it seems as if Nina is a name that could always be just a bit more popular, and given the slight stirrings the name has had since the mid-'70s, it may well start to become more visible. Variations: *Neena, Ninelle, Ninet, Nineta, Ninete, Ninetta, Ninette, Ninita, Ninnette, Ninotchka, Nynette.*

NOEL *(French)* Christmas. Names that reflect the seasons in some way are starting to become very popular, and Noel is no exception. Traditionally, parents named their baby boys and girls born on Christmas day with a variation of

Noel, but today's parents have taken the liberty of giving the name to children who are born throughout the month of December. Variations: *Noela, Noelani, Noele, Noeleen, Noelene, Noeline, Noell, Noella, Noelle, Noelline, Noleen, Nowell.*

Names from Nature

Nature can be a great resource for baby names, though girls' names always seem to have the upper hand in this category. Although maybe some parents in the '60s went overboard when naming their kids Nutmeg, Tofu, and Earth, all in all, Mother Nature is still a good place to turn to for names that are a bit different, but still fitting.

One way to personalize your choice is to name your baby after the birthstone or flower of her birthday month. Following are the flowers and gemstones for each month:

JANUARY	**Birthstone:** *garnet*	**Flower:** *carnation*
FEBRUARY	**Birthstone:** *amethyst*	**Flower:** *violet*
MARCH	**Birthstone:** *aquamarine*	**Flower:** *jonquil*
APRIL	**Birthstone:** *diamond*	**Flower:** *sweet pea*
MAY	**Birthstone:** *emerald*	**Flower:** *lily of the valley*
JUNE	**Birthstone:** *pearl*	**Flower:** *rose*
JULY	**Birthstone:** *ruby*	**Flower:** *larkspur*
AUGUST	**Birthstone:** *peridot*	**Flower:** *gladiolus*
SEPTEMBER	**Birthstone:** *sapphire*	**Flower:** *aster*
OCTOBER	**Birthstone:** *opal*	**Flower:** *calendula*
NOVEMBER	**Birthstone:** *topaz*	**Flower:** *chrysanthemum*
DECEMBER	**Birthstone:** *turquoise*	**Flower:** *narcissus*

NORA *(Greek)* Light. Variation: *Norah.*

NOREEN *(English)* Diminutive of Nora, light. Variations: *Noreena, Norene, Norina, Norine.*

NORMA *(Latin)* Pattern. Though Norma was once fashionable enough to belong to several movie actresses including Norma Shearer, off the screen the name always seemed to belong to mothers and grandmothers and never little girls. Though a similar-sounding name—Martha—has caught on in some circles, Norma doesn't seem as if it will have the same clout. Variation: *Normah.*

Slightly Daring Choices

NADETTE *(German)* Brave bear.

NAIA *(Hawaiian)* Dolphin.

NAIDA *(Greek)* Water nymph. Variations: *Naiad, Nayad, Nyad.*

NAILAH *(Arabic)* One who succeeds. Variation: *Naila.*

NAIMA *(Arabic)* Content. Variations: *Naeemah, Naimah.*

NARA *(Japanese)* Oak tree.

NARDA *(Latin)* Scented lotion.

NARELLE *(Australian)* Unknown definition.

NATANE *(Native American: Arapaho)* Daughter.

NATANIAH *(Hebrew)* Gift of God. Feminine version of Nathan. Variations: *Natania, Nataniela, Nataniella, Natanielle, Natanya, Nathania, Nathaniella, Nathanielle, Netana, Netanela, Netania, Netaniah, Netaniela, Netaniella, Netanya, Nethania, Nethaniah, Netina.*

NATESA *(Hindu)* Lord of the dance.

NEALA *(Irish)* Champion. Feminine version of Neil. Variations: *Nealie, Nealy, Neeli, Neelie, Neely, Neila, Neile, Neilla, Neille.*

NERISSA *(Greek)* Sea snail. Variations: *Nerisa, Nerise.*

NEVADA *(English)* The state. Like Montana, Nevada is quickly becoming one of the more popular girls' names that are taken from a state. This trend seems to be spreading overseas as well—the name Nevada is also popularly used in Great Britain.

NISSA *(Hebrew)* Examine. Variation: *Nisa.*

NITA *(Hindu)* Friendly. Variations: *Neeta, Nitali.*

NOIRIN *(Irish)* Honorable light.

NOLA *(English)* White shoulder. Variations: *Nolah, Nolana.*

NOLETA *(Latin)* Reluctant. Variation: *Nolita.*

NONA *(Latin)* Ninth. Variations: *Nonah, Noni, Nonie, Nonna, Nonnah.*

Living on the Edge

NADEZDA *(Czech)* Unknown definition. Variation: *Nadeia.*

NAJAT *(Arabic)* Safe. Variation: *Nagat.*

NAJIBA *(Arabic)* Well born. Variations: *Nagiba, Nagibah, Najibah.*

NAJLA *(Arabic)* Pretty eyes. Variations: *Nagla, Najila, Najlaa, Najlah.*

NANA *(Hawaiian)* Spring month.

NANABAH *(Native American: Navajo)* Wife of a tribal chairman.

NANALA *(Hawaiian)* Sunflower.

NANDANA *(Hindu)* Happiness. Variations: *Nandini, Nandita.*

NANEK *(Hawaiian)* Merciful. Variations: *Naneka, Naneki, Naneta.*

NANI *(Hawaiian)* Beautiful.

NANISE *(Polynesian)* Gracious.

NANVAH *(Hebrew)* Lovely.

NARCISSA *(Greek)* Daffodil. Variations: *Narcisa, Narcisse, Narkissa.*

NARESHA *(Hindu)* Leader.

NARILLA *(English, Gypsy)* Unknown definition. Variation: *Narrila.*

NASRIN *(Arabic)* Rose. Variation: *Nasreen.*

NASYA *(Hebrew)* Miracle of God. Variation: *Nasia.*

NATA *(Native American)* Creator.

NATIVIDAD *(Spanish)* Christmas.

NATKA *(Russian)* Promise.

NATSU *(Japanese)* Summer. Variations: *Natsuko, Natsuyo.*

NAYANA *(Hindu)* Beautiful eyes.

NAYO *(African: Nigerian)* She is our joy.

NAZIHAH *(Arabic)* Trustworthy.

NAZIRA *(Arabic)* Equal. Variation: *Nazirah.*

NECI *(Latin)* On fire.

NEDA *(Czech)* Born on Sunday. Variations: *Nedda, Neddie, Nedi.*

NEDAVIAH *(Hebrew)* God is charitable. Variations: *Nedavia, Nedavya, Nediva.*

NEEMA *(African: Swahili)* Born during good times.

NEENAH *(Native American: Winnebago)* Running water.

NEMERA *(Hebrew)* Leopard.

NENET *(Egyptian)* Goddess.

NEOLA *(Greek)* Young girl. Variation: *Neolah.*

NEPA *(Arabic)* Walking backward.

NERA *(Hebrew)* Light. Variations: *Neria, Neriah, Neriya.*

NERIDA *(Greek)* Sea nymph. Variations: *Nerice, Nerina, Nerine, Nerisse, Neryssa, Rissa.*

NEVA *(Spanish)* Snow.

NEVIAH *(Hebrew)* Forecaster. Variation: *Nevia.*

NEZA *(Slavic)* Lamb. Variation: *Neysa.*

NIABI *(Native American)* Young deer.

NIAMH *(Irish)* Bright.

NIBAL *(Arabic)* Arrow.

NIKE *(Greek)* Goddess of victory. Variation: *Nika.*

NILI *(Hebrew)* An acronym for "The glory of Israel will not repent."

NILSINE *(Scandinavian)* Victory of the people.

NIMA *(Hindu)* Tree. Variations: *Neema, Neemah, Nema.*

NITARA *(Hindu)* Settled.

NITSA *(Greek)* Shining girl.

NITUNA *(Native American)* Daughter.

NIVA *(Hebrew)* Talk. Variation: *Neva.*

NIXIE *(German)* Water nymph.

NOELAN *(Hawaiian)* Divine mist.

NOGA *(Hebrew)* Morning light.

NORNA *(Scandinavian)* Fate.

NORRIS *(English)* Last name.

NOULA *(Greek)* Grace. Variation: *Noulah.*

NOURA *(Arabic)* Light. Variation: *Nourah.*

NOVA *(Latin)* New. Variation: *Novah.*

NOVELLA *(Spanish)* New little thing.

NOVIA *(Spanish)* Girlfriend.

Tried and True Classics

OCTAVIA *(Latin)* Eighth. Octavia is a wonderfully intriguing name. The name brings up images of reruns of the old British series *I, Claudius*, which exhibited some of the more decadent characteristics of the Roman Empire. Most everyone will admit to liking the name, but you'll have to be brave to give it to your own daughter. Variations: *Octavie, Ottavia.*

OLGA *(Russian)* Holy. The two Olgas who are perhaps best known are a saint from the tenth century and the petite gymnast Olga Korbut, who helped bring a new grace to the name in this country during the 1976 Summer Olympics. Olga is still one of the more popular names in Russia today, but it is also widely used across Europe. Variations: *Elga, Ola, Olenka, Olesya, Olia, Olina, Olka, Olli, Olly, Olunka, Oluska, Olva, Olya, Olyusha.*

OLIVIA *(Latin)* Olive tree. Olivia, currently very popular and hovering near the top ten list in this country, has a long and illustrious history in the arts and on TV. Though it's often associated with actress Olivia De Havilland and Australian singer Olivia Newton-John, Olivia made a much earlier appearance in literature, in Shakespeare's play *Twelfth Night*. Today its popularity seems to stem from its wide usage on TV: Olivia was not only the name of the sainted mother on the '70s show *The Waltons*, but has also appeared as a character in several soap operas. Parents like the name because it has eloquence and sophistication, and yet a down-home, almost southern feel to it. Variations: *Lioa, Lioia, Liovie, Liv, Olia, Oliva, Olive, Olivet, Olivette, Olivine, Ollie, Olva.*

OPHELIA *(Greek)* Help. Variation: *Ofelia.*

ORALIE *(French)* Golden. The "Ora" part of Oralie is actually the feminine version of "oro," which in Spanish means gold. While gold technically isn't a jewel, many of the girls' names that contain this root first began to be popular, appropriately enough, in the '80s, when names that sounded rich and sophisticated were all the rage. One variation of this name, Oriel, represents the angel of fate; and the popularity of a similar-sounding name, Ariel, (which parents began to flock to after the success of the Disney movie *The Little Mermaid*) seem to have set the stage for a more widespread acceptance of these unusual but beautiful names. Variations: *Oralee, Oralia, Orelie, Oriel, Orielle, Orlena, Orlene.*

Slightly Daring Choices

OCEAN *(English)* Ocean. Variations: *Oceana, Oceania.*

ODELE *(German)* Wealthy. Variations: *Oda, Odeela, Odela, Odelia, Odelinda, Odell, Odella, Odelle, Odelyn, Odila, Odile, Odilia.*

ODELIA *(Hebrew)* Praise God. Variation: *Odeleya.*

ODERA *(Hebrew)* Plow.

ODESSA *(Greek)* Long journey.

ODETTE *(French)* Wealthy. Variation: *Odetta.*

OLA *(Polish)* Protector of men; (Scandinavian) Ancestor's relic. Variations: *Olesia, Olesya.*

OLEDA *(English)* Noble. Variations: *Oleta, Olethea.*

OLENA *(Russian)* Brilliant light. Variation: *Olenya.*

OLESIA *(Polish)* Protector of humanity.

OLIANA *(Hawaiian)* Flowering evergreen.

OLINA *(Hawaiian)* Happy. Variations: *Oleen, Oline.*

OLINDA *(Latin)* Perfumed.

OLISA *(African)* God.

OLYMPIA *(Greek)* Mount Olympus, home of the Greek gods. Variations: *Olimpia, Olympya, Pia.*

ONDREA *(Czech)* Fierce woman. Variation: *Ondra.*

ONEIDA *(Native American)* Anticipation. Variations: *Onida, Onyda.*

ONELLA *(Greek)* Light.

OPAL *(English)* Gem. Some of the old-fashioned jewel names, like Opal, were pretty common around the 1900s. Today, while Ruby and Jade are quickly becoming hot names in the United States, Opal doesn't seem to be keeping up. Variations: *Opalina, Opaline.*

OPHIRA *(Hebrew)* Gold. Variation: *Ofira.*

OPRAH *(Hebrew)* A fawn. Talk show personality Oprah Winfrey has made this uncommon name famous. Variations: *Ofra, Ofrat, Ofrit, Ophra, Ophrah, Ophrat, Ophrit, Oprah, Orpa, Orpha, Orphy.*

ORA *(Latin)* Prayer. Variation: *Orra.*

ORAH *(Hebrew)* Light. Variations: *Ora, Orali, Orit, Orlee, Orli, Orlice, Orly.*

ORELA *(Latin)* Revelation.

ORENDA *(Native American)* Magic spell.

ORIANA *(Latin)* Sunrise. Variations: *Oraine, Oralia, Orane, Orania, Orelda, Orelle, Oriane.*

ORINO *(Japanese)* Weaver's loom. Variation: *Ori.*

ORIOLE *(English)* Bird. Variations: *Auriel, Orella, Oriel, Oriola.*

ORLAIN *(African-American)* Unknown definition.

ORLENDA *(Russian)* Female eagle. Variation: *Orlinda.*

ORSA *(Latin)* Female bear. Variations: *Orsala, Orsaline, Orsel, Orselina, Orseline, Orsola.*

ORTHIA *(Greek)* Straight.

ORYA *(Russian)* Peace. Variation: *Oryna.*

OSEN *(Japanese)* Thousand. One of the more popular Japanese superstitions is that numbers that are rounded off are luckier than odd numbers that are left intact. Osen is one of the many names that grew out of this superstition.

OTYLIA *(Polish)* Wealth.

OZERA *(Hebrew)* Help.

Living on the Edge

OBA *(African: Nigerian)* Goddess of the river.

OBEDIENCE *(English)* Loyalty.

OBELIA *(Greek)* Needle.

OBIOMA *(African: Nigerian)* Kind.

OCIN *(Native American)* Rose.

ODDRUN *(Scandinavian)* Point. Variations: *Oda, Odd, Oddr.*

ODDVEIG *(Scandinavian)* Woman with a spear.

ODE *(African: Nigerian)* Born while traveling.

ODEDA *(Hebrew)* Powerful.

ODELETTE *(French)* Little song. Variations: *Odelet, Odette.*

ODHARNAIT *(Irish)* Green. Variations: *Orna, Ornat.*

ODINA *(Native American: Algonquin)* Mountain.

ODIYA *(Hebrew)* Song of God.

OFA *(Polynesian)* Love.

OGIN *(Native American)* Rose.

OHELA *(Hebrew)* Tent.

OKTAWJA *(Polish)* Eighth.

OLABISI *(African: Nigerian)* To increase.

OLABUNMI *(African)* Award.

OLANIYI *(African: Nigerian)* Wealth.

OLATHE *(Native American: Shawnee)* Beautiful.

OLAUG *(Scandinavian)* Devoted to ancestors.

OLDRISKA *(Czech)* Prosperous ruler. Variations: *Olda, Oldra,*

Oldrina, Olina, Oluse.

OLVYEN *(Welsh)* White footprint.

OLWEN *(Welsh)* White footprint. Variations: *Olwenn, Olwin, Olwyn, Olwyne.*

OMA *(Arabic)* Leader.

OMANA *(Hindu)* Lady.

OMEGA *(Greek)* Last letter of the Greek alphabet.

OMEMEE *(Native American)* Pigeon.

ONA *(Lithuanian)* Grace.

ONAIWAH *(Native American)* Alert. Variation: *Onawa.*

ONATAH *(Native American)* God of corn.

ONDINE *(Latin)* Little wave. Variations: *Ondina, Ondine, Ondyne, Undina, Undine.*

ONI *(African: Nigerian)* Desired.

ONIATARIO *(Native American: Iroquois)* Beautiful lake. Variation: *Ontario.*

ONIDA *(Native American)* The one we search for.

ONORA *(Latin)* Honor. Variations: *Onoria, Onorine.*

OONA *(Irish)* Unity. Variations: *Oonagh, Oonah.*

OPA *(Native American: Choctaw)* Owl.

ORANGE *(English)* Orange. Variation: *Orangetta.*

ORFHLAITH *(Irish)* Golden lady. Variations: *Orflath, Oria, Oriana, Oriane, Orianna, Orla, Orlagh, Orlaith, Orlann, Orlene.*

ORITHNA *(Greek)* Mythological daughter of the king of Athens.

ORNICE *(Hebrew)* Pine tree. Variations: *Orna, Ornit.*

ORQUIDEA *(Spanish)* Orchid.

OSEYE *(African: Nigerian)* Happy one.

OSYKA *(Native American: Choctaw)* Eagle.

OSYTH *(English)* Unknown definition.

OTILIE *(Czech)* Wealthy.

OTTHILD *(German)* Successful in battle. Variations: *Ottila, Ottilia, Ottilie, Otylia.*

OTZARA *(Hebrew)* Wealth. Variation: *Ozara.*

The Most Popular Girls' Names from the 1980s

Name trends are somehow affected by the decade's events, and in the '80s, the names that parents chose seemed to have the sound of money to them. Or maybe we were just watching too many of those nighttime soap operas that starred people with too much money.

1. Jennifer
2. Sarah
3. Nicole
4. Jessica
5. Katherine
6. Stephanie
7. Elizabeth
8. Amanda
9. Melissa
10. Lindsay
11. Rebecca
12. Lisa
13. Rachel
14. Lauren
15. Andrea
16. Christina
17. Emily
18. Kristen
19. Megan
20. Angela
21. Crystal
22. Kelly
23. Julie
24. Erin
25. Amy
26. Kimberly
27. Michelle
28. Laura
29. Danielle
30. Jacqueline
31. Mary
32. Heather
33. Tiffany
34. Christine
35. Shannon
36. Erica
37. Katie
38. Renee
39. Maria
40. Susan
41. Monica
42. Natalie
43. Courtney
44. Amber
45. Diana
46. April
47. Dana
48. Dawn
49. Samantha
50. Victoria

OUIDA *(English)* Famous soldier.
OURANIA *(Greek)* Heavenly one.
OVYENA *(Welsh)* Unknown definition.
OWENA *(Welsh)* Well born. Feminine version of Owen.
OYA *(Native American: Miwok)* To give a name to something.

Tried and True Classics

PAGE *(French)* Intern. Page is a girls' name that isn't used too frequently, but when it is, it seems to command a sense of respect and power. One prominent Paige who certainly fits this definition is Paige Rense, the editor of the magazine *Architectural Digest*, who transformed the publication into one of the foremost influences in the industry. Paige also appeared as a character on the 1980s TV show *Knots Landing*, played by Nicollette Sheridan. The name Page will probably continue to be used sparingly, but when it does appear, it will always pack a punch. Variation: *Paige*.

PAMELA *(Greek)* Honey. Despite the omnipresence of former *Baywatch* vixen Pamela Anderson, the name actually has quite a number of strong literary connections. Pamela's first known usage was by author Sir Philip Sidney in his work entitled *Arcadia*, which dates from the very end of the sixteenth century. Next, it appeared in a popular novel entitled *Pamela* by author Samuel Richardson in the middle of the eighteenth century. Latter-day authors who were actually christened with the name include Brits Pamela Moore and Pamela Hansford Johnson. Pamela fell into the top ten list from the '50s through the '70s, but then tended to fall off in popularity. Ms. Anderson could very well bring the name back into popular usage once again. Variations: *Pam, Pamala, Pamalia, Pamalla, Pamelia, Pamelina, Pamella, Pamilia, Pamilla, Pammela, Pammi, Pammie, Pammy*.

PARIS *(Greek)* The city. In keeping with the current trend toward naming girls after cities, states, and regions, Paris is right up there as a name for a baby girl. Über-rich hotel heiress/party girl Paris Hilton has brought this name into the limelight of late. Variations: *Parisa, Parris, Parrish.*

PATRICIA *(Latin)* Noble. Feminine version of Patrick. Though Patricia has a long, esteemed history dating from the sixth century, when it began to be used within the Catholic church, a surge in Patricia's popularity can clearly be distinguished from the time that one of Queen Victoria's granddaughters was given the name. From there, it basically exploded in both Great Britain and the United States. This fervor lasted until well into the '70s. As with many other formal names, even though Patricia may be the given name, it's more likely that you'll use one of Patricia's nicknames. And when parents are choosing the name today, they are leaning toward one of the more exotic variations listed here. Famous Patricias include actresses Patty Duke and Patricia Neal. Variations: *Pat, Patreece, Patreice, Patria, Patric, Patrica, Patrice, Patricka, Patrizia, Patsy, Patti, Pattie, Patty, Tricia, Trish, Trisha.*

PAULA *(Latin)* Small. Feminine version of Paul. Variations: *Paola, Paolina, Paule, Pauleen, Paulene, Pauletta, Paulette, Paulie, Paulina, Pauline, Paulita, Pauly, Paulyn, Pavla, Pavlina, Pavlinka, Pawlina, Pola, Polcia, Pollie, Polly.*

PEARL *(Latin)* Pearl. Variations: *Pearla, Pearle, Pearleen, Pearlena, Pearlette, Pearley, Pearline, Pearly, Perl, Perla, Perle, Perlette, Perley, Perlie, Perly.*

PENELOPE *(Greek)* Bobbin weaver. Penny is a great worldly name that dates back to the ancient Greek myth in which Penelope remained faithful to Odysseus. Famous Penelopes include actresses Penelope Ann Miller, Penelope Cruz, and Penny Marshall. Variations: *Lopa, Pela, Pelcia, Pen, Penelopa, Penina, Penine, Penna, Pennelope, Penni, Penny, Pinelopi, Piptisa, Popi.*

PERRY *(French)* Pear tree; (Greek) Nymph of mountains. Perry started out as a boys' name that was actually a nickname for Peregrine. Parents began to consider the name for their daughters around the middle of this century, but it seems to be so rarely used by either sex that it has remained a gender-neutral name even after all these years. Variations: *Peri, Perrey, Perri, Perrie.*

PHILIPPA *(Greek)* Lover of horses. Feminine version of Philip. Variations: *Philipa, Philippine, Phillipina, Pippa, Pippy.*

PHOEBE *(Greek)* Brilliant. Variations: *Pheabe, Phebe, Pheby, Phobe.*

PHYLLIS *(Greek)* Green tree branch. Variations: *Philis, Phillis, Philliss, Phillys, Phylis, Phyllida, Phylliss.*

POLLY *(English)* Variation of Molly, which in turn is a diminutive form of Mary. In the minds of some people, the name Polly will forever be connected with a cracker-eating parrot or the goody-two-shoes in the novel by author Eleanor H. Porter, Pollyanna. Variations: *Pauleigh, Pollee, Polley, Polli, Pollie, Pollyann, Pollyanna, Pollyanne.*

PRISCILLA *(Latin)* Old. Once upon a time, Priscilla seemed to have the same kind of reputation as Polly, since it was a popular Puritan name; its most famous bearer was Priscilla Alden. Today, however, the widow of Elvis Presley, Priscilla Presley, has given new visibility to this name and single-handedly altered its reputation from prim and proper to smart and alluring. Variations: *Precilla, Prescilla, Pricilla, Pris, Priscila, Priss, Prissie, Prissilla, Prissy, Prysilla.*

Slightly Daring Choices

PADGETT *(Greek)* Wisdom. Variations: *Padget, Paget, Pagett, Pagette.*

PADMA *(Hindu)* The lotus. Variations: *Padmasundara, Padmavati, Padmini.*

PALILA *(Hawaiian)* Bird.

PALLAS *(Greek)* Another name for Athena, goddess of the arts; goddess of wisdom.

PALMA *(Latin)* Palm.

PALMER *(English)* Palm tree. Last name. Variations: *Ilmirah, Palima, Pallimirah, Pallma, Pallmara, Pallmyra, Palma, Palmira, Palmyra.*

PALOMA *(Spanish)* Dove. Variations: *Palloma, Palometa, Palomita, Peloma.*

PANA *(Native American)* Partridge.

PANDITA *(Hindu)* Scholar.

PANDORA *(Greek)* All-gifted. Variations: *Panda, Pandorra, Panndora.*

PANNA *(Hindu)* Emerald.

PANOLA *(Native American: Choctaw)* Cotton.

PANTHEA *(Greek)* All the gods.

PANYA *(African: Swahili)* Mouse.

PANYIN *(African: Ghanian)* First-born of twins.

PAPINA *(Native American: Miwok)* Vine on an oak tree.

PARTHENIA *(Greek)* Virginal. Variations: *Parthania, Parthena, Parthenie, Parthina, Parthine, Pathania, Pathena, Pathenia, Pathina.*

PARVANI *(Hindu)* Celebration. Variation: *Parvina.*

PARVATI *(Hindu)* The goddess Devi.

PARVIN *(Hindu)* Star. Variation: *Parveen.*

PASCALE *(French)* Child of Easter. Feminine version of Pascal. Variations: *Pascalette, Pascaline, Pascalle, Paschale.*

PASHA *(Greek)* Of the ocean. Variation: *Palasha.*

PATIENCE *(English)* Patience. Variations: *Paciencia, Patient.*

PELA *(Hawaiian)* Pretty. Variation: *Bela.*

PELAGIA *(Greek)* The ocean; (Polish) Sea-dweller. Variations: *Pelage, Pelageia, Pelagie, Pelegia, Pelgia, Pellagia.*

PERDITA *(Latin)* Lost.

PERSEPHONE *(Greek)* The goddess of spring and rebirth.

PERSIS *(Latin)* From Persia. Variation: *Perssis.*

PETA *(Greek)* Rock. Feminine version of Peter. Variations: *Petra, Petrice, Petrina, Petrona.*

PETRONELLA *(Latin)* Roman clan name. Variations: *Pernel, Pernelle, Peronel, Peronelle, Petrina, Petronelle, Petronia, Petronilla, Pier, Pierette.*

PETRONILLA *(Scandinavian)* Stone. Variations: *Pella, Pernilla, Pernille, Petrine.*

PETULA *(Latin)* Sassy. Variation: *Petulah.*

PETUNIA *(English)* Flower.

PHILADELPHIA *(Greek)* City, brotherly love. Variations: *Philli, Phillie.*

PHILANA *(Greek)* Lover of people.

PHILANTHA *(Greek)* Lover of flowers.

PHILBERTA *(English)* Bright.

PHILOMENA *(Greek)* Beloved. Variations: *Filomena, Philomene, Philomina.*

PIA *(Latin)* Pious.

PILAR *(Spanish)* Pillar.

PIPER *(English)* Bagpipe player.

PIRENE *(Greek)* The daughter of the river god, Achelous.

PITA *(African)* Fourth daughter.

PIXIE *(English)* Tiny.

PLACIDA *(Spanish)* Calm. Variation: *Plasida.*

PLEASANCE *(English)* Pleasure. Variations: *Pleasant, Pleasants, Pleasence.*

POPPY *(Latin)* Flower. Variation: *Popi.*

PORTIA *(Latin)* Roman clan name. Variations: *Porcha, Porscha, Porsche, Porschia, Porsha.*

POSALA *(Native American: Miwok)* Flower.

PRECIOUS *(English)* Precious. Variations: *Precia, Preciosa.*

PRIMA *(Latin)* First. Variations: *Primalia, Primetta, Primina, Priminia, Primula.*

PRIMAVERA *(Italian)* Spring.

Most Popular Girls' Names from the 1990s

In the 1990s, girls' names had a wealthy ring to them. One thing you can be sure of is that parents continued to select names for their kids that reflected the times they're were living in—or the years they were nostalgic about. Because some things never change!

1. Ashley
2. Jessica
3. Amanda
4. Sarah
5. Brittany
6. Megan
7. Jennifer
8. Nicole
9. Stephanie
10. Katherine
11. Caitlin
12. Lauren
13. Rachel
14. Samantha
15. Heather
16. Elizabeth
17. Danielle
18. Christina
19. Emily
20. Amber
21. Melissa
22. Tiffany
23. Lindsey
24. Kristen
25. Kayla
26. Rebecca
27. Michelle
28. Kelly
29. Chelsea
30. Courtney
31. Crystal
32. Amy
33. Laura
34. Kimberly
35. Allison
36. Erica
37. Alicia
38. Jamie
39. Katie
40. Erin
41. Mary
42. Alyssa
43. Kelsey
44. Andrea
45. Alexandra
46. Christine
47. Angela
48. Jacqueline
49. Casey

40\. Shannon

PRIMROSE *(English)* First rose.

PRINCESS *(English)* Royal title. Variations: *Prin, Princesa, Princessa.*

PRISMA *(Greek)* Cut glass. Variation: *Prusma.*

PRUDENCE *(Latin)* Wariness. Variations: *Pru, Prudencia, Prudie, Prudu, Prudy, Prue.*

PRUNELLA *(Latin)* Small plum.

PURITY *(English)* Pure.

Living on the Edge

PAAVANA *(Hindu)* Pure.

PAAVANI *(Hindu)* The Ganges River.

PACA *(Spanish)* Frenchman.

PAKA *(African: Swahili)* Kitten.

PALA *(Native American)* Water.

PALAKIKA *(Hawaiian)* Hawaiian version of Frances. Variation: *Farakika.*

PANGIOTA *(Greek)* All holy.

PANPHILA *(Greek)* She loves all. Variations: *Panfila, Panfyla, Panphyla.*

PANSY *(English)* Flower. Variations: *Pansey, Pansie.*

PARTHENOPE *(Greek)* Ancient mythological figure.

PASUA *(African: Swahili)* Born by cesarean section.

PATEREKIA *(Hawaiian)* Aristocrat. Variation: *Pakelekia.*

PATI *(Native American: Miwok)* Twisting willows.

PATIA *(Spanish)* Leaf.

PAUSHA *(Hindu)* Month in the Hindu year.

PAVANA *(Hindu)* Wind. Variation: *Pavani.*

PAX *(Latin)* Peace.

PAZ *(Hebrew)* Gold. Variations: *Paza, Pazia, Paziah, Pazice, Pazit,*

Paziya, Pazya.

PEAKALIKA *(Hawaiian)* She brings happiness. Variation: *Beatarisa, Biatirisa.*

PEDZI *(African)* Last child.

PEKE *(Hawaiian)* Bright.

PELEKA *(Hawaiian)* Bright. Variations: *Beke, Bereta.*

PELEKILA *(Hawaiian)* Primitive. Variations: *Peresekila, Peresila, Perisila.*

PELENAKINO *(Hawaiian)* Strong as a bear. Variations: *Berenadeta, Berenadino.*

PELIAH *(Hebrew)* God's miracle. Variation: *Pelia.*

PELIKA *(Hawaiian)* Peaceful. Hawaiian version of Freda. Variation: *Ferida.*

PELIPA *(Native American)* Lover of horses.

PELULIO *(Hawaiian)* Emerald. Variation: *Berulo.*

PEMBA *(African)* Meteorological power.

PENDA *(African: Swahili)* Beloved.

PENI *(Native American)* His mind.

PENINAH *(Hebrew)* Coral. Variations: *Peni, Penie, Penina, Penini, Peninit.*

PENINIYA *(Hebrew)* Hen. Variation: *Peninia.*

PEONY *(English)* Flower.

PEPITA *(Spanish)* God will add. Diminutive feminine form of Joseph. Variations: *Pepa, Peta.*

PERACH *(Hebrew)* Blossom. Variations: *Perah, Pericha, Pircha, Pirchia, Pirchit, Pirchiya, Pirha.*

PERFECTA *(Spanish)* Perfect.

PHEAKKLEY *(Cambodian)* Loyal.

PHEDRA *(Greek)* Bright. Variations: *Faydra, Fedra, Phadra, Phaedra, Phedre.*

PHEODORA *(Greek)* Gift from God. Feminine version of Theodore.

PIEDAD *(Spanish)* Devotion.

PILI *(African: Swahili)* Second-born.

PILIKIKA *(Hawaiian)* Strong. Variation: *Birigita.*

PILILANI *(Hawaiian)* Close to heaven.

PILISI *(Greek)* branch.

PILUKI *(Hawaiian)* Leaf.

PINEKI *(Hawaiian)* Peanut.

PINGA *(Hindu)* Bronze.

PINGJARJE *(Native American: Apache)* Small deer.

PINQUANA *(Native American: Shoshone)* Fragrant.

POCAHONTAS *(Native American: Algonquin)* Capricious.

POLETE *(Hawaiian)* Small. Variations: *Poleke, Polina.*

POLLYAM *(Hindu)* Goddess of the plague.

POLYXENA *(Greek)* Very hospitable.

POMAIKAI *(Hawaiian)* Fortunate.

POMONA *(Latin)* Apple.

PONI *(African)* Second daughter.

PRAGYATA *(Hindu)* Wisdom.

PRARTHANA *(Hindu)* Prayer.

PRATIBHA *(Hindu)* Tolerance.

PREMA *(Hindu)* Love.

PREMLATA *(Hindu)* Vine.

PRIBISLAVA *(Czech)* To help glorify. Variations: *Pribena, Pribka, Pribuska.*

PRIYA *(Hindu)* Beloved. Variations: *Priyal, Priyam, Priyanka, Priyasha, Priyata, Priyati.*

PROSERPINE *(Roman)* Mythological queen of the underworld.

PROTIMA *(Hindu)* Prominent Indian dancer.

PSYCHE *(Greek)* The soul.

PTAYSANWEE *(Native American: Sioux)* White buffalo.

PUA *(Polynesian)* Flowering tree.

PUAKAI *(Hawaiian)* Ocean flower. Variation: *Pua.*

PUAKEA *(Hawaiian)* White flower.

PUALANI *(Hawaiian)* Flower. Variation: *Puni.*

PUANANI *(Hawaiian)* Beautiful flower.

PULUPAKI *(Polynesian)* Flower wreath.
PURNIMA *(Hindu)* Full moon.
PYRRHA *(Greek)* Red.

Tried and True Classics

QUEEN *(English)* Queen. Variations: *Queena, Queenation, Queeneste, Queenette, Queenie, Queeny.*

QUINCI *(English)* The fifth son's estate. Variations: *Quincie, Quincy.*

QUINN *(Gaelic)* Advisor. Variation: *Quincy.*

QUINTINA *(English)* Fifth. Quintina and all of its melodious variations are often used when a daughter's birth falls under very specific categories: Frequently, a girl named Quintina will either be the fifth child in a family or born on the fifth day of a certain month. Some parents even choose the name when their daughter is born in the month of May, the fifth month of the year. Personally, I'd reserve it for a daughter who is born in the fifth month, on the fifth day, at *5:55 in the morning.* Variations: *Quin, Quinella, Quinetta, Quinette, Quintana, Quintessa, Quintona, Quintonice.*

Slightly Daring Choices

QUIANA *(American)* Grace. Variation: *Quianna.*

Living on the Edge

QUAHAH *(Native American: Pueblo)* White coral beads.

QUARTILLA *(Latin)* Fourth.

QUBILAH *(Arabic)* Agreement.
QUERIDA *(Spanish)* Beloved.
QUESTA *(French)* Hunter.
QUETA *(Spanish)* Home ruler.
QUITERIE *(French)* Peaceful.

Tried and True Classics

RACHEL *(Hebrew)* Lamb. Rachel is essentially one of the oldest names in the Bible. It has proven to be a popular name in this country ever since the Puritans first arrived in the 1600s. After the Puritans broke through with its more common use, it remained popular among parents who wished their daughters to eventually emulate the mother of Joseph in the Bible, and as time went on, parents from all walks began to see the beauty in the name. Of late, Rachel has consistently appeared in the top twenty names list, possibly due in part to the popularity of the TV show *Friends* and Jennifer Aniston's character, Rachel Green. Variations: *Rachael, Racheal, Rachele, Rachell, Rachelle, Rae, Raelene, Raquel, Raquela, Raquella, Raquelle.*

RAFAELA *(Spanish)* God heals. Feminine version of Raphael. Variations: *Rafa, Rafaelia, Rafaella, Rafella, Rafelle, Raffaela, Raffaele, Raphaella, Raphaelle, Refaela, Rephaela.*

RAMONA *(Spanish)* Wise protector. Feminine version of Raymond. Many parents casting around for a suitable name for their daughters will remember Ramona primarily as the impish character in the children's books by author Beverly Cleary.

REBECCA *(Hebrew)* Joined together. The first Rebecca known to us was the Biblical wife of Isaac and the mother of Jacob. Other famous Rebeccas since then have been Rebecca of Sunnybrook Farm from Kate Douglas's novel, as well as another literary figure, novelist Rebecca West. Novelist Daphne du Maurier also wrote a novel called *Rebecca*, later turned into a movie by Alfred Hitchcock. Name-watchers point to du Maurier's book as the main influence that put Rebecca on the map back in the '40s. Variations: *Becca, Becky, Reba, Rebbecca, Rebbie, Rebeca, Rebeccah, Rebecka, Rebeckah, Rebeka, Rebekah, Rebekka, Rebekke, Rebeque, Rebi, Reby, Reyba, Rheba.*

REGAN *(Irish)* Son of the small ruler. Variation: *Reagan.*

REGINA *(Latin)* Queen. Variations: *Raenah, Raina, Raine, Rainy, Rana, Rane, Rayna, Regena, Reggi, Reggie, Reggy, Regi, Regie, Regiena, Regine, Reginia, Reginna, Reinette, Reyna.*

RENÉE *(French)* Reborn. French names with accent marks appeared to be pretty popular during the '70s and Renée fit right in. The Latin version of Renée is Renata, and it was commonly used by people in the Roman Empire for their daughters. Somewhere between back then and the 1600s, Renata turned into Renée; Renata rarely appears anymore. Variations: *Renata, Renay, Rene, Renelle, Reney, Reni, Renia, Renie, Renni, Rennie, Renny.*

RHODA *(Greek)* Rose. Of course, the most famous Rhoda that most of us know is Rhoda Morgenstern, Valerie Harper's successful TV role. Rhoda's roots are actually Biblical—the name first appeared in the New Testament Book of Acts—and it was commonly used during the late 1800s. Variations: *Rhodante, Rhodanthe, Rhodia, Rhodie, Rhody, Roda.*

RHONDA *(Welsh)* Grand. Variations: *Rhonnda, Ronda.*

RICARDA *(Italian)* Powerful ruler. Feminine version of Richard. Variations: *Rica, Ricca, Richarda, Richel, Richela, Richele, Richella, Richelle, Richenda, Richenza, Ricki, Rickie, Ricky, Riki, Rikki, Rikky.*

RITA *(Spanish)* Pearl. Diminutive of Margarite. Rita reached its height during the '40s with the popularity of the actress Rita Hayworth. Other famous Ritas are singer Rita Coolidge and actress Rita Moreno. No wonder the name isn't more widely used! Variations: *Reeta, Reta, Rheta, Rhetta.*

Famous Female Authors and Artists

Some parents read Shakespeare aloud during pregnancy, in the hopes that some of that culture just may rub off on their kids later on. Others play Mozart for their unborn baby, from the results of the pregnancy test to the delivery room, hoping that the child will grow into a musical prodigy. Who knows if this sort of stuff rubs off on kids, but if you're looking for inspiration from the creative world, here are some examples:

AGATHA CHRISTIE
ALICE WALKER
CHARLOTTE BRONTË
ELIZABETH BARRETT BROWNING
FRIDA KAHLO
GEORGIA O'KEEFFE
GLORIA STEINEM
JANE AUSTEN
LAURA INGALLS WILDER
MAYA ANGELOU
NORA EPHRON

ROBERTA *(English)* Bright fame. Feminine version of Robert. Variations: *Bobbet, Bobbett, Bobbi, Bobbie, Bobby, Robbi, Robbie, Robby, Robena, Robertena, Robertha, Robertina, Robin, Robina, Robine, Robinette, Robinia, Robyn, Robyna, Rogan, Roynne.*

ROCHELLE *(French)* Little rock. Variations: *Rochele, Rochell, Rochella, Roshele, Roshelle.*

ROLANDA *(German)* Famous land. Feminine version of Roland. Variations: *Rolande, Rollande, Rolonda, Rolonde.*

ROMA *(Italian)* Rome.

RONNI *(English)* Strong counsel. Feminine version of Ronald. Variations: *Ronnette, Ronney, Ronnica, Ronny.*

ROSALIND *(Spanish)* Pretty rose. Variations: *Rosalina, Rosalinda, Rosalinde, Rosaline, Rosalyn, Rosalynd, Rosalyne, Rosalynn, Roselind, Roselynn, Roslyn.*

ROSANNA *(English)* Combination of Rose and Anna. Variations: *Rosana, Rosannah, Rosanne, Roseana, Roseanna, Roseanna, Roseannah, Rosehannah, Rozanna, Rozanne.*

ROSE *(Latin)* Flower. Flower names have been making a comeback, and Rose seems to be the runaway leader. It has Victorian overtones, it's elegant, and it's also becoming extremely popular as a middle name. Variations: *Rosabel, Rosabell, Rosabella, Rosabelle, Rosalee, Rosaley, Rosalia, Rosalie, Rosalin, Rosella, Roselle, Rosetta, Rosette, Rosey, Rosi, Rosie, Rosita, Rosy, Ruza, Ruzena, Ruzenka, Ruzsa.*

ROSEMARY *(Latin)* Dew of the sea. Variations: *Rosemaree, Rosemarey, Rosemaria, Rosemarie.*

ROSSALYN *(Scottish)* Cape. Feminine version of Ross. Variations: *Rosslyn, Rosslynn.*

ROXANNE *(Persian)* Dawn. Variations: *Roxana, Roxane, Roxann, Roxanna, Roxianne, Roxie, Roxy.*

RUBY *(English)* Jewel. Ruby was part of the first wave of jewel names that began to hit right after the Civil War. Today, Ruby is slowly beginning to become more popular. Variations: *Rube, Rubey, Rubie, Rubye.*

RUTH *(Hebrew)* Companion. Variations: *Ruthe, Ruthella, Ruthelle, Ruthetta, Ruthi, Ruthie, Ruthina, Ruthine, Ruthy.*

Slightly Daring Choices

RAE *(Hebrew)* Lamb. Variations: *Raeann, Raelene, Ray, Raye, Rayette.*

RAINBOW *(English)* Rainbow.

RAINELL *(English)* Newly created, combination of "rain" and "elle." Variation: *Rainelle.*

RAISA *(Hebrew)* Rose. Variations: *Raise, Raisel, Raissa, Raisse, Raizel, Rayzil, Razil.*

RAJA *(Arabic)* Anticipation. Variations: *Raga, Ragya, Rajya.*

RALPHINA *(English)* Wolf-counselor. Feminine version of Ralph. Variation: *Ralphine.*

RAMAA *(Hindu)* Lovely. Variations: *Ramana, Ramani.*

RAMIA *(African)* Fortune-teller.

RAMLA *(African: Swahili)* Predicts the future.

RANA *(Spanish)* Frog. Variations: *Raniyah, Ranna, Ranya.*

RANDA *(Arabic)* Tree.

RANI *(Hindu)* Queen. Variations: *Rania, Ranique, Ranita.*

RANIELLE *(African-American)* God is my judge. Variation of Danielle.

RANITA *(Hebrew)* Song of joy. Variations: *Ranice, Ranit, Ranite, Ranitra, Ranitta.*

RANYA *(Hindu)* To gaze.

RASHA *(Arabic)* Gazelle.

RASIA *(Greek)* Rose. Variations: *Rasine, Rasya.*

RAVEN *(English)* The bird. Variation: *Ravenne.*

RAYA *(Hebrew)* Friend.

RAYNA *(Hebrew)* Song of the Lord. Variations: *Raina, Rana, Rane, Rania, Renana, Renanit, Renatia, Renatya, Renina, Rinatia, Rinatya.*

RAYYA *(Arabic)* Quenched thirst.

RAZI *(Hebrew)* Secret. Variations: *Razilee, Razili.*

RAZIAH *(Hebrew)* Secret of God. Variations: *Razia, Raziela,*

Razilee, Razili, Raziya.

RAZIYA *(African: Swahili)* Agreeable.

REA *(English)* Manly. Variations: *Rhia, Ria.*

REIKO *(Japanese)* Very pleasant child. Variation: *Rei.*

REMY *(French)* Champagne. Variations: *Remi, Remie.*

REN *(Japanese)* Lotus.

RENA *(Hebrew)* Melody. Variation: *Reena.*

RENITA *(Latin)* Defiant. Variation: *Reneeta.*

RESEDA *(Latin)* Flower.

REUBENA *(English)* Behold a son. Feminine version of Reuben. Variations: *Reubina, Rubena, Rubenia, Rubina, Rubine, Rubyna.*

REUMA *(Hebrew)* Lofty. Variation: *Raomi.*

REVA *(Hindu)* Sacred river.

REVAYA *(Hebrew)* Satisfied. Variation: *Revaia.*

REXANA *(Latin)* King and grace. Combination of Rex and Anna. Variations: *Rexanna, Rexanne.*

REZA *(Czech)* Harvest. Variation of Teresa. Variations: *Rezi, Rezka.*

RHEA *(Greek)* Earth. Variations: *Rhia, Ria.*

RHETA *(Greek)* Eloquent.

RHIANNON *(Welsh)* Goddess. Variations: *Rheanna, Rheanne, Rhiana, Rhiann, Rhianna, Rhiannan, Rhianon, Rhuan, Riana, Riane, Rianna, Rianne, Riannon, Riannon, Rianon, Riona.*

RIA *(Spanish)* Mouth of a river.

RIANE *(Irish)* Feminine version of Ryan.

RIDA *(Arabic)* Content. Variations: *Radeya, Radeyah.*

RILLA *(German)* Stream. Variations: *Rilletta, Rillette.*

RIMA *(Arabic)* Antelope.

RIMONA *(Hebrew)* Pomegranate.

RIN *(Japanese)* Park.

RINA *(English)* Newly created.

RINDA *(Scandinavian)* Ancient mythological figure. Variation: *Rind.*

RISA *(Latin)* Laughter. Variations: *Rise, Risha, Riza.*
RISHONA *(Hebrew)* Initial.
RISSA *(Greek)* Nickname for Nerissa, a sea nymph.
RODA *(Polish)* Rose.
RODERICA *(German)* Famous ruler. Feminine version of Roderick. Variations: *Rica, Roderiqua, Roderique.*
ROHANA *(Hindu)* Sandalwood. Variation: *Rohanna.*
ROMAINE *(French)* One from Rome. Variation: *Romayne.*
ROMANA *(Polish)* Citizen of Rome.

Watch Those Initials

Okay, you've finally picked the name you want to give your new baby. It sounds great with your last name, and you've selected a middle name that works well, too. Hold on—there's still one more thing you should consider: What do the initials spell out?

Frequently, parents-to-be agonize so much over choosing a name for their baby that once they've settled on a great name, they breathe a huge sigh of relief and forget about it until the birth certificate needs to be signed. Unfortunately, this little oversight could cause years of agony for your child later on—just think of a poor kid whose name is Ashleigh Sarah Stanford. Think of your grown daughter refusing to wear anything with a monogram or your adult son covering up the monogram on his suitcase before he ever gets to the airport.

So watch those initials. Make sure they don't spell out anything offensive or that could call attention to the combination. If you've overlooked this little detail, you may have some more name work to do!

ROMOLA *(Latin)* Woman from Rome. Variations: *Romella, Romelle, Romi, Romolla, Romula, Romy.*

RONA *(Scandinavian: Norwegian)* Rough isle. Variations: *Rhona, Roana, Ronella, Ronelle, Ronna.*

RONI *(Hebrew)* Joy is mine. Variations: *Ronia, Ronice, Ronit, Ronli.*

RONIYA *(Hebrew)* Joy of God. Variations: *Ronela, Ronella, Ronia.*

RONNELL *(African-American)* Feminine version of Ron. Variations: *Ronell, Ronelle, Ronnel.*

ROSAMOND *(German)* Famous protector. Variation: *Rosamund.*

ROSCHAN *(Hindu)* Dawn. Variations: *Rochana, Rochani, Roschana, Roshan, Roshana, Roshanara, Roshni.*

ROSELANI *(Hawaiian)* Heavenly rose.

Living on the Edge

RAANANA *(Hebrew)* Fresh. Variation: *Ranana.*

RABAB *(Arabic)* Pale cloud.

RABIAH *(Arabic)* Breeze. Variations: *Rabi, Rabia.*

RACHAV *(Hebrew)* Large. Variation: *Rahab.*

RADHA *(Hindu)* Prosperity; success.

RADHIYA *(African: Swahili)* Agreeable.

RADINKA *(Czech)* Active.

RADMILLA *(Slavic)* Industrious for the people. Variation: *Radmila.*

RADOMIRA *(Czech)* Glad and famous.

RADOSLAVA *(Czech)* Glorious and happy.

RADOSLAWA *(Polish)* Glad for glory. Variation: *Rada.*

RAFA *(Arabic)* Well-being. Variation: *Rafah.*

RAFYA *(Hebrew)* God heals. Variations: *Rafia, Raphia.*

RAGHIDA *(Arabic)* Happy.

RAGNBORG *(Scandinavian)* Counsel. Variations: *Ragna, Ramborg.*

RAGNILD *(German)* Power. Variations: *Ragnhild, Ragnhilda, Ragnhilde, Ragnilda, Ranillda, Renilda, Renilde.*

RAI *(Japanese)* Next. Variation: *Raiko.*

RAIDAH *(Arabic)* Guide.

RAJALAKSHMI *(Hindu)* Goddess of fortune. Variation: *Raji.*

RAJANI *(Hindu)* Night. Variations: *Rajana, Rajni.*

RAJATA *(Hindu)* King. Variation: *Raji.*

RAJNANDINI *(Hindu)* Princess.

RAKU *(Japanese)* Pleasure.

RAN *(Scandinavian)* Goddess of the sea.

RANJANA *(Hindu)* Beloved.

RANVEIG *(Scandinavian)* Housewife. Variation: *Ronnaug.*

RASHEDA *(Turkish)* Righteous. Feminine version of Rashid. Variations: *Rasheeda, Rasheedah, Rasheida, Rashidah.*

RATHNAIT *(Irish)* Grace. Variations: *Ranait, Rath.*

RATI *(Hindu)* Goddess of love.

RATRI *(Hindu)* Night.

RAVVA *(Hindu)* The sun.

RAWIYA *(Arabic)* Tell a story. Variations: *Rawiyah, Rawya.*

RAWNIE *(Gypsy)* Lady.

REHEMA *(African: Swahili)* Compassion.

REI *(Japanese)* Appreciation.

REICHANA *(Hebrew)* Aromatic. Variations: *Rechana, Rehana.*

REKHA *(Hindu)* Line.

REMAZIAH *(Hebrew)* Sign from God. Variations: *Remazia, Remazya.*

REMEDIOS *(Spanish)* Help.

RHIANVYEN *(Welsh)* Fair maiden.

RHONWEN *(Welsh)* Slender, fair. Variations: *Ronwen, Roweena, Roweina, Rowena, Rowina.*

RHU *(Hindu)* Pure.
RIGBORG *(Scandinavian)* Strong fortification.
RIGMOR *(Scandinavian)* Powerful courage.
RIHANA *(Arabic)* Sweet basil.
RIKU *(Japanese)* Land. Variation: *Rikuyo.*
RIOGHNACH *(Irish)* Queen. Variation: *Riona.*
RITIKA *(Hindu)* Active.
RITZPAH *(Hebrew)* Coal. Variations: *Ritzpa, Rizpah.*
RIVA *(Hebrew)* Joined. Variations: *Reva, Rivah.*
RIVKA *(Hebrew)* Noose. Variations: *Rifka, Rifke, Riki, Rivai, Rivca, Rivcka, Rivi, Rivvy.*
ROKUKO *(Japanese)* Sixth-born.
ROSALBA *(Latin)* White rose.
ROSCISLAWA *(Polish)* Glory in conquest.
ROSTISLAVA *(Czech)* One who seizes glory. Variations: *Rosta, Rostina, Rostinka, Rostuska.*
ROULA *(Greek)* Defiant. Variation: *Rula.*
ROYALE *(French)* Royal. Variations: *Royalene, Royall, Royalle.*
RUANA *(Hindu)* Indian violin.
RUCHI *(Hindu)* Love.
RUCHIKA *(Hindu)* Attractive.
RUDELLE *(German)* Famous. Variation: *Rudella.*
RUDRA *(Hindu)* Plant.
RUFARO *(African: Zimbabwean)* Happiness.
RUFINA *(Latin)* Red-haired. Feminine version of Rufus.
RUKAN *(Arabic)* Confident.
RUKIYA *(African: Swahili)* To arise.
RUKMINI *(Hindu)* Golden.
RUNA *(Scandinavian)* Secret lore. Variation: *Rula.*
RUPAL *(Hindu)* Beautiful. Variations: *Rupala, Rupali, Rupinder.*
RUQAYYA *(Arabic)* Arise. Variations: *Ruqayah, Ruqayyah.*
RURI *(Japanese)* Emerald.
RUSALKA *(Czech)* Wood nymph.
RUT *(Czech)* Devoted companion.

RUTA *(Hawaiian)* Friend.
RUWAYDAH *(Arabic)* Graceful walk.
RYBA *(Czech)* Fish.

Tried and True Classics

SAMANTHA *(English)* His name is God. Samantha is widely considered to be the feminine version of Samuel, and though it's been around for centuries, it wasn't until the TV series *Bewitched* first appeared in the 1960s that this name really took off. Samantha was a well-regarded but little-used name in Britain in the mid-'60s but, when *Bewitched* started airing in England, the popularity of the name soared, and Samantha turned into one of the top names for girls. Besides Samantha Stevens, another famous Samantha was Samantha Eggar, a British actress who was popular in the '60s. Variations: *Sam, Samella, Samentha, Sammantha, Sammee, Sammey, Sammi, Sammie, Sammy, Semanntha, Semantha, Simantha, Symantha.*

SANDRA *(Italian)* Protector of men. Shortened from Alessandra (Alexandra); feminine version of Alessandro (Alexander). Variations: *Sandee, Sandi, Sandie, Sandrea, Sandria, Sandrina, Sandrine, Sandy, Saundra, Sondra, Zana, Zandra, Zanna.*

SARAH *(Hebrew)* Princess. Sarah was once primarily notable for its popularity as a name for Jewish girls, but now Sarah hovers among the most popular names for all daughters in the United States. In the Bible, Sarah was the wife of Abraham, and the name has been well used and well liked in both Great Baritain and the United States since Puritan times. Famous Sarahs today include actresses Sarah Jessica Parker, and Sara Gilbert, from the *Rosanne* show in the '90s. Though some fear Sarah will become overused if its popularity continues, others believe that it's destined to be a timeless classic. Variations: *Sadee, Sadie, Sadye, Saidee,*

Saleena, Salena, Salina, Sallee, Salley, Sallianne, Sallie, Sally, Sallyann, Sara, Sarai, Saretta, Sarette, Sari, Sarita, Saritia, Sarra.

SASHA *(Russian)* Protector of men. Feminine diminutive version of Alexander. Variations: *Sasa, Sascha.*

SAVANNA *(Spanish)* Treeless. Place name. Savanna is hot. It seems that in every other movie, as well as many books, the name of the female protagonist who must jump through hoops and face seemingly insurmountable challenges all in 300 pages or 90 minutes, is named Savanna. Melinda Dillon played Savannah in the movie *The Prince of Tides*, and Whitney Houston played Savannah in the movie *Waiting to Exhale*. Variations: *Savana, Savanah, Savannah, Savonna, Sevanna.*

SCARLETT *(English)* Red. Variations: *Scarlet, Scarlette.*

SEBASTIANE *(Latin)* One from an ancient Roman city. Feminine version of Sebastian. Variations: *Sebastiana, Sebastienne.*

SELA *(Polynesian)* Princess.

SELENA *(Spanish)* From Celine (*Greek*), Goddess of the moon. Though Selena's first use was as a Greek goddess, the name began to become popular in the 1800s when a countess in Britain went by the name of Selina. At present, this name is becoming increasingly popular in the Hispanic community because of the late singer Selena Quintanilla. Variations: *Celena, Celina, Celinda, Celine, Celyna, Salena, Salina, Salinah, Sela, Selene, Selina, Selinda, Seline, Sena.*

SERENA *(Latin)* Serene. If you'd like your daughter to be cute and a little bit mischievous, then Serena is a good name for her. Serena was alter ego to Samantha in the sitcom *Bewitched*, and Serena was always doing things to get Samantha into trouble. Variations: *Sareen, Sarena, Sarene, Sarina, Sarine, Sereena, Serenah, Serenna, Serina.*

SHANICE *(African-American)* Newly created. Variations: *Shaneice, Shanese, Shaniece, Shanise, Shannice.*

SHANIKA *(African-American)* Newly created. Variations: *Shaneeka, Shaneeke, Shanicka, Shanikah, Shaniqua, Shanique, Shenika.*

SHANNON *(Irish)* Ancient. Though Shannon is thoroughly Irish in its origin, it has primarily only been used as a last name in that country. It first appeared as a girls' name in the United States, in fact, back in the 1930s. Britain had only started to discover the name by 1950. Bucking the tide, many parents then began to use it for their sons, but the female habit of totally assimilating a boys' name has taken over, and today Shannon is mostly thought of as a girls' name. Variations: *Shanan, Shann, Shanna, Shannah, Shannan, Shannen, Shannie, Shanon.*

SHARLENE *(English)* Woman. Feminine version of Charles. Variations: *Sharleen, Sharleyne, Sharlina, Sharline, Sharlyne.*

SHARMAINE *(Latin)* Roman clan name. Variations: *Sharma, Sharmain, Sharman, Sharmane, Sharmayne, Sharmian, Sharmine, Sharmyn.*

SHARON *(Hebrew)* A plain. Sharon is a pretty name that feels just a bit dated, since it regularly appeared on lists of the top twenty most popular girls' names in the '40s, '50s, and '60s. Variations: *Sharan, Sharen, Sharin, Sharona, Sharonda, Sharone, Sharran, Sharren, Sharron, Sharronda, Sharronne, Sharyn, Sheren, Sheron, Sherryn.*

SHAUNA *(Hebrew)* God is good. Feminine variation of John. Variations: *Shaunda, Shaune, Shauneen, Shaunna, Shawna, Shawnda, Shawnna.*

SHAVONNE *(Hebrew)* God is good. Feminine variation of John. Variations: *Shavon, Shavone, Shevon, Shevonne, Shivonne, Shyvon, Shyvonne.*

SHAWN *(Hebrew)* God is good. Another feminine variation of John. Variations: *Sean, Shawnee, Shawni.*

Female Figures from Greek Mythology

There's a wealth of interesting names to ponder when it comes to female mythological figures. Think about some of these exotic, melodious names:

APHRODITE: *Goddess of love and beauty*
ARTEMIS: *Goddess of nature*
ATHENA: *Goddess of wisdom*
DEMETER: *Goddess of the earth*
ERIS: *Goddess of debate*
HERA: *Goddess of marriage and childbirth*
HESTIA: *Goddess of the home*
IRIS: *Goddess of the rainbow*
NIKE: *Goddess of victory*
PERSEPHONE: *Goddess of spring and rebirth*
RHEA: *Mother of Zeus*
SELENE: *Goddess of the moon*

SHELBY *(English)* Estate on a ledge. Shelby is most commonly thought of as a name for boys and as a last name, but it is currently one of the hottest names for baby girls. Julia Roberts played a woman named Shelby in the movie *Steel Magnolias*, and the rest is history. Variations: *Shelbee, Shelbey, Shellby.*

SHELLEY *(English)* Meadow on a ledge. Variations: *Shellee, Shelli, Shellie, Shelly.*

SHIRLEY *(English)* Bright meadow. Though Shirley was a common name for boys from Puritan times all the way through to the mid-1800s, two female Shirleys—almost a century apart—helped to turn the tide. The first was a novel by Charlotte Brontë entitled *Shirley*, but the second was perhaps the most famous Shirley in the history of the world—Shirley Temple. Although theirs is an uncommon name today, a number of famous Shirleys from decades past helped the name to remain popular throughout the '60s: Shirley Jones, Shirley Jackson, and Shirley MacLaine. Variations: *Shirlean, Shirleen, Shirlene, Shirlynn, Shurly.*

SHONA *(Irish)* God is good. Feminine variation of John. Variations: *Shonah, Shone.*

SIBYL *(Greek)* Seer, oracle. When most people hear the name Sibyl today, they think of the woman with multiple personality disorder. More than a century earlier, however, a novel written by Benjamin Disraeli entitled *Sybil* helped to popularize the name. Actress Cybill Shepherd has also helped to add some glamour to the name in recent years. Variations: *Sibbell, Sibel, Sibell, Sibella, Sibelle, Sibilla, Sibyll, Sibylla, Sybel, Sybella, Sybelle, Sybil, Sybill, Sybilla, Sybille, Sybyl.*

SIGOURNEY *(English)* Unknown definition. The most well-known Sigourney is actress Sigourney Weaver.

SIMONE *(French)* God listens. Feminine version of Simon. Simone may initially resemble Renée, since it was a French name that was popular in the '70s, however, Simone has a much more timeless quality, perhaps owing to the actress Simone Signoret and the author Simone de Beauvoir. Look for the name to become more popular in the future. Variations: *Simona, Simonetta, Simonette, Simonia, Simonina, Symona, Symone.*

SOLANGE *(French)* Dignified. Variation: *Solance.*

SONIA *(Slavic)* Wisdom. Variation of Sophia. Variations: *Sonja, Sonya.*

SOPHIA *(Greek)* Wisdom. Sophia and its close relation Sophie have both zoomed onto the top ten list in the United States and Great Britain. The names have had a great deal of exposure from celebrities, starting with the seemingly ageless Sophia Loren, continuing with the novel and movie *Sophie's Choice*, and singer Sophie B. Hawkins. Sophie holds a slight edge over Sophia in popularity. Variations: *Sofi, Sofia, Soficita, Sofka, Sofya, Sophey, Sophie, Sophy, Zofe, Zofia, Zofie, Zofka, Zosha, Zosia.*

STACY *(Greek)* Resurrection. Diminutive of Anastasia. Variations: *Stace, Stacee, Stacey, Staci, Stacia, Stacie, Stasee, Stasia.*

STELLA *(Latin)* Star.

STEPHANIE *(Greek)* Crown. Feminine version of Stephen. Stephanie is turning into one of those perennially popular names. It has a timeless quality that parents like and sounds like a name that will fit the shy, retiring girl as well as the active and more outgoing daughter. Famous Stephanies include Princess Stephanie, and actresses Stephanie Zimbalist and Stefanie Powers. When Stephanie first became popular back in the 1970s, few people would have foreseen that the name would still be hot decades later, but it regularly appears on the list of the top twenty-five names for girls. Variations: *Stefania, Stefanie, Steffi, Stepania, Stepanie, Stephana, Stephanine, Stephannie, Stephena, Stephene, Stepheney, Stephenie, Stephine, Stephne, Stephney, Stevana, Stevena, Stevey, Stevi, Stevie.*

STOCKARD *(English)* Last name.

STORM *(English)* Storm. Variations: *Stormi, Stormie, Stormy.*

SUSAN *(Hebrew)* Lily. Susan today tends to appear more frequently as a middle name than as a first name, but some of its exotic variations are beginning to be used more often. Variations: *Susann, Susanna, Susannah, Susanne, Susetta, Susette, Susi, Susie, Susy, Suzan, Suzane, Suzanna, Suzannah, Suzanne, Suzetta, Suzette, Suzi, Suzie, Suzy, Zsa Zsa, Zusa, Zuza.*

SVETLANA *(Czech)* Star. Variations: *Svetla, Svetlanka, Svetluse, Svetluvska.*

SYDNEY *(French)* Feminine version of Sidney. Saint Denis. Variations: *Sydnie, Sydny.*

SYLVIA *(Latin)* From the forest. Variations: *Silvana, Silvia, Silvianne, Silvie, Sylva, Sylvana, Sylvanna, Sylvee, Sylvie.*

Slightly Daring Choices

SABINA *(Latin)* Roman clan name. Variations: *Savina, Sebina.*

SABRA *(Hebrew)* Rest. Variations: *Sabrah, Sabre, Sabreen, Sabreena, Sabrena, Sabrinna, Sebra.*

SADIRA *(Persian)* Lotus tree.

SAFFRON *(English)* Flower. Variations: *Saffren, Saffronia, Saphron.*

SAFI *(Hindu)* Friend.

SAGE *(Latin)* Wise. Variations: *Saige, Sayge.*

SAINT *(English)* Holy.

SAKARI *(Hindu)* Sweet one.

SAKI *(Japanese)* Cape.

SALMA *(Hindu)* Safe. Variation: *Salima.*

SALVADORA *(Spanish)* Savior.

SAMAR *(Arabic)* Night talk.

SAMARA *(Hebrew)* Protected by God. Variations: *Samaria, Sammara.*

SAMIA *(Arabic)* Understanding. Variations: *Samihah, Samira, Samirah.*

SAMINA *(Hindu)* Happy. Variations: *Sameena, Sameenah.*

SAMIRA *(Hebrew)* Evening talk.

SAMUELA *(Hebrew)* God has heard. Feminine version of Samuel. Variations: *Samelle, Samuella, Samuelle.*

SAMYA *(Arabic)* To rise up. Variations: *Samiya, Samiyah.*

SANCIA *(Latin)* Holy. Variations: *Sancha, Sanchia, Santsia, Sanzia.*

SANDEEP *(Punjabi)* Enlightened.

SANSANA *(Hebrew)* Leaf of the palm.

SANTANA *(Spanish)* Saint.

SANYA *(Hindu)* Born on a Saturday.

SAPPHIRE *(Hebrew)* Jewel. Variations: *Safira, Saphira, Sapir, Sapira, Sapirit, Sapphira, Sephira.*

SARAB *(Arabic)* Fantasy.

SARONNA *(African-American)* Unknown definition.

SATIN *(French)* Satin.

SATO *(Japanese)* Sugar.

SATORIA *(African-American)* Unknown definition.

SELIMA *(Hebrew)* Peace. Variation: *Selimah.*

SEMA *(Greek)* Omen.

SENALDA *(Spanish)* Sign.

SEPTEMBER *(English)* Month.

SEPTIMA *(Latin)* Seventh.

SERACH *(Hebrew)* Plenty.

SERAPHINA *(Hebrew)* Angel. Variations: *Sarafina, Serafina, Serafine, Seraphine, Serofina.*

SHAKIRA *(African-American)* Newly created. Variations: *Shakera, Shaketa, Shakirah, Shakirra.*

SHALENA *(African-American)* Newly created.

SHALONDA *(African-American)* Newly created. Putting the prefix "Sha-" before the suffix of a popular name—like "Londa"—or placing it before an independent name—like "Linda"—is another popular way that African-Americans are creating new names for their daughters. Though the "La-" prefix seems to be more popular, "Sha-" presents an original, though not entirely unfamiliar, way to create a new name.

SHAMICA *(African-American)* Newly created. Variations: *Shameeka, Shameka, Shamika, Shamikah.*

SHANDRA *(African-American)* Variation of Sandra.

SHANELLE *(African-American)* Newly created.

SHAYLEEN *(African-American)* Unknown definition.

SHEA *(Hebrew)* Request. Variations: *Shay, Shayla, Shaylee.*

SHEBA *(Hebrew)* Pledged daughter. Short for Bathsheba.

SHEELA *(Hindu)* Gentle. Variation: *Sheeli.*

SHEINA *(Hebrew)* Beautiful. Variations: *Shaina, Shaindel, Shaine, Shana, Shayna, Shayndel, Sheindel, Shona, Shoni, Shonie.*

SHELIYA *(Hebrew)* My God. Variations: *Sheli, Shelia, Shelli.*

SHENANDOAH *(Native American: Algonquin)* Beautiful girl from the stars.

SHERA *(Hebrew)* Light.

SHERICE *(American)* A plain. Variations: *Sharice, Shericia.*

SHOSHANA *(Hebrew)* Rose. Variations: *Shosha, Shoshanah, Shoshanna.*

SHYLA *(Hindu)* The goddess Parvati.

SIDONIE *(French)* From Sidon, a town in the ancient Middle East. Variations: *Sidaine, Sidonia, Sidony, Sydonia, Syndonia.*

SIDRA *(Latin)* Stars.

SIERRA *(English)* Mountain. Variation: *Siera.*

SIGRID *(Scandinavian: Norwegian)* Beautiful victory. Variation: *Siri.*

SILVA *(Latin)* Forest. Variations: *Silvaine, Silvana, Silvania, Silvanna, Silvia, Silviana.*

SKYLER *(Dutch)* Shelter. Variations: *Schuyler, Skye.*

SOLANA *(Spanish)* Sunshine. Variations: *Solenne, Solina, Soline, Souline, Soulle, Zelena, Zelene, Zelia, Zelie, Zelina, Zeline.*

STANISLAVA *(Czech)* Glorious government. Variations: *Stana, Stanuska, Stinicka.*

STAR *(English)* Star. Variations: *Starla, Starlene, Starr.*

STARLING *(English)* Bird.

SUMMER *(English)* The season. Variations: *Somer, Sommer.*

SUNSHINE *(English)* Sun. Variations: *Sunnie, Sunni, Sunita, Sunny.*

Muslim Girls' Names

For girls, virtuous names rule in the Muslim tradition, although they aren't directly derived from the Koran, as is the case with Muslim boys' names. Fatima is "daughter of the prophet," and Ayasha means wife. Whether for boys or girls, Muslim names. Muslim names are—like Native American names—derived from nature and everyday objects, as well as admirable character qualities. Examples of such names that have a positive meaning include Tahira (pure) and Malak (angel) for girls. Other names include:

ALIMA	**JAMILA**	**QITURAH**
AMINA	**KALILA**	**SANA**
AYASHA	**LATAVIA**	**TAHIRA**
BASIMAH	**LILITH**	**TAKIA**
FATIMA	**MALAK**	**ZAKIA**
GENNA	**MEDINA**	
IMAN	**NOURA**	

Living on the Edge

SABRIYYA *(Arabic)* Patience. Variations: *Sabira, Sabirah, Sabriyyah.*

SACAJAWEA *(Native American: Shoshone)* Unknown definition. Variation: *Sacagawea.*

SACHI *(Japanese)* Bliss. Variation: *Sachiko.*

SADA *(Japanese)* Virginal.

SADHANA *(Hindu)* Devotion.

SADHBH *(Irish)* Goodness. Variations: *Sabha, Sabia, Sadbha, Sadhbha, Saidhbhe, Saidhbhin, Sive.*

SADZI *(Native American)* Sun heart.

SALAMA *(African: Swahili)* Security.

SALE *(Hawaiian)* Princess. Variations: *Kala, Kalai, Kale, Kela, Sarai, Sera.*

SAMEH *(Arabic)* One who forgives.

SAMHAOIR *(Irish)* Unknown definition.

SATYARUPA *(Hindu)* Truth. Variation: *Satarupa.*

SAUDA *(African: Swahili)* Dark-skinned.

SAWA *(Japanese)* Swamp.

SAWNI *(Native American: Seminole)* Echo. Variation: *Suwanee.*

SAWSAN *(Arabic)* Lily.

SAYO *(Japanese)* Evening birth.

SCENANKI *(Native American: Creek)* Unknown definition.

SEASON *(Latin)* Season.

SHONAK *(Native American: Pima)* Creek.

SHRILEKHA *(Hindu)* Good writing.

SHU *(Chinese)* Tender.

SIF *(Scandinavian)* Relationship. Variation: *Siv.*

SIGELE *(African: Malawian)* Left.

SIGNE *(Scandinavian: Norwegian)* Beautiful. Variations: *Signa, Signild, Signilda, Signilde.*

SIGNY *(Scandinavian)* New victory. Variations: *Signe, Signi.*

SIGRUN *(Scandinavian)* Secret victory.

SIGYN *(Scandinavian)* Victory.

SIHAM *(Arabic)* Arrow.

SIHU *(Native American)* Flower.

SIKO *(African)* Crying.

SILENCE *(English)* Quiet.

Tried and True Classics

TABITHA *(Aramaic)* Gazelle. About the only character in the hit TV series *Bewitched* whose name hasn't caught on among baby-naming parents is that of the irrepressible Darren. As with Samantha and Serena, the show was single-handedly responsible for promoting the name Tabitha into popular culture. It continues to be used quite frequently, even today, almost thirty years later. Variations: *Tabatha, Tabbitha, Tabby, Tabetha, Tabotha, Tabytha.*

TALIA *(Hebrew)* Dew. Talia is a sweet and unique name that its fans feel is terribly underexposed. Most of us are familiar with the name through the actress Talia Shire, who appeared in many of the *Rocky* movies. However, its history is a bit loftier: In the Old Testament, Talia was the name of one of the angels who escorted the sun from dawn to dusk. Variations: *Talie, Talley, Tallie, Tally, Talora, Talya, Thalie, Thalya.*

TAMARA *(Hebrew)* Palm tree. Variations: *Tama, Tamah, Tamar, Tamarah, Tamarra, Tamera, Tami, Tamma, Tammara, Tammee, Tammera, Tammey, Tammie, Tammy, Tamor, Tamour, Tamra, Thamar, Thamara, Thamarra.*

TANISHA *(African-American)* Newly created. Variations: *Taneesha, Taneisha, Tanesha, Taneshea, Tanicha, Taniesha, Tanitia, Tannicia, Tannisha, Tenecia, Teneesha, Teneisha, Tenesha, Teniesha, Tenisha, Tinecia, Tiniesha, Tynisha.*

TARA *(Irish)* Hill. Of course, the most famous Tara around was the plantation in *Gone with the Wind*. Scarlett's home seems to have served as the catalyst for the increasing presence of this name in the United States and in England. Variations: *Tarah, Taran, Tareena, Tarena, Tarin, Tarina, Tarra, Tarrah, Tarren, Tarryn, Taryn, Taryna, Teryn.*

TASHA *(Russian)* Christmas. Diminutive of Natasha. Variations: *Tashina, Tashka, Tasia.*

TATIANA *(Russian)* Feminine version of Tatius, ancient Slavic king. Variations: *Latonya, Tahnya, Tana, Tania, Tanis, Tanka, Tannia, Tannis, Tarnia, Tarny, Tata, Tatianna, Tatyana, Tatyanna, Tonia, Tonya, Tonyah.*

TAYLOR *(English)* Tailor. Variations: *Tailor, Talor, Tayler.*

TERESA *(Greek)* Harvest. Teresa and all of its variations are wonderfully feminine names that are as timely today as they were back in the '60s, when they first started to become popular in the United States. Two Catholic saints made this name part of the lexicon: Saint Teresa of Avila from the sixteenth century and Saint Therese from nineteenth-century France, who was commonly referred to as a little flower. And of course, there is also Mother Teresa. Variations: *Terasa, Teree, Terese, Teresia, Teresina, Teresita, Teressa, Teri, Terie, Terise, Terrasa, Terresa, Terresia, Terri, Terrie, Terrise, Terry, Terrya, Tersa, Terza, Tess, Tessa, Tessie, Tessy, Theresa, Therese, Theressa, Thereza, Thersa, Thersea.*

TESSA *(Polish)* Beloved by God. Variations: *Tess, Tessia, Tessie.*

THELMA *(Greek)* Will. Variation: *Telma.*

THEODORA *(Greek)* Gift of God. Feminine version of Theodore. Theodora has been one of those unexpectedly popular names that appear from nowhere basically overnight. It's a weighty name that also shows its fun side through its abbreviated version, Theo. Theodora has only begun to catch on, so look for more girls with this name over the next twenty years. Variations: *Teddy, Teodora, Theadora, Theda, Theodosia.*

TIFFANY *(Greek)* God's appearance. Modern version of Theophania. As the '80s went, so did certain baby names, and Tiffany was one of these. In the anything-goes decade of luxury, Tiffany was one of the most popular girls' names around. Even earlier, in the '70s, the name was especially popular with African-American parents. Tiffany first got its start back in ancient Greece, when it was commonly given to girls who were born on January sixth, also known as the Epiphany. But in the modern era, as with many other names that seem to come out of nowhere, this one was in a movie: Audrey Hepburn in *Breakfast at Tiffany's* put this name on the map in the 1960s. Variations: *Tifani, Tiff, Tiffaney, Tiffani, Tiffanie, Tiffiney, Tiffini, Tiffney, Tiffy.*

TOBY *(Hebrew)* God is good. Feminine version of Tobias. Toby seems like a great name for a little girl who aspires to play Little League or even a female corporate executive. Variations: *Tobe, Tobee, Tobey, Tobi, Tobie.*

TORI *(Japanese)* Bird.

TRACY *(English)* Summer. Variation of Teresa. Tracy was one of the more popular gender-neutral names back in the '60s when it was in the middle of its transition from boys' name to girls' name. Today, other gender-neutral names are more popular, but a number of famous Tracys may renew interest in this name: Tracy Chapman, Traci Ullman, and Tracy Austin. Variations: *Trace, Tracee, Tracey, Traci, Tracie, Trasey, Treacy, Treesy.*

TRICIA *(English)* Noble. Short for Patricia, feminine version of Patrick. Variations: *Treasha, Trichia, Trish, Trisha.*

TRIXIE *(English)* She brings happiness. Variation of Beatrice. Trixie is perhaps best known as the name of Ed Norton's wife on *The Honeymooners*. Surprisingly, it is catching on as a childhood nickname for the more formal Beatrix. Variations: *Trix, Trixi, Trixy.*

Top Girls' Names of 2000

1. Emily
2. Hannah
3. Madison
4. Ashley
5. Sarah
6. Alexis
7. Samantha
8. Jessica
9. Taylor
10. Elizabeth
11. Lauren
12. Alyssa
13. Kayla
14. Abigail
15. Brianna
16. Olivia
17. Emma
18. Megan
19. Grace
20. Victoria
21. Rachel
22. Anna
23. Sydney
24. Destiny
25. Morgan
26. Jennifer
27. Haley
28. Jasmine
29. Nicole
30. Kaitlyn
31. Amanda
32. Natalie
33. Katherine
34. Miranda
35. Alexandra
36. Stephanie
37. Maria
38. Savannah
39. Chlöe
40. Rebecca
41. Sophia
42. Mackenzie
43. Allison
44. Isabella
45. Amber
46. Mary
47. Danielle
48. Gabrielle
49. Andrea
50. Jordan

Slightly Daring Choices

TABIA *(African: Swahili)* Talented.

TABINA *(Arabic)* Follower of Mohammed.

TACEY *(English)* Quiet. Variations: *Tace, Tacita.*

TAFFY *(Welsh)* Beloved.

TALE *(African: Botswana)* Green.

TALISA *(African-American)* Variation of Lisa. Variation: *Telisa.*

TALISE *(Native American: Creek)* Beautiful water.

TALITHA *(English)* Girl. Variations: *Taleetha, Taletha, Talicia, Talisha, Talita.*

TALLIS *(English)* Forest.

TALLULAH *(Native American: Choctaw)* Leaping water. Variations: *Tallula, Talula, Talulah, Talulla.*

TALYA *(Hebrew)* Dew or rain. Variation: *Talia.*

TAMAS *(Hindu)* Night. Variations: *Tamasa, Tamasi, Tamasvini.*

TAMASINE *(English)* Twin. Feminine version of Thomas. Variations: *Tamasin, Tamsin, Tamsyn, Tamzen, Tamzin.*

TAMI *(Japanese)* People. Variations: *Tamie, Tamiko.*

TARAL *(Hindu)* Rippling.

TASIDA *(Native American)* Rides a horse.

TASMINE *(English)* Twin. Feminine version of Thomas. Variation: *Tasmin.*

TATE *(Scandinavian)* Bubbly. Variation: *Tatum.*

TEAGAN *(Welsh)* Pretty. Variations: *Tegan, Teige.*

TEMPERANCE *(Latin)* Moderation.

TEMPEST *(French)* Storm.

TERENA *(Latin)* Roman clan name. Feminine version of Terence. Variations: *Tereena, Terenia, Terina, Terrena, Terrina, Teryna.*

THALEIA *(Greek)* To bloom. Variation: *Thalia.*

THEA *(Greek)* Goddess.

THOMASINA *(English)* Twin. Feminine version of Thomas.

Variations: *Thomasa, Thomasena, Thomasine, Toma, Tomasina, Tomasine, Tommi.*

THORA *(Scandinavian)* Thor's battle. Variations: *Thordia, Thordis, Thyra, Tyra.*

TIA *(Spanish)* Aunt. Variations: *Tiana, Tianna.*

TIARA *(Spanish)* Crown. Variation: *Tiera.*

TIBERIA *(Latin)* Tiber River. Variations: *Tibbie, Tibby.*

TIERNAN *(Gaelic)* Lord. Variation: *Tierney.*

TIFARA *(Hebrew)* Festive. Variations: *Tiferet, Tifhara.*

TIGRIS *(Irish)* Tiger.

TIMOTHEA *(Greek)* Honoring God. Feminine version of Timothy. Variations: *Timaula, Timi, Timie, Timmi, Timmie.*

TIPONYA *(Native American)* Owl eating an egg.

TIPPAH *(Native American: Chickasaw)* Unknown definition.

TIRA *(Hebrew)* Camp.

TIRION *(Welsh)* Gentle.

TISH *(English)* Happiness. Variation of Letitia. Variation: *Tisha.*

TOPAZ *(Latin)* Jewel.

TOPSY *(English)* The topsail. Variations: *Toppsy, Topsey, Topsie.*

TORA *(Japanese)* Tiger; (Scandinavian) Thunder.

TRINITY *(Latin)* Triad. Variations: *Trini, Trinita.*

TRISTA *(Latin)* Sad. Variations: *Trgsta, Tristan, Tristen, Tristin, Tristina, Tristyn.*

TRYPHENA *(Greek)* Delicacy. Variations: *Triphena, Tryphana, Tryphene, Tryphenia, Tryphina.*

TUESDAY *(English)* Tuesday.

TULA *(Native American: Choctaw)* Apex; (Hindu) The astrological sign Libra.

TWYLA *(African-American)* Newly created. Variations: *Twila, Twylla.*

TYANA *(African-American)* Newly created.

TYESHA *(African-American)* Newly created. Variation: *Tyisha.*

TYLER *(English)* Last name.

Living on the Edge

TALIBA *(Arabic)* Seeker of knowledge. Variation: *Talibah.*

TALMA *(Hebrew)* Hill.

TALUTAH *(Native American: Sioux)* Red.

TAM *(Vietnamese)* Heart.

TAMA *(Japanese)* Jewel.

TAMAH *(Hebrew)* Marvel. Variation: *Tama.*

TAMAKI *(Japanese)* Bracelet. Variations: *Tamako, Tamayo.*

TAMANNA *(Hindu)* Want.

TAMIKA *(Japanese)* Child of the people. Variations: *Tamike, Tamiko, Tamiya, Tamiyo.*

TAMOHARA *(Hindu)* The sun.

TAMRIKA *(African-American)* Newly created. Variation: *Tamreeka.*

TANAKA *(Japanese)* Swamp dweller.

TANAY *(African-American)* Newly created. Variation: *Tanee.*

TANAYA *(Hindu)* Daughter. Variation: *Tanuja.*

TANE *(Japanese)* Seed.

TANI *(Japanese)* Valley.

TANITH *(Irish)* Estate. Variations: *Tanita, Tanitha.*

TANNISHTHA *(Hindu)* Devoted.

TANSY *(Greek)* Immortality.

TANVI *(Hindu)* Young woman.

TAO *(Chinese)* Apple.

TAPASYA *(Hindu)* Bitter.

TAQIYYA *(Arabic)* Devotion. Variations: *Takiyah, Takiyya, Takiyyah, Taqiyyah.*

TATSU *(Japanese)* Dragon.

TAULAKI *(Polynesian)* Waiting.

TAWIA *(African)* Born after twins.

TAWNIE *(English)* Child. Variation: *Tawny.*

TAYANITA *(Native American: Cherokee)* Beaver.

TEAMHAIR *(Irish)* Hill.

TEGVYEN *(Welsh)* Lovely maiden. Variation: *Tegwyn.*

TENNILLE *(French)* Last name. Variation: *Tenille.*

TENUVAH *(Hebrew)* Fruit and vegetables. Variation: *Tenuva.*

THADDEA *(Greek)* Brave. Feminine version of Thaddeus. Variations: *Thada, Thadda.*

THALASSA *(Greek)* Ocean.

THANA *(Arabic)* Thanksgiving.

THANDIWE *(South African)* Affectionate.

THEONE *(Greek)* Godly. Variations: *Theona, Theoni, Theonie.*

THETA *(Greek)* Greek letter. Variation: *Thetis.*

THU *(Vietnamese)* Autumn. Variation: *Tu.*

THURAYYA *(Arabic)* Star. Variations: *Surayya, Surayyah, Thuraia, Thuraypa, Thurayyah.*

THUY *(Vietnamese)* Gentle.

TIRTHA *(Hindu)* Ford.

TIRZA *(Hebrew)* Kindness. Variations: *Thirza, Tirza, Tirzah.*

TISA *(African: Swahili)* Ninth child.

TISHRA *(African-American)* Newly created. Variation: *Tishrah.*

TITANIA *(Greek)* Giant. Variation: *Tita.*

TITILAYO *(African: Nigerian)* Eternal happiness.

TIVONA *(Hebrew)* Nature lover.

TIWA *(Native American)* Onion.

TIWOLU *(Native American)* Chicken hawk sitting on eggs.

TOHUIA *(Polynesian)* Flower.

TOIREASA *(Irish)* Strength. Variations: *Treise.*

TOKI *(Japanese)* Chance.

TRILBY *(English)* Literary name that dates from the Victorian era. Variations: *Trilbie, Trillby.*

TRINH *(Vietnamese)* Virgin.

TUHINA *(Hindu)* Snow.

TUKI *(Japanese)* Moon. Variations: *Tukiko, Tukiyo.*

Tried and True Classics

UMA *(Hindu)* Flax; (Hebrew) Nation.
URSULA *(Latin)* Little female bear. Variations: *Ursala, Ursella, Ursola, Ursule, Ursulina, Ursuline.*

Slightly Daring Choices

ULA *(Irish)* Jewel from the ocean.
ULIMA *(Arabic)* Wise. Variation: *Ullima.*
ULRICA *(German)* Wolf power.
ULRIKA *(Scandinavian)* Noble ruler. Variation: *Ulla.*
ULTIMA *(Latin)* The end. Variation: *Ultimah.*
UMALI *(Hindu)* Generous.
UMAYMA *(Arabic)* Little mother.
UNA *(Irish)* Lamb; (Latin) One.
UNITY *(English)* Oneness. Variation: *Unita.*
UNN *(Scandinavian)* Love.
UPALA *(Hindu)* Beach.
URANIA *(Greek)* Heavenly. Once upon a time in nineteenth-century Great Britain, there were a number of parents who thought it ought to be all the rage to name their daughters after Greek goddesses and muses. Urania, the muse of astronomy, was one of those names. A handful of parents might be tempted to use it today. Variations: *Urainia, Uraniya, Uranya.*
URBANA *(Latin)* Of the city. Variation: *Urbanna.*

Living on the Edge

UCHENNA *(African: Nigerian)* God's will.
UDELE *(English)* Wealthy. Variations: *Uda, Udella, Udelle.*
UDIYA *(Hebrew)* Fire of God. Variations: *Udia, Uriela, Uriella.*
UINISE *(Polynesian)* Fair victory.
UJILA *(Hindu)* Bright light. Variations: *Ujala, Ujjala, Ujvala.*
ULU *(African: Nigerian)* Second-born girl.
ULUAKI *(Polynesian)* First.
ULVA *(German)* Wolf.
UME *(Japanese)* Plum blossom. Variations: *Umeki, Umeko.*
UMEEKA *(Hindu)* The goddess Parvati.
UMIKO *(Japanese)* Child of the sea.
UM-KALTHUM *(Arabic)* Mother of a plump-cheeked baby. Variation: *Um-Kalsum.*
UMM *(Arabic)* Mother.
UMNIYA *(Arabic)* Desire.
URANJA *(Polish)* The muse of astronomy.
URBI *(African: Nigerian)* Princess.
URIT *(Hebrew)* Brightness.
USHA *(Hindu)* Dawn. Variation: *Ushas.*
USHI *(Chinese)* Ox.
USHMIL *(Hindu)* Warm. Variation: *Ushmila.*
USHRIYA *(Hebrew)* God's blessing. Variation: *Ushria.*
UT *(Vietnamese)* East.
UTA *(Japanese)* Song. Variation: *Utako.*
UWIMANA *(African: Rwandan)* Daughter of God.

Tried and True Classics

VALENTIA *(Latin)* Healthy. Variations: *Valence, Valencia, Valene, Valentina, Valentine, Valenzia.*

VALERIE *(Latin)* Strong. A popular name during the Roman Empire, Valerie tends to be underused today. Famous Valeries include actresses Valerie Harper, Valerie Bertinelli, and Valerie Perrine. Although some parents may feel that the name sounds like a relic from the 1960s, others will feel slightly nostalgic about the name and choose it for their own daughters. Variations: *Val, Valaree, Valarey, Valaria, Valarie, Vale, Valeree, Valeria, Valeriana, Valery, Vallarie, Valleree, Vallerie, Valli, Vallie, Vally.*

VANESSA *(Greek)* Butterflies. Variations: *Vanesa, Vanesse, Vania, Vanna, Vannessa, Venesa, Venessa.*

VANNA *(Cambodian)* Golden; also newly created from Savanna.

VELMA *(English)* Newly created. From Thelma. Variation: *Vellma.*

VERA *(Slavic)* Faith. Vera was at its height in both the United States and Britain during the flapper days of the 1920s. Variations: *Veera, Veira, Verasha, Viera.*

VERONICA *(Latin)* True image. Variations: *Veranique, Vernice, Veron, Verona, Verone, Veronice, Veronicka, Veronika, Veronike, Veroniqua, Veronique.*

VESTA *(Latin)* Goddess of the home. Variations: *Vessy, Vest.*

VICTORIA *(Latin)* Roman goddess of victory. Victoria is a name that has had a number of spurts in popularity since the days of the early Roman Empire, when it was one of the most frequently bestowed names for girls. It lay dormant until Queen Victoria took the throne in Britain in the

1800s, when it began to be used with some regularity until she died after the turn of the century. The name was resurrected again in the 1940s and has remained in common usage ever since. Victoria's nicknames are also very popular today. Variations: *Torey, Tori, Toria, Torie, Torrey, Torri, Torrie, Torrye, Tory, Vicki, Vickie, Vicky, Victoriana, Victorina, Victorine, Victory, Vikki, Vikky, Vitoria, Vittoria.*

VIOLA *(Latin)* Violet.

VIOLET *(Latin)* Violet. Variations: *Viola, Violetta, Violette.*

VIRGINIA *(Latin)* Virgin. Variations: *Vergie, Virgy, Virginie, Vegenia, Virginai, Virgena, Virgene.*

VIVIAN *(Latin)* Full of life. Actress Vivien Leigh was responsible for the name's first burst of popularity in the United States in the 1940s. Ever since actress Julia Roberts played a hooker named Vivian in the movie *Pretty Woman*, the name has started to appear on birth certificates with a little bit more regularity. Variations: *Viv, Viva, Viveca, Vivecka, Viveka, Vivia, Viviana, Viviane, Vivianna, Vivianne, Vivie, Vivien, Vivienne.*

Slightly Daring Choices

VALESKA *(Polish)* Glorious ruler.

VALONIA *(Latin)* Shallow valley.

VALORA *(Latin)* Brave. Variations: *Valoria, Valorie, Valory, Valorya.*

VANA *(Polynesian)* Sea urchin.

VANDA *(Czech)* Variation of Wanda. Tribal name. Variation: *Vandah.*

VANDANI *(Hindu)* Honor. Variation: *Vandana.*

Top Girls' Names of 2001

1. Emily
2. Hannah
3. Kaitlyn
4. Madison
5. Sarah
6. Hailey
7. Ashley
8. Brianna
9. Samantha
10. Jasmine
11. Elizabeth
12. Katherine
13. Anna
14. Kayla
15. Alexis
16. Abigail
17. Megan
18. Alyssa
19. Taylor
20. Jessica
21. Lauren
22. Destiny
23. Kaylee
24. Rachel
25. Olivia
26. Madeline
27. Victoria
28. Makayla
29. Emma
30. Mackenzie
31. Grace
32. Nicole
33. Sydney
34. Julia
35. Natalie
36. Chlöe
37. Jordan
38. Jennifer
39. Morgan
40. Stephanie
41. Rebecca
42. Isabella
43. Allison
44. Arianna
45. Alexandra
46. Savannah
47. Jacqueline
48. Christina
49. Maria
50. Gabriella

VANECIA *(English)* Venice; Italian city. Variations: *Vanetia, Vanicia, Venecia, Venetia, Venezia, Venice, Venise, Venize.*

VANORA *(Welsh)* White wave. Variation: *Vannora.*

VARANA *(Hindu)* River.

VARDA *(Hebrew)* Rose. Variations: *Vardia, Vardice, Vardina, Vardis, Vardit.*

VARSHA *(Hindu)* Rain shower. Variation: *Varisha.*

VEDA *(Hindu)* Knowledge, wisdom. Variation: *Veeda.*

VEDETTE *(Italian)* Sentry. Variation: *Vedetta.*

VEERA *(Hindu)* Strong.

VEGA *(Arabic)* Falling star; (Scandinavian) Star.

VELINDA *(African-American)* Variation of Melinda. Variation: *Valinda.*

VENUS *(Latin)* Roman goddess of love. Variations: *Venise, Vennice, Venusa, Venusina.*

VERENA *(Latin)* True. Variations: *Vereena, Verene, Verina, Verine, Veruchka, Veruschka, Verushka, Veryna.*

VERITY *(Latin)* Truth. Variations: *Verita, Veritie.*

VERNA *(Latin)* Springtime. Variations: *Vernetta, Vernie, Vernita, Virna.*

VESPERA *(Latin)* Evening star.

VEVINA *(Irish)* Kind woman.

VIANNA *(African-American)* Unknown definition.

VIDA *(Hebrew)* Beloved. Variations: *Veda, Veeda, Veida, Vidette, Vieda, Vita, Vitia.*

VIDONIA *(Portuguese)* Vine branch. Variations: *Veedonia, Vidonya.*

VILLETTE *(French)* Small town.

VILMA *(Russian)* Variation of Wilma.

VINA *(Spanish)* Vineyard. Variations: *Veina, Venia.*

VINCENTIA *(Latin)* To conquer. Feminine version of Vincent. Variations: *Vincenta, Vincentena, Vincentina, Vincentine, Vincetta, Vinia, Vinnie.*

VIRIDIS *(Latin)* Green. Variations: *Virdis, Virida, Viridia, Viridiana.*

VIRTUE *(Latin)* Virtue.

VITA *(Latin)* Life. Variations: *Veeta, Vitel, Vitella.*

VLADIMIRA *(Czech)* Famous ruler. Variation: *Vladmira.*

VLADISLAVA *(Czech)* Glorious ruler. Variations: *Ladislava, Valeska.*

VONDRA *(Czech)* A woman's love.

Living on the Edge

VACHYA *(Hindu)* To speak.

VAILEA *(Polynesian)* Water that talks.

VALA *(German)* Chosen.

VALDA *(Norse)* Ruler. Variations: *Valida, Velda, Vellda.*

VANAJA *(Hindu)* Daughter from the woods.

VANALIKA *(Hindu)* Sunflower.

VANETTA *(English)* Newly created.

VANI *(Hindu)* Voice.

VANIKA *(Hindu)* Small forest.

VANJA *(Scandinavian)* God is good.

VASHTI *(Persian)* Beautiful.

VASUNDHARA *(Hindu)* Earth.

VATUSIA *(African)* The dead leave us behind.

VEATA *(Cambodian)* Wind.

VELESLAVA *(Czech)* Great glory. Variations: *Vela, Velina, Velinka, Velka, Veluska.*

VELIKA *(Slavic)* Great. Variation: *Velia.*

VERBENA *(Latin)* Holy plants. Variations: *Verbeena, Verbina.*

VERDAD *(Spanish)* Truth.

VICA *(Hungarian)* Life.

VIDYA *(Hindu)* Instruction.

VIGDIS *(Scandinavian: Norwegian)* War goddess. Variation: *Vigdess.*

VIGILIA *(Latin)* Alert.

VIKA *(Polynesian)* Victory. Variation: *Vikaheilala.*
VIMALA *(Hindu)* Lovely.
VINH *(Vietnamese)* Gulf.
VISOLELA *(African)* Unlimited imagination.
VORSILA *(Czech)* Little she-bear.
VYOMA *(Hindu)* Sky. Variation: *Vyomika.*

Tried and True Classics

WANDA *(German)* Wanderer. Variations: *Wandi, Wandie, Wandis, Wonda, Wonnda.*

WENDY *(English)* Wendy first appeared as the name of a character in the novel *Peter Pan.* Variations: *Wenda, Wendee, Wendey, Wendi, Wendie, Wendye, Windy.*

WHITNEY *(English)* White island. Of course, singer Whitney Houston is the primary reason why this name has rapidly traveled from being a corporate success-track name for boys in the early '80s to one of the more popular names for girls in the '90s. Variations: *Whitnee, Whitnie, Whitny, Whittney.*

WILHELMINA *(German)* Feminine version of William, Will + helmet. Variations: *Wiletta, Wilette, Wilhelmine, Willa, Willamina, Williamina.*

WILLOW *(English)* Tree.

WILMA *(German)* Feminine version of William, Will + helmet. Variations: *Wilmette, Wilmina, Wylma.*

WINIFRED *(Welsh)* Holy peace. Winifred is a pretty name that is both delicate and powerful. The name was at its height in popularity during the nineteenth and early twentieth centuries among English and Scottish parents. Today Americans are beginning to fall for the sweet quality of the name. Look for Winifred to become more widely used in the coming years, especially with the letter "y" replacing one of the vowels in the name. Variations: *Win, Winifrede, Winifride, Winifryde, Winne, Winni, Winnie, Winny, Wyn, Wynn.*

WYNONAH *(Native American)* First-born. Variations: *Wenona, Wenonah, Winona, Winonah, Wynnona.*

Top Girls' Names of 2002

1. Emily
2. Madison
3. Hailey
4. Kaitlyn
5. Hannah
6. Sarah
7. Brianna
8. Ashley
9. Alexis
10. Abigail
11. Emma
12. Samantha
13. Olivia
14. Elizabeth
15. Jasmine
16. Katherine
17. Alyssa
18. Lauren
19. Isabella
20. Anna
21. Kayla
22. Grace
23. Jessica
24. Sophia
25. Taylor
26. Makayla
27. Madeline
28. Megan
29. Sydney
30. Mackenzie
31. Rachel
32. Kaylee
33. Victoria
34. Allison
35. Natalie
36. Destiny
37. Jennifer
38. Chlöe
39. Mia
40. Savannah
41. Morgan
42. Jordan
43. Julia
44. Nicole
45. Kylie
46. Gabriella
47. Alexandra
48. Isabel
49. Rebecca
50. Ariana

Slightly Daring Choices

WALDA *(German)* Ruler. Feminine version of Waldo. Variations: *Wallda, Welda, Wellda.*

WALIDA *(Arabic)* Newborn. Variation: *Walidah.*

WALKER *(English)* Last name. Variation: *Wallker.*

WALLIS *(English)* One from Wales. Feminine version of Wallace. Variations: *Wallie, Walliss, Wally, Wallys.*

WELENA *(Hawaiian)* Springtime. Hawaiian version of Verna.

WHITLEY *(English)* White field.

WHOOPI *(French)* Unknown definition. Actress Whoopi Goldberg has made this less common name famous.

WILDA *(English)* Willow. Variations: *Willda, Wylda.*

WILFREDA *(English)* Peaceful will. Feminine version of Wilfred.

WILONA *(English)* To desire.

WINDA *(African: Swahili)* Hunt.

WINEMA *(Native American: Miwok)* Female chief.

WINTER *(English)* Winter.

WISDOM *(English)* Wisdom.

WREN *(English)* Bird.

WYANET *(Native American)* Beautiful.

WYETTA *(African-American)* Feminine version of Wyatt.

WYNELLE *(African-American)* Variation: *Wynette.*

WYNN *(Welsh)* Fair, white. Variations: *Winne, Wynne.*

WYOME *(Native American: Algonquin)* Big field.

Living on the Edge

WACHIW *(Native American: Sioux)* Girl who dances.
WAFA *(Arabic)* Faithful. Variations: *Wafiyya, Wafiyyah.*
WAHCHINTONKA *(Native American: Sioux)* Patient.
WAIPSHWA *(Native American: Wanapum)* One who carries.
WAJA *(Arabic)* Noble. Variations: *Wagiha, Wagihah, Wajiha, Wajihah.*
WAKANDA *(Native American)* Magical. Variation: *Wakenda.*
WALANIKA *(Hawaiian)* True image. Hawaiian version of Veronica. Variations: *Walonika, Welonika.*
WALBURGA *(German)* Strong protection. Variations: *Walberga, Wallburga.*
WALENTYA *(Polish)* Healthy.
WANAAO *(Hawaiian)* Sunrise.
WANAAONANI *(Hawaiian)* Beautiful sunrise.
WANAKA *(Hawaiian)* Hawaiian version of Wanda.
WANETA *(Native American)* One who moves forward. Variations: *Wanetta, Wanette, Wannetta, Wannette.*
WANIKA *(Hawaiian)* God is good.
WAPIN *(Native American: Potawatomi)* Sunrise.
WARDA *(German)* Protector. Feminine version of Ward. Variations: *Wardia, Wardine.*
WASEME *(African: Swahili)* People talking.
WASHI *(Japanese)* Eagle.
WASHTA *(Native American: Sioux)* Good.
WASULA *(Native American: Sioux)* Bad hair.
WATSEKA *(Native American: Potawatomi)* Woman.
WATTAN *(Arabic)* Homeland.
WAUNA *(Native American: Miwok)* Calling geese.
WAYLAHSKISE *(Native American: Shawnee)* Graceful.
WAYNOKA *(Native American: Cheyenne)* Clean water.
WEAYAYA *(Native American: Sioux)* Sunset.

WEEKO *(Native American: Sioux)* Beautiful girl.

WEETAMOO *(Native American: Pocasset)* Lover. Variations: *Weetamoe, Weetamore, Wetamoo, Wetemoo.*

WEHINAHPAY *(Native American: Sioux)* Sunrise.

WICAHPI *(Native American: Sioux)* Star. Variation: *Wicapi.*

WICAHPI ISNALA *(Native American: Sioux)* Long star. Variation: *Wicapi Isnala.*

WICAHPI WAKAN *(Native American: Sioux)* Holy star. Variation: *Wicapi Wakan.*

WIDAD *(Arabic)* Love.

WIHAKAYDA *(Native American: Sioux)* Youngest daughter.

WIKOLIA *(Hawaiian)* Victorious.

WILA *(Hawaiian)* Faith.

WINNE-COMAC *(Native American: Algonquin)* Fertile land.

WINOLA *(German)* Enchanting friend.

WISIA *(Polish)* Victorious.

WITASHNAH *(Native American: Sioux)* Chaste.

WIYAKA-WASTEWIN *(Native American: Sioux)* Pretty feather.

WLADYSLAWA *(Polish)* Glorious ruler.

X

Tried and True Classics

XANDRA *(Spanish)* Protector.

Slightly Daring Choices

XAVIERA *(English)* New house. Feminine version of Xavier, Xaviera is the name of a saint from the sixteenth century. Variations: *Xavier, Xavyera.*

XENIA *(Greek)* Hospitable. Variations: *Xeenia, Xena.*

XIN *(Chinese)* Elegant, beautiful.

XYLIA *(Greek)* Forest. Variations: *Xyla, Xylina, Xylona.*

Living on the Edge

XANTHE *(Greek)* Yellow. Variations: *Xantha, Xanthia.*

XANTHIPPE *(Greek)* Wife of Socrates.

XIANG *(Chinese)* Fragrant.

XIAO-NIAO *(Chinese)* Small bird.

XIAO-XING *(Chinese)* Morning star.

XUAN *(Vietnamese)* Spring.

Tried and True Classics

YASMINE *(Arabic)* Flower. Though Jasmine, the name from which Yasmine is derived, is the more well-known variation of this name, Yasmine will become more popular in time, simply because many parents will want to put their unique spin on what is becoming a relatively popular name. In fact, Yasmine first became popular in the United States back in the 1920s because of a play entitled *Hassan*, by playwright James Flecker, in which the female protagonist was named Yasmin. Variations: *Yasmeen, Yasmeena, Yasmena, Yasmene, Yasmin, Yasmina.*

YOKO *(Japanese)* Child of the ocean. Yoko Ono, artist and widow of late Beatle John Lennon, has made this name famous.

YOLANDA *(Greek)* Purple flower. Yolanda first appeared as the name of a saint in thirteenth-century Spain, and later belonged to Hungarian royalty. Though some parents might feel the name is dated and too unusual to use today, it's clear that others disagree. Variations: *Eolanda, Eolande, Iolanda, Iolande, Yalanda, Yalinda, Yalonda, Yola, Yoland, Yolande, Yolane, Yolette, Yoli, Yolonda, Yulanda.*

YVETTE *(French)* Arrow's bow.

YVONNE *(French)* Yew wood. Yvonne is a name that conjures up images of black-and-white dramas from the '40s, when Yvonne was often chosen as the name of the unsuspecting tragic female heroine. Some parents today, however, may feel that the name is cool because of their exposure to the '60s sitcom *The Munsters* starring Yvonne De Carlo. Variations: *Yvetta, Yvette, Yvone.*

Top Girls' Names of 2003

1. Emily
2. Emma
3. Madison
4. Hannah
5. Hailey
6. Sarah
7. Kaitlyn
8. Isabella
9. Olivia
10. Abigail
11. Madeline
12. Kaylee
13. Alyssa
14. Grace
15. Sophia
16. Lauren
17. Brianna
18. Alexis
19. Sydney
20. Megan
21. Chlöe
22. Ashley
23. Samantha
24. Taylor
25. Elizabeth
26. Anna
27. Mia
28. Kayla
29. Makayla
30. Riley
31. Zöe
32. Jordan
33. Kylie
34. Allison
35. Katherine
36. Rachel
37. Lily
38. Ella
39. Julia
40. Isabelle
41. Natalie
42. Morgan
43. Ava
44. Mackenzie
45. Victoria
46. Paige
47. Abby
48. Jessica
49. Jasmine
50. Savannah

Slightly Daring Choices

YAEL *(Hebrew)* Mountain goat. Variations: *Jael, Yaala, Yaalat, Yaela, Yaella.*

YAMINA *(Arabic)* Ethical. Variations: *Yaminah, Yemina.*

YAMINI *(Hindu)* Night.

YARDENA *(Hebrew)* To descend. Variation: *Jardena.*

YARINA *(Russian)* Peace. Variation: *Yaryna.*

YARMILLA *(Slavic)* Market seller.

YASHILA *(Hindu)* Successful.

YASHNA *(Hindu)* Prayer. Variation: *Yashnah.*

YELENA *(Russian)* Light. Variation of Helen. Variation: *Yalena.*

YEMINA *(Hebrew)* Strong. Variation: *Yemena.*

YESENIA *(Arabic)* Flower. Variations: *Yecenia, Yesnia, Yessenia.*

YESHARA *(Hebrew)* Direct.

YEVA *(Russian)* Life. Variation: *Yevka.*

YIESHA *(Arabic)* Woman.

YONINA *(Hebrew)* Dove. Variations: *Yona, Yonah, Yoninah, Yonit, Yonita.*

YORI *(Japanese)* Honest.

YOSHA *(Hindu)* Woman.

YOSHE *(Japanese)* Lovely.

YOVELA *(Hebrew)* Rejoicing.

YUKI *(Japanese)* Snow. Variations: *Yukie, Yukiko.*

YULA *(Russian)* Young. Variation of Julia. Variations: *Yulenka, Yuliya, Yulya.*

Living on the Edge

YAA *(African: Ghanian)* Born on Thursday.

YACHI *(Japanese)* Good luck. Variations: *Yachiko, Yachiyo.*

YACHNE *(Hebrew)* God is good. Variation: *Yachna.*

YAFFA *(Hebrew)* Beautiful.

YAHIVIKA *(Native American: Hopi)* Spring.

YAKI *(Japanese)* Snow. Variations: *Yukie, Yukika, Yukiko.*

YAKIRA *(Hebrew)* Dear. Variations: *Yekara, Yekarah.*

YALIKA *(Native American)* Spring flowers.

YALUTA *(Native American)* Women talking.

YAMKA *(Native American)* Flower blooming.

YANAHA *(Native American: Navajo)* She confronts an enemy. Variation: *Yanaba.*

YARDENIYA *(Hebrew)* God's garden. Variations: *Jardenia, Yardenia.*

YARKONA *(Hebrew)* Green.

YASHODHANA *(Hindu)* Prosperous. Variation: *Yashwina.*

YASHODHARA *(Hindu)* Renowned.

YASU *(Japanese)* Calm. Variations: *Yasuko, Yasuyo.*

YE *(African: Ghanian)* First-born of twins.

YEHUDIT *(Hebrew)* Praise. Variations: *Yudi, Yudit, Yudita, Yuta, Yutke.*

YEJDE *(African: Nigerian)* She resembles her mother.

YENENE *(Native American)* Sorceress.

YENTA *(Hebrew)* An elderly female busybody or gossip. Variations: *Yente, Yentel, Yentele, Yentil.*

YIN *(Chinese)* Silver.

YOCHEVED *(Hebrew)* God's glory. Variation: *Yochebed.*

YOI *(Japanese)* Born in the evening.

YOKI *(Native American)* Bluebird.

YOKKAKO *(Japanese)* Four days.

YOLOTA *(Native American)* Farewell to spring.

YOLUTA *(Native American)* Seed.
YON *(Burmese)* Rabbit.
YONKELA *(African-American)* Unknown definition.
YOSHIKO *(Japanese)* Quiet. Variations: *Yoshi, Yoshie, Yoshiyo.*
YOSHINO *(Japanese)* Fertile land.
YOUNG-IL *(Korean)* Excellence.
YOUNG-SOON *(Korean)* Tender flower.
YU *(Chinese)* Jade.
YURIKO *(Japanese)* Lily child.
YUSRA *(Arabic)* Rich. Variations: *Yusrivva, Yusrivvah.*
YUTKIYE *(Native American)* Chicken hawk hunting.

Tried and True Classics

ZELDA *(German)* Woman warrior. Famous Zeldas include the wife of author F. Scott Fitzgerald.

ZOE *(Greek)* Life. Zoe is perhaps the most popular "Z" name for girls in this country, and it seems to have picked up steam in the '90s. The first Zoe surfaced in the third century A.D.; she was later martyred as a saint. Today parents can choose to add an umlaut above the "e" or to leave it as is. Parents will continue to look to Zoe for a daughter they expect to have considerable artistic talent. Variations: *Zoey, Zoie.*

Slightly Daring Choices

ZADA *(Arabic)* Fortunate. Variations: *Zaida, Zayda.*

ZAFINA *(Arabic)* Triumphant.

ZAFIRA *(Arabic)* Success. Variation: *Zafirah.*

ZAHARA *(Hebrew)* Shine. Variations: *Zahari, Zaharit.*

ZAHAVA *(Hebrew)* Golden. Variation: *Zahavah.*

ZAHIRA *(Arabic)* Bright. Variations: *Zaheera, Zahirah.*

ZAHRA *(Arabic)* Blossom. Variations: *Zahara, Zahirah, Zahrah, Zara, Zuhra.*

ZAIRA *(Italian)* Princess. Variations: *Zarah, Zaria, Zayeera.*

ZAKIYA *(African: Swahili)* Pure. Variation: *Zakiyah.*

ZANETA *(Polish)* God is gracious.

ZARA *(Hebrew)* Dawn. In the '90s, names that have a "z," "x," or "q" in them were popular, but parents still liked names that weren't totally unfamiliar. Zara fits the bill nicely, as it is close to both Tara and Sarah. It is also the name of the daughter of Princess Anne in Britain. Variations: *Zarah, Zaria.*

ZARINA *(Hindu)* Golden.

ZARITA *(Spanish)* Princess. Variation of Sarah.

ZEFFA *(Portuguese)* Rose.

ZELLA *(German)* Hostile one.

ZELMA *(German)* Divine helmet.

ZEMIRA *(Hebrew)* Song.

ZEMORAH *(Hebrew)* Tree branch. Variation: *Zemora.*

ZENAIDA *(Greek)* Wild dove.

ZENANA *(Hebrew)* Woman. Variations: *Zena, Zenia.*

ZENDA *(Hebrew)* Holy.

ZENOBIA *(Greek)* Strength of Zeus. Zenobia is a powerful name that served a queen in the third century A.D. in the early Roman Empire. Novelists Nathaniel Hawthorne and Edith Wharton both used the name in their stories.

ZEPHYR *(Greek)* Wind from the west. Variations: *Zefir, Zephira, Zephyra.*

Top Girls' Names of 2004

1.	Madison	11.	Olivia
2.	Emma	12.	Hailey
3.	Abigail	13.	Paige
4.	Riley	14.	Emily
5.	Chlöe	15.	Grace
6.	Hannah	16.	Ava
7.	Alexis	17.	Aaliyah
8.	Isabella	18.	Alyssa
9.	Mackenzie	19.	Faith
10.	Taylor	20.	Brianna

ZEPPELINA *(English)* Definition unknown.

ZERA *(Hebrew)* Seeds.

ZERALDINA *(Polish)* Spear ruler.

ZERDALI *(Turkish)* Wild apricot.

ZERLINDA *(Hebrew)* Beautiful dawn. Variation: *Zerlina.*

ZERREN *(English)* Flower.

ZESIRO *(African: Ugandan)* First of twins.

ZETTA *(Hebrew)* Olive. Variations: *Zeta, Zetana.*

ZEVIDA *(Hebrew)* Present. Variation: *Zevuda.*

ZHANE *(African-American)* Unknown definition.

ZILLA *(Hebrew)* Shadow. Variations: *Zilah, Zillah, Zylla.*

ZILPAH *(Hebrew)* Dignity. Many of the girls' names that begin with "Z" are Biblical in origin, and Zilpah is no exception, first appearing in the Book of Genesis as the name of Jacob's mistress. If you wander around old cemeteries, you'll find the name Zilpah on many of the headstones. Variations: *Zillpha, Zilpha, Zulpha, Zylpha.*

ZIMRIAH *(Hebrew)* Songs. Variations: *Zimria, Zimriya.*

ZINA *(English)* Hospitable. Variation: *Zena.*

ZINNIA *(English)* Flower. Variations: *Zinia, Zinnya, Zinya.*

ZIPPORA *(Hebrew)* Little bird. Biblical wife of Moses. Variations: *Cipora, Tzipeh, Tzipora, Tzippe, Zipeh, Zipora, Ziporah, Zipporah.*

ZIRAH *(Hebrew)* Coliseum. Variation: *Zira.*

ZITA *(Greek)* Seeker. Variation: *Zitella.*

ZIVA *(Hebrew)* Brilliant. Variations: *Zeeva, Ziv.*

ZOLA *(Italian)* Piece of earth.

ZONA *(Latin)* Belt.

ZONIA *(English)* Unknown definition.

ZONTA *(Native American: Sioux)* Honest.

ZORA *(Slavic)* Dawn. Variations: *Zara, Zorah, Zorra, Zorrah.*

ZORINA *(Slavic)* Golden. Variation: *Zorana.*

ZUDORA *(Hindu)* Laborer.

Living on the Edge

ZAHREH *(Persian)* Happiness.
ZAINAB *(Hindu)* Plant.
ZAKAH *(Hebrew)* Pure. Variations: *Zaka, Zakia, Zakiah.*
ZAKIYYA *(Hindu)* Pure. Variations: *Zakia, Zakiah, Zakiyyah.*
ZALIKA *(African: Swahili)* Well born.
ZALTANA *(Native American)* Tall mountain.
ZAN *(Chinese)* Support; favor; praise.
ZARIFA *(Arabic)* Graceful.
ZAWADI *(African: Swahili)* Present.
ZAYIT *(Hebrew)* Olive.
ZAYNAB *(Arabic)* Plant. Variation: *Zainab.*
ZAZA *(Hebrew)* Action. Variation: *Zazu.*
ZBYHNEVA *(Czech)* To get rid of anger. Variations: *Zbyha, Zbysa.*
ZDENKA *(Czech)* Variations: *Zdena, Zdenicka, Zdenina, Zdeninka, Zdenuska.*
ZDESLAVA *(Czech)* Glory is here. Variations: *Zdevsa, ZdeVska, Zdisa, Zdiska, Zdislava.*
ZEA *(Latin)* Grain. Variation: *Zia.*
ZEBORAH *(African-American)* Variation of Deborah.
ZEFIRYN *(Polish)* Goddess of the west wind.
ZEHARA *(Hebrew)* Light. Variation: *Zehorit.*
ZEHAVA *(Hebrew)* Gold. Variations: *Zahava, Zehovit, Zehuva, Zehuvit.*
ZEHIRA *(Hebrew)* Careful.
ZEL *(Persian)* Cymbal.
ZELENKA *(Czech)* Fresh.
ZELFA *(African-American)* Unknown definition.
ZEYNEP *(Turkish)* Ornament.
ZHEN *(Chinese)* Pure.
ZHO *(Chinese)* Character.

ZHONG *(Chinese)* Honest.
ZHUO *(Chinese)* Smart.
ZIGANA *(Hungarian)* Gypsy.
ZIHNA *(Native American)* Spinning.
ZIRACUNY *(Native American: Kiowa)* Water fiend.
ZITKALA *(Native American: Sioux)* Bird.
ZITKALASA *(Native American: Sioux)* Red bird.
ZITOMIRA *(Czech)* To live famously. Variations: *Zitka, Zituse.*
ZIVANKA *(Czech)* Alive. Variations: *Zivka, Zivuse, Zivuska.*
ZLATA *(Czech)* Golden. Variations: *Zlatina, Zlatinka, Zlatka, Zlatuna, Zlatunka, Zlatuse, Zlatuska.*
ZLHNA *(Native American: Hopi)* Spinning.
ZOCHA *(Polish)* Wisdom.
ZOHERET *(Hebrew)* She shines.
ZUBA *(English)* Unknown definition.
ZUBAIDA *(Arabic)* Marigold. Variations: *Zubaidah, Zubeda.*
ZULEIKA *(Arabic)* Brilliant.
ZULEMA *(Hebrew)* Peace. Variation: *Zulima.*
ZURI *(African: Swahili)* Beautiful.
ZUWENA *(African: Swahili)* Good. Variation: *Zwena.*
ZUZANA *(Czech)* Rose.
ZUZELA *(Native American: Sioux)* A wife of Sitting Bull.
ZYTKA *(Polish)* Rose.